THE
CRITICAL
YEAR

Harper's Weekly, Sept. 1, 1866

JOHNSON BEFRIENDS THE NEGRO

AMERICAN CLASSICS

The Critical Year

A STUDY OF ANDREW JOHNSON
AND RECONSTRUCTION

HOWARD K. BEALE

Professor of History
The University of Wisconsin

WITH ILLUSTRATIONS

FREDERICK UNGAR PUBLISHING CO.
New York

Printed in the United States of America

Library of Congress Catalog Card No. 58-9332

TO

PROFESSOR EDWARD CHANNING

THIS BOOK IS AFFECTIONATELY DEDICATED

Foreword to the 1958 Edition

THE DEMAND on the part of libraries and students of history for a new printing of my book, *The Critical Year,* which has now been out of print for a quarter of a century, is gratifying indeed. That a book is read by successive generations of people interested in history makes it seem important to have it available again. Reissuing a book written thirty-four years ago and published twenty-eight years ago has, however, its dangers. Would one say the same things now? What would one change? How much should the book be rewritten? After a thorough rereading I decided there was so little that I should wish to change that the volume ought to be reissued as it stands.

Two things ought perhaps to be mentioned. When the book was written, and even when it was published in 1930, recent changes in regard to the status of the Negro in American democracy were only beginning. I was then interested in race relations, but at that time, in two great northern universities as free from bias about the Negro as any in the country and in the high school maintained by one of them, I had never encountered anybody that capitalized the word "Negro," or anyone that refused to capitalize it. In the intervening years capitalizing "Negro," along with numerous other matters, has become an important symbol of an attitude toward race. I should, therefore, today capitalize the word.

In the intervening years, too, a long search for further evidence supporting Conklin's claim that the word "person" was deliberately inserted into the Fourteenth Amendment so that the Amendment might apply to corporations has led me to doubt this story. In the twenties, Conklin's story fitted theories about economic interpretation then current. Since that time, no new evidence has appeared supporting his story, and I have come to believe that, though he was in a position to know what happened, either a bad memory or a desire to win the suit for his client led him to give inaccurate testimony at the time of *San Mateo* v. *the Southern Pacific Railroad* in 1882. In other matters I am glad to see reprinted what I said many years ago.

Three other matters concerning the original publication of this book do seem in retrospect worthy of comment.

This study was inspired by Edward Channing, to whose curiosity and intuition I owe the suggestion of the problem I studied. After a month of exploring manuscript collections in the Library of Congress, I returned to Cambridge frightened at the overwhelming proportions of the task. "All right," barked Professor Channing, "go ahead if you wish and do a history of the sugar beet in a county of Utah. If, however, you wish to amount to something, then you'd better stick to a problem that may conquer you, but that will be worth solving if you can conquer it." I was discouraged, too, at twenty-four, by the warning I had heard in Washington that a man twenty years my senior and already a professor in a first-rate institution, had been working on a Johnson for ten years. "What? Old——?" snorted Professor Channing, thumbs in armholes of his vest and paunch and red cheeks puffed out beyond their always awesome proportions. "Don't you let old——worry you. You go ahead and do

your job." Throughout the study, Professor Channing's
provocative monosyllabic ejaculations and questions provided stimulation. His intuitions were remarkable. His high
expectations prodded one to do his best. One did not let
"the Old Man" down, then or later, if one could help it.

The book was written at the height of the vogue for
economic interpretation of history. It was natural, then,
perhaps inevitable, that economic motives for the conflict
of 1866 should have been discovered. Because of the chapter
in this volume on "economic issues," I have often been
credited with being a disciple of Charles A. Beard. In 1927,
in their *Rise of American Civilization*, Charles and Mary
Beard published a brief passage without documentation
describing the economic forces in the struggle over Southern
policy. But this present volume had been finished, with the
chapter on "economic issues" included, three years before
the Beards published their brief statement of the same thesis.
The Beards had not seen my findings, nor I the Beards'
statement, about economic issues in 1866. I later came to
know Beard well and was subsequently much influenced by
him, but at the time of the writing of this book I owed to
Beard only that general influence which his two books on
the Constitution and Jeffersonian democracy had exerted
on all of our generation maturing in the twenties. We were
all likely to see strong economic motivation in many phases
of history because of the pioneering Charles Beard had done
in this field. Yet actually, it was the searching questions of
two of my teachers, William E. Dodd and Frederick Jackson
Turner, and their stressing of economic motivations, that
first suggested to me the chapter on "economic issues." One
of the remarkable experiences of my historical career is that
I have heard little expounded as "new" in these last thirty-

five years that Frederick Jackson Turner had not already said
in those strangely disorganized, rambling comments on history that constituted Turner's lectures and that opened to
Turner's students new insights and exciting questions in
many fields where he never got around to writing at all. And
so what has always been described as Beardian in this particular volume came directly out of classes and conversations
with Turner.

The writing of this book illustrates, in the second place, a
phenomenon of historiography often repeated in historical
work about other times and places, namely, that when new
interpretations are made they are often presented almost
simultaneously by several people, who came upon them
independently of each other. So far as I know, the thesis
of this book concerning the role of economic issues in the
decision about Reconstruction was unique among the various revisionists of the twenties except for the brief, unsup-
ported statements of the Beards. On the other hand, what
I did toward the rehabilitation of Johnson and the moderates
was part of a group rehabilitation accomplished by several
of us working at the same time without knowledge of each
other's findings. The book was part of a great flowering of
interest in rethinking the old interpretations of the Johnson
era. I finished the manuscript of this book in July, 1924, and
put it aside to spend fourteen months abroad on a Harvard
traveling fellowship "to get to know Europe." I got it revised
in time to take the Ph.D. with it only in January, 1927. In
Oxford, England, at tea at the Samuel Eliot Morisons' in
November, 1924, I heard from Professor Morison a fairly
detailed description of another dissertation so nearly like
this one that I could not sleep that night, but Professor
Morison could not remember who had told him of it. The

next day he sent word that he had remembered that the dissertation was one Merle Curti had described to him a few weeks before, and I realized that the dread rival was my own manuscript that my friend Merle Curti had been generously publicizing.

The chronology of the various works on Johnson is interesting. The first two to appear after the completion of this manuscript in July, 1924, were the brief account taken from this work in manuscript form by Professor Morison himself, with full acknowledgement of the source, in his *Oxford History of the United States,* and the Beard account in the *Rise of American Civilization,* written without knowledge of this thesis. Both Morison and Beard published in 1927. In 1928 Robert W. Winston's *Andrew Johnson* appeared, and in 1929 Lloyd P. Stryker's. While the polishing up of this manuscript was under way, George Fort Milton, with that charm that could always command assistance of numerous historians for whatever he was writing, persuaded Professor Schlesinger to suggest things he ought to use; and Professor Schlesinger, who had sat on my thesis committee, suggested this dissertation then on file at Harvard. When Professor Schlesinger was too busy to write Milton what was in it, Milton wrote me asking to digest my own thesis for him and then subsequently, before I had found a publisher, Milton asked me to read and criticize the galley proofs of his *Age of Hate,* which I declined to do lest anyone suspect I had got material out of them for my own work. In the meantime, Claude Bowers had written his *Tragic Era,* and that was in press at Houghton Mifflin while I was seeking a publisher. This prevented Houghton Mifflin from considering my manuscript, which both Samuel E. Morison and William E. Dodd had recommended to them. The Bowers

book appeared in 1929 just in time for me to read it and
inject a comment on it into the galley proofs of my bibli-
ography. My own book appeared in mid-1930 and, after I
had found a publisher, I read and criticized Milton's *Age
of Hate*, which had remained in galley proof for nearly two
years and appeared late in 1930 after mine was out. Charles
W. Thompson's *Fiery Epoch* in 1931 completed the group
of Johnson-centered books all written simultaneously.

The Critical Year has been unavailable for some years.
If anything, World War II and the efforts to deal with
defeated peoples at its close make this study of similar
problems following the American Civil War more pertinent
than ever. Hence this study of the reasons why the North
decided to abandon the mild program of Lincoln and Johnson, which would have welcomed Southerners back to full
equality with other people, and why the North instead
decided to try to remould the South on a Northern model
through occupation troops and Negro ballots, is once more
offered to the interested public.

HOWARD K. BEALE

Madison, Wisconsin
May 26, 1958

Preface

THE choice of reconstruction policy made by the North at the end of the American Civil War has long puzzled me. Why should a Northern people, not normally vindictive, have adopted toward the defeated South a policy which their grandchildren generally condemn as both harsh and unwise? War hatred was explicable; but post-war vindictiveness, following so closely the early magnanimity which the North, eager for the return of normal peace relations, apparently shared with its great generals and martyred president, was difficult to understand. Andrew Johnson has interested me, too. How did a man of his inadequate capacity for public office happen to favor the program that posterity has adjudged wise, while the "great and able" men of the time insisted upon a policy now condemned as mistaken? Furthermore, since Johnson was neither a fool nor a contemner of the popular will, I have not been convinced by Rhodes's simple explanation that the unreasoning obstinacy of Johnson and the South in the face of an overwhelming popular verdict for the Fourteenth Amendment was responsible for the subsequent extremes of reconstruction. At the suggestion of Professor Channing, I have studied the period between Grant's gesture of magnanimity at Appomattox and the inauguration of Stevens's harsh plan during the early months of 1867, my effort having been to explain the decision said to be indicated in the Congressional election of 1866.

The Sumner Manuscripts in the Widener Library revealed a strongly organized Radical minority hard at work to convert a passive but unconvinced majority—a minority fully aware of the difficulties of the task, but determined to win if indefatigable labor and earnestness of purpose could bring victory. The Johnson Manuscripts in Washington proved rich in a variety of political opinion. Gradually the task narrowed down to an understanding of the complex political situation which determined the outcome of the 1866 election. The study centered in a threefold problem: Johnson's motives, aims, and personality; the steady development of the well-organized Radical Party from the position of a determined minority to the irresistible mastery of 1867; and the influences, particularly economic and psychological, the campaign methodology and propaganda, that actually swayed the ordinary voter of 1866.

An extended study of campaign correspondence and speeches has led me to revise completely the traditional reasons for the decision in favor of Radical reconstruction. I have made no attempt to judge the wisdom of the policy. An understanding of what Northerners believed to be the condition of the South is more important than a survey of the actual situation there. I have tried throughout to sift the claims of party leaders for the true issues and the motives of their protagonists. And particularly have I been interested in economic factors, until now neglected, which my research has indicated were significant influences in the decision of reconstruction.

Beside the extensive collections of Johnson and Sumner manuscripts, the papers of other prominent men have been consulted. I have read hundreds of campaign pamphlets and speeches in pamphlet form, not because they shed light on the true condition of the country, but because they contain the kind of information upon which the voter had to depend in making his choice at the polls. For the same reason newspapers of the period are significant. Printed writings of contemporaries, letters and memoirs, official documents, and campaign histories, however inaccurate, have proved important, too, because they show the actual influences that decided the election.

A debt of appreciation is due several who have aided me in my task. Professor Edward Channing was the inspirer of the work itself, and to his stimulating personality and sympathetic interest I owe much. Professor Frederick J. Turner has made helpful suggestions. To Professor Andrew C. McLaughlin I am indebted for my first interest in the reconstruction period. To the argumentative bent of my fellow-worker, Paul Buck, I owe many little criticisms during the progress of the study. To my friend, John K. Snyder, I am grateful for valuable assistance in the final revision of the manuscript. I wish also to thank Mr. Briggs and the staff of the Widener Library, Mr. Worthington C. Ford, Mr. John C. Fitzpatrick, Mr. Thomas P. Martin, and others in the Manuscript Division of the Library of Congress, the Chicago Public Library, and the staff of the Harper Memorial Library in Chicago, for their kindness in facilitating my research. For painstaking assistance in proof-reading I am indebted to my friends Stanley Barney Smith, Lawrence C. Jenks, and Paul E. Everett.

Contents

Illustrations

THE
CRITICAL
YEAR

Chapter I

INTRODUCTION

LINCOLN lived until Lee had surrendered and the Confederate government had fled in April, 1865. He saw the Union preserved and freedom for the blacks assured. But the fundamental conflict between two social and economic orders entered upon its final stage only after the fighting ceased. Then an industrialized Northeast, dominated by business principles that were to create the machine-made America of today, faced an agrarian South and West contending for those time-honored principles of frontier individualism and plantation aristocracy which had dominated an America that was passing. This peace-time struggle for supremacy in the newly preserved Union continued until the victory at the polls in November, 1866, decided that henceforth New England bred economics and social standards, rather than those of frontier and plantation, should rule America.

Men who contested the Congressional elections of 1866 recognized that the issue at stake was far-reaching in its significance. But the true import of the decision then made was revealed to the commonalty only with the slow passage of years. The defeat of Johnson meant the triumph of Stevens. Military rule and negro supremacy supplanted slowly re-

1

viving democratic institutions in the South. A gradual restoration of Southern institutions was set aside for a complete reconstruction of Southern society upon a Northern model. Subjugation superseded conciliation. The "solid South" was created out of political diversity. But far more important was the fact that, in the North, war hatred displaced economic issues in politics during fifteen years of "waving the bloody shirt." A righteous and domineering portion of the North, driven by the vindictive fury of Stevens and the misguided idealism of Sumner, undertook the task of chastening a prostrate South. And under cover of this, a minority group fastened upon the whole country an economic system that had failed for thirty years to make headway against a combined West and South. Southern policy and nationally important economic issues were open questions in 1866. The election, however, assured the subjugation of the South to Northern military rule for a number of years, and, holding the South impotent, enabled the Radicals to force their economic policies upon Northern opponents. By the time Radical domination of the South had spent itself in failure, the new economic order was firmly established in the country beyond danger from attack. What might have happened is left to the speculative philosopher. To the historian falls the task of analyzing the factors which brought the enactment of the Radical program in 1867.

For many years war hatred and partisan bias bred prejudiced historians of post-bellum politics. We find most writers of the war generation consistent in their view of the struggle of 1866. Southerners, they claimed, except negroes and a few loyal whites, were traitors clamoring to get into power only that they might bring about by the ballot what their arms had failed to accomplish—the destruction of the government. The equally disloyal Democrats were waiting to join forces with restored rebels. Andrew Johnson, once courageously loyal, but perverted by the guiles of traitors and the dream of power, was using the great authority that war had bestowed upon the executive to reinstate rebels in a dominant position in Washington. Realizing that not only the gains of the costly Civil War were at stake, but their country itself was endangered, the people repudiated Johnson and his schemes, and returned to Congress a loyal majority that imposed the Radical program upon the South, and saved the country.

A later group of historians, of whom Rhodes and Dunning are eminent examples, looked back at the period from the vantage point of a generation that, without being actors in the bitter conflict, had witnessed the failure of Radical reconstruction. To them "Democrat" and "traitor" were not synonymous; Republican politics or a black skin failed to make every scoundrel virtuous. They realized that the reconstruction period was troubled with perplexing problems. The Democratic and Southern attitude they viewed without hostility; and along with Southern faults and mistakes, they pictured the sufferings of the South and the injustice done it. In Andrew Johnson they saw a loyal and well-meaning, but foolish and erring politician, whose incapacity in the presidency brought disaster to both sections of the country. These writers recognized the election of 1866 as the crisis of reconstruction. Until that election, it was doubtful whether the people favored Johnson's plan or that of the Radicals; in that election the people chose between the two plans and decided overwhelmingly in favor of a moderate Congressional program. Johnson, repudiated by the people upon whose support he had staked all, should have heeded their verdict. His influence could have won the Southern states to ratify the Fourteenth Amendment. Then Congress would have readmitted them to the Union;[1] reconstruction would have been peaceably accomplished; and the Radicals would have been powerless before a popular moderate policy. Instead, Johnson stubbornly defended his own repudiated program, defied Congress, the people, and common sense, and advised the Southern states to refuse to ratify the Amendment. His stubbornness, and the Southern intractability which it encouraged, drove a moderate majority of Congressmen and voters into the arms of the extremists, and led to the establishment of military rule of the South, and the hardships of negro supremacy. This is substantially Rhodes's interpretation of the election.

Some eminent historians hold that the extreme Radical program was necessary to humble the South and rebuild the Union; others think that the Fourteenth Amendment offered a reasonable solution; many, including Rhodes, feel that Johnson's policy was wise had he been qualified as a statesman to carry it out successfully. But whatever their view of the program adopted, these later historians generally agree in their interpretation of the election, and Johnson's part in it. Even Southerners have joined in denouncing Johnson as his own and the South's worst enemy, and in laying at the door of his well-meaning but fatal stubbornness in 1866, the blame for their suffering under Radical reconstruction.

These later historians,[2] like the earlier prejudiced ones, have failed to see the larger economic and social aspects of the struggle over reconstruction. Over-emphasis of Southern

[1] Dunning is much less certain of this than Rhodes.
[2] In their *Rise of American Civilization*, the Beards have proved themselves exceptions, but they necessarily treat this period only cursorily.

policy and the negro has blinded writers to other factors ultimately more significant than any political policy for the South. The reconstruction controversy had two phases: one which concerned the South and its post-war problems, and one which concerned social and economic disputes, old as the nation itself, in which the Civil War had been but an interlude. The whole controversy of Radicals and Conservatives needs retelling in the light of recent investigations and of this broader interpretation.

A clear understanding of the struggle cannot be gleaned from what leaders in Congress said were the issues, nor from what the chief actors of one party or the other wrote in their memoirs to justify past actions; it cannot be obtained from impressions that men consciously sought to convey, nor from honest opinions formed in the light of later events. The reasons for the decision of 1866 must be sought in a study of motives actually at work as they found expression in newspapers, private correspondence, local campaign speeches, and political sermons. From these sources the complexity of the political situation becomes manifest and the crucial nature of the campaign apparent. Johnson's stand both before and after the balloting is explained if not justified. The difficulty, even hopelessness of his position, becomes impressive. In spite of obvious mistakes and shortcomings, Johnson becomes more worthy of respect. Furthermore, the study presents a valuable cross-section of American politics, revealing political campaign methods. It illustrates the height that post-bellum prejudice can attain; it indicates what a skilful manipulation of popular passions and the employment of campaign propaganda can accomplish; it strikingly evidences the ability of newspapers and a well-ordered campaign to misrepresent and eternally damn opponents. As a silent commentary on the American political system and the hopelessness of knowing the truth or voting wisely, the campaign of 1866 is eloquent.

Many Radicals were honestly convinced of the wickedness of the South and the danger of restoring rebels to political rights. The campaign was in part an attempt to determine the wisest policy for the South. A conflict of temperament did arise, strangely analogous to the recent post-bellum attitude toward Germany, between a group who could see security only in crushing the South to impotence, and a group who believed that generosity in trusting defeated Southerners to return in loyalty to the Union was the only safeguard of a peaceful future. But the rôle of the Fourteenth Amendment, which Rhodes felt was the great issue at stake, has been misunderstood. It was not in reality one simple measure, but four distinct enactments lumped into one for Radical purposes. Only with two parts of it did the Conservatives seriously quarrel. Johnson was not much more dissatisfied with it as a final settlement than Sumner would have been. Johnson felt that the extreme measures advocated by Stevens could be prevented only by a stand in 1866 against any important legislation, until Congress recognized the right of Southern states to a vote in government, whenever they should send properly loyal representatives to Washington. Consequently, he opposed a measure half of which he would have accepted if passed by a Congress representative of the whole country. Sumner and Stevens, on the other hand, could support the Amendment as a convenient halting ground where more timid persons could be prepared for the next advance toward extreme measures. Negro suffrage and military rule of the South were distinctly issues in the struggle, but issues which Radical leaders

suppressed whenever possible as too extreme for the voters of
1866 until they had been further "educated." The Fourteenth Amendment was a more discussed but a confused issue,
whose exact relation to the campaign nobody understood.
Safest of all was the condition and temper of the South.
This was the most debated topic of the period. But it was
used by both sides merely as a means of converting voters to
a preconceived policy based on other considerations. Few
Conservatives or Radicals made an effort to determine the
true situation in the South. Both sides gathered there only
such evidence as would support their respective causes in the
North. Policies for the South were, then, issues in the
struggle of Radicals and Conservatives for control of the
country, but they were complex and confused issues.

The very terms "reconstruction" and "Radical" were mis-
nomers. In the South the period might be called one of
Northern attempts at reconstruction. It was more exactly a
destruction of the South as it had been, for the destructive
process was permanent, whereas the new Radical structures
lasted only while supported by Northern force. Real reconstruction did not come until Southerners were free to work it
out for themselves. Furthermore, the so-called "Radicals"
were radical only on reconstruction, only on questions affecting not themselves but a distant and rival section of the
country. On the great economic questions of the day, the
"Radicals" were in general conservative, and the opponents
of their reconstruction policy tended toward radicalism of
an agrarian type.

While many became Radicals because of honest conviction
concerning the South, others had economic or political reasons for desiring permanent rule by the Republican Party,
and supported the policy of Stevens from a realization that

the political supremacy they desired could be made permanent only by excluding the Southern States until a Republican Party based on negro constituencies could control that region. One group in the North was determined to use the opportunity to remake the very character of the government. Some followers of Hamilton's ideals had always wished to efface state lines and create a strong, completely centralized government freed from all checks and balances. Some with a vision of the future national scope of business and its relation to the federal government, and others with a desire to gain complete political control of the country, sought to remodel the government to make Congress supreme. Only Johnson's tenacity in holding to the older theories prevented the establishment of a parliamentary system with Congress omnipotent in a Washington where checks and balances had been scrapped, and with the central government all-powerful in a nation from which state lines had been obliterated.

Underneath the quarrel over "reconstruction" lay great economic differences that had divided men for generations, and new problems that were to become great political issues before the century closed—the regulation of big corporations, government subsidies to business, taxation and government expenditures, currency and banking problems, and the tariff. On many of *these* questions Johnson could have secured more support than Stevens or Sumner. The business interests and economically conservative groups of the country had learned by discouraging experience of pre-war decades that they could make no headway in these matters in normal times. They realized that should the South be restored, South and West could outvote the conservative business groups. The Radicals had enjoyed the sweets of power and unexpected favor for their economic interests. They had no intention of returning to the hopeless minority fight their fathers had made as Whigs. To keep the economic questions in the background until the Southern problem was settled and their power secure, was therefore essential. A campaign of denunciation and vituperation would accomplish this end by keeping war hatreds alive. Personal defamation, shouts of "Copperhead" and "traitor" against political and economic opponents, unreasoning passion, rodomontade—claptrap rather than issues—dominated the campaign. The Radicals were eminently successful. After November, 1866, they were supreme. During long years when "reconstruction" monopolized Northern politics, unperceived changes took place, the nation-wide significance of which overshadows temporary experiments in remaking an unwilling South; a new social and economic order under Radical favors grew to maturity; the Age of Big Business dawned; and the factors underlying modern agrarian unrest gained strength.

Chapter II

JOHNSON AND HIS POLICY

BOTH Andrew Johnson and his Southern policy were important factors in the decision of reconstruction. Man and policy have alike been distorted by hostile interpretation and need to be repictured more accurately. Of the true character of Andrew Johnson we know surprisingly little. Yet for several years he inspired more hatred, stirred more discussion, than any other individual in the land. As man and as executive, his every act swelled this storm of controversy. No political speaker failed to talk of him. But those who really knew him were few.

The animosity of reconstruction days has printed a very definite picture of our Seventeenth President upon tradition; but it is not Andrew Johnson. It is the caricature that his calumniators in Congress and the press fastened upon him, rather a political bogy, a personified policy, than the man who lived in the White House. His enemies worked effectively, for the popular conception of Johnson is that of a vulgar, drunken tailor; a soap-box ranter; an illiterate, ill-mannered, intemperate fellow, stubborn, intolerant, quarrelsome; honest and well-meaning, but a fool, pliant in the hands of traitors, Copperheads, or anybody who would

toady to him; a "spiteful, inflated, and unprincipled ego-
tist"; an "insolent, clownish drunkard" whose excesses disgraced the White House, whose family could not be recognized by respectable society, whose lack of dignity and incapacity in office made us hang our heads in shame before
foreign nations. Time has considerably toned down the picture, but our fathers' generation could never have looked on
Andrew Johnson without contempt.

He has always been charged with egotism. He did talk
overmuch of himself. But this habit arose rather from a
sense of inferiority than from egotism. He had entered
manhood unable to read; his wife had taught him to write.
By his own merit and perseverance, he had risen from the
stratum of a poor journeyman tailor to the presidency. He
had lived among a proud slave-holding aristocracy who had
snubbed him and scorned him. But his humble origin had
proved a political resource which he had learned to exploit.
Had others boasted of it, his rise from tailor's bench to White
House might have had popular appeal. For the President to
do so, was bad taste. Besides, there was something effeminate,
contemptible in the tailor's trade. It had not the glamor
that rail-splitting had shed over another president from
the frontier. And when Radicals began to ridicule his trade
and social inferiority, they hit upon the most sensitive spot
in his armor; [1] they recalled all the indignities and mortifica-
tions of a long unhappy career. His boasting was a shield
for a naturally sensitive soul. In most matters Johnson
lacked assurance, sought advice, hesitated in full realization
of his own shortcomings. He truly said of himself: "The
elements of my nature, the pursuits of my life, have not

[1] See, e.g., John J. Craven, *Prison Life of Jefferson Davis*, 244.

made me either in my feelings or in my practice aggressive. My nature, on the contrary, is rather defensive in its character." [2]

In spite of popular belief, there can be no question of Johnson's sobriety. It was a day of hard drinking, but Johnson was not one of the hard drinkers. No evidence exists of his ever drinking to excess during his senatorship or war-governorship.[3] Then came the fatal day of his inauguration as vice-president when he was unquestionably drunk. The spectacle was distressing to sober men throughout the country. Anti-administration Radical papers, Copperhead papers, and scandal-mongers published the news with glee. Most conservative journals printed it in shame. Sumner sought to impeach Johnson. But the story was hushed up. Some papers printed the explanation; many did not.

Johnson had just recovered from typhoid fever, and had

[2] *New York Herald*, Aug. 19, 1866.

[3] Contemporary enemies like Stewart (*Reminiscences*, 194), and even historians like Rhodes (*History of the United States from the Compromise of 1850*, V, 618) repeat the charges of inebriety as facts but present no evidence. Clifton R. Hall (*Andrew Johnson Military Governor of Tennessee*, 219) says, "The habit of indulging in intoxicants, afterwards reputed as Johnson's most conspicuous personal failing as president, had, of course, been formed long before." Mr. Hall's authorities for this allegation are two: Charles A. Dana, writing thirty years after the event, when he says, Johnson "brought out a jug of whisky . . . and then made it about half and half water. The theoretical, philosophical drinker pours out a little whisky and puts in almost no water at all—drinks it pretty nearly pure—but when a man gets to taking a good deal of water in his whisky, it shows he is in the habit of drinking a good deal. I noticed that the Governor took more whisky than most gentlemen would have done, and I concluded that he took it pretty often." (*Recollections of the Civil War*, 106); and Carl Schurz, writing forty-three years afterward, when he says, "It happened twice or three times that, when I called upon him, I was told by the attendant that the Governor was sick and could not see anybody; then, after the lapse of four or five days, he would send for me, and I would find him uncommonly natty in his attire, and generally 'groomed' with especial care. He would also wave off any inquiry about his health. When I mentioned this circumstance to one of the most prominent Union men of Nashville, he smiled, and said that the Governor had 'his infirmities,' but was 'all right' on the whole." (*Reminiscences*, III, 96.) Slim evidence, indeed, for so grave an accusation!

not wanted to come to Washington, but Lincoln had insisted. On the morning of the inauguration, Johnson still felt weak from his illness. Just before he entered the Senate chamber a friend gave him some whisky to strengthen him for the ceremony. He took too much, or was over-sensitive to whisky; at any rate, it went to his head, and he made a sorry, jumbled speech. McCulloch,[4] Doolittle,[5] Hamlin [6] who accompanied him to the capitol, and Crook [7] testify to the truth of this explanation. There is no proof that Johnson was ever again intoxicated.

But this slip gave a handle to the Radicals. They later called up this occasion, and began to speak of him as the "drunken tailor." On February 22, 1866, on April 18, and during his "Swing 'round the Circle," whenever he made one of his disjointed extemporaneous speeches, they accused him of drunkenness. Papers all over the country printed the accusation, and spoke of his special train as a traveling bar-room. Thousands of good people hung their heads in shame at the thought of a "drunken" President.

That Johnson never again drank to excess seems certain from the fact that the Radicals did not use it as an impeach-ment charge. They searched diligently but found no evidence that could be used even in a political trial.[8] But better proof exists. Welles confides in the unprinted portions of his diary that Grant had to leave the Presidential party at Cleveland

[4] H. McCulloch, *Men and Measures*, 373.

[5] *Century Magazine*, LXXXV (1912), 198.

[6] Schouler (*History of the United States*, VII, 8) says that Hamlin's statement of the facts was preserved in the Johnson MSS., but it does not seem to be there now. See also Charles E. Hamlin, *Hannibal Hamlin*, 497.

[7] Body-guard to Lincoln, Johnson, Grant, Hayes, Garfield, and Arthur. Col. Wm. H. Crook, *Through Five Administrations*, 82.

[8] David M. Dewitt, *The Impeachment and Trial of Andrew Johnson*, 420. H. McCulloch, *op. cit.*, 393-394. McCulloch declares that "there were few public men whose character and conduct would have sustained as severe a scrutiny." The testimony itself Winston found in the Document Room in Washington.

because he had drunk too heavily; [9] he speaks of the drunkenness of Senators Chandler [10] and Howard [11] of Michigan; and he pictures Robert Johnson as an habitual drunkard, a great trial to his father, and relates how he provided a ship and sent Robert on a long cruise under charge of a depend-

able captain to relieve the President of anxiety over his escapades. [12] On the occasion of the inauguration as vice-president, Welles frankly recorded that Johnson was drunk, and hoped there was an explanation. [13] Yet at no other time did Welles even in the privacy of the expurgated sections of

---

[9] Welles MS. Diary, Sept. 17, 1866.

[10] *Ibid.*, Dec. 5, 1866. "Chandler is steeped & steamed in whisky—is coarse, vulgar and reckless."

[11] *Ibid.*, Dec. 5, 1866. "Howard also drinks, but has more culture and is better educated, yet he is an . . . unfit man for Senator."

[12] *Ibid.*, April 24, April 27, and Sept. 19, 1866.

[13] *Ibid.*, March 4, 1865—(II, 252). References to Welles's Diary are always to the manuscript which varies considerably in places from the printed version (See H. K. Beale, "Is the Printed Diary of Gideon Welles Reliable?", *Am. Hist. Rev.*, XXX [1925], 547). Where there is, as there usually is, a corresponding passage in the published edition, the volume and page are cited in parentheses as here.

his diary mention Johnson's drinking. McCulloch says, "For nearly four years I had daily intercourse with [Johnson], frequently at night, and I never saw him when under the influence of liquor. I have no hesitation in saying that whatever may have been his faults, intemperance was not among them." [14] In a contemporary letter to his friend Talbot, McCulloch declared that "the reports in regard to his habits of personal indulgence are . . . utterly destitute of foundation—slanders of which the authors will themselves be ashamed when the heat of party passion shall have subsided." [15] Doolittle testified, "My relations to him have been such that I have seen him frequently, in the early morning hours, at mid-day and in the evening. I have had frequent conversations with several of the members of his Cabinet, and with his private secretaries, and I tell you as a fact that ought to be published to the world as an answer to the most infamous charges that have been circulated against him, that there is not one word of truth in the charges that Mr. Johnson is intemperate." [16]

Shortly after the unfortunate inaugural incident, Lincoln testified to a doubting cabinet member, "I have known Andy Johnson for many years; he made a bad slip the other day, but you need not be scared; Andy ain't a drunkard." [17] A Leipzig paper in describing Johnson's personal habits, told that before dinner he took a glass of whisky as an appetizer, and that "various fine wines [were] then brought in, of which the President [took] but very little, closing the meal

[14] "There was no liquor in his room. . . . His luncheon, when he had one, was, like mine, a cup of tea and a cracker." H. McCulloch, *op. cit.*, 374.
[15] *New York Herald*, Oct. 5, 1866.
[16] Speech at the Academy of Music, Philadelphia, May 19, 1866, *Speeches of Hon. Edgar Cowan . . . Jas. R. Doolittle . . . Hugh McCulloch (National Union Club Documents)*, 12.
[17] H. McCulloch, *op. cit.*, 373.

uniformly with another ration of coffee." [18] Gobright who reported the Chicago tour for the Associated Press,[19] Jefferson Davis,[20] Major Truman who was Johnson's private secretary,[21] Crook, Johnson's body-guard,[22] and even Parson Brownlow [23] testified to Johnson's sobriety. Welles, McCulloch, Doolittle, Truman, and Crook were honorable men in a position to know; Lincoln's word cannot be doubted; the German newspaper could have had no possible motive for falsehood. Brownlow and Davis were Johnson's enemies. No trustworthy contradiction exists. Johnson's habitual intoxication existed only in wild rumors, in disproved stories such as Beecher's,[24] in mendacious campaign propaganda, in the Radical press, and in the memoirs of old men who could only have known by hearsay or who like Dana and Schurz, able to know the truth, had personal axes to grind in repeating rumors that would hurt an old enemy. Such testimony is worthless. But Johnson's Fourth of March slip set the tone of the Radical campaign, and laid him open to indignities.

In his astounding book [25] published in 1867, General Baker, war-time head of the Secret Service, printed at length the evidence taken at the trial of a Mrs. Cobb. The

18 Article in a Leipzig (Germany) newspaper, reprinted in the *New York Herald*, Aug. 13, 1866.

19 Gobright was grilled by the impeachment investigators. "Testimony Taken before the Judiciary Committee . . . in the Investigation of the Charges against Andrew Johnson," *Reports of Committees*, 40 Cong., 1 Sess., ser. no. 1314, House Report no. 7, 525-532.

20 J. J. Craven, *op. cit.*, 245.

21 *Century Magazine*, LXXXV (1913), 438.

22 Crook "never once saw him under the influence of liquor." As he was with Johnson almost constantly in Washington and on the Chicago trip, his knowledge should be exact. As he disliked Johnson until he knew him well, and admired Grant, Hayes, and Lincoln, his testimony should be impartial.

23 Robert W. Winston, *Andrew Johnson*, 104. Winston could not find any charge of drinking in Tennessee newspapers.

24 *Infra*, 78-79.

25 Lafayette C. Baker, *History of the U. S. Secret Service*.

manifest purpose was, without subjecting the author to libel prosecution, to stigmatize the President by innuendo as a keeper of harlots, to picture the White House under Johnson as a house of prostitution. He described the manipulations of a group of women who acted as pardon-brokers, selling for cash the pardons they wrung from Johnson by appeals to his sympathy; he insinuated that their success lay in power they held over the President. Baker does not prove that these women were more than pretty flirts who capitalized their smiles with department clerks, though undoubtedly some had unsavory reputations.[26] But even Baker's account shows, if read carefully, that whatever influence these women did have, was with Robert Johnson and not with the President.[27] Andrew Johnson's heart always melted before the pleadings of a woman, especially a pretty one, even in the stern days of his war-governorship, but no evidence has ever been adduced to show that he was other than strictly honorable in his connections with them. The picture that Baker seeks to paint has no other substantiation than wild rumors in opposition papers. The singularity and sensationalism of his story, and the fact that it was written in anger at his dismissal, make his charges quite untrustworthy. On the other

[26] Baker and this troupe of women were entirely discredited before the House investigating committee that would have been only too glad to use their testimony. H. McCulloch, *op. cit.*, 394; R. W. Winston, *op. cit.*, 414–416.

[27] Other evidence exists against Robert, who was at this time private secretary to his father. It was soon after this that Johnson's anxiety over his son became so great that Welles and Seward contrived to send the son abroad on a warship. An Illinois lieutenant of Trumbull wrote of Robert: "There is too much whiskey in the White House, and harlots go into the Private Secretary's office unannounced in broad daylight. Mrs. C[obb] did that since the trial while a friend of mine was waiting for an audience . . . and she came out leaning on the arm of a drunken son of the Prest. There were a large number . . . waiting . . . and saw it all." N. B. Judd to L. Trumbull, Feb. 14, 1866, Trumbull MSS., LXIV. Robert was a notorious debauchee; the profligacy of the son was easily turned by Johnson's enemies into ill repute for the father.

hand, abundant reliable evidence, the known regularity of his life, and his devotion to his large family, all testify to Johnson's high character.

Johnson's reputation suffered from the enmity of newspaper men. In whatever he did or said, he was vigorous and picturesque, a type that reporters idolize or victimize. Never popular with any group, he was particularly hated by press correspondents, because like Grant he dealt with them brusquely when they interfered with the efficient administration of the War. In Tennessee he had no time for interviews; he was indifferent to their favor. Even when he meant to be polite, pressure of important affairs often made him curt. With importunate reporters he dealt summarily. While he was the popular War Governor, newspapers lauded him; his daring and vigor made him a favorite in sensational stories. Correspondents bided their time and bore their grudges. After he became president they saw their chance and wreaked all the accumulated grievances of the years upon his head.[28]   *   *   *   *

To destroy this old picture is easier than to draw a new one, for Johnson defies intimacy. Of only average height, he was none the less broad-shouldered and imposing. His complexion was swarthy, his features good. He had sparkling, penetrating eyes. A mass of thick dark hair topped his head. Deep lined into his countenance was a look of mingled determination and distress. A stolidity resulting from patient suffering under accustomed hardship, and a somber serious-mindedness not often relieved by any sign of joviality, were characteristic. His greatest physical asset was a voice, mellow and pleasing in tone, but of such power that,

[28] E.g., Dana's story of his drunkenness in Tennessee, *op. cit.*, 106.

without appearing to raise it, he could make himself heard
to the outer edge of vast throngs of people. His manner and
the peculiar magnetism of his personality as he spoke to a
crowd, lent a vigor and dignity to speeches that in print were
unimpressive.

Yet it was Johnson's extemporaneous speeches that most
seriously injured his reputation. His training had been in
upland Tennessee political campaigning. To auditors he
carried conviction. Reported in a newspaper, especially an
unfriendly one, his speeches became jumbled harangue. His
Tennessee habit of parrying words with the crowd gave
opposition reporters a coveted opportunity to belittle him.
Against skilful heckling he could not maintain his dignity.
Taken out of their surroundings, Johnson's extemporaneous
speeches are undignified, sometimes illiterate, often in bad
taste. But the political gathering of the day was accustomed
to his kind of stump oratory from senators, governors of
states, and ministers. Johnson's outbursts compare favorably
with speeches of John A. Logan, Thad Stevens, Senator
Chandler, Senator Wade, Governor Oglesby, Governor
Brownlow, or Wendell Phillips, who denounced him for lack
of dignity.[29] Had his sentiments been Radical, his speeches
would have won him praise from the men whom they
"shocked." But they did supply enemies with an extraordinary stock of ridicule.

His prepared addresses and messages were impressive.[30]
Johnson's very enemies testify to "his clear and forcible
powers of expression" and his ability, "when calm and collected," to state his opinions impressively.[31] His messages to

[29] The speeches of the scholarly Sumner were exceptional.
[30] Whether he wrote them himself or sought aid, as with his first
annual message, from men like Bancroft, matters little. The ideas were
his if not the phraseology.
[31] *Christian Examiner,* LXXXI (November, 1866), 404.

Congress remain models of clarity and convincing reason; and in his own day, not even the suspicious Welles guessed that he did not write them himself.

Johnson was methodical, as no president had been since John Quincy Adams. He instituted what the White House had never before boasted—a system of records of all business transacted. His letter-books were carefully preserved as were all letters received. He even kept scrap-books of the times. The vast collection of records and papers thus preserved testifies to Johnson's orderliness and administrative efficiency, as does the expedition with which he handled the quantity of work that reconstruction and the new pardon system imposed upon his personal staff. He revolutionized the administration of the executive offices.

His industry was amazing. When he came to Washington in the spring of 1865, he was still weak from typhoid fever. All summer he was ill. Welles repeatedly urged him to take a rest, or at least a sail.[32] In the latter part of June he was so weak that strong will power could no longer sustain him, and for ten days he had to drop work.[33] But ill as he was, he stayed on in Washington through the summer heat of 1865 and 1866. He arose early and retired late. All day he received throngs of office-hunters, pardon-seekers, advice-givers, who crowded his ante-rooms.[34] Numerous delegations of petitioners or well-wishers from North and South paid their respects, and often received a speech in return. Johnson

[32] E.g., Welles MS. Diary, July 9, 24, and Aug. 1, 1865—(II, 329, 342, 347).
[33] H. McCulloch to S. M. Forbes, July 3, 1865, McCulloch MSS., II.
[34] When the cabinet did not meet and no official visitors were to be received, as was often the case during the summer, Johnson was victimized by the ante-room crowd from early morning until evening. For a description of the crowds of rebels that monopolized his time see Whitelaw Reid, *After the War*, 304-308.

did not know how to turn people away. Our presidents until recently have been expected to make themselves available to a pestiferous horde of callers. But with Johnson, to the usual crowd were added swarms of Southerners with grievances to air or pardons to seek, and useless congratulatory committees. These throngs occupied long hours with trifles, while important matters waited. Many a leader of Northern opinion despaired and went home discouraged because this host of nonentities deprived him of the President's ear, or angry because the President's time was monopolized by ex-rebels. Eventually his friends protested, and the crowd was at last thinned out, but that was not until the fall of 1866.[35]

Aside from these interviews, Johnson was a busy man. He read long reports, heard opinions of advisers, formulated policies, handled the routine of administration, held frequent cabinet meetings, and wrote letters, telegrams, and orders to subordinates all over the country. His days were long and difficult. Doolittle tells how "assiduously and . . . industriously" Johnson worked "from the early morning hours till late at night."[36] He rose at seven in winter and six in summer. Until ten he wrote, read, and studied; he was an omnivorous reader. From ten to eleven he interviewed visitors; at eleven he lunched; from twelve to one he met his cabinet or received distinguished callers, and then again admitted the throngs of pardon-seekers and place-hunters. If he got time he took a walk at three, but often he received the swarms of callers without relief until dinner at four. At dinner he discussed the news of the day with his nearest

---

[35] On Oct. 3, 1866, the *New York Herald* commented that the "President's edict against office brokers . . . [was] having a salutary effect and [was] greatly lessening the amount of his daily labor."

[36] Speech at the Academy of Music, Philadelphia, May 19, 1866, *Speeches of Hon. Edgar Cowan . . . Jas. R. Doolittle . . . Hugh McCulloch* (*National Union Club Documents*), 12.

friends. Then at five he retired with a cat and a huge coffee pot to his study, where he worked until midnight, reading, writing, and holding conferences with intimates. At eight he emerged long enough to have tea with his family. The endurance of the man who in ill health, under strain of abuse and oppressively weighty problems, could work from six in the morning until midnight month after month without vacation or recreation, is appalling. This calm, taciturn, hard-working human being is hardly recognizable as the bawling drunken demagogue of the Radical newspapers.

Regularity and hard work were not even relieved by normal recreations. When Johnson became president, he had never attended a theater, and he saw only a few plays in Washington. He remarked once that he had been to a circus, and to a minstrel show, and had enjoyed them; but that he never found time for such diversions, because he preferred to read and study. His only relaxation was a drive or an occasional picnic with his grandchildren. This attitude made White House festivities somber observances of duty. There were more dinners and receptions than in the succeeding administrations; they were dignified, sometimes brilliant; but they were solemn, never gay.

Except for Robert, the President's family was respected and accepted without question in Washington society. His daughters, Mrs. Patterson and Mrs. Stover, were women of great charm and tact.[37] His eldest daughter, Senator Patterson's wife, presided over the household and was a gracious hostess. In the background was Mrs. Johnson, an invalid in an upper room, known only to family intimates. Her pres-

[37] Even Mrs. John A. Logan, wife of one of Johnson's bitterest enemies, who saw Washington society through many decades, testified to this. *Reminiscences of a Soldier's Wife*, 226, 240. See also H. McCulloch, *op. cit.*, 406.

ence there was not generally known; only twice did she appear in public. But she was a good woman and intelligent; she had been an invaluable aid to Johnson ever since the penniless, obscure days when she taught him to write. To her he was passionately devoted, and she remained his most trusted counselor. Johnson's body-guard testifies that "her influence was a strong one, and it was exerted in the direction of toleration and gentleness." She was sweet-faced and sweet-spirited; Johnson's response to the slightest movement of her hands or her "Now, Andrew," evidenced his respect and her influence. She was slowly dying of old-fashioned consumption. The death of her eldest son, the debauchery of her next, and the bitter attacks on her husband, made her life unhappy. Indeed, she said she had been "more content when her husband was an industrious young tailor." [38] To understand Johnson one must picture him in this family group, surrounded by his four children, a son-in-law and five grandchildren, with his patient, gentle, invalid wife in their midst.

*   *   *   *

Johnson's devotion to duty was tireless. He was doggedly persistent, dauntlessly courageous. Even his enemies admitted his rugged honesty, his "great native force of intellect and exceeding strength of will . . . his love for the Union [and] his genuine patriotism." [39] It was these characteristics that had made him the notable leader of pre-war Tennessee, the fearless Senator of 1861 who alone among Southerners remained loyally at his post, and the efficient War Governor under great trial and personal danger in whom Lincoln felt

[38] The description of Mrs. Johnson comes from one of the few who ever mentions her. W. H. Crook, *op. cit.,* 87.
[39] *Christian Examiner,* LXXXI (November, 1866), 404. McCulloch (*op. cit.,* 406) says that in "intellectual force he had few superiors."

complete confidence. By ridicule the Radicals burlesqued these same traits and certain up-country Tennessee peculiarities into grave faults. Crude Johnson was, of course, but his was the crudity of the American frontier of which his countrymen were proud. In another time and place he would have been a popular idol.

Just before the election of 1866, the unemotional, non-committal Secretary of the Treasury wrote, "Men may differ with him in regard to his manner of dealing with the States recently in rebellion, but no fair man could have been with him, as I have been during the trying eighteen months of his administration, without being impressed with his love of country and his devotion to duty, with the unselfishness and uprightness of his character, and the honesty of his purposes." [40]   *   *   *   *

Weaknesses Johnson had, too. One was inordinate faith in his own power of persuasion. He felt that if only he could present his case in person to the people and appeal to their wisdom and sense of justice, they would unquestionably support him. His trip to Chicago wrought great harm, but he seemed not to realize that it was injuring him.[41] His faith in his ability to win votes on the Southern question, led him to neglect really effective issues.

Johnson was never popular. A peculiar magnetism he did have that attracted people who talked with him personally. George L. Stearns, a Boston Radical, was temporarily won by an interview.[42] Yet he possessed none of the personal

[40] H. McCulloch to W. H. Talbott, *New York Herald*, Oct. 5, 1866.

[41] This trip did cure him of extemporaneous speaking. Through the ordeal of impeachment he admirably preserved his dignity and his silence, in strong contrast to most of his Congressional denunciators. But he learned his lesson too late.

[42] He was so much impressed that he asked and got Johnson's permission to publish the conversation. Oct. 8, 1865, Johnson MSS., LXXVIII.

charm that gives men popularity. He could sway a crowd; he could impress individuals. But he never succeeded in making men love him. When he led, it was by force of will.

Johnson's reserve deprived him of intimate friends. He was exasperatingly non-committal. Often this was an advantage. He listened well; in an interview he could let the other man do all the talking, agree without committing himself, and send the man away satisfied without avowing his own view. More often his reserve hurt him. In cabinet meetings he listened patiently to all opinions, but seldom expressed one. Welles frequently recorded in his diary what he had suggested to the President with the remark that he "seemed to agree," and later the comment that he had not acted on the advice. Of all things Johnson most needed the coöperation of close friends. Welles, McCulloch, Doolittle, Randall, Browning, Cowan, the Blairs, Ewing, Stanton, Seward were with him constantly; they had access to him for private conversation at any hour of the day or night. They advised; they wrote reports; they argued with him. But none of them really knew Johnson. Welles was probably as good a friend as any. Yet from the diary it is evident that Johnson never really confided in him. In a galaxy of extraordinarily life-like portraits, Johnson, the center of them all, is the one Welles fails to vivify. His was an inscrutable soul. In the midst of exciting times, surrounded by crowds of people, he remained lonely in the White House.

Indecision was another failing. Amid a bewilderment of conflicting advice and professed friendship, Johnson was perplexed. Since he was not directly in touch with Northern sentiment, he had to depend upon advisers who were. But whom was he to trust? The Blairs, Welles, Seward, and Stanton distrusted one another, and warned him each against the other. Radicals, moderate Republicans, moderate Democrats, Copperheads, and Southerners tendered advice and denounced each other. Torn between opposing factions, Johnson hesitated, and did nothing. Early in 1866 a moderate program aggressively sponsored, drastic changes in federal offices and the cabinet, a break with extreme Radicals, would have won his policy a party. But he hesitated for months, reluctant to break the Union Party, while the Radicals through vigorous leadership won Moderate after Moderate to their cause.

Johnson's very courage and determination once he had made up his mind were often converted from virtues into faults. He did not know how to compromise. His mind had one compartment for right and one for wrong, but no middle chamber where the two could commingle. When Johnson did finally become convinced of the justice or rectitude of a cause, all the powers of earth could not turn him from it. He could bear insult, personal danger, obloquy; but he could not yield his point. He could not accept the situation as he found it, turn partial support to his ends, or yield on details to attain large advantages. In the restoration of the Southern States, Johnson saw the salvation and future happiness of the country; fundamental principles were at stake; both his duty and his honor were involved. He could gladly face death or political ruin, but he could not be swerved from the path whither every fiber of his passionate soul told him duty led. His admirable, courageous, but ruinous determination was based on the same inflexible sense of honor that underlay Sumner's unreasoning opposition. In other times and other men, Americans have lauded this quality. But it was disastrous at a time when infinite tact, yielding here, forcing there, was necessary. Johnson failed to carry the day

—yet he failed but by a little and under great odds, and on reconstruction and constitutional interpretation the future has vindicated him. Had the balance of events turned slightly the other way—had he succeeded—this very uncompromising sense of duty which brought obloquy upon his name would have been accredited the highest virtue of a great man. Johnson possessed those characteristics that make men blessed or damned, famous or infamous, because chance leads them to success or failure.

* * * *

Johnson, responsible for enforcing the country's laws, had to face the Southern situation immediately upon his inauguration. First in the field with a constructive policy, he was rebuilding the South while others were still debating. He was convinced that this Southern problem must be settled before other issues were considered.

Fundamentally Johnson's program was based upon conviction that kindness and generosity alone would restore the Union, upon confidence in the Southern people as essentially good, and upon faith in democracy as practicable even in time of crisis. Johnson believed that, aside from a few indispensable guarantees, the details of readjustment should be left to the loyal people of the states in question, whom he considered infinitely better fitted to work out their problems than military officers or Northern politicians. "If a State is to be nursed until it again gets strength, it must be nursed by its friends, not smothered by its enemies," he declared.[43] And again, "The only safety of the nation lies in a generous and expansive plan of conciliation, and the longer this is delayed, the more difficult will it be to bring the North and the South into harmony . . . The idea of legislating for one-

[43] *Speeches of Andrew Johnson,* edited by F. Moore, 483-484.

third of the population of the country, and passing constitutional amendments without allowing them any voice in
the matter . . . is full of danger to the future peace and
welfare of the nation. They cannot be treated as subjugated
people or as vassal colonies without a germ of hatred being
introduced, which will some day or other, though the time
may be distant, develop mischief of the most serious character." [44] He believed that the observance of political equality as a matter of justice would encourage the people of the
South to be "more and more constant and persevering in
their renewed allegiance," while military force would be
"contrary to the genius and spirit of our free institutions,
and exhaustive of the national resources." [45]

Johnson had spent a lifetime fighting a Southern aristocracy. He was proud of being a plebeian, and looked upon
himself as the great guardian of the rights of the common
man. Now he saw in New England a new type of aristocracy,
based upon Hamiltonian principles of government for "the
rich and the well born" and upon the new business principles of government for the benefit of industry. This new
Northeastern civilization seemed to Johnson as dangerous
to Jacksonian principles and the welfare of the common man
as had the rule of the old slavocracy. He had opposed, too,
the determination of a minority of great slave-holders to
impose their ideas upon the rest of the country, and could
not now brook a New England civilization which avowed the
purpose of remolding the South to fit New England standards. He saw in this new type of Hamiltonian centralism a
serious menace to the Jeffersonian principle of states' rights
upon which his political beliefs were grounded. While John-

[44] *Boston Evening Commercial*, July 21, 1866.
[45] Proclamation, April 2, 1866, James D. Richardson, *Messages and Papers of the Presidents*, VI, 431-432.

son had disliked the slave system, he was none the less a Southerner who understood the negro problem. Abolitionism had been anathema. And much that New England now demanded seemed to smack of it. Besides, he could not believe New Englanders entirely sincere in their denunciations of the disunionism of Southerners. In February, 1861, he had pointedly enumerated New England's past demands for disunion.[46] Her new determination to keep Southern states out, he regarded as a new form of opposition to the Union for which he had risked life and reputation. For a combination of reasons, then, he felt a strong prejudice against New England, and, as a Southerner, could not sympathize with her 1866 ambitions.

He was a democrat, too. His greatest boast was that he was a common man, the friend of common men. "I am a Democrat now," he had said in 1862; "I have been one all my life; I expect to live and die one . . . they shall never divert me from the polar star by which I have ever been guided from early life—the great principles of Democracy upon which this Government rests." [47] His training had bred in him implicit faith in the people and distrust of politicians. On the eve of civil war he had said, "We have some bad men in the South . . . and we have some bad men in the North, who want to dissolve this Union in order to gratify their unhallowed ambition . . . If the question could be taken away from politicians; if it could be taken away from the Congress of the United States, . . . [the people] would settle it without the slightest difficulty, and bid defiance to secessionists and disunionists." [48] He told a delegation from the Cleveland Convention: "We must return to constitutional

[46] *Cong. Globe*, 36 Cong., 2 Sess., 769.
[47] *Ibid.*, 37 Cong., 2 Sess., 586.
[48] *Ibid.*, 36 Cong., 2 Sess., 767.

limits establishing the great fact that ours is a government of limited powers with a written constitution, with boundaries both national and State, and that these limitations and boundaries must be observed and strictly respected if free government is to exist; and, coming out of a rebellion, we ought to demonstrate to mankind that a free government cannot live on hate and distrust." [49] To deny Southerners the rights of self-government because they could not be trusted to govern themselves properly, seemed to Johnson a betrayal of democratic principles.

Though Johnson stood ready to punish the man who was in arms against the government, he was just as willing to welcome him back to full fellowship when he showed himself repentant and once more loyal. In the very definition of repentance and loyalty inhered the fundamental conflict between Johnson and the Radicals. Repentance to Johnson meant sorrow for having taken up arms against the government, and, as a proof thereof, repudiation of debts incurred in rebellion; loyalty connoted a present desire to maintain the Union, and live under the Constitution with slavery and the right of secession eliminated. But the Radicals saw in Southerners no repentance short of condemning themselves, their soldiers, and their leaders as sinners against God and traitors against the government, no loyalty short of repudiating their own society and adopting Northern political, economic, and social standards. Between these two points of view, there was a gulf that could have been bridged only by tolerance and earnest effort on both sides.

Johnson's program of restoration followed that of Lincoln, yet carried out virtually the policy that he had advocated long before he became vice-president. The basic

[49] *New York Herald*, Sept. 26, 1866.

terms were laid down in two proclamations of May 29, 1865. One granted amnesty with restoration of property,[50] except slaves, to all but fourteen excepted classes of former Confederates when they should take a solemn oath of allegiance.[51] But he restored confiscated lands generously and issued pardons freely to those who asked, provided they showed evidence of future loyalty. "I did not expect to keep out all who were excluded from the amnesty, or even a large number of them," he later explained, "but I intended they should sue for pardon, and so realize the enormity of their crime." [52] The second proclamation appointed Holden Provisional Governor of North Carolina with "all the powers necessary and proper to enable such loyal people of the State of North Carolina to restore said State to its constitutional relations to the Federal Government." [53] A convention was to amend the constitution of the state, but no person should be a delegate or vote for a delegate to this convention unless he had subscribed to the amnesty oath, and had been a qualified voter under the state law before the passage of the ordinance of secession. Determination of future qualifications for electors and office-holders was left entirely to the state. This second proclamation ordered the restoration of federal revenue officers, postal service, and courts. Subsequent proclamations soon set in motion the wheels of reorganization in Mississippi, Georgia, Texas, Alabama, South Carolina, and Florida. Similar provisional governments had been established under Lincoln in Tennessee, Louisiana,

---

[50] Except where legal proceedings under confiscation laws had already been instituted.

[51] J. D. Richardson, *op. cit.,* VI, 310.

[52] Conversation with G. L. Stearns, *Boston Daily Advertiser,* Oct. 23, 1865. Also Johnson MSS., LXXIX.

[53] J. D. Richardson, *op. cit.,* 312.

Virginia, and Arkansas. By July, then, all Secessia was in process of political rehabilitation.

* * * *

When Johnson announced this policy of leniency, he was denounced by the Radicals for inconsistency. As War Governor of Tennessee, he had dealt severely with traitors. While vice-president and during the assassination furor, he had daily proclaimed that treason should be made odious and traitors should be punished. So summarily, indeed, did he handle the accomplices in Lincoln's assassination that he was criticized for excessive harshness. Now men said he had suddenly reversed his position, and they sought to guess the influence that had brought the change. His policy was in reality fundamentally the same in 1866 as it had been in 1863; [54] it was merely at first misunderstood.

When Johnson made his stirring Senatorial speeches against traitors, the Union was in danger; and to the Union Andrew Johnson showed as complete devotion as did Charles Sumner to the negro. When Johnson was War Governor of Tennessee, that state was the scene of a bitter battle for the very life of the nation. Johnson stopped at nothing in defense of the Union against traitors in arms. When he became president, the victory was won and Lee had surrendered, but the War was by no means over. Johnston's forces were still in the field against Sherman. The problem that had worried Lincoln and Grant and Lee, Johnson still faced—the danger of guerrilla warfare. Grant and Sherman, with Lincoln, bent every effort to sparing the country its prolonged agonies, for they, like Johnson, who had seen it in Ten-

[54] As War Governor he had urged Lincoln to oppose the Wade-Davis proposal and had urged speedy restoration as soon as loyalty was assured. A. Johnson to M. Blair, Nov. 24, 1863, E. McPherson, *Political Manual* (1867), 73. See also R. W. Winston, *op. cit.*, 252-257, 522-525.

nessee, knew what it meant, as Stanton and Stevens and Sumner could not. Johnson's threats against treason, then, were hurled at desperate leaders who were threatening to scatter the Southern forces in guerrilla bands more dangerous than actual armies.

In April the shock of Lincoln's assassination had made even wise men temporarily lose their heads. In issuing his proclamation of May 2, which accused Davis and other prominent Southerners of complicity in the murder of Lincoln, Johnson had the advice of calm and sage men as well as the opinion of Stanton and Holt who wrote it. Full comprehension of the tension, the distrust, the panic of April and May, 1865, is possible only through feeling the rapidity of the popular pulse as it beat out its rhythm of terror and hatred in the numberless letters that poured in upon such men as Johnson, Sumner, and Joseph Holt, the stern, suspicious Judge-Advocate-General.[55] Nearly everybody was infected by the spasm of fear and wild rumor that overcame the country.[56] Scarcely a Southern leader escaped suspicion. Even benign old Welles was swept off his feet. It is little wonder that in this atmosphere Johnson's ire was aroused against the leading Confederates of whose complicity in Lincoln's murder his Secretary of War, and Attorney-General, and Judge-Advocate-General claimed to have positive proof. Only gradually did passions cool and excitement subside, as slowly the truth of Booth's fanatical intrigue was divulged. By the end of May, however, the War was actually over, the Southern armies were safely demobolized, and guerrilla

[55] The Holt MSS. present an admirable picture of this phase of the opening days of Johnson's administration.

[56] E.g., a lengthy epistle from J. Hamilton of New York gave the details of a Southern plot to assassinate Lincoln, Johnson, Stanton, Grant, and others and put General Sherman in power because of his leniency toward the South. May 29, 1865, Stanton MSS., XXVII.

warfare was no longer an imminent danger but an easily forgettable chimera.

Johnson did long to inflict exemplary punishment upon a few leading traitors. "I shall go to my grave," he wrote in 1868, "with the firm belief that Davis, Cobb, Toombs, and a few others of the arch-conspirators and traitors should have been tried, convicted, and hanged for treason . . . If it was the last act of my life I'd hang Jeff Davis as an example. I'd show coming generations that, while the rebellion was too popular a revolt to punish many who participated in it, treason should be made odious and arch-traitors should be punished." [57] ·The criticism aroused by Stanton's conduct of the trial of Booth's co-conspirators, and his own repugnance toward military tribunals, kept him from yielding to the pressure for a military trial of Davis. Johnson desired an example, not revenge. He knew only too well that a military trial would make Davis a martyr. For two years he kept Davis in confinement while he sought legal means to try him. But Chase would not ride the Virginia circuit until the last vestiges of military rule were withdrawn and the habeas corpus restored,[58] and Johnson's legal advisers never found the means of surmounting this obstacle. It was, however, only when open warfare with the Radicals overbalanced all other considerations, that Johnson gave up his efforts to bring Davis to trial.

While Johnson was threatening leading traitors, he was quietly formulating in cabinet his plan of leniency for the

[57] A. Johnson to B. C. Truman, Aug. 3, 1868, *Century Magazine,* LXXXV (1913), 438.
[58] S. P. Chase to A. Johnson, Oct. 12, 1865, Johnson MSS., LXXIX; S. P. Chase to G. W. Brook, District Judge, March 20, 1866, *ibid.,* XCI; S. P. Chase to J. W. Schuckers, Sept. 24, 1866, Chase MSS., 2nd ser., III; J. W. Schuckers, *Life and Public Services of Salmon Portland Chase,* 535-543.

masses. The very North Carolina Proclamation issued on May 29 had been drawn up while Lincoln was yet alive, discussed at his last cabinet meeting, and postponed only to enable Stanton who had drawn it up to furnish the other cabinet members with copies. As soon as Lincoln's funeral was over, the proclamation was again considered, changed somewhat, and made applicable to North Carolina instead of Virginia whose existent loyal government presented complications. This and the Amnesty Proclamation carefully drawn by Speed were agreed upon while Seward, whom Radicals later blamed [59] for Johnson's so-called reversal of policy, was still confined to his house.[60]

Johnson's close advisers favored moderation. The cabinet agreed upon the policy of the proclamations except that Dennison, Speed, and Stanton would have included negro suffrage, and Speed and Stanton would have dealt more severely with the leaders. Grant and Sherman urged moderation and speedy restoration; their opinion carried weight. Grant, whose prestige and friendliness gave him influence over Johnson, attended cabinet meetings and was constantly in consultation with the President. After their subsequent quarrel Johnson wrote, "Grant . . . meant well for the first two years, and much that I did that was denounced was through his advice." [61] Welles and McCulloch, Seward when he was sufficiently recovered, and Senator Doolittle were frequently with the President. The Blairs were intimate advisers.[62] In fact, it was to Blair's home at Silver Spring, just

[59] James G. Blaine, *Twenty Years of Congress*, II, 66-70; Sumner's Speech, reported in the *New York Herald*, Oct. 3, 1866; O. O. Howard, *Autobiography*, II, 277. Seward gladly accepted credit for molding Johnson's policy, New York speech, *New York Tribune*, Sept. 4, 1866.

[60] Welles MS. Diary, May 8 and 9, 1865—(II, 301).

[61] A. Johnson to B. C. Truman, Aug. 3, 1868, *Century Magazine*, LXXXV (1913), 439.

[62] Sumner's speech, *New York Herald*, Oct. 3, 1866.

out of Washington, that Johnson had retired to avoid the public gaze and recover his dignity, after his drunken inauguration as vice-president. Friends who stood by him then naturally retained influence. Preston King was so close to the President that when Mrs. Lincoln left and Johnson took possession, this New York politician went to the White House to live with him until his family arrived. All summer King remained in Washington to advise.[63] At the very moment when Sumner and Wade were rejoicing at Johnson's Radicalism, Doolittle wrote home to his wife, "Johnson is all right . . . God is still with us. O, if we are only true to the country all will yet be safe . . . Mr. Johnson, King and myself are a trio whose hearts & heads sympathize more closely and more deeply than any other trio in America just now." [64] These close friends of Johnson all favored moderation.[65]

Radicals went to call on Johnson, did most of the talking, and interpreted his taciturnity into approval. The President was a good listener, non-committal even with close friends. The Radicals assumed that a courageous loyalist from the South who had suffered grievously at the hands of rebels would seek revenge. They read *their* meaning into the word "traitor" in his speeches. Blinded by their own enthusiasm, they congratulated themselves that he was their tool. Then when time disillusioned them, they accused Johnson of a political somersault. Some blamed Seward. Others said wheedling of Southern aristocrats who had snubbed him before the War had wrought the change, in a man who would

[63] J. G. Blaine, *op. cit.*, II, 11; Welles MS. Diary, May 12 and July 24, 1865—(II, 305, 340); G. Welles to Mrs. Welles, Aug. 6 and Sept. 24, 1865, Welles MSS., LIX.

[64] April 26, 1865, State Hist. Soc. of Wis., *Proceedings* (1909), 291

[65] They were not "rebels" or Copperheads, but the same moderate Union men who had advised Lincoln.

sell his soul for social recognition.[66] Still others accused him of ambition to build a party of Southerners and Westerners, "traitors" and "Copperheads," that would retain him in the Presidency. These men, if sincere, did not know Johnson. The truth was that the development of his policy had been steady and logical from beginnings under Lincoln and his own experiments in Tennessee to its final form late in 1865.

To the application of his policy Johnson gave personal attention. He appointed provisional governors who called conventions chosen on the basis of the amnesty oath and the old qualifications for voting. The conventions amended state constitutions, determined future suffrage qualifications, and then arranged elections of legislatures and governors. These legislatures chose United States senators and held elections for members of the House of Representatives. Meanwhile the provisional governors and troops remained. Only when he was convinced that he could do so safely, did Johnson turn over the state governments to the elected officials.

The whole problem was made infinitely more difficult for Johnson by the foolish acts of Southerners themselves. Southern legislators whom he was trying to help were as uncompromising on the one side as Northern Radicals were on the other. In fact, during 1865 Southern extremists caused Johnson more concern than did those of the North. Then when Southerners went to the polls, they elected their old leaders, often unpardoned, sometimes notorious rebels, instead of the less prominent candidates who had a passive war record. To put faith in former leaders was natural, but extremely impolitic. It ruined what chance Johnson's policy

[66] J. G. Blaine, *op. cit.*, II, 68-70; J. D. Fuller, Dec. 27, 1865, Pastor of Tremont Temple, Boston, to C. Sumner, Sumner MSS., LXXV.

had of immediate success. Besides, unreasonable and hot-headed editors and politicians talked wildly. Returned soldiers took in general a rational view of the situation, but many of them could not undo the damage wrought by a few noisy agitators.[67]

In handling this trying situation Johnson displayed unusual patience and wisdom. With one eye on Northern politics, he untiringly counseled the South to be reasonable and tactful. After the election in 1865 he wired Governor Holden, "The results of the recent elections in North Carolina have greatly damaged the prospects of the State in the restoration of its Governmental relations. Should the action and the spirit of the Legislature be in the same direction, it will greatly increase the mischief already done, and might be fatal. It is hoped the action and spirit manifested by the Legislature will be so directed as rather to repair than to increase the difficulties under which the State has already placed itself." [68] The President advised the Southern members-elect not to present themselves at the organization of Congress. "It will be better policy," he said, "to present their certificates of election after the two Houses [are] organized which will then be a simple question under the Constitution of the members taking their seats. Each House must judge for itself the election returns and qualifications of its members." [69] When the Mississippi Legislature hesitated about ratifying the Thirteenth Amendment, he wired, "Failure to adopt the Amendment will create the belief that the action

[67] Even Sidney Andrews, a Radical journalist who found little good in the South, reported the ex-soldiers "the best citizens" in the South, and warned his Radical friends that the Union depended on "the bearing of the men who were privates and minor officers in the armies of Lee and Johnston." *Atlantic Monthly*, XVII (February, 1866), 242.

[68] Nov. 27, 1865, Johnson MSS., "Telegrams."

[69] A. Johnson to B. F. Perry, Nov. 27, 1865, *ibid.*, LXXXI, and "Telegrams."

of the convention abolishing Slavery, will hereafter by the same body be revoked . . . I trust in God, that the Legislature will adopt the amendment, and thereby make the way clear for the admission of Senators and Representatives to their seats in the present Congress." [70] To South Carolina and Georgia he wired similar counsel.[71]

Lenient as he was, there were limits beyond which Johnson would not yield. As an evidence of loyalty prerequisite to a special pardon, he required an amnesty oath. Southerners attempted to vote on the strength of this oath before they had been pardoned. Johnson promised to try to pardon all who deserved it by the time their votes were needed, but he emphatically forbade their voting until the pardon was granted.[72] When unpardoned rebels were elected, the President refused to allow them to assume office. Humphreys was not recognized as Governor of Mississippi until Johnson saw fit to pardon him; [73] in New Orleans Monroe was suspended from the mayoralty until he had made application and received a pardon.[74] Later after sufficient time for application had passed, Johnson refused altogether to allow Semmes of Mobile, still unpardoned, to occupy an office for which he had been chosen.[75] Johnson knew how to be firm when he chose.

To the wisdom of Johnson's choice of provisional governors even the Radicals testified.[76] In coöperation with these governors Johnson worked out the details of Southern

[70] A. Johnson to Gov. W. L. Sharkey, Nov. 1, 1865, *ibid.,* "Telegrams."
[71] A. Johnson to Gov. Perry, Oct. 28, 1865, and A. J. to Gov. Johnson, Nov. 26, 1865, *ibid.,* "Telegrams."
[72] A. Johnson to Gov. Johnson, Sept. 29, 1865, and A. J. to Gov. Holden, Sept. 21, 1865, *ibid.,* "Telegrams."
[73] A. Johnson to Maj. Gen. Thomas, Nov. 19, 1866, *ibid.,* "Telegrams."
[74] Edward McPherson, *Political Manual* (1866), 28.
[75] *New York Herald,* Oct. 2, 1866.
[76] E.g., M. Howard of Hartford to G. Welles, July 27, 1865, Welles MSS., LIX.

policy. He kept in close touch with each of them, wrote letters, sent telegrams, interviewed prominent Southerners and Northern travelers in Secessia, studied reports, and heard and gave advice. He well realized the delicacy of his task. To move too speedily, he, too, felt would endanger the Union cause. He spoke plainly to a group of Virginians: "In going into the recent rebellion against the Government of the United States the people of the South erred; and in returning . . . I am free to say that all the responsible positions and places *ought to be confined distinctly and clearly to men who are loyal.* If, for instance, there are only five thousand loyal men in a State, or a less number, but sufficient to take charge of the political machinery of the State, *those five thousand men, or the lesser number, are entitled to it, if all the rest should be otherwise inclined.* I look upon it as fundamental that the *exercise of political power should be confined to loyal men.*" [77] But "loyal men" according to Johnson were either those not excepted by the classification of May 29 or those excepted but specially pardoned after having subscribed to the amnesty oath. To swell the ranks of loyalty Johnson favored full restoration of property and civil rights to men sincerely anxious to return to good citizenship.[78]

He enlisted the aid of prominent Southerners applying for pardon. For example, when Joseph E. Brown, an 1860 secessionist and War Governor of Georgia, was imprisoned in Washington after the War, Johnson released him, talked with him, and sent him home on parole to serve the Union cause. "I think," the President told Stanton, "that his return home can be turned to good account. He will at once

---

[77] Reply to "Virginia Resolutions," Johnson MSS., LXXXVI. Italics are Johnson's.
[78] He issued an order that land should be restored when a pardon was granted to ex-rebels. E. McPherson, *op. cit.* (1866), 12-13.

go to work and do all that he can in restoring the State. I
have no doubt that he will act in good faith. He can not,
under the circumstances, act otherwise." [79] Brown became a
strong advocate of the Union and of acceptance of Northern
terms of reconstruction. He became a United States senator; in 1868 he voted for Grant; he was forced into the
Democratic Party in 1872 only by Republican excesses.
Such another pardoned leader was Alexander H. Stephens,
Vice-President of the Confederacy. After release from
prison, he labored sedulously under Johnson's surveillance
for moderation among Southerners.[80] Yet Johnson urged
Stephens not to run for office. "It would be exceedingly impolitic," he wired, "for Mr. A. H. Stephen's [sic] name to be
used in connection with the Senatorial election. If elected
he would not be permitted to take his seat . . . He stands
charged with Treason, and no disposition has been made of
his case. His present position will enable him to do far more
good than any other." [81] Stephens had emphatically refused
to allow his name to stand lest it embarrass the President.[82]
But he was elected over this protest. His telegram to Johnson explained even this much heralded "defiance" of Congress. "I was elected yesterday to the United States Senate,"
it runs, ". . . under circumstances particularly embarras-
ing [sic] which will be fully explained by mail. An effort
may be made to impress you with the belief that this was the
result of a disposition . . . to oppose the policy of the Administration . . . My full conviction is that it sprung from
an earnest belief whether erroneous or not, that it would most

[79] June 3, 1865, Stanton MSS., XXVII.
[80] See, e.g., Alex. H. Stephens, *Recollections,* 544, 546-548.
[81] A. Johnson to Maj. Gen. Steedman, Nov. 24, 1865, Johnson MSS.,
"Telegrams."
[82] J. S. Harris of Milledgeville, Ga., to A. Johnson, Dec. 29, 1865, *ibid.,*
LXXXIII.

effectually aid that policy which it is well known I am faith-
fully laboring to carry out." [83] Stephens did greatly aid
Johnson. He even helped persuade the Georgia Legislature
to pass laws securing negroes the very civil rights that the
Radicals were seeking to impose by Congressional action.[84]

In applying this same policy of giving Southerners an
active interest in peace and union, Johnson encouraged them
to organize a militia that Radicals denounced as preparation
for another civil war. September 1, 1865, he wired Governor
Parsons of Alabama, "I would suggest for your consideration the propriety of raising in each county an armed
mounted *posse comitatus* organized under your Militia Law
and under such provisions as you need to secure their loyalty
and obedience to your authority and that of the Military
Authorities, to repress crime and arrest criminals. A similar
organization by me in Tennessee when Military Governor
worked well. Governor Sharkey has begun to raise such a
force in Mississippi. It seems to me that in some such way
your citizens would be committed to the cause of Law and
Order and their loyalty to the Union would become not
merely passive but active. In any event while Society is
reörganizing, the people would themselves by Vigilance Committees or by like unauthorized, spontaneous, and quasi-
illegal manner endeavor to repress lawlessness and punish
marauding. And it seems preferable to give this natural
impulse a proper legal shape and control than to have it
illegal and uncontrolled." [85] When Schurz protested against
the Mississippi militia, and encouraged General Slocum in
prohibiting it, Johnson wired in rebuke: "I presume General Slocum will issue no order interfering with Governor

[83] Feb. 1, 1866, *ibid.*, "Telegrams."
[84] A. H. Stephens to A. Johnson, March 23, 1866, *ibid.*, XCI.
[85] *Ibid.*, "Telegrams."

Sharkey in restoring functions of the State Government without first consulting the Government . . . It is believed there can be organized in each county a force of citizens or militia to suppress crime, preserve order, and enforce the civil authority . . . which would enable the Federal Government to reduce the Army and withdraw to a great extent the forces from the State . . . The great object is to induce the people to come forward in defense of the State and Federal Government . . . The people must be trusted with their Government." [86]

In the relations between military and civil authorities Johnson faced a problem. He knew that military authority was necessary in portions of the South; even when he declared by proclamation that the rebellion had ended, he announced against the advice of many of his friends that "the President's proclamation does not remove martial law, or operate in any way upon the Freedmen's Bureau in the exercise of its legitimate jurisdiction." [87] He wished civil and military officers to coöperate in hastening the return of normal conditions. Military commanders were ordered to "aid and assist the . . . provisional governor" and to "abstain from in any way hindering, impeding, or discouraging the loyal people from the organization of a State government." [88] Where the military and civil authorities did coöperate, good government and order were rapidly restored. Where they did not, Johnson sometimes backed the military, as when he upheld General Thomas's suspension of an order of the Legislature of Mississippi to disarm all negroes; [89] he

[86] Carl Schurz, *Reminiscences*, III, 192. Also C. Schurz to C. Sumner, C. Schurz, *Speeches, Correspondence, and Political Papers*, I, 269.
[87] E. McPherson, *op. cit.* (1866), 17.
[88] J. D. Richardson, *op. cit.*, VI, 312-314.
[89] A. Johnson to Gen. Thomas, Dec. 12, 1865, Johnson MSS., LXXXII.

sometimes supported the civil authorities, as when he upheld
in Florida the arrest of General Foster's officers for fast
riding in violation of civil ordinances,[90] and when he ordered
an imprisoned sheriff in Mississippi to be released, Lieutenant Colonel Gibson who had arrested him to be relieved of
his command, and the general in charge to "direct that no
military interference be had against civil process respecting
the matter." [91] Johnson's maxim was never to allow the military force to interfere "in any case where justice [could]
be attained through the medium of civil authority." [92]

Three demands Johnson did make of the Southern States:
repeal of the ordinances of secession, ratification of the
Thirteenth Amendment, and repudiation of the rebel debts,
Confederate and state. But even these fundamental and unquestionably just conditions, Johnson was determined to secure by voluntary action. He would not use force beyond
withholding pardons or delaying recognition of individual
officials, but he advised and persuaded, and used every line
of Southern influence to secure their adoption. For example,
when he heard through Governor Holden that the North
Carolina Convention had tabled a law prohibiting the payment of the war debt of the state,[93] Johnson wired, "Every
Dollar of the Debt created to aid the rebellion against the
United States should be repudiated . . . forever . . . It
. . . cannot be recognized by the people of any state, pro-
fessing themselves loyal to the Government of the United
States, and in the Union . . . I trust and hope, that the
people of North Carolina, will wash their hands of every-

90 New York Herald, Dec. 20, 1866.
91 A. Johnson to Maj. Gen. P. J. Osterhaus, Nov. 3, 1865, Johnson MSS.,
"Telegrams."
92 E. D. Townsend to D. Tillson, April 17, 1866, E. McPherson, op. cit.
(1866), 17.
93 E. McPherson, op. cit. (1866), 19.

thing that partakes in the slightest degree of the Rebellion." [94] The next day the tabled resolution of repudiation was called forth and passed, 84-12. From Georgia Governor Johnson wired, "We need some aid to repeal the war debt. Send me word on the subject." [95] Johnson responded, "The people of Georgia should not hesitate one single moment in repudiating every single Dollar of debt created for the purpose of aiding the rebellion against the Government of the United States. . . . It should at once be made known at home and abroad, that no debt contracted for the purpose of dissolving the Union of the States, can, or ever will be paid." [96] Ten days later the Georgia Convention passed the repudiation ordinance, 133-117.[97] The South Carolinians quibbled to a degree that must have exasperated Johnson, and their Convention finally adjourned without repudiating the state debt; but it did repeal the ordinance of secession, and declared slavery abolished "by action of the United States authorities." [98] Johnson displayed infinite tact and patience, but upon his three demands he stood firm.

He also urged upon the states protection of the civil rights of negroes. "There is no concession required on the part of the people of Mississippi," he told Governor-Elect Humphreys, "or the Legislature, other than a loyal compliance with the laws and constitution of the United States, and the adoption of such measures, giving protection to all freedmen or freemen, in person and property without regard to color, as will entitle them to resume all their constitutional relations in the Federal Union . . . There is no disposition,

94 Oct. 18, 1865, Johnson MSS., "Executive Mansion Letters," printed in E. McPherson, *op. cit.* (1866), 19.
95 Oct. 27, 1865, E. McPherson, *op. cit.* (1866), 20.
96 Oct. 28, 1865, Johnson MSS., "Telegrams."
97 E. McPherson, *op. cit.* (1866), 20.
98 *Ibid.* (1866), 22-24.

arbitrarily, on the part of the Government, to dictate what their action should be, but on the contrary, simply and kindly advise a policy that is believed will result in restoring all the relations which should exist between the States comprising the Federal Union." [99]

Johnson realized that the basis of Southern representation would have to be changed to prevent Southern power in Congress from being actually increased by the Thirteenth Amendment which automatically abolished the old three-fifths rule. Hence he suggested in January, 1866, a compromise amendment which read: "Representatives shall be apportioned among the several States . . . according to the number of qualified male voters, as prescribed by each State. Direct taxes shall be apportioned among the several States . . . according to the value of all property subject to taxation in each State." [1] But his proposal was ignored. He had doubted the propriety of making this amendment in January. By July he believed that the question could never be permanently settled until all the states were represented, but that the menace of over-representation of the South was a mere bugbear anyway since no change could occur until after the census-taking of 1870, by which date a proper remedy could have been determined. [2]

Johnson even favored limited negro suffrage. But he believed that this was a matter for the states to decide. [3] Southerners must be allowed to work out the problem for them-

[99] Nov. 17, 1865, Johnson MSS., "Telegrams."

[1] The proposal was made to Senator Dixon, and was published in the *National Intelligencer*, Jan. 29, 1866. There is a copy in the Johnson MSS., XCV, in Wm. G. Moore's handwriting.

[2] Interview with Johnson, *Boston Evening Commercial*, July 21, 1866.

[3] On his trip South on the President's behalf, Watterson assured the people that the Chases and Sumners would never drive Johnson from the position that the suffrage question belonged to the states. H. M. Watterson to A. Johnson, June 27, 1865, Johnson MSS., LXVIII.

selves. Johnson knew the mutual hatred of poor white and
negro.[4] He felt that the negro would fare better in the hands
of the old slave-holding class than under Northerners and
poor white loyalists. In his first message to Congress, he said,
"The freedmen, if they show patience and manly virtues,
will sooner obtain a participation in the elective franchise
through the States than through the General Government,
even if it had power to intervene." [5] As a citizen of Tennessee
Johnson would have sought the suffrage for intelligent and
property-holding negroes, and ex-soldiers; [6] as President he
could only recommend it to the states. "I hope and trust," he
wrote Governor Sharkey of Mississippi, "your convention
[will grant this qualified suffrage], and, as a consequence,
the Radicals, who are wild upon negro franchise, will be completely foiled in their attempt to keep the southern States
from renewing their relations to the Union by not accepting
their senators and representatives." [7] Universal suffrage,
Johnson, a Southerner who knew the negro, could not favor.

* * * *

Through the summer and fall the people watched Johnson's program in operation, and on the whole, approved. In
September the Wisconsin Convention supported Johnson by
a huge majority.[8] Senator Dixon repeatedly [9] and Babcock
as late as April,[10] promised the overwhelming approval of
Connecticut voters. In February men like Cochrane of New

[4] Conversation of A. Johnson with G. L. Stearns, *Boston Daily Advertiser*, Oct. 23, 1865. Also Johnson MSS., LXXIX.
[5] J. D. Richardson, *op. cit.*, VI, 360.
[6] Conversation with G. L. Stearns cited above.
[7] Aug. 15, 1865, E. McPherson, *op. cit.* (1866), 19.
[8] The old abolitionist element was completely snowed under. J. R. Doolittle to A. Johnson, Sept. 8, 1865, Johnson MSS., LXXVI.
[9] E.g., Sept. 26, 1865, *ibid.*, LXXVII.
[10] J. F. Babcock to G. Welles, April 6, 1866, Welles MSS., LX.

York,[11] Geiger of Ohio,[12] and General Sherman in Missouri,[13] declared that, whatever the politicians did, the people would support Johnson. Grant testified to the popularity of the Moderate cause.[14]

The hearty support of nearly all the great Union generals, Grant, Sherman, Thomas, Hancock, Meade, Schofield, Ewing and war governors like Morton of Indiana and Andrew of Massachusetts won for Johnson's cause great prestige with the people.[15] Beecher offered thanks that "God has raised you up for such a crisis & endowed you with the ability and disposition, to serve the Nation rather than yourself or any mere party." [16]

Radical leaders realized the strength of popular support of Johnson. Just before the first veto the shrewd Chicago journalist, Charles H. Ray, wrote Trumbull, "I greatly fear that the result of the disposition that many of our friends counsel will be to drive him into the enemy's ranks. Now take my prophecy on one thing: If he will agree to your bill giving the freedmen the civil rights that the whites enjoy, and if he halts at that, and war is made on him because he will not go to the extent of negro suffrage, he will beat all who assail him. The party may be split, the government may go out of Republican hands; but Andy Johnson will be the cock of the walk." [17] After the veto and Johnson's much denounced February speech, Loring wrote from the Massachusetts Legislature, "I find a peculiar desire for delay, & a reluctance to move against the President. . . . I am

11 J. Cochrane to A. Johnson, Feb. 12, 1866, Johnson MSS., LXXXVI.
12 J. H. Geiger to J. R. Doolittle, Feb. 11, 1866, *ibid.*, LXXXVI.
13 W. T. Sherman to A. Johnson, Feb. 11, 1866, *ibid.*, LXXXVI.
14 U. S. Grant, *Personal Memoirs*, 510-511.
15 R. W. Winston, *op. cit.*, 340, 347.
16 H. W. Beecher to A. Johnson, Oct. 23, 1865, Johnson MSS., LXXIX.
17 Feb. 7, 1866, Trumbull MSS., LXIII.

somewhat astonished at the affection manifested for a man, whose course towards the party which elected him, entitles him to anything but affection." [18] In November, 1865, Wade dubbed Johnson "a knave or a fool," but feared he had a majority of the people behind him.[19] Morton, later to become a bitter opponent, wrote Johnson, "Since the publication of your message, I have conversed with a number of the first men in New York, in the financial and commercial departments of business, and have found all to heartily approve it. . . . The great body of the people in the North will endorse your doctrines and policy, and this the members of Congress will find out before they are ninety days older." [20]

Johnson's annual message commending his policy to Congress was masterful. Charles Francis Adams wrote, "The annual message, and the report of the Secretary of the Treasury, raised the character of the nation immensely in Europe; I know of nothing better in the annals even when Washington was chief and Hamilton his financier." [21] Watterson, Bancroft, and General Dix agreed with this verdict.[22] Even Lowell praised it.[23] Sheridan, Commander of the Military Division of the Gulf, after Schurz's condemnatory report was in Johnson's hands, wrote praising the Presi-

[18] G. B. Loring to C. Sumner, Feb. 26, 1866, Sumner MSS., LXXVII.

[19] B. F. Wade to C. Sumner, Nov. 1, 1865, *ibid.*, LXXV.

[20] Dec. 7, 1865, Johnson MSS., LXXXII. Other leaders who later became Radicals testified at this time to the popularity of his policy. Gen. J. T. Pratt of Connecticut to A. Johnson, Sept. 11, 1865, *ibid.*, LXXVI; A. Badeau, Grant's staff assistant, to E. B. Washburne, Oct. 20, 1865, Washburne MSS., XVI. Forney of the *Philadelphia Press* believed in December that if the party opposed Johnson, it would "go to pieces." J. W. Forney to C. Sumner, Dec. 26, 1865, Sumner MSS., LXXV.

[21] C. F. Adams to Sidney Brooks, Hugh McCulloch, *Men and Measures,* 219-220; also *Detroit Advertiser and Tribune,* Dec. 6, 1865.

[22] H. M. Watterson to A. Johnson, Dec. 7, 1865, J. A. Dix to A. Johnson, Dec. 7, 1865, Geo. Bancroft to A. Johnson, Dec. 6, 1865, Johnson MSS., LXXXII. Bancroft who had written the message for Johnson watched with special interest its effect, and wrote, "*All* of all parties applaud the ground you have taken."

[23] *North Am. Rev.,* CII (January, 1866), 250-260.

dent's position. "We can well afford," he said, "to be lenient to this last annoyance, impotent ill feeling. . . . It is so hard by any species of legislation to correct this feeling, magnanimity is the safest and most manly course. How hard it would be to change the opinions of Mr. Wendell Phillips and make him a Vallandigham democrat by any species of legislation. I have the most abiding faith in the solution of the question of a restored Union, if we can only wait and trust to a little time and the working of natural causes." [24] Had a referendum been taken in December, 1865, Johnson's policy would have been approved overwhelmingly.[25] How popular support was diverted from Johnson to the Radicals is the story of the campaign.

[24] P. H. Sheridan to A. Johnson, Nov. 26, 1865, Johnson MSS., LXXXI.
[25] Rhodes concedes this. *History of the United States*, V, 549.

Chapter III

RECRUITING THE RADICAL RANKS

"THERE is no doubt," declared Senator Wade, "that if by an insurrection [the colored people] could contrive to slay one half of their oppressors, the other half would hold them in the highest respect and no doubt treat them with justice." [1] "With malice toward none, with charity for all . . . let us strive on . . . to do all which may achieve a just and lasting peace," urged Lincoln. Both men were Republicans.

Faction in the Republican Party was, indeed, no new phenomenon in 1866. From its very inception the anti-slavery movement had included moderates and extremists. The latter steadily grew in power from the days when Garrison was ostracized and Lovejoy murdered, until in 1867 they controlled Congress. A few earnest men with fanatical perseverance had conquered a nation. With success the objectives broadened, but Thad Stevens and Ben Wade led the same movement in 1867 that Lovejoy and Garrison had served thirty years earlier. The anti-slavery movement had embraced abolitionists who, with religious fervor, attacked slavery by fair means or foul wherever it existed; and more

---

[1] B. F. Wade to C. Sumner, Nov. 1, 1865, Sumner MSS., LXXV. Even if these lines were written in passion, the vindictiveness of a man who could commit this suggestion to paper is significant.

51

moderate men who opposed only the extension of slavery under the national ægis in national territories. The two groups coöperated as long as the Republicans were an opposition party. Victory brought disagreement, and even after the outbreak of the War factional differences within his party caused Lincoln as much concern as did Southern generals.[2]

In attacking the Union, Southerners welded together the diverse elements of Republicanism, and even drove many Democrats into the "Union Party." But the Radicals never entirely ceased agitation. They insisted upon unconstitutional general abolition at a time when Lincoln knew that even partial emancipation as a war measure would destroy the Union. The Emancipation Proclamation did not satisfy them. Lincoln, however, moderate from temperament and national policy alike, stood his ground against Radical denunciators, and moved only as political wisdom and the safety of the Union dictated.

But as the War progressed, its very purpose changed. In 1861 Lincoln led a Northern majority that placed the preservation of the Union above all questions of slavery; an extreme minority favored abolition. By 1863 the majority supported the moderate emancipation sponsored by Lincoln, and extremists were already suggesting equality of civil rights; the boldest talked of negro suffrage. Once more Lincoln was attacked as too moderate. In the first two years of the War, on the theory that the states were still in the Union, Congress seated all members legally elected by a loyal portion of the voters in a Unionist district of the seceding states. But the Thirty-eighth Congress, meeting in

2 The clamors of dissentious Republicans during the winter of 1860-1861 made satisfactory appointments to office difficult. Carl R. Fish, "Lincoln and the Patronage," *Am. Hist. Rev.*, VIII (1902), 53.

1863, refused to recognize members from any portion of a state that had seceded.[3] Thus Congress gradually evolved a new theory of the status of Southern states at the very time when Lincoln, acting on the original Northern contention that a state could not secede, was working toward the restoration of normal relations with parts of seceded states inside of the Union lines.

Then when the Emancipation Proclamation and prospects of the Thirteenth Amendment threatened its *raison d'être,* the old abolition group organized a campaign against Lincoln's reconstruction policy; during the summer of 1864, Radicals sought to repudiate Lincoln, and put Frémont in his place as president. The Davis bill [4] proposed a more extreme substitute for the program outlined in Lincoln's Proclamation of Amnesty and Reconstruction of December 8, 1863. When the bill fell before a pocket veto in July, 1864, Lincoln was denounced by its Radical sponsors.[5] The Wade-Davis Manifesto [6] attacked him in language comparable to that later applied to Johnson. *Brownson's Review* scathingly denounced him.[7] In April Medill of the *Chicago Tribune* favored rejecting him unless he remodeled his cabinet on Radical lines. "Lincoln has some very weak and foolish traits of character," Medill stated. "If he had reasonable political sagacity and would cut loose from the semi-copperheads in his Cabinet and about him, if he would put live, bold, vigorous radicals in their places no human power could prevent his nomination." Otherwise, thought Medill,

---

[3] Frederick W. Moore, "Representation in the National Congress from the Seceding States, 1861-65," *Am. Hist. Rev.,* II (1897), 279, 461.

[4] For Davis's speech supporting it, see *Cong. Globe,* 38 Cong., 1 Sess., Appendix, 82.

[5] George W. Julian, *Political Recollections,* 246; J. G. Blaine, *Twenty Years of Congress,* I, 514.

[6] *New York Tribune,* Aug. 5, 1864.

[7] *Brownson's Quarterly Review,* I, nat. ser. (April, 1864), 210-223.

Grant would be nominated.[8] Julian, who served on a committee to promote Chase's candidacy in 1864, tells us, "The opposition to Mr. Lincoln . . . was secretly cherished by many of the ablest and most patriotic men of the party. The extent of their opposition in Congress can never be known. . . . Mr. Lincoln's nomination was nearly unanimous, . . . but of the more earnest and thorough-going Republicans in both Houses of Congress, probably not one in ten really favored it. It was not only very distasteful to a large majority of Congress but to many of the most prominent men of the party throughout the country. During the month of June the feeling against Mr. Lincoln became more and more bitter and intense, but its expression never found its way to the people." [9] Blaine says Lincoln's veto of the Davis bill met "violent opposition from the more radical members of both Houses. If Congress had been in session at the time, a very rancorous hostility would have been developed against the President." [10] To save the country from McClellan, the Radicals scampered back to the fold, and supported Lincoln in the election. After the election, however, they began a persistent campaign of opposition to Lincoln's mildness toward the South.[11]

Lincoln's restoration policy was liberal toward the South, kindly, forgiving, moderate. Sumner, Wade, and Stevens fought this policy under his régime as they did later under Johnson. All through the War even in his own state, Lincoln was bitterly opposed by the Radicals in his party, especially

8 J. Medill to E. B. Washburne, April 12, 1864, Washburne MSS., LI.
9 G. W. Julian, op. cit., 238, 243.
10 J. G. Blaine, op. cit., II, 43.
11 For a discussion of this opposition see Chas. H. McCarthy, *Lincoln's Plan of Reconstruction*, 190-383.

the old abolitionists and the Germans.[12] On the very day of his assassination a New York Radical had written Sumner bitterly denouncing Lincoln's "magnanimity" as "the great word with the disloyal."[13] In February a Philadelphia Republican wrote, "We voted for Lincoln here pretty much upon the choice of evils principle. Some are expressing their regret, & not in measured terms, that they voted for him at all."[14]

Proof, if proof be needed,[15] of Lincoln's desire for speedy restoration, exists in the steps already taken in Louisiana, Virginia, Arkansas, and Tennessee, in the story of the Hampton Roads Conference, in his kindly nature, and in the events of the last week of his life. On Tuesday night of that week, Lincoln responded to serenaders in a carefully prepared speech. In it he outlined his ideas. He said:

"Reconstruction . . . is fraught with great difficulty. Unlike a case of war between independent nations, there is no authorized organ for us to treat with—no one man has authority to give up the rebellion for any other man. We simply must begin with and mold from disorganized and discordant elements. Nor is it a small additional embarrassment that we, the loyal people, differ among ourselves as to the mode, manner, and measure of reconstruction. . . . The question whether the seceded states, so called, are in the Union or out of it . . . has not been, nor yet is, a practically material one and . . . any discussion of it, while it thus remains practically immaterial, could have no effect other than

[12] Arthur C. Cole, "President Lincoln and the Illinois Radical Republicans," *Miss. Valley Hist. Rev.,* IV (1918), 417.
[13] A. P. Grunger to C. Sumner, Sumner MSS., LXXIII.
[14] J. Penington to C. Sumner, Feb. 4, 1865, *ibid.,* LXXII.
[15] Blaine insists that: "Beyond his experiment with the 'Louisiana plan' Mr. Lincoln had never given the slightest indication either by word or deed as to the specific course he would adopt." *Op. cit.,* II, 49.

the mischievous one of dividing our friends. As yet, whatever it may hereafter become, that question is bad as the basis of a controversy, and good for nothing at all—a merely pernicious abstraction. We all agree that the seceded States, so called, are out of their proper practical relation with the Union, and that the sole object of the government, civil and military, in regard to those States, is to again get them into that proper practical relation. I believe that it is not only possible, but in fact easier, to do this without deciding or even considering whether these States have ever been out of the Union, than with it. Finding themselves safely at home, it would be utterly immaterial whether they had ever been abroad. Let us all join in doing the acts necessary to restoring the proper practical relations between these States and the Union, and each forever after innocently indulge his own opinion whether in doing the acts he brought the States from without into the Union, or only gave them proper assistance, they never having been out of it. . . . The question is not whether the Louisiana government, as it stands, is quite all that is desirable. The question is, will it be wiser to take it as it is and help to improve it, or to reject and disperse it? . . . If . . . we recognize and sustain the new government of Louisiana, . . . we encourage the hearts and nerve the arms of the 12,000 to adhere to their work, and argue for it, and proselyte for it, and fight for it, and feed it, and grow it, and ripen it to a complete success. The colored man, too, in seeing all united for him, is inspired with vigilance, and energy, and daring, to the same end. Grant that he desires the elective franchise, will he not attain it sooner by saving the already advanced steps toward it than by running backward over them? Concede that the new government of Louisiana is only [to] what it should be as the egg is to the fowl, we shall sooner have the fowl by hatching the egg than by smashing it." [16]

The day before he was shot, Lincoln told Welles, "Civil government must be reëstablished as soon as possible;— there must be courts, and law, and order, or society would be broken up—the disbanded armies would turn into robber bands and guerrillas, which we must strive to prevent." [17]

At his last cabinet meeting he urged serious consideration of what was to become Johnson's North Carolina Proclamation; he considered it the greatest question then before them. It seemed to him "providential" that the "rebellion was crushed just as Congress had adjourned, and there were none of the disturbing elements of that body to hinder and embarrass us. If we were wise and discreet, we should reanimate the States and get their governments in successful operation, with order prevailing and the Union reëstablished, before Congress came together in December. . . . He hoped there would be no persecution, no bloody work, after the war was over. None need expect he would take any part in hanging or killing those men, even the worst of them. We must extinguish our resentments if we expect[ed] harmony and union. There was too much of a desire on the part of some of our very good friends to be masters, to interfere with and dictate to those States, to treat the people not as fellow-citizens; there was too little respect for their rights. He did not sympathize in these feelings." [18]

---

[16] *Complete Works of Abraham Lincoln* (Nicolay and Hay), XI, 85-91.

[17] Welles MS. Diary, April 13, 1865—(II, 279). This passage, though not so indicated in the printed edition, was added a few days later with the penciled note in Welles's hand, "to be inserted as it was written after the President was assassinated."

[18] Gideon Welles, "Lincoln and Johnson," the *Galaxy*, XIII (1872), 526. This is an elaboration of the diary account, and was written eight years later; but the corroboration of the brief diary statement and Welles's usual accuracy give it more value than the ordinary memoir.

When Schuyler Colfax urged the necessity of calling Congress into extra session, the President replied that "he should put it off as long as possible"; he merely promised that he would give "sixty days notice . . . if he convened one." [19] Blaine testified that when Lincoln died he "had only allayed and postponed—not removed, . . . [the] conflict with Congress." [20] Julian, another Radical, insists that Lincoln's "well-known views on . . . reconstruction were as distasteful as possible to radical Republicans," and reminds us that in Lincoln's "last public utterance, only three days before his death, he had declared his adherence to the plan of reconstruction . . . which . . . so stirred the ire of Wade and Winter Davis as an attempt of the Executive to usurp the powers of Congress." [21] Seward reminded men that the Radicals had denounced Lincoln until he became a martyr, and predicted that assassination would raise Johnson, too, "to the pinnacle of a martyr's fame and glory." [22] Whether in spite of the Radicals Lincoln could have succeeded where Johnson failed, is still a moot question.[23] He would have had advantages which Johnson lacked. His personality won him friends. Victory in war had given him prestige. He was a consummate politician. His ability in handling men and turning situations to his advantage was phenomenal. Firmness in him was tempered by diplomacy that Johnson knew not. Four years of difficult experience had taught him many lessons. He was a Northerner, and

[19] Speaker Colfax to the Editors of the *National Republican,* June 4, 1866, Welles MSS., "Scrap-books."
[20] J. G. Blaine, *op. cit.,* II, 35.
[21] G. W. Julian, *op. cit.,* 256.
[22] Speech at Niagara, *New York Herald,* Sept. 2, 1866.
[23] Blaine says Lincoln "had acquired so complete an ascendency over the public mind . . . that any policy matured and announced by him would have been accepted by a vast majority of his countrymen." *Op. cit.,* II, 7. Perhaps this was true, but Blaine had forgotten in 1886 that in 1865 he and his friends had no faith in Lincoln and were denouncing him as they later did Johnson.

had his fingers on the popular pulse. Most important of all, he was personally at the head of a great party machine; innumerable wires of influence led to his office; through innumerable other wires he controlled the vast political mechanism. Johnson succeeded to the office, but not to the keys of the party machinery. When Lincoln died the Radicals were a mere faction. The mass of the party was behind him. He might have maintained his leadership in spite of Radical attacks. But a study of the times makes one question this assumption. He would have been subjected to the same abuse; his policy would have met the same opposition.[24] The very qualities that enabled him successfully to meet opposition during the War and lead the North to victory, would have brought criticism during reconstruction. Lincoln was great as few men are; Johnson was an ordinary human being. Yet Lincoln and his ideas of restoration had bitter enemies within his own party whose denunciations only his martyrdom silenced. The same men who savagely attacked Johnson had nearly ruined Lincoln. At the very time of his assassination the Radicals were planning the campaign against him which they later launched against Johnson.[25]

For months only the necessity of winning the War and Lincoln's popularity with the masses, had restrained the Radicals. In the interval of celebration between Lee's surrender and Lincoln's death, they had no time to organize an effective opposition; but that they were about to do so is evidenced by their correspondence.[26] On April 10, a Boston friend of Sumner wrote to encourage that senator by telling

---

24 Just after the first veto, Feb. 24, 1866, T. W. Bartley of Cincinnati wrote Johnson: "The same men, who now denounce you, declared here in Cincinnati last Spring, that Abraham Lincoln's death was Providential." Johnson MSS., LXXXVIII.

25 After Lincoln was safely dead Republican leaders wished the public to forget their disagreement with him.

26 The Sumner and Stevens MSS. furnish abundant examples.

him of a meeting of Franklin Street merchants who with
hisses had silenced Willard, a Lincoln man and former idol
of Republicans. He hoped that by the next Congress "Old
Abe" would retire from his "false position." [27] While Lincoln
was in Richmond Stanton remarked to Welles and Seward
"that it was quite as pleasant to have the President away,
that he (Stanton) was much less annoyed." [28] In the light
of Stanton's now known relations with the Radicals, this is
significant. More than a month before Lincoln was shot,
Phillips wrote to Sumner, "Well—my point is, there's ample
public opinion to sustain your course—it only needs a reputable spirited leader to make this *evident*—So when the
Senate closes make, or accept if offered, an opportunity to
sound one bugle note . . . & set the tone for the summer.
We have six months to work in (barring extra session) & if
you'll begin an agitation—we will see that it reaches the
Senate room by December." [29] Only three days before his
death Lincoln himself publicly mentioned the attacks upon
him which had come to his knowledge in spite of his pre-
caution to avoid them. [30]

Though they had hesitated in publicly defying him, the
Radicals were frank in expressing relief at Lincoln's death.
After criticizing his leniency, a St. Louis Radical declared
that "God has clearly indicated that this is not his policy." [31]
B. Gratz Brown, a more famous Radical of that city, wrote
Johnson, "Sad as was the atrocity which deprived us of a
President whose heart was all kindness . . . I yet believe
that God in His providence has called you to complete the

[27] G. F. Williams to C. Sumner, Sumner MSS., LXXIII.
[28] Welles MS. Diary, March 30, 1865—(II, 269).
[29] March 10, 1865, Sumner MSS., LXXII.
[30] *Complete Works of Abraham Lincoln* (Nicolay and Hay), XI, 85.
[31] J. E. Yeatman, President of the Western Sanitary Commission, to A.
Johnson, April 19, 1865, Johnson MSS., LIX.

work of rebuilding this nation that it might be stamped with the idea of radical democracy in all its parts." [32] Another wrote, "In the good Providence of the Almighty Ruler of events, you have been placed at the most exalted situation in the world. The people of this great nation will now 'thank God, and take courage,' believing, as they must, that the days of criminal clemency to traitors are over; that milk-and-water and the oath of allegiance, will not longer be relied on, as sovereign remedies for treason and rebellion." [33] Yet another phrased it: "His work was done—the assassin has done his—& Johnson's begins! His firmer hand, strengthened by the last act—was just what was wanted, & it has come." [34] Morrill of Maine found it "truly most difficult to speak candidly of the elements of [Lincoln's] character without offending the public sense at this time so keenly sensitive from memory of recent events." [35] Radical preachers and press joined in voicing the belief that Lincoln's assassination was an act of God to strengthen presidential policy. A few hours after Lincoln died the Radicals met in political caucus to consider "the necessity of a new Cabinet and a new line of policy less conciliatory than that of Mr. Lincoln," and Julian who was present reports: "While everybody was shocked at his murder, the feeling was nearly universal that the accession of Johnson to the Presidency would prove a godsend to the country." [36]

* * * *

[32] April 22, 1865, *ibid.*, LX.
[33] T. Fiske to A. Johnson, April 20, 1865, *ibid.*, LIX.
[34] H. S. Sanford to C. Sumner, May 4, 1865, Sumner MSS., LXXIII.
[35] June 12, 1865, *ibid.*, LXXIII. See also C. P. Smith, chairman of N. J. Union State Ex. Comm., to A. Johnson, April 15, 1865, Johnson MSS., LVIII, and G. L. Stearns to C. Sumner, May 8, 1865, Sumner MSS., LXXIII.
[36] G. W. Julian, *op. cit.*, 255.

During Johnson's first month in office the Radicals were jubilant; they expected to find him sympathetic with their vindictive mood, if not an easy tool. They set out to dominate him. "I pray you keep President Johnson true," Loring urged Sumner.[37] Schurz felt he "must be talked to as much as possible" to keep him out of "the hands of his old associations," [38] and wrote several times to dissuade him from allowing elections in the Southern states until Congress convened.[39] Chief Justice Chase wrote a speech which he tried to get Johnson to deliver, advocating universal loyal suffrage for the South.[40] The day after Lincoln's death, Wade, Julian, and others of the Committee on the Conduct of the War called on Johnson; they saw him again the following Monday. Schurz tried often to see him. Wade and Sumner talked to him several times. Wade was delighted at the President's bitterness toward traitors.[41] Sumner wrote Wendell Phillips, reassuring him in regard to Johnson.[42] He even discussed negro suffrage with the President. In the Radical caucus on May 12 both Wade and Sumner announced that the President was with them even to the extent of negro suffrage.[43] But their jubilation was short-lived. On May 29 Johnson's proclamations disillusioned them.

Some Radicals did still seek to win the President. In July Stevens wrote him, "Can you not hold your hand and wait the action of Congress?" [44] Late in June Sumner begged Schurz to "make one more effort to arrest the policy of the

---

[37] April 17, 1865, Sumner MSS., LXXIII.
[38] C. Schurz to C. Sumner, July 3, 1865, *ibid.*, LXXIV, and C. Schurz, *Speeches, Correspondence, and Political Papers*, I, 267.
[39] C. Schurz to C. Sumner, July 3, 1865, Sumner MSS., LXXIV.
[40] April, 1866, Johnson MSS., LXIV.
[41] G. W. Julian, *op. cit.*, 257.
[42] W. Phillips to C. Sumner, May 5, 1865, Sumner MSS., LXXIII.
[43] G. W. Julian, *op. cit.*, 263.
[44] July 6, 1865, Johnson MSS., LXX.

President." [45] In August he urged Mrs. Eames and her husband to persuade Welles to change the President's policy or to resign.[46] "Again, therefore . . . I entreat you," he wrote McCulloch in September, "give us peace . . . I write simply in the hope of inducing you to help produce a *right-about-face* in the present policy." [47] After a two hours' interview the same month, Fessenden still felt the President was sound in sentiment except on negro suffrage, and thought "time and firmness and prudence on our part [would] bring him right." [48] Even in November Senator Howard expressed "confidence—that Mr. Johnson will stand with us" since "there is no other place for him." [49]

June, however, found most of the leading Radicals despondent. Sumner felt the proclamations would "divide the North," and "give the Democrats an opportunity to organize." "Nothing since Chancellorsville," he wrote Welles, "has to my mind been so disastrous to the National Cause, & to the cause of peace. Alas! that this blow should be struck by our own administration!" [50] Even the irrepressible Thad Stevens was disheartened. His scribbled notes to Sumner are cries of despair. "I see the President is precipitating things . . . I fear before Congress meets he will have so be-deviled matters as to render them incurable . . . I almost despair of resisting Executive influence." [51] Again, "Is it possible to devise any plan to arrest the government in its ruinous course? When will you be in Washington? Could we collect bold men enough to lay the foundation of a party to take the helm of this government, and keep it off

[45] June 22, 1865, Sumner-Schurz Letters, and C. Schurz, *op. cit.*, I, 265.
[46] Welles MS. Diary, Aug. 19, 1865—(II, 363).
[47] Sept. 16, 1865, McCulloch MSS., II.
[48] H. Wilson to C. Sumner, Sept. 9, 1865, Sumner MSS., LXXIV.
[49] J. M. Howard to C. Sumner, Nov. 12, 1865, *ibid.*, LXXV.
[50] June 15, 1865, Welles MSS., LVIII.
[51] May 10, 1865, Sumner MSS., LXXIII.

the rocks?" [52] Two weeks later: "Is there no way to arrest the insane course of the President . . . ? Can you get up a movement in Massachusetts? I have thought of trying it at our State Convention . . . If something is not done the President will be crowned king before Congress meets." [53]

Even after the Radicals became hopeless of dominating Johnson, they moved cautiously, for they dreaded the blame for splitting the party. During the summer Harlan, Dana, and Wilson wrote Sumner counseling patience until the people could be prepared for extreme measures.[54] "We must try," Stevens wrote, "to keep out of the ranks of the opposition—the danger is that so much success will reconcile the people to almost anything." [55] That the people even in New England were not in sympathy with extreme measures these leaders well knew. In sending Sumner the resolutions of a Radical meeting he had organized in Salem, Loring apologized: "They are not in exactly the phrase I should like; but I found it hard to bring some of the Committee up to the mark." [56] In the summer of 1865 the Radical cause was veritably a "policy in search of a party."

* * * *

Sumner, Stevens, and their friends were not men to sit down in discouragement before even great obstacles. They immediately began to organize a campaign. First of all, delay was necessary. Attorney-General Speed encouraged Boutwell with the assurance that nothing more would be done at present. "If there is delay," Boutwell felt, "all will

---

52 June 3, 1865, *ibid.*, LXXIII.
53 June 14, 1865, *ibid.*, LXXIII.
54 J. Harlan to C. Sumner, Aug. 21 and Sept. 11, 1865; C. A. Dana to C. Sumner, Sept. 1, 1865; H. Wilson to C. Sumner, Sept. 9, 1865, *ibid.*, LXXIV.
55 T. Stevens to C. Sumner, Aug. 17, 1865, *ibid.*, LXXIV.
56 May 6, 1865, *ibid.*, LXXIII.

be well." [57] About the same time Harlan, in urging Sumner not to break with Johnson, said, "I know the potency of your great idea of the duty of a statesman to *create* rather than to be controlled by circumstances. But this 'creation' requires time." [58] Stearns pleaded with Sumner to "give more time at the Convention to arguments in favor of delay than to the direct question." [59] "The only hope I do have," said P. W. Chandler after discovering Johnson's strength in Philadelphia and Boston, "is to gain time for emigration & suffering to do their work . . . Delay, delay, delay, on one ground & another until the devils are civilized." [60] Schurz and Phillips urged delay.[61] Grosvenor, however, best stated the Radical program when he said, "If we cannot yet control public opinion on the direct suffrage issue, or hold a sure majority in Congress on that, perhaps other topics, nearer to the popular appreciation, may serve to unite enough to prevent final action for the present. Meantime we will educate." [62] Though they put on a bold front, the Radicals realized that they must play for time while they "educated" the people.[63]

Propaganda was a term little used, but in its methods the Radicals were skilled. A great campaign to "educate" Northerners to extreme measures was launched. Sumner's faith in its success was superb. When others were discouraged he wrote Welles, "What you say . . . although not new to me, is indescribably painful . . . But I have faith in my country. The right will prevail. The present policy

[57] G. S. Boutwell to C. Sumner, June 12, 1865, *ibid.*, LXXIII.
[58] June 15, 1865, *ibid.*, LXXIII.
[59] Aug. 28, 1865, *ibid.*, LXXIV.
[60] Feb. 12, 1866, *ibid.*, LXXVI.
[61] C. Schurz to C. Sumner, July 3, 1865, *ibid.*, LXXIV, and C. Schurz, *op. cit.*, I, 266. W. Phillips to C. Sumner, May 5, 1865, Sumner MSS., LXXIII.
[62] M. M. Grosvenor to C. Sumner, Nov. 5, 1865, *ibid.*, LXXV.
[63] The Sumner, Stevens, and Johnson MSS. abound in evidence of this.

will come to shame & disaster . . . I tremble to think how much of agitation, Trouble & strife the Country must pass through in order to recover from the false move which has been made. *The discussion has begun & it will not stop until Human Rights are recognized & the Providence of God is vindicated.*" [64] Sumner had fought in the once-disparaged anti-slavery movement. He knew what determined leadership and faith in a cause could accomplish.

"Education" had two purposes. It sought to convince the North that the South could not be trusted and that the administration policy was therefore dangerous to Northern interests; it aimed by a gradual process to win people to the use of force and to negro rights—eventually to the negro equality necessary to maintain Radicals in power, but revolting to thousands of loyal Northerners. Disparagement of Johnson, the great advocate of moderation, would serve both objects.

Constant discussion and agitation was the method of "education." The Radicals used newspapers, speeches, pamphleteering, and the machinery of the old abolitionist cause. They sent agents to gather evidence against the South. They used every device known to politicians to promote their ceaseless discussion in Congress and party gatherings. They attacked Johnson, and then abused him for striking back under great provocation. Congressional committees became mere agencies for propagating their ideas. While the Committee of Fifteen is at work, said Sumner, "Congress will occupy itself with the ideas. This discussion will go on for months. I do not see how it can be stopped; nor do I think it desirable to stop it . . . The single point to be reached is *the assertion of jurisdiction by Congress.* One person will

64 July 4, 1865, Welles MSS., LIX.

reach this point by one road and another by another road. Provided it is reached, it is not of much importance how this is accomplished. Therefore, I hope that all will speak and ventilate their theories." [65] Many took advantage of the Radical movement to further selfish ambition; many justified dubious means by the worthiness of the cause, the necessity of success, and the methods of the opposition; many saw in the struggle only righteous methods advancing a holy cause. Whatever the motive, Radicals joined in the effort to "educate" the people.

During the summer Unionist state conventions in Maine, Pennsylvania, and Massachusetts were made vehicles of propaganda. In them Johnson was attacked; Radical tenets were given publicity. Sumner praised two of the resolutions of the Pennsylvania Convention. "Such a voice from Pennsylvania has salvation in it," he rejoiced. Then he inquired anxiously, "Pray what was the feeling of your Convention? Give me a hint about your State. Can anything be done to stop this wretched experiment which the Prest. is making?" [66] Stevens tried "to get up a soldier's convention to denounce the President's policy." [67]

Chief Justice Chase stumped New England for negro suffrage.[68] Winter Davis gave a Radical harangue at Chicago on the Fourth of July. Stevens and Sumner in their respective state conventions delivered speeches that struck the key-note of the whole campaign. Leaders urged silent friends to speak.[69]

[65] C. Sumner to C. Schurz, Dec. 25, 1865, Sumner-Schurz Letters, and C. Schurz, op. cit., I, 374.
[66] C. Sumner to T. Stevens, Aug. 20, 1865, Stevens MSS., IV.
[67] T. Stevens to C. Sumner, Oct. 25, 1865, Sumner MSS., LXXIV.
[68] E.g., Welles MS. Diary, July 25, 1865—(II, 343).
[69] E.g., C. Sumner to C. Schurz, June 19, 1865, Sumner-Schurz Letters; J. M. Scovel to C. S., Oct. 23, 1865, Sumner MSS., LXXIV; J. M. Howard to C. Sumner, Nov. 12, 1865, ibid., LXXV.

One long series of campaign speeches and pamphlets kept the Radical views before the public from the summer before Lincoln's death until Radicals were supreme in 1867. Wide circulation was given to these speeches and essays in newspapers or pamphlets. Important speeches were printed *in extenso.* The New York *Independent* paid Sumner one hundred dollars each for articles on equal rights.[70] In April, 1865, Norton and Stearns of Boston helped organize a new journal [71] "to advocate advanced opinions," and claimed to have enough capital behind it to start with a circulation of 40,000. Thousands of copies of speeches of men like Sumner and Stevens were published—at government expense if made in Congress, otherwise by private subscription—and distributed over the North under government frank. The correspondence of leading Radicals is burdened with thanks for speeches sent, or requests for extra copies. Friends helped in the circulation.[72] Funds existed for the purpose.[73]

[70] T. Tilton to C. Sumner, Oct. 20, 1865, Sumner MSS., LXXIV.
[71] The *Nation.* G. L. Stearns to C. Sumner, April 30, 1865, *ibid.,* LXXIII.
[72] E.g., Sumner sent a bundle of speeches with the frank upon them to Walker of Brookfield, Mass. A. Walker to C. Sumner, Jan. 5, 1866, *ibid.,* LXXVI. On February 24, 1866, F. W. Ballard of New York wrote Sumner, "I have been hard at work today addressing speeches to the right persons here & elsewhere and shall find a market for every copy I have on hand." *Ibid.,* LXXVII.
[73] Individuals contributed, as when Cephas Brainerd sent Sumner a check for $10 to pay for all the copies of his recent speech that it would buy. Feb. 27, 1866, *ibid.,* LXXVI. Stearns published in a pamphlet containing negro suffrage speeches of W. D. Kelley, W. Phillips, and Fred Douglass, this introductory letter: "I am distributing 10,000 copies to antislavery men in all the Free States; but, desiring to increase the number to 100,000 or more, invite you to aid its circulation, on the following plan:— If you will send me what money you can spare for this object, I will forward to you, free of postage, such number as you may send for at the rate of twenty copies for every dollar, or one hundred copies for every four dollars." In the fall of 1865 Stearns raised $50,000 in Boston, New York, and Philadelphia, and with it sent out 100,000 newspapers and 50,000 pamphlets per week. G. L. Stearns to C. Sumner, Oct. 11, 1865, *ibid.,* LXXIV. Stearns alone printed 20,000 to 40,000 copies of Sumner's

The old Loyal Publication Society kept actively at work for negro suffrage.[74] * * * *

Even more effective "educational" material was provided by reports of travelers and correspondents in the South. Reliable information was difficult to secure at best; conditions in the South varied from town to town; apparently trustworthy pieces of evidence were often contradictory. Even when unbiased, the reports from the South were of questionable value.[75] Most of them, however, were not unprejudiced, but were written in an effort to support partisan views.[76] The South was a prolific source of campaign material, and the Radicals made good use of it.

Prominent men traveled through the South, and then in letters, books, or speeches described conditions there. Conditions they saw agreed surprisingly with their political sentiments. Salmon P. Chase, for instance, found a degree of intelligence among the negroes that was amazing. Whitelaw Reid spent several months collecting material for an interesting book that was avidly read. Its descriptions are vivid; it has the earmarks of fairness; it contains some details that substantiate Johnson's view. But the central theme served Reid's party, for it pictured the haughty, unbroken, defiant Southern people that Reid expected to meet, and the intelligence and industry among negroes that Radicals wanted to find. Many of the officers of the widely

Worcester speech. Oct. 12, 1865, *ibid.,* LXXIV. F. W. Bird gave $350 to pay for circulating his and Kelley's speeches. He requested Sumner to supply Kelley with the names of "lawyers and ministers" to whom to send it. March 21, 1866, *ibid.,* LXXVII.

[74] E.g., it published as a pamphlet Count Gasparin's letter to Johnson insisting on negro suffrage.

[75] *Infra,* chap. VI.

[76] E.g., Schurz wrote to his wife, "I have found all my preconceived opinions verified most fully, no, more than that." C. Schurz, *op. cit.,* I, 268.

discussed Freedmen's Bureau wrote reports to convince the public of the necessity of continuing their bureau—and hence their offices.

The most important single contribution to Radical literature on the South, was the report of Carl Schurz, German political refugee, immigrant, Civil War general, and Radical agitator. This report was made in writing to Johnson, then called for by Sumner, to be spread upon the records of Congress, and finally broadcasted over the country in pamphlet form at government expense. Schurz was an able writer, a prominent national figure. He inspired confidence. Because of the character of the man and the "impartiality" of his evidence, his report had great influence. Johnson was bitterly denounced for his refusal to heed it. Yet Schurz proves to be but another collector of Radical propaganda. Johnson knew that Schurz favored negro suffrage; he had urged Johnson to accept it, and had told him it would "become a subject of general and fierce discussion—not only among extremists but among men of moderate views." [77] Although he knew Schurz's beliefs, Johnson sent him South, because he wished to use men of diverse opinions and supposed that he would make a fair report. At the same time Harvey M. Watterson, father of the famous Kentuckian, was dispatched on a similar tour. The two sets of contemporaneous letters provide an interesting contrast, and throw light on Johnson's method of weighing conflicting evidence in forming judgment. The President was glad to hear what an advocate of negro suffrage would think after he had been South; what he could not have known was that Schurz's own object was not to serve his president or his country by

[77] June 6, 1865, Johnson MSS., LXVI. In the same letter Schurz had denied the power of the executive to appoint civil governors and had predicted trouble between Johnson and Congress.

gathering unbiased information, but to collect material for
Radical propaganda.

Schurz was working hand in glove with the Sumnerites.
Sumner had been urging him to make a speech, as he would
be "listened to—and read." [78] When Johnson asked him to
tour the South, Schurz wrote Sumner of the offer, and told
him he feared he could not afford to go, as he had a family to
support and would have to pay an extra premium on his
insurance policy if he made the trip. Sumner hurriedly
responded; "You *must go*. Let me know the *extra* premium
on your policy. The friends of the cause here will gladly
pay it. I write this in earnest and as business. Send me the
bill; and do you go at once on the journey." [79] Stanton told
Schurz that it was "absolutely necessary" to the Radical
cause that he go.[80] Sumner's friends hired and sent with
Schurz the best "phonographer" in Boston, a man already
experienced in collecting material for the Radicals, since he
had toured the South with the Freedmen's Commission.
Arrangements were made for Schurz to publish articles in a
Boston newspaper, and after some deliberation, the *Daily
Advertiser* was chosen. Five letters from Schurz appeared
over the signature "Observer," and then since his identity
became known the articles ceased. The Senator's god-speed
was, "We shall conquer." [81] While Schurz was gone Sumner
kept in correspondence with him. "Let them begin at once,"
he wrote, "with complete justice to the negro. Preach this
doctrine—talk it wherever you go. You will be sustained
. . . Be of good cheer. We shall win this battle easier than

---

[78] June 15 and 19, 1865, Sumner-Schurz Letters. The first is printed
in C. Schurz, *op. cit.,* I, 263.

[79] June 22, 1865, Sumner-Schurz Letters, and C. Schurz, *op. cit.,* I, 265.

[80] C. Schurz to Mrs. Schurz, June 16, 1865, *ibid.,* I, 264.

[81] C. Sumner to C. Schurz, June 29 and July 11, 1865, Sumner-Schurz
Letters. The latter is printed in C. Schurz, *op. cit.,* 267.

any of the others." [82] A little later he added, "I fear that you will make your journey too short. Should you not prepare for the future by gathering details and proofs?" [83]

When the President learned the true personal purpose of Schurz's journey, he telegraphed a rebuke which Schurz never forgave. "The people," Johnson wired, "must be trusted with their government . . . The main object of Major General Carl Schurz's mission to the South was to aid as far as practicable in carrying out the policy adopted by the Government for restoring the States to their former relations with the Federal Government. It is hoped such aid has been given." [84] When Schurz returned to Washington, Johnson was polite, but showed no interest in a report he knew to be intentionally warped.

The report was a collection of detailed evidence to substantiate the Radical contention that Southerners were unrepentant, and could not be trusted to return to the Union without safeguards against their malevolence toward negroes, national government, and Northerners—in short, that Johnson's policy was dangerous. Had Schurz reached this conclusion after open-minded investigation, the report would have justified an alteration in executive policy. Instead, he reached it before he began his tour. The South described was not the South Schurz saw, but the South that he and his Radical friends determined in advance it would be expedient to picture. What made the report insidious was the fact that Schurz, secretly under pay of Johnson's enemies, used the pretense of an impartial investigation for Johnson, to gather *only* such evidence as would injure Johnson and the South, and support partisan purposes of a Northern faction.

82 July 11, 1865, letter cited above.
83 Aug. 28, 1865, Sumner-Schurz Letters.
84 Aug. 30, 1865, Stanton MSS., XXVIII.

Sumner promised to call for the report in the Senate as soon as the President's message was read.[85] Meantime he urged Schurz to make a speech. The report he pronounced "all that I had expected; very able, elaborate, complete, full of facts and ideas." [86] In one of his letters to Johnson, Schurz admitted that he was painting the dark side, and that the spirit of many planters was commendable; but he thought that none could really get the idea of free labor.[87] From New Orleans he wrote his wife: "If the President insists on taking a wrong course, he should not be surprised if, later, I take the field against him with the entire artillery that I am now collecting. He will find the guns rather heavy." [88] The report was the strongest argument of the Radicals; as "impartial evidence" of a capable observer, it won many moderates to the Radical policy.

* * * *

The Radicals early plotted how to capture the party machinery in Congress. In August Stevens wrote Sumner, "Get the rebel states into a territorial condition, and [negro suffrage] can be easily dealt with. That I think should be our great aim. Then Congress can manage it— We need a good committee on elections— I fear Davis— Can he be brought right—to exclude all rebel state members until final reorganization?" [89] Wade and Fessenden prepared "to make vigorous opposition." [90] Morrill impressed upon Sumner the need of a definite plan and organization before Congress should meet.[91] In November Radicals were gathering in

[85] Nov. 15, 1865, Sumner-Schurz Letters, and C. Schurz, *op. cit.*, I, 278.
[86] Dec. 25, 1865, Sumner-Schurz Letters, and C. Schurz, *op. cit.*, I, 374.
[87] Aug. 18, 1865, Johnson MSS., LXXIII.
[88] Sept. 2, 1865, C. Schurz, *op. cit.*, I, 270.
[89] Aug. 26, 1865, Sumner MSS., LXXIV.
[90] C. Sumner to Mrs. Eames, quoted in Welles MS. Diary, Aug. 19, 1865—(II, 363).
[91] Oct., 1865, Sumner MSS., LXXIV.

Washington. A definite plan had been formulated, and key men picked to carry it out. Speaker Colfax arrived several days early, was serenaded, and delivered a carefully prepared speech which was widely circulated.[92] A party caucus met and agreed to details. Stevens presented a resolution to establish a Joint Committee of Fifteen of the two Houses to which all questions concerning admission of members from the seceding states should be submitted without debate.[93]

When Congress convened, Radicals controlled it. Colfax was reëlected Speaker. Eight of the fifteen appointed to the Joint Committee were Radicals.[94] Before the President's message was read, Sumner presented a series of Radical resolutions that pointedly ignored Johnson's policy and all that he had done.

The President did not try to dictate to Congress about the admission of Southerners. He upheld the right of that body to decide upon the qualifications of its members. He urged Southerners not to present themselves at the opening of Congress as a matter of right, but to stay away until Congress was organized so that each case could be decided upon its merits. He did, however, wish to establish the right of the Southern states to representation, provided the individuals they sent were acceptable to Congress. To this end he urged Maynard of Tennessee to present himself for recognition as a test case. Maynard was unquestionably loyal; no personal objection to him could exist. But through McPherson, the Clerk of the House, whom they controlled, the Radicals struck Maynard's name from the roll. Maynard's vocif-

92 Welles MS. Diary, Dec. 1, 1865—(II, 385).

93 Welles and Johnson both saw in this a Radical intrigue, but Johnson was confident it would be "knocked in the head" by the necessity of admitting Maynard. *Ibid.*, Dec. 3, 1865—(II, 387).

94 One of these, Fessenden, later repented, and voted against removing Johnson from office in the impeachment trial.

crous protest when the roll was read went ignored, and he was denied his seat. Then before the reading of Johnson's message, the resolution establishing the Joint Committee of Fifteen was rushed through Congress.[95] Of this resolution, Morton, who later became a Radical, wrote Johnson, "The joint resolution which has passed the house . . . is cunningly devised and is intended to entrap your friends in such a manner they cannot escape." [96] Indeed, all of these measures were railroaded through Congress by strict party votes. Before the moderate members of the party realized what was happening, the Radicals were in control.[97] The editor of the New York *Independent* wrote Stevens, "The way in which you have opened Congress & thrown down the gauntlet to the President's policy has pleased our Radical friends hereabouts so thoroughly that we are all hearty, merry, and tumultuous with gratitude." [98]

* * * *

Neither Congress nor Radical leaders made any effort to coöperate with Johnson, to secure his approval of measures or to confer with him. Individual Moderates did consult him freely. But the only notice the Committee of Fifteen took of Johnson was a resolution presented to him by Fessenden, Reverdy Johnson, and Washburne, expressing desire "to avoid all possible collision or misconstruction between the Executive and Congress in regard to the relative positions of Congress and the President." It stated that the Committee "thought it exceedingly desirable that, while this subject was under consideration by the Joint Committee, no

95 *Cong. Globe*, 39 Cong., 1 Sess., 3-10.
96 Dec. 7, 1865, Johnson MSS., LXXXII.
97 Welles says, "The new Members, and others weak in their understandings, were taken off their legs, as was designed, before they were aware of it." MS. Diary, Dec. 5, 1865—(II, 392).
98 T. Tilton to T. Stevens, Dec. 6, 1865, Stevens MSS., V.

further action in regard to reconstruction should be taken by the President, unless it should become imperatively necessary." "Mutual respect," it continued, "would seem to require mutual forbearance on the part of the Executive and of Congress." Johnson replied cordially to this that, while he considered it desirable that reconstruction should be advanced as rapidly as might be consistent with the public interest, still he desired to secure harmony of action between Congress and the Executive, and it was not his intention to do more than had been done for the present.[99] There all coöperation ended.

Meantime the Radicals began the campaign of abuse and misrepresentation that reached its height only in the political heat of September. In November a Philadelphia Radical had said, "In this man Johnson we see the instincts of 'the mean white' cropping out. He cannot shake off the bootlicking proclivity born & bred in him toward the . . . aristocracy of the south, miserable fool!"[1] The *Chicago Tribune* launched a bitter personal attack.[2] Fred Douglass declared that though Jeff Davis was a criminal, he did stand by his friends, and that much could not be said for Andrew Johnson.[3] William Thayer of Boston thought it necessary to make Johnson "identify himself" so thoroughly "with the Rebels, that the Country [could] not escape from the conclusion that he [was] a vile, sneaking traitor who [had] obtained political goods on false pretenses."[4]

On January 8 the House passed a resolution seeking to take the removal of troops from the South out of Johnson's

99 B. B. Kendrick, *Journal of the Joint Committee of Fifteen,* 40-41.
1 S. Penington to C. Sumner, Nov. 28, 1865, Sumner MSS., LXXV.
2 *Chicago Tribune,* Feb. 7, 1866.
3 Speech at Brooklyn, *New York Tribune,* Jan. 30, 1866.
4 W. W. Thayer to C. Sumner, Feb. 21, 1866, Sumner MSS., LXXVII.

hands.[5] When Johnson intimated to Dixon that he would have to veto the bill providing negro suffrage for the District of Columbia, and then suggested a new basis of representation and taxation,[6] Radicals pounced upon what he had meant as a bid for harmony, and accused him of trying to usurp all powers of government, and dictate to Congress. Stevens denounced this "utterance of one at the other end of the avenue," and declared that "centuries ago, had it been made to Parliament by a British king it would have cost him his head." [7] He spoke of the President as "an alien enemy, a citizen of a foreign State, . . . not . . . legally President." [8] Sumner characterized his message accompanying the Grant and Schurz reports as a "whitewashing" affair.[9] Wendell Phillips "arraigned and abused" him in what Sherman termed "a shameless manner," classed him with Arnold and Burr, and declared that he had taken Jeff Davis's place as leader of the Confederacy.[10]

Both Johnson and his policy were subjected to a gross misrepresentation that increased as the elections drew nearer. Some of it resulted from the usual wildness of Dame Rumor, but a large portion was an integral part of the Radical campaign.[11] A Washington dispatch of the *Tribune* stated: "It has now come to light that the instructions under which the Freedmen's Bureau in Louisiana was so completely disrupted in November, its 300 schools brought to a close soon afterward, the freedmen and discharged colored soldiers

---

[5] *Cong. Globe,* 39 Cong., 1 Sess., 137. It passed 94-37, with 51 not voting.
[6] *National Intelligencer,* Jan. 29, 1866.
[7] Jan. 31, 1866, *Cong. Globe,* 39 Cong., 1 Sess., 536.
[8] *Ibid.,* Appendix, 129.
[9] Speech in Senate, Dec. 19, 1865, *ibid.,* 79.
[10] *Ibid.,* Appendix, 129.
[11] When it served their purpose, Radicals even circulated reports that Johnson favored measures which he consistently opposed; then they denounced him as inconsistent when he did not act on these Radical rumors.

arrested as vagrants in the streets of New-Orleans, without trial or process of law, and the orphans of freedmen returned to former slave holders as apprentices, were imparted by the President himself, and that Gen. Fullerton acted in accordance with Executive instructions." [12] Fullerton declared the statement wholly untrue in regard to both himself and Johnson.[13] But the papers that printed the falsehood gave no place to the counteracting denial. Kelley of Philadelphia spread the tale that Johnson "had established a Rebel newspaper in Memphis, . . . given a government press & materials for the office, put in charge a Rebel officer as Editor & taken away the government patronage from Brownlows [sic] Paper in Knoxville," which in violation of law he had "given to this secession paper." [14]

Accusations of complicity in the murder of Lincoln were kept in circulation.[15] Stories of Johnson's drunkenness were propagated by extremists long before the party broke with the President.[16] Rumors of this kind spread epidemic-like with extraordinary effect. As usual with scandal, they needed no proof to gain popular credence; yet once they were diffused, no amount of convincing denial could undo the damage wrought. One of many such stories was that which Henry Ward Beecher, though friendly to Johnson, believed and helped to circulate. Senator Pomeroy of Kansas had told Postmaster Lincoln of Brooklyn, who told Beecher (and undoubtedly others), who wrote Representa-

---

12 *New York Tribune*, Feb. 21, 1866.

13 J. S. Fullerton to A. Johnson, Feb. 23, 1866, Johnson MSS., LXXXVII.

14 T. T. Davis, M.C., to A. Johnson, Feb. 17, 1866, *ibid.*, LXXXVII.

15 Some of them started among Johnson's Tennessee enemies. E.g., J. H. Holmes to C. Sumner, Feb. 27, 1866, Sumner MSS., LXXVII. Radicals claimed that Johnson did not dare to remove Stanton because the latter had proof of this charge. F. P. Blair to A. Johnson, Sept. 20, 1866, Johnson MSS., CI.

16 E.g., J. Howe to A. Johnson, Sept. 23, 1865, *ibid.*, LXXVII.

tive Defrees of Indiana, who sent the letter to McCulloch, who showed it to Welles—that he, Pomeroy, called at the White House and found "the President, his son, and son-in-law, all drunk and unfit for business, that the President kept a mistress at the White House, etc." [17] When cornered, Senator Pomeroy disavowed stating that he had seen the President drunk; what he had seen was Robert Johnson "in liquor"; he thought he had seen Johnson's son-in-law in the same condition.[18] Yet even Beecher had passed the story on as fact. Less scrupulous Radicals were spreading the tales of Johnson's White House harem of harlots. During the winter the trial of Mrs. Cobb and General Baker's gross stories of Presidential profligacy burst upon the public. Baker, the confidant of Stanton, had had the effrontery to set up a system of espionage in the White House, putting a spy at the very door to watch the President and his callers. Radicals who knew them to be false, allowed these scurrilous rumors to be utilized in their campaign [19] because by casting contempt on Johnson, they helped to defeat his policy.

Under such provocation, Johnson's forbearance was notable; his two single outbursts of retort in kind merely punctuate the long months of dignified silence under a torrent of abuse, when the Tennessee politician in him must have longed to jump into the fray.

In these early months Johnson would have been willing to

[17] Welles MS. Diary, March 16, 1866—(II, 453).
[18] *Ibid.*, March 23, 1866—(II, 461).
[19] So far did the leaders carry their antagonism to the President that some Radical constituents lost patience. One wrote Trumbull, "In my judgment Congress is employing its time and wisdom to very little purpose—not to say with consummate folly." There is "terrible hazard" in "*smart*" men employing all their wisdom, all their faculties to create, construct, manufacture, an issue or issues of conflict with the President . . . Congress would far better manifest its wisdom, its patriotism . . . in providing the ways & means" of restoring "a still unrestored Union . . . than in combatting the Prest's views." J. Marsh to L. Trumbull, Jan. 8, 1866, Trumbull MSS., LXIII.

coöperate with Congress, but the Radicals avoided him. Moderates in Congress tried to bring President and Congress together. But Johnson was becoming increasingly convinced that the Radicals' various proposals were part of a consistent intrigue to keep the South out, to make their own rule in Congress secure, and to make Congress omnipotent by changing the very form of our government. He was losing hope of finding a solution save on the firm ground of opposition to all changes until the loyal members from seceded states were admitted.

Then, early in February, Congress sent Johnson the Freedmen's Bureau Bill just at the time when Moderates were trying to secure the admission of Tennessee members. He did favor protection for the negroes, but he preferred that the states give it. Besides, there was already a Freedmen's Bureau which under his interpretation of the law would continue for one year after he should declare the war at an end. He objected, moreover, to several details of the bill. But Trumbull, its Moderate author, thought he had Presidential approval for the measure. Moderates felt that if only the President could be induced to sign the bill, Moderate Republican opinion would rally to his support, and more extreme measures would be forestalled, whereas a veto would throw many moderate men into the Radical ranks, and greatly widen the breach between Congress and the President. In Tennessee's "admission," Moderates saw a chance to win Johnson's signature for the bill. Recognition of Tennessee was still dear to his heart. Of her loyalty there was little question even in Radical minds. To "admit" her, would in no way endanger the Union; it would please the President; it would establish the Moderate principle; and it would remove Conservative fears that Radicals were determined to go to extremes.

Johnson was seeking advice from both friends and opponents of the bill, and was still apparently undecided. On February 9, General Fullerton presented a report naming five objections which finally formed a partial basis of the veto message.[20] On the twelfth, in an estimate submitted at the President's request, he named twenty million dollars as the minimum cost of the Bureau under the new bill.[21] On February 13 Johnson told Welles he had not yet received the bill, but "apprehended he should experience difficulty in signing it." [22] But the same day he wrote Governor Hamilton of Texas, "Much will depend upon the future proceedings of your Convention. I am still hopeful that matters will take a different turn here and that loyal representatives will be admitted to take their seats . . . from all the States." [23] With the Tennessee question in mind, he must have been planning to sign the Freedmen's Bureau Bill in the hope of bringing about that "different turn." On the sixteenth Morgan "greatly disturbed" Sumner and Wilson by predicting that the representatives from Tennessee would be "admitted before the close of [the] next week." He repeated this to Welles on the seventeenth, but Welles felt certain that Johnson would not be influenced by the "scheme to . . . induce him to surrender his principles in order to get the Tennesseans in their seats." [24] To the most sanguine, the "admission" of Tennessee was conceivable only if the President did not veto the Freedmen's Bureau Bill. On the seventeenth Representative Davis urged Johnson to sign the bill because

20 Johnson MSS., LXXXVI.
21 Ibid., LXXXVI.
22 Welles MS. Diary, Feb. 13, 1866—(II, 432).
23 Johnson MSS., "Telegrams."
24 Welles MS. Diary, Feb. 17, 1866—(II, 434).

"it would strengthen [his] friends in sustaining the position they [had] taken in regard to the admission of representatives." [25] As late as this there was a general hope that the President and a Congress controlled by Moderates might return to amicable relations through "admission" of Tennessee on the one hand, and approval of the Freedmen's Bureau Bill on the other.

But at the crucial moment the Radicals played a trump card. In the Committee of Fifteen, the Southern states had been apportioned among four subcommittees. To the most moderate of these,[26] Tennessee affairs had been assigned. This subcommittee reported a simple declaratory resolution: "WHEREAS the people of Tennessee have presented a Constitution and asked admission into the Union, and which on due examination is found to be Republican in its form of Government; *be it enacted*, . . . that the State of Tennessee shall be one, and is hereby declared to be one of the United States of America, on an equal footing with the other states in all respects whatever." Congress would unquestionably have adopted this resolution. But because of Stevens's rule, forced through on the opening day by use of the party whip, this resolution could be voted upon by either House only if the Joint Committee approved it. Now the power that the Stevens resolution gave the Radicals became evident. On February 15 Bingham presented the subcommittee's resolution to the Committee of Fifteen. On February 17 Williams of Oregon met it with a motion that the whole subject of Tennessee be referred to a select committee of three members, to be appointed by the Chairman, with instructions to

25 Johnson MSS., LXXXVII.

26 Grimes, Grider, and Bingham. All three were Moderates, although Bingham was to become a Radical; on each of the other committees, two out of three were Radicals.

report thereon to the Joint Committee at the next meeting. His motion was adopted by an 8-7 vote; Fessenden appointed three Radicals, Williams, Conkling, and Boutwell, in place of the three Moderates of the old subcommittee.[27]

The new subcommittee offered a substitute resolution under which Tennessee was to be admitted only after a majority of her electors had ratified certain guarantees: repudiation of the rebel debt, payment of the Union debt, permanent incorporation into her constitution of a disavowal of secession, and disfranchisement and disbarment from office, for five years, of all who had aided or adhered to the late rebellion.[28] This resolution Johnson and the Conservatives could not support.[29] Probably the Radicals did not expect its adoption. In any case, this manœuver upset hopes of a compromise, and furnished evidence satisfactory to Johnson that negotiation with Congress was useless. One vote in the Committee of Fifteen overturned Moderate efforts to bring the President and Congress together. Had Fessenden voted with the Moderates as he finally did in the impeachment trial, the Freedmen's Bureau Bill might not have been vetoed.

Stevens was a good actor. He had persistently sought to provoke a break by insulting the President and thwarting his wishes. His Radical cohorts in the Committee had added the last straw that made the veto inevitable. Yet on February 20 he walked into the Committee and announced in surprised indignation that an event had happened since yesterday that had materially changed his attitude toward the "expediency and propriety" of action on Tennessee. Under the party lash

27 B. B. Kendrick, *Journal of the Committee of Fifteen*, 63-67.
28 *Ibid.*, 68.
29 It denied the "right" of Tennessee to representation, and it contained the punitive clause that later made the Fourteenth Amendment unpalatable.

and the previous question, he then rushed through Congress a resolution that no senator or representative should be admitted into Congress until Congress should declare his state "entitled to such representation." Next he announced, without telling the nature of the terms first proposed and the later substitution, that the Committee of Fifteen had been earnestly considering the admission of Tennessee when the veto message made it impossible.[30] Keeping Tennessee out of the Union was added to the list of Johnson's·misdeeds.

Aside from widening the breach between Johnson and Congress, the veto in itself did no·irremediable damage to the Conservative cause. Thomas Ewing praised it, and assured Johnson that "the legal profession" and "thinking conservative" men would sustain him.[31] The veto message was an able, dignified, convincing state paper that won new praise for the President. Many Moderate Republicans wished he had signed the bill; his refusal gave the Radicals a further handle against him. But after all, there was a Freedmen's Bureau in operation, and by existing law it would continue to function for at least a year. This veto lost Johnson few friends. Congress sustained it. Many Republican leaders over the country and a majority of the people appeared to approve.   *   *   *   *

[30] For six hours the Democrats and a few Moderates tried to get the floor or postpone the vote by dilatory tactics, but Stevens would not yield or withdraw his motion of the previous question; by means of his whip and insistence that opposition to his resolution meant "simply a return of the rebels of 1861," Stevens, under the excitement of the veto, got reluctant Republicans committed against Johnson on a purely party vote. *Cong. Globe*, 39 Cong., 1 Sess., 943-950. Johnson's speech of February 22 stimulated the Senate to passing the bill, 26-19, though Sherman and others strenuously protested. *Ibid.*, 981-984. General Sherman wrote his brother, "You will be ashamed of it ten·years hence." Feb. 23, 1866, W. T. Sherman MSS., XVIII.

[31] Feb. 22, 1866, Johnson MSS., LXXXVII. See also T. Ewing to J. Sherman, Feb. 12, 1866, Ewing MSS., "Letter-book."

Then came the Washington's Birthday speech before opinion had had time to crystallize. Its intrinsic significance has been magnified unreasonably. Read today, it is surprising only because of the mildness of language that "shocked and humiliated the country." Johnson accused the Radicals of encouraging his assassination—a foolish charge. The Radicals would have celebrated Johnson's death with glee as the removal of the only insurmountable obstacle to their plans; but even Johnson in the calm of his study would not have thought them capable of stooping to plot it. He called Forney a "dead duck." Then in Tennessee fashion, urged on by the crowd of serenaders, he named Sumner and Stevens as traitors who were seeking to destroy the Union by their extreme, illegal measures; he described them as setting up a directory comparable in power to that of the French Revolution.[32] Otherwise, the speech was unremarkable. It merely expressed, honestly and forcibly, Johnson's views. It was not in good taste; but in comparison with Radical utterances which provoked it, and the abusive language that denounced it, the speech shows gentlemanly forbearance. Many praised it as a master-stroke. Seward approved it.[33] Weed wired to assure Johnson that the Union was "now a fixed fact."[34] Welles wished the personalities had been omitted, but otherwise commended it as "earnest, honest, and strong."[35] The non-partisan *New York Herald* applauded it. In March General Sherman optimistically wrote, "I think from the tone in Congress and outside," the passage of words "between the President & Congress has done good, for

[32] This parallel was suggested by Stevens's implication that the ancestors of the present Congress had cut off the head of one Charles of England for offenses similar to Johnson's.
[33] "Your speech is triumphant and the country will be happy." W. H. Seward to A. Johnson, Feb. 23, 1866, Johnson MSS., "Telegrams."
[34] Feb. 23, 1866, *ibid.*, "Telegrams."
[35] Welles MS. Diary, Feb. 23, 1866—(II, 439).

it has proven to the party" that "being drawn hopelessly into the ways of Stevens & Sumner" would irredeemably have surrendered "the political power into the hands of the combination of democrats and anti-war men that were laying low and chuckling at the evident mistake." [36] Other friendly opinion regretted the political indiscretion of the speech, and feared that it would weaken the President's case against Radical vituperation. But most of the evidence of humiliation and shame is found in the Radical press. There it was not the speech as delivered that shocked men accustomed to campaigning of the 'Sixties, but the picture which the Radicals drew of its surroundings, and the open accusations and insidious innuendoes of drunkenness. Repeated reiteration that loyal men were humiliated made them believe they were.

On the day of the Presidential outburst, Radicals in Congress engineered a commemoration of the death of Winter Davis, a Radical politician and enemy of Lincoln and Johnson, with all the solemnity that had marked the Lincoln memorial service of ten days earlier. Johnson and his friends stayed away, and left the ceremony a Radical celebration, but they were irritated, as was intended. The same night, a large and enthusiastic Johnson meeting was staged in Cooper Institute in New York. Seward's speech there had a happier effect than Johnson's in Washington, and was more discreet. Throughout the country the holiday was utilized for political meetings.

The next morning and for several successive days the more sensational Radical papers hurled hitherto unequalled abuse at Johnson on the pretext of his speech. The more dignified

---

[36] W. T. Sherman to J. Sherman, March 5, 1866, W. T. Sherman MSS., XVIII.

Tribune told its readers how "pained" and "appalled" every thoughtful man was. It first reported Johnson drunk, but later, insisting he was sober, declared his "performance" could not be palliated even by inebriety.[37] The *Philadelphia Press* spoke of the "grief and dismay" of "a betrayed and despairing people" at "the most deplorable spectacle since that of the 4th of March last." [38] "This last loose and disjointed harangue," it said, had dispelled any doubts "that the Chief Magistrate of the United States is frequently disqualified from speaking intelligently or intelligibly." It declared that this most recent of his "diatribes" would "diffuse every honest brow with shame." [39]

Senator Sherman can best speak the general moderate judgment: "I ask you, Senators, whether the President of the United States, regarding him as he is; a man who never turned his back upon a foe, personal or political; a man whose great virtue has been his combative propensity; as a man who repelled insults here on the very spot where I now stand, when they came from traitors arming themselves for the fight; can you ask him, because he is President, to submit to insult? Every sentiment of manhood, every dictate of our nature, would induce a man, when he heard these words (the enumerated insults of Stevens, Sumner, and Phillips) uttered, in the heat of passion, to thrust them back. When a man becomes President he has none the less the feelings of manhood . . . It is one of the peculiarities of his character that he has not the gentleness of the late President, and yet

---

[37] *New York Tribune,* Feb. 23 and 24, 1866. "The Copperheads," it said, "and late Rebels have everywhere applauded, cheered, fired guns over, and in every way evinced their delight in, those deplorable utterances. *They* have no shadow of doubt that the President is henceforth their own." *Ibid.,* Feb. 27, 1866.

[38] *Philadelphia Press,* Feb. 25, 1866.

[39] *Ibid.,* Feb. 24, 1866.

. . . the very courage with which he resists opponents wherever they present themselves, we commended five years ago
as the highest virtue of Andrew Johnson's life." [40]

The speech was harmful chiefly because it opened the
flood-gates to a torrent of abuse that in the end overwhelmed
him. He would have been denounced anyway. But as long as
he maintained dignified silence he occupied a strong position.
When he came down out of the reserve of the Presidency
and entered the fray, he lost his strongest defense, and made
himself merely one of many in a campaign disgraceful for
its personalities.   *   *   *   *

After the Senate sustained the veto of the Freedmen's
Bureau Bill, the Radicals determined to secure a two-thirds
majority in that body. That veto had been sustained by a
vote of 18-30. The Radicals worked constantly on senators
whose Conservatism was doubtful.[41] But they employed a
more certain weapon than persuasion. Through skilful use of
an unmerciful party whip, and the breaking of a pair by
Senator Morrill of Maine, they unseated one of the Johnson
senators, Stockton of New Jersey.[42] Trumbull and all but one
of his Judiciary Committee colleagues, declared Stockton's
election legal; no question was raised until his unseating became necessary to override vetoes. When the vote was taken,
four of the five Republicans of the Judiciary Committee, and
several other Republican senators voted for Stockton's right
to his seat. His election by the legislature seems to have been
unquestionably valid. The vote stood 21-20 in favor of
Stockton. Wright, who was sick in New Jersey, had paired

---

[40] Speech in the Senate, Feb. 26, 1866, *Cong. Globe*, 39 Cong., 1 Sess.,
Appendix, 129.
[41] They did win Morgan, Willey, and Stewart, who had voted to sustain
the first veto, but who voted to override the second.
[42] This proceeding is recorded in the *Cong. Globe*, 39 Cong., 1 Sess., 1564-
1573, 1589-1602, 1635-1648, 1666-1679.

with Morrill. Although Morrill never directly communicated with Wright, he had Stockton wire him the day before this vote that he would, after allowing a reasonable time for Wright to return, break his pair. A telegram that morning announced that Wright was too ill to be moved before the middle of the next week. After the vote had been taken, the Radical senators bombarded Morrill on the floor of the Senate, shouting to him to vote; finally he told the Secretary to call his name and voted nay, breaking his pair with the sick New Jersey Senator. The vote stood 21-21. Then Stockton, who had refrained from voting in his own cause, recorded his aye, and the motion declaring Stockton entitled to his seat was passed, in spite of Morrill's plighted word. This was on Friday. On Tuesday, the subject was reconsidered. By that time Stewart of Nevada had been belabored by the Radicals into absenting himself and Riddle into changing his vote. Stockton by vote of the Senate was denied the right to vote. No effort had been made to bring Wright to Washington as Friday's vote had been considered final. But when on Monday the reconsideration was announced, Wright was notified. He agreed to be there by Thursday or withdraw his pair, which he claimed still held. Just before the vote, another message from New Jersey announced that Wright would be carried to Washington against his doctor's orders, to vote the next morning. But the Senate ignored Wright's telegraphed plea for delay, and with the aid of Morrill's broken word, unseated Stockton, 23-20.[43] Had Stockton not been unseated, the veto of the Civil Rights Bill would have

---

[43] Van Winkle, Doolittle, Howard, and Williams who had been paired on the earlier vote, now voted, two for and two against the bill. Morrill, ashamed to face a vote, formed a new pair with Foster and stayed away. Even so, had Wright been present, Dixon could have been carried in on a stretcher, Stockton could have voted against denying himself the right to vote, and then could have cast the third vote necessary to prevent his own unseating.

been sustained in spite of defections from Johnson, for two votes would have sustained it, and Dixon who lay ill was ready to be carried in on a stretcher in case his vote would uphold the veto. With a Congress led by men using these means to carry their extreme measures, Johnson felt there was no hope of coöperation should he yield on any number of bills.   *   *   *   *

Senator Stewart of Nevada, one of the wavering supporters of the first veto, now proposed a compromise measure based on universal suffrage and universal amnesty. Hope of winning both Congress and the President to its support was voiced in Moderate Republican circles. But the veto of the Civil Rights Bill defeated what chances of success this measure ever had.[44]

Whether Johnson might gain enough moderate support by approval of that bill to strengthen him against more extreme measures was a question on which his advisers did not agree. Governor Cox of Ohio urged him to sign the bill. "Few people have read it through," he said. "They judge of it by synopses of its provisions which have been published very briefly in the country papers. They fasten their minds upon the fact that the bill declares that the freedmen shall have the same rights of property and person, the same remedies for injuries received & the same penalties for wrongs committed, as other men— This they approve, and they know that you and I and all true Union men have constantly desired this result— They do not look much at the means employed to enforce the provisions of the bill—they do not care much about or very well understand them. . . . Under these circumstances, and especially in view of the fact

[44] Kendrick thinks this the best plan offered, one which all parties would have accepted. *Op. cit.,* 252-255.

that the persistent efforts which have been made by the extremists to create distrust of your motives and intentions are recoiling, and every day adds to the strength of your position before the country, I believe it will be well to *strain a point* in order to meet the popular spirit and impulse rather than to make a strict construction of duty the other way." [45] Signing the bill, said Beecher, "would go far to *harmonize the feelings* of men who should never have differed. . . . It has been sought for several months, to detatch [*sic*] from you the sober and reflecting class of men. The passage of this bill will, in a great degree, frustrate the influence of those who have sought to produce the impression that you had proved untrue to the cause of liberty and loyalty. . . . Assuming that it is Constitutional, I only say that it will through all the north & west give great strength to you, to sign it." [46]

On the other hand, Senator Cowan of Pennsylvania wrote, "Don't hesitate for a moment to veto the '*Civil Rights Bill.*' To do otherwise will be fatal—and no argument will remain to us— They will then be able to claim power to do anything —even to conferring the right of suffrage upon the people of the States—negroes or anybody. Be careful to put it distinctly as a question of *power*—not of policy—indeed it might be recommended to the States with propriety." [47]

Johnson himself had been strengthened, by the increasing bitterness of the controversy, in his conviction that admission of the legality of any important legislation with the Southern states still unrepresented, would merely enable the Radicals to proceed to extremes. At a crucial moment when the bill was in Johnson's hands, Stevens deepened this con-

[45] March 22, 1866, Johnson MSS., XCI.
[46] March 17, 1866, *ibid.*, XCI.
[47] March 23, 1866, *ibid.*, XCI.

viction by another of his diatribes. He had the Clerk read into the record of the House the *World's* statement that Johnson was an "insolent clownish drunkard," and that the consulate "was scarcely more disgraced" by the horse which the "drunken and beastly Caligula" raised to it, than was the vice-presidency by the election of Andrew Johnson, that "insolent, drunken brute in comparison with whom Caligula's horse was respectable." If his slanderers, jeered Stevens, could make the people believe that the President ever uttered the speech of February 22, then this comparison with Caligula's horse was an apt one. "But," he added with a sneer, "we all know he never did utter it." [48] This attack of Stevens contributed only incidentally to the veto, but it evidenced the unreasonableness that did help convince Johnson of the danger of yielding on the Civil Rights Bill.

The message that accompanied the veto ranks among the ablest of state papers; [49] its strength was recognized at the time even by Radicals. Had not Stockton been unseated, this veto like the first would have been sustained [50] in spite of the new converts [51] to Radicalism. The people were still reluctant to follow the Radical lead.[52] This veto was just another in a long series of unfortunate events. No one was important; the accumulation wrought disaster.

During the remainder of the session Johnson vetoed several other measures: [53] a bill admitting the State of Colorado to the Union; an act establishing the New York and Mon-

[48] March 10, 1866, *Cong. Globe,* 39 Cong., 1 Sess., 1308.
[49] The Supreme Court ultimately justified Johnson's veto on the ground of unconstitutionality. Civil Rights Cases, 109 *U. S.,* 3.
[50] *Supra,* 89-90.
[51] Morgan, Willey, and Stewart.
[52] See, e.g., J. S. Wilson to L. Trumbull, March 6, 1866, and D. L. Phillips to L. Trumbull, March 22, 1866, Trumbull MSS., LXIV.
[53] Radicals predicted he would veto the Habeas Corpus Bill, but he and Stanbery favored this act.

tana Iron Mining and Manufacturing Company; the same measure disguised as a bill to erect the Territory of Montana into a surveying district; another Freedmen's Bureau bill; and a bill making Nebraska a state. Of these vetoes Congress overrode one,[54] and sustained the others.[55]

* * * *

Meantime the Joint Committee of Fifteen had been at work, successfully carrying out the Radical plan of killing time and allowing all to "speak and ventilate their theories" until Congress and the people should be "educated." For five months it had been collecting "the evidence" which "as reported," was to "show the necessity of interference by Congress."[56] On January 20 it did report an amendment basing representation on population, but providing that whenever the right to vote should be abridged because of race or color, those denied the ballot should be excluded from the basis of representation. The amendment was defeated in the Senate when Sumner and three other ultra-Radicals joined with nine Democrats and nine Moderates in opposing it.[57] No further proposal was made by the Committee for several weeks.

All through the winter the Fifteen talked, heard evidence, and criticized Johnson's policy. Now and then proposals were made for amendments to the Constitution. But not until April 30 did the Committee present a definite program. It did so then only under constant goading,[58] even from the

---

[54] The veto of the new Freedmen's Bureau Bill.
[55] Nebraska was excluded by a "pocket veto."
[56] C. Sumner to C. Schurz, Dec. 25, 1865, Sumner-Schurz Letters, and C. Schurz, *Speeches, Correspondence, and Political Papers*, I, 375.
[57] *Cong. Globe*, 39 Cong., 1 Sess., 337, 1289.
[58] E.g., *New York Times*, April 23 and 24, 1866; and the *Boston Traveller*, April 23, 1866.

Radical press,[59] which began to fear that in the absence of a plan the people might come to accept Johnson's policy as better than none.

Up to this time the subcommittees had been taking testimony. When evidence sufficient for the purpose of the Radical managers had been collected, an eight hundred page report was published,[60] of which one hundred thousand copies were distributed at government expense.[61] The four subcommittees meeting to hear evidence, formed a great American Court of Star Chamber sitting for the conviction of the South in an *ex parte* case. The Committee sought not to learn the truth about the South, but to convince the people of the efficacy of the Radical program. The examination of witnesses was no taking of testimony, for the South unheard stood precondemned. The Committee chose its witnesses carefully. Radical Freedmen's Bureau officers determined what men would be "able and fit to give information" to the Committee; they selected chiefly "Union men" whose "loyalty" was "undoubted." [62]

Of the witnesses examined for all Secessia, twelve thought the South expected compensation for the slaves emancipated and the property destroyed during the War; three thought they did not. Seventy-three thought the Freedmen's Bureau and the maintenance of troops in the South necessary; ten thought them unnecessary. Eighty-seven had seen evidence of general hostility toward the freedmen and of occasional

---

[59] The *Nation*, II (March 22, April 12, 1866), 358, 454; the *New York Tribune*, April 21, 1866.

[60] *Report of the Joint Committee on Reconstruction at the First Session of the Thirty-ninth Congress.*

[61] *Cong. Globe*, 39 Cong., 1 Sess., 3325-3326.

[62] E.g., J. W. Sharp from Petersburg to T. Stevens, Jan. 17, 1866, Stevens MSS., VI. Later Sharp wrote, "The best man that I can find to give evidence before your Committee is Mr. Thomas Whitworth a venerable gentleman who loudly denounced Secession as the greatest evil that could fall on Virginia." Feb. 9, 1866, *ibid.*, VI.

cruelty; thirty-six had not. Fifty-nine declared the freedmen were anxious to work and suited to free labor; four
gave a negative answer. Of white hostility to free labor for
the negro, eleven bore witness; four declared there was none.
Twenty-eight declared the South was reluctant to pay taxes
and its share of the national debt; one declared it was ready
to pay its full share. Forty-two thought the pardons and
executive leniency had had a bad effect; two thought their
influence good. Fifty pronounced secession principles and
states' rights doctrines prevalent in the South; fourteen
pronounced them dead. Ninety-two saw indications of hostility to the Union; thirty-six thought Southerners friendly
toward it. Seventy-one related manifestations of hostility
toward Southern Union men and Northerners; fifteen saw
none. The one-sidedness of the testimony, however, is easily
explicable when one does what the publishers of the report
did not do—collate with the above figures an analysis of the
witnesses called. Of one hundred forty-four summoned, one
hundred fourteen were men whose private interests and
prejudices strongly biased them against Southerners, or
made them eager to paint the picture as black as possible,
while only thirty had an interest in restoration. Seventy-
seven were Northerners living in the South; sixty-seven were
Southerners. Of the one hundred fourteen classed here as
naturally favoring continuance of military rule, ten were
Northern travelers in the South, ten were Northern office-
holders in the South, thirty-eight were Northern army
officers, fifteen were Northern Freedmen's Bureau officers,
three were Northerners living in the South, twenty-one were
Southern white loyalists, and eight were negro "loyalists."
Of the thirty who were not a priori anti-Southern, sixteen
were white citizens of the South, mostly ex-Confederates

like Robert E. Lee; two were provisional governors; one,[63] was a governor; seven were Southern state officers; and four, including Alexander H. Stephens, were members-elect to Congress. But the testimony is even more disproportionate than the figures indicate. Witnesses were merely answering questions categorically put to draw out certain answers. Men like Lee, Stephens, and Humphreys whose answers would be adverse to committee wishes, when called in at all, were asked very few of the tabulated questions, or else their answers were not recorded. The answers they did give were distorted in compiling these astounding statistics. Thus whenever a witness admitted under persistent questioning one case of maltreatment of a negro, he was registered as giving evidence of "a general hostility and occasional cruelty toward the freedmen." Lee is listed as declaring that the South was hostile toward Union men on the basis of his answering to a question twice put him, "They might avoid them." [64] Patently useless as this evidence was to an unbiased investigator, it made priceless campaign material. That was what the Radicals sought.[65]

* * * *

When finally presented to Congress, the Committee plan provoked a long discussion. To secure passage in the Senate, the punitive third section was remodeled. Counter plans were suggested. Unsuccessful efforts were made by Conservatives to separate the four amendments and have their respective provisions go to the country on their merits. Johnson, the

[63] Humphreys of Mississippi.
[64] *Report of the Joint Committee on Reconstruction at the First Session of the Thirty-ninth Congress,* part II, 132; part IV, 181.
[65] After a thorough study of the Joint Committee of Fifteen, Kendrick concludes that its chief purpose was to bring the people to the Radical way of thinking, in order that they might vote right in the approaching elections. B. B. Kendrick, *op. cit.,* chap. V.

Conservatives, and the South would almost certainly have accepted parts of the Amendment had they been accompanied by a guarantee of admission of Southern States upon ratification.[66] Lumping all four into one amendment made Johnson's opposition inevitable. Besides, Congress made it doubtful whether these demands were actually final, by refusing to approve the accompanying bill providing for the admission of the Southern States when they should ratify. In spite of the opposition, however, the Amendment was passed, and hurriedly sent to the states for approval.

Connecticut and Tennessee ratified before Congress adjourned, and Tennessee was "admitted" to the Union. But even this fulfillment of Johnson's long-cherished desire was made unpalatable. By a stringent registry law,[67] the Radicals had denied the vote to enough Conservatives in Tennessee to gain control of the Legislature, and Governor Brownlow had long since distanced Northern Radicals in Radicalism. When the Amendment arrived in Tennessee, the Legislature had adjourned and gone home. Brownlow recalled it, and gathered together the Radical members. But the opponents of the Amendment in the Lower House prevented a quorum by absenting themselves. Tennessee Radicals were determined. They had fifty-four members; fifty-six made a legal quorum. Hence two Conservative members, Williams and Martin, were arrested, forcibly detained during the vote, and counted present, though they refused to answer

---

[66] *Infra*, 199 ff., 205-206.

[67] *Report of the Joint Committee on Reconstruction at the First Session of the Thirty-ninth Congress*, part I, 30-32. The registry law cancelled all old registrations; it laid down severe qualifications for voting; it gave the county clerk power to decide under these tests who should vote. The bill was railroaded through the Legislature by Radical leaders under the previous question with little discussion, and no chance for amendment. The minority, whose constituents would be disfranchised by the law, could do nothing but absent themselves in an effort to prevent a quorum. See S. P. Walker to A. Johnson, Feb. 18, 1866, Johnson MSS., LXXXVII.

the roll call.[68] In this manner, the Fourteenth Amendment was ratified by a minority in Tennessee. Brownlow wired the Senate in terms insulting to Johnson, and Congress, without awaiting an official notification, passed a bill admitting Tennessee. The method of ratification and the precipitation of Congressional acceptance of it, were exasperating to Conservatives. The mode of announcement was derisive. Brownlow wired, "We have ratified the Constitutional amendment in the House—43 for it, 11 against it, two of Andrew Johnson's tools not voting. Give my respects to the dead dog of the White House." [69]

In the bill to admit Tennessee, Johnson faced a skilfully contrived dilemma. The preamble stated the Radical theory of the status of the seceded states. If Johnson signed the measure, he gave his official approval to the Congressional plan; if he vetoed it, all the opprobrium of depriving Tennessee of representation would fall upon him. On a suggestion from Senators Doolittle, Cowan, Hendricks, and Guthrie,[70] he avoided both horns of the dilemma by approving the bill in a message which denied the utterances of the preamble, and waved them aside as mere *obiter dicta*. The Radicals could only denounce the message as unconstitutional. Tennessee members were seated, and Johnson maintained his own position.

*   *   *   *

In their campaign for recruits the Radicals wielded a weapon against Johnson more powerful and more insidious than all the abusive speeches their orators could compose.

---

[68] J. C. Grant and J. S. Brien, Nashville friends, wired Johnson the details. *Ibid.*, July 19, 1866, "Telegrams." Also *New York Tribune*, July 18-21, 1866.

[69] *Cong. Globe*, 39 Cong., 1 Sess., 3957.

[70] J. R. Doolittle to A. Johnson, July 23, 1866, Johnson MSS., XCVII.

They had influence in his own official family. Stanton and probably Speed were actively coöperating with Johnson's enemies; Harlan sympathized with them; Dennison's position was doubtful.

In May, 1865, Speed, Stanton, and Dennison all favored negro suffrage.[71] In June Speed assured Boutwell that he was "unequivocally" for it "as necessary for whites as well as blacks," and that nothing was needed to insure its establishment but delay.[72] Harlan approved negro voting but advised against making it a prerequisite to readmission, since it would not be just to force it upon the South while the North refused to grant it. "We must," he wrote Sumner, "look at things as they are, and not as they should be, in estimating the probabilities of success."[73] He protested, however, that he still held the same views as Sumner, and was merely stating practical facts. Harlan praised Johnson,[74] but at the same time contemplated the ultimate triumph of the Radical program.[75] In December Sumner assured Welles that both Harlan and Speed opposed Johnson's policy.[76] In January he said he knew three members of the cabinet who fully concurred with the extreme Radicals. "Why," said he, "one of them has advised and urged me to prepare and bring in a bill which should control the action of the President and wipe out his policy."[77] Welles mournfully confided to his diary, "Sumner is truthful and

[71] Welles MS. Diary, May 9, 1865—(II, 301).
[72] G. S. Boutwell to C. Sumner, June 12, 1865, Sumner MSS., LXXIII. See also J. Speed to C. Sumner, June 17, 1865, ibid., LXXIII.
[73] June 15, 1865, ibid., LXXIII.
[74] He is "as firm as a rock," he wrote Washburne, "and as inflexibly right on all the main points involved in the great struggle as the most ardent could desire." June 12, 1865, Washburne MSS., XC.
[75] J. Harlan to C. Sumner, June 15, Aug. 21, 1865, Sumner MSS., LXXIII, LXXIV.
[76] Welles MS. Diary, Dec. 8, 1865—(II, 394-395).
[77] Ibid., Jan. 13, 1866—(II, 417).

therefore his statement is reliable." [78] Harlan privately denied that the first veto "was advised & supported by every member of the cabinet"; but he warned against correction of this rumor, unless it was time "to make war on the President." [79]

Speed used his cabinet position to serve Radical friends in Congress. Harlan was unquestionably more sympathetic to the Radicals than to Johnson. Both gave their confidence to Radical enemies of the President, and yet remained in the cabinet until the Philadelphia Convention forced them openly to avow their views; then they resigned. It was loyalty to the Union Party rather than sympathy with the Radical leaders that controlled Dennison. When he could no longer remain really true to both Johnson and the party, he resigned voluntarily; while he remained, he gave the President loyal support.

Not so Stanton, who refused to resign at all. When Lincoln died Stanton was leaning toward Radicalism, but his admiration for Lincoln might have held him true, had that president lived. His devotion to country was undoubted. His courage of conviction was like Johnson's, over-developed into stubbornness. Neither Johnson nor Stanton was a man with whom it was easy to get along. Lincoln, appreciating their worth, had by skilful handling drawn out the best in each. Johnson was no manager of men; and he failed to understand Stanton. During the War Stanton had expressed only admiration for Johnson. But the latter's war career was a perpetual altercation with the War Department, and Stanton was no man to bear criticism without resentment, however free it might be from personal strictures. Although

[78] *Ibid.*, Jan. 15, 1866—(II, 417).
[79] J. Harlan to L. Trumbull, Feb. 26, 1866, Trumbull MSS., LXIV.

he supported Johnson in many quarrels with his own generals, this backing may have emanated from the President; had Stanton writhed ever so much under it, support that Lincoln wished accorded would still have borne Stanton's signature. The eulogistic acceptance of Johnson's resignation in 1865 may have been written in the White House. Stanton probably cherished secret resentment over the conflicts between Johnson and the Tennessee generals. In any case, Johnson failed to inspire in him the confidence which had bound him closely to Lincoln.

On Lincoln's death, Stanton went over to the extremists. Outwardly he supported Johnson; secretly he sympathized, consulted, and coöperated with the Sumnerites to the injury of the President. Yet he clung to his cabinet position. This tortuous duality of Stanton was an element in Johnson's weakness in the election of 1866.

Lincoln died on Saturday morning; Sunday morning Johnson's first cabinet meeting discussed the general policy of reconstruction. Johnson urged exemplary punishment of leading rebels, and Stanton presented his reconstruction plan discussed two days before under Lincoln. That evening several Congressmen who had attended a Radical conclave the day before, met, probably by appointment, in Stanton's rooms in the War Department. Stanton read them the future North Carolina Proclamation which had been considered in cabinet earlier in the day, and they discussed it.[80] The submission of this important and still confidential cabinet matter to a group of Radicals, illustrates Stanton's tactics.

[80] Welles MS. Diary, April 16, 1865—(II, 291). Sumner, Gooch, Dawes, and others were present. The demand of Sumner to know what provision had been made for negro suffrage was not in the original MS. Diary, but was added at a later date, probably when Welles wrote the *Galaxy* account stating that Sumner secured the incorporation of a passage providing for negro suffrage.

Only a month after Lincoln's death, Fessenden wrote Stanton, "I hope Andy will have sense and firmness enough to resist all intrigues until Congress meets, when they can be taken care of . . . If, by any chance, I can aid you . . . count upon me, at a moment's warning. I shall be happy to fight by your side." [81] Winter Davis, Trumbull, Howard, Forney, Curtin, Colfax, and other Radical leaders were in intimate correspondence with Stanton during this first year of Johnson's administration.[82] In September Stanton visited Radical friends in New England. He stopped first at Newport, and then with Sumner,[83] whose Worcester speech he found none too radical. He told Sumner that he approved "every sentiment, every opinion and word of it." [84] In December Sumner was surprised that Welles did not know of Stanton's opposition to Johnson's policy. Until that time, however, neither Welles, McCulloch, nor Dennison had ever heard Stanton explicitly advocate negro suffrage.[85] When the call for the Philadelphia Convention was issued in July, 1866, Stanton refused either to endorse it, or to resign. He kept in close touch with Speed and Dennison after they did resign to join the Radicals.[86] In September Tichnor and Fields offered him space in the *Atlantic Monthly* for whatever he wished to publish about his decision to remain in the cabinet.[87] During the campaign he supplied Radical leaders with cabinet information which they used effectively to gain votes.[88]

[81] May 23, 1865, Stanton MSS., XXVII.
[82] *Ibid.*, XXVII-XXXI.
[83] W. C. Gibbs to C. Sumner, Sept. 14, 1865, Sumner MSS., LXXIV.
[84] Welles MS. Diary, Dec. 8, 1865—(II, 394).
[85] *Ibid.*, Dec. 8 and 18, 1865—(II, 394, 398).
[86] J. Speed to E. Stanton, Sept. 12, 1866, Stanton MSS., XXX; and W. Dennison to E. Stanton, Oct. 16, 1866, *ibid.*, XXXI.
[87] Tichnor and Fields to H. Wilson, and H. Wilson to E. Stanton, Sept. 15, 1866, *ibid.*, XXX, and Sept. 17, 1866, *ibid.*, XXXI.
[88] E.g., C. A. Dana to E. Stanton, Nov. 13, 1866, *ibid.*, XXXI. The Stanton MSS. give ample evidence of his coöperation with the Radicals.

Rumors of his resignation, however, never failed to alarm the Radicals. In September Bingham of Ohio wrote, "The people rely on you *alone* of all the Administration to stand by them in the contest for the Amendment." [89] Governor Cony of Maine, Forney, White of the *Chicago Tribune*, Morton after his conversion, and other Radicals joined in urging him to stay in the cabinet, even though he had "to endure the obloquy of a false appearance for the accomplishment of our common efforts." [90] Randall spoke truth when he said, "Stanton will not leave—it is given to me in a reliable shape—that the radicals insist on his remaining." [91]

In the cabinet his power for good or evil was enormous. He controlled agencies upon which any policy of reconstruction depended for success. Both the regular army and the Freedmen's Bureau were under his direction. He appointed officers of both. Their reports came to him and could be suppressed or widely published as he chose. The President had two secretaries, Browning [92] and Morrow. But the rush of reconstruction business necessitated additions to the staff. Consequently, the War Department detailed Colonel Long, Colonel Wright Reeves, Major William C. Moore, and General Mussey to help Johnson's service.[93] By providing his private secretaries, Stanton was in a position to learn his best-guarded secrets. Welles thinks he had a regular spy system to watch the President and report his conversations.[94] The only government telegraph was in the War Office. There every incoming message was received under Stanton's surveillance, and was subject to delay or loss. Every telegram

[89] Sept. 3, 1866, Stanton MSS., XXX.

[90] *Ibid.*, XXX-XXXI. See also "Stanton and the Cabinet," *New York Herald*, Aug. 1, 1866.

[91] S. J. Randall to A. Johnson, Oct. 31, 1866, Johnson MSS., CV.

[92] Browning died within the year, and Robert Johnson took his place.

[93] W. H. Crook, *Through Five Administrations*, 85.

[94] Welles MS. Diary, Dec. 26, 1865—(II, 403 footnote). This is a note inserted later.

that Johnson sent, went through this same department. Much of Johnson's correspondence with Southern provisional governors was by wire. Even the complaints of the governors against the War Department, and Johnson's replies, passed through the hands of this unsympathetic secretary. The efficient administration of the whole Executive Department was dependent upon a cordiality between Secretary of War and President which did not exist. A few incidents will illustrate the possibilities of the situation.

When the papers of the military trial of Mrs. Surratt were sent by the court to the War Department, they contained a note on behalf of the court recommending mercy; when they reached President Johnson this note was not among them. Critics of Johnson's policy knew that the note had been sent. Hence Johnson was put in the light of refusing the court's plea for clemency and harshly condemning to death on the gallows a woman whose guilt was doubtful. When he learned of its existence, he publicly announced that the note of mercy had never reached him. But since Mrs. Surratt had been hanged, and an impression of harshness had been created, the later explanation did Johnson little good.[95]

The President and cabinet were unanimous in rejecting Sherman's terms to General Johnston. But Sherman's motives had been good. Johnson delegated Grant to handle the matter personally, and so kindly did he do it that the incident but increased Sherman's friendship for him. The question was settled in cabinet meeting on Friday. Strict secrecy was enjoined. Yet Saturday afternoon Stanton told

[95] Stanton and Holt share the guilt in the suppression of the recommendation of mercy. W. H. Crook, *op. cit.*, 90. David M. Dewitt, *The Assassination of Abraham Lincoln*, 133-139, 223-255. W. G. Moore, "Notes," *Am. Hist. Rev.*, XIX (1913), 108. R. W. Winston, *Andrew Johnson*, 285-291.

Sumner the whole story, and in the Sunday newspapers he published over his own signature full details of the Sherman terms and the cabinet discussion, colored by insinuations of disloyalty and treachery on Sherman's part.[96] This public statement surprised both President and cabinet. It temporarily discredited Sherman, one of the strong advocates of moderation.[97]

When Governor Brownlow failed in his efforts to secure a quorum in his reconvened legislature, he asked General Thomas to arrest enough recalcitrant members to form one. On July 14 Thomas wired to Washington to know whether he should make the requested arrests. *Three days later* the telegram was delivered to Johnson who directed Stanton to wire emphatic orders to abstain from meddling in local politics.[98] But during the three days' delay, in the absence of instructions, the two necessary members had been arrested and forcibly held while the Amendment was ratified.

At the time of the New Orleans riot, another telegram to the President was delayed. Had Stanton not withheld it, the President would have sent orders that would have prevented the riot.[99] Baird's telegram was not delivered to Johnson until the day after the riot, three days after it had been sent. Stanton later admitted that he had withheld it intentionally.[1] The riot brought untold abuse upon Johnson and was an effective election argument for the Radicals.

[96] Welles MS. Diary, April 22 and 23, 1865—(II, 295).
[97] Rhodes proves Stanton guilty of deliberate misrepresentation and uses strong terms to express his disapproval of his part in the incident. He thinks that Stanton "accustomed to act impulsively on insufficient knowledge . . . lost his head . . . in vehement rage." *History of the United States,* V, 171-175.
[98] Order of E. M. S. to Gen. Grant, July 17, 1866, Stanton MSS., XXX.
[99] *Infra,* 349-350.
[1] In January, 1867, when the special Congressional committee appointed to investigate the New Orleans riot was about to report, Eliot, the Radical chairman, warned Stanton that Boyer was going to charge in a minority report "that the tragical conclusion of the whole would have been

Such examples might be multiplied. But it is evident that Stanton controlled excellent opportunities for working injury to Johnson's cause, while at the same time covering his tracks beyond detection then or now. Johnson's weakness in his cabinet is patent. Yet he hesitated to break with the Radicals in it. Speed, Harlan, and Dennison were finally forced to resign only by a manœuvre of Johnson's friends. The President at least suspected Stanton's loyalty. Welles, the Blairs, and McCulloch repeatedly gave warning against him;[2] numerous correspondents furnished evidence of his duplicity. In January, 1866, Johnson was considering his removal.[3] But he hesitated, and did not move to oust him for more than two years. Then it was too late.

* * * *

Through the first half of 1866 Johnson lost, and the Radicals gained, first one leader and then another; there was slow but steady flow of popular support from Conservative to Radical ranks. The factors that made Radical recruits of leading Moderates are significant. When Governor Morton of Indiana went to Europe in December, 1865, he was still

avoided or prevented had it not been that the Secretary of War kept to himself unanswered, the dispatch of Gen. Baird." Eliot sent word to Stanton that he might "meet this charge on the threshold." D. L. Eaton to E. Stanton, Jan. 7, 1867, Stanton MSS., XXXI. In answer Stanton admitted failure to forward the telegram. "I saw no reason," he said, "to instruct him to withdraw protection from a convention sanctioned by the Governor, and in the event of any attempt at arrest General Baird's interference would bring up the case with all the facts for such instructions as might be proper." E. M. S. to T. D. Eliot, Jan. 30, 1867, Stanton MSS., XXXI.

[2] For some reason Seward and Weed supported Stanton.

[3] Comstock confided to his diary, "Stanton has been not doing some things with reference to general that he wished & doing some things not wished, for army. Gen. spoke to Mr. J. about it & was told he would be sustained, intimating that Mr. S. would not stay long." C. B. Comstock MS. Diary, Jan. 15, 1866.

a staunch supporter of Johnson.[4] Indeed, he was entrusted with a secret mission to Emperor Napoleon.[5] A little later Johnson offered him the Austrian mission. After the first veto, Representative Stilwell of Indiana wired Johnson, "Govr Morton is much better and able to accept a cabinet position. If you desire it his brother-in-law . . . will go after him." [6] What effect Johnson's failure to accept this suggestion had on Morton's course is indeterminable. On his return in March the ex-governor stopped for a long interview in which he urged Johnson to sign the Civil Rights Bill. When he got back to Indiana in April, he found the Republicans hesitating between Johnson and the Radicals, and the Democrats jubilant, hopeful of success, denouncing the Republicans, and supporting Johnson. It was undoubtedly the attitude of the Democrats whom he had fought all through the War, and the inevitability of an alliance between them and Johnson after the veto of the Civil Rights Bill that swung Morton into the Radical camp; [7] for on the negro problem, on Southern policy, on opposition to centralization, and on dread of New England control, Morton and Johnson agreed. Be that as it may, on June 20 Morton came out strong-fistedly at the head of Indiana Radicals.

For a year John Sherman tried to hold a moderate con-

[4] His Richmond speech on September 29 had a powerful influence favorable to Johnson. For years Morton and the Radical followers of Julian had been enemies in state politics.

[5] The object was to secure what official communications could not have attempted without undue strain of relationships, the withdrawal of the French troops from Mexico. R. R. Hitt says Morton confided this to him while on his death bed. Wm. D. Foulke, *Life of Oliver P. Morton*, I, 457. A letter from Morton to Johnson reporting the French situation and counseling patience and peace, substantiates Hitt's story. Dec. 29, 1865, Johnson MSS., LXXXIII.

[6] Feb. 21, 1866, *ibid.*, "Telegrams," 33.

[7] W. D. Foulke, *op. cit.*, 466-468. His key-note speech at Masonic Hall on June 20 indicates this, too.

ciliatory course, and in this his general-brother unceasingly encouraged him. Before Congress opened he talked with Johnson several times, and thought him "kind and patient with all his terrible responsibility." [8] By February he was worried. "A widening breach," he wrote, "is taking place in the Union Party. Not only for my own sake but for the good of the country, I will keep quiet as possible on political questions in the hope to do good by conciliation." [9] After the first veto and the Washington's Birthday speech, Sherman ably defended the President and his policy in the Senate. But then he began to waver. "Our difficulties here are not over," he wrote. "Johnson is suspicious of every one, and I fear will drift into his old party relations. If so, he will carry with him but little force & prestige, and will soon be in deserved disgrace." [10] He criticized Johnson's opposition to the Civil Rights Bill and Fourteenth Amendment which he believed were entirely consistent with his original policy. But Sherman was no Radical even in July; he had complete confidence in the South; his only hate was for Copperheads; he was ready to offer general amnesty and repeal the test oaths, as soon as the South agreed to "a firm basis of representation." [11] He felt Congress had "failed in a plain duty" in not allowing "legal senators & representatives to take their seats." [12] What turned Sherman irreconcilably from Johnson, was the latter's "betrayal" of the party that elected him. Recurringly, fears of his going over to the "Copperheads" had haunted Sherman.[13] By July 8, that senator was convinced of Johnson's determination to split the Union

8 Nov. 10, 1865, W. T. Sherman MSS., XVII.
9 J. Sherman to W. T. Sherman, Feb. 15, 1866, *ibid.*, XVIII.
10 J. Sherman to W. T. Sherman, March 20, 1866, *ibid.*, XVIII.
11 J. Sherman to W. T. Sherman, July 2, 1866, *The Sherman Letters*, 271.
12 J. Sherman to W. T. Sherman, July 8, 1866, W. T. Sherman MSS., XIX.
13 *Ibid.*, XVII-XVIII.

Party, and fraternize with Copperheads. The President's preëlection replacement of Union office-holders by "Copperheads" roused Sherman's ire and completed his transformation into a Radical.[14]

John A. Bingham of Ohio, another original Moderate, was apparently driven to Radicalism when Johnson refused to accept the Fourteenth Amendment. He would have sustained the President's first veto of the Freedmen's Bureau Bill.[15] He did uphold the veto of the Civil Rights Bill,[16] and made an able speech defending Johnson's stand. He favored protection of negro rights, but maintained that only the states had power to provide it. It was in his ardent advocacy of the civil rights guarantee by constitutional amendment that he deserted the President. His desire for the high tariff on wools which Radical leaders were dangling temptingly before the dazzled eyes of his sheep-raising constituents, gave added zest to his attacks on Johnson.

Among Johnson's most powerful backers was the *New York Herald*. That sheet agreed with his economic tenets; it approved his Southern policy. It read the popular mind, and maintained until September that the election would bring success to the Conservatives. It deserted Johnson because the Maine elections and the failure of the New York Convention to nominate Dix, emphasized in telling fashion the fatal effect of the Democracy's failure to keep itself in the background of the Conservative movement.[17] Belief that

[14] Late in life he gave Johnson's split with the party, and the Black Codes and Ku Klux Klan as the causes of his conversion to Radicalism. J. Sherman to W. T. Sherman, Oct. 26, 1866, *The Sherman Letters*, 278; J. Sherman, *Recollections*, I, 369.

[15] The House did not vote on the overriding of the veto, as the Senate, to which the bill was returned, voted to sustain the veto.

[16] On this vote he was paired against the bill with Hubbard and Williams who favored it. He thought the bill unconstitutional.

[17] Mr. Phillips of the editorial staff wrote Johnson an interesting series of letters explaining the motives and attitude of Mr. Bennett and the

Johnson's originally good chances were ruined by Democratic selfishness drove a paper which sought popularity above all else to belated support of the Fourteenth Amendment as the lesser of evils.

John A. Logan, a pre-war Democrat and war general, at first supported Johnson. In June, 1865, he vociferated the right of the states alone to control suffrage, and roused loyal applause by shouting that the Southern States were in the Union and had never been out. He noisily accepted Johnson's program.[18] During the next year he watched the trend of affairs and adroitly avoided further committing himself politically until he could jump into the fray on the winning side. His speeches were mere rodomontade.[19] During the winter Johnson appointed him minister first to Mexico and then to Japan, but he declined. Army friends in New Orleans represented him as favoring speedy restoration, because he hoped to be able to invade Mexico.[20] In May a Johnson aide reported, "I have had an interview with Col. John Logan and am perfectly satisfied that he will be an active worker against the radicals at the next election. He is bitterly denounced by the extreme radicals as a traitor to his party." [21] Then the Radicals of Illinois nominated him for Congress, and he suddenly became one of the bitterest of Johnson's calumniators. His unfathomable vagueness makes it impossible to determine why he turned against Johnson;

Herald. One on September 16 explains the somersault of that week. W. B. Phillips to A. Johnson, Johnson MSS., CI. See also the editorial columns of the *Herald.*

18 This was after the full announcement of Johnson's plan of restoration. Speech at Cooper Institute meeting, *New York Herald,* June 8, 1865.

19 He denounced slavery and bombastically lauded the soldier boys; he urged education of negroes. But his speeches reveal nothing of his politics. Speech at Cooper Institute meeting, June 7, 1865, and speech at Louisville, Ky., July, 1865, Geo. F. Dawson, *Life and Services of Gen. John A. Logan as Soldier and Statesman,* 109.

20 J. H. Black to A. Johnson, Oct. 12, 1866, Johnson MSS., CIII.

21 A. J. Allen to A. Johnson, May 21, 1866, *ibid.,* XCV.

probably because of political ambition. In any case, in the early summer of 1866 he threw his military prestige and his noisy vituperation into the Radical balance.

Lyman Trumbull of Illinois was another Moderate who only reluctantly deserted the President. In introducing the Freedmen's Bureau and Civil Rights bills, he tried to coöperate with Johnson. His tone was not antagonistic even when he urged passage of the Civil Rights Bill over the veto.[22] Ray wrote in April, "I *know* that Trumbull has no desire to quarrel with the President; I know that his instincts and aspirations are for a Democratic policy and that he has been very unwillingly forced into antagonism to Mr. Johnson by a party pressure that he could not resist. His letters to me are full of regrets over what has happened; and I believe that he is yet hopeful of a readjustment of the relations between our wing of the party and the President on a satisfactory and harmonious basis." Trumbull felt ill-used, however, by Johnson's vetoes, for at an early stage he had read both bills to Johnson, and had stood ready to accept modification. Ray was "sure he would never *never* have committed his fortunes to their success," had he not thought that he had Presidential approval. Trumbull, he said, feels that "he has been misled by the President himself. I think he must have misunderstood his words. . . . He has no heart to follow out the course that his friends have marked down for his guidance." [23] Party pressure finally forced him into reluctant opposition.

Undoubtedly many Moderates succumbed to Radical proselytism because they feared ridicule, calumniation, and party ostracism if they firmly stood their ground, and be-

---

[22] *Cong. Globe,* 39 Cong., 1 Sess., 1755 ff.
[23] C. H. Ray, former editor of the *Chicago Tribune,* to M. Blair, April 10, 1866, Johnson MSS., XCIII.

cause they dreaded the opprobrious cry of "traitor" which party leaders hurled at Conservatives. Ray succinctly analyzed the political situation, and hit upon the causation of many a Radical conversion, when he said, "Those fellows in Washington . . . are egging each other on to all sorts of excesses—not because they individually wish for the laws that they are voting for every day;—but because they are afraid of being suspected of conservatism if they hold back." [24]   *   *   *   *

Whether the break in the Union Party was inevitable is not determinable. Had Johnson and Congress both been tolerant, common ground might have been found. But the Radicals were avowedly extremists who used extreme methods to educate people to extreme ends. Johnson's greatest strength would have lain in the practice of tolerance and kindness, for it was upon the Moderates of all parties that his program depended, and yet Johnson was by nature incapable of preaching even tolerance tolerantly. The President was immovable in his belief in a conciliatory policy toward the South and the efficacy of democratic self-government and freedom of thought, even when applied to Southerners. An unrelenting group of Congressmen were convinced that the only security for good government in the South and the only safety for their own economic and political system, lay in imposing that system forcibly upon the rest of the country. Between these elements agreement was perhaps impossible. But the majority of people upon whom both factions depended stood somewhere between President and Radicals, more tolerant, more open-minded, more powerful than either, and in June still undecided.

[24] *Ibid.*

Chapter IV

MODERATE THIRD PARTY MOVEMENT

IN 1866 a third party, rightly captained, would have had an unusual chance of success. The political situation was anomalous. Technically there were two parties; actually there was chaos. During the War but two parties had subsisted: supporters of the government and an opposition—termed Union and Democratic parties. When the War ended and peace-time issues again began to interest men, the stage was set for a political upheaval.

The Union Party was a war-time combination of Republicans of pre-war days with War Democrats. Republicans and Democrats had differed too fundamentally to remain long united except under stress of war. Hence the Union Party would inevitably split into its component parts. The Republican Party itself was a hodge-podge of varying political and economic groups fasciated by a common hatred of slavery. The elimination of that institution cut the bands, and let the old elements of Republicanism fall apart. Furthermore, many old Copperheads would now support Conservative Republicans on peace-time issues. On reconstruction many good Republicans of slavery days found themselves in closer sympathy with former "Doughfaces" than with the Radical leaders of their own party. On economic

113

questions most War Democrats and many Republicans agreed more nearly with Copperheads, even with Rebels, than with Radicals. War had made strange bedfellows who could no longer lie together.

Slavery had divided political society vertically into two main groups, Republicans and Democrats; the War had divided the Democrats again into War and Peace Democrats; and reconstruction split Republicans into Radicals and Moderates. The termination of the conflict had unboxed a Pandora's collection of economic and political issues long confined, first by the slavery controversy and then by war. Consequently, the four vertical political groups were now horizontally cross-sectioned, not only by the question of expediency of specific guarantees to be exacted from the South, by feeling toward the negro, and by the dispute over states' rights and checks and balances in the federal government, but by the old economic lines that had separated the commercial and industrial class from agriculturalists since the very beginnings of our history. Until new parties could be organized around these new issues, or until some single issue could be found that would perform the function that first slavery, and then the War, had exercised in holding together the anti-Southern party, political groupings would remain chaotic.   *   *   *   *

Johnson's task was to formulate a platform and organize a party. He had two choices. He could form a party around some of the economic issues upon which he and Sumner differed as fundamentally as they did on Southern policy; or he could make reconstruction the paramount issue and build a party around his policy. Had Johnson chosen the former course, he would have found many of his Radical opponents ranged against him on the new issues, too, but he would have won from the Sumner party many of its Western supporters. Eastern Radicals knew this, and hoped to keep the Southern question so interesting that other issues would be forgotten.

Since the Southern problem was urgent, Johnson turned to it first. Had he succeeded in his restoration policy, he would have found himself at the head of a Southern and Western party which could have restored agrarian social and economic ideals to their old dominance in the country, greatly altering the course of America's second industrial revolution. He felt, however, that he must first of all get the South back into the full fellowship of states. The Radicals opposed him in this, and the field of conflict was determined.

*   *   *   *

Organization of a party was important. Many of Johnson's friends advised the launching of a new, conservative movement, active and well organized, that would include moderates of both old parties. Doolittle had written in October, "Sumner & Stevens are flooding the country [with their speeches]. It is wrong for us to wait until prejudices and passions, and hate of the South, and avarice, and ambition shall all be joined together hand in hand, before wise statesmanship magnanimity and returning affection and loyalty can have a fair chance." [1]

In December Harvey Watterson wished "to join . . . in the construction of that National Administration party," on which reposed "the sole hope of the country." "With this constantly before me," he wrote, "I have endeavored . . . to urge the necessity for a liberal spirit toward men and measures; to counsel an abandonment of the old cant about

[1] J. R. Doolittle to A. Johnson, Oct. 10, 1865, Johnson MSS., LXXIX.

abolitionism, and a recognition of the new and future relations of the sections; of consigning the war and its passions to a common grave; and of looking to no party in the North, but to the discretion and sound impulses of the whole people for relief." [2] "The only practical question left," declared Campbell of Ohio, "is whether the impracticable radical zealots who seem to be 'instigated by the devil and fatally bent on mischief' shall gobble us all up and run us on their infernal train to national perdition, or whether fair minded men will assert their independence and organize a party *on the basis of the Presidents* [sic] *patriotic policy* which is heartily approved by the mass of the people." [3] Morton of Indiana and Bennett of the *New York Herald*, both keen political observers, joined in the plea. [4]

Governor Cox and his Ohio friends drew up a definite plan which they were certain would put Johnson in a "winning position." It included constitutional protection for the freedmen; "a vote on the admission of Tennessee members . . . to compel individual Congressmen to show their hands"; a ballot on the amendment providing a "voting basis" of representation, to "show the country that New England selfishness is not willing to accept any basis . . . that diminishes her power"; and, finally, organization of party machinery with the patronage "in the hands of men who know how to wield it." [5]

Radical apprehension of the effectiveness of a new moderate party was evidenced by Brownson of *Brownson's Quarterly Review*, who said, "I fear such men as Doolittle, Dixon & Raymond, backed as they are by the Administra-

[2] H. M. Watterson to A. Johnson, Dec. 7, 1865, *ibid.*, LXXXII.
[3] L. D. Campbell to Senator D. P. Patterson, Jan. 22, 1866, *ibid.*, LXXXV.
[4] O. P. Morton to A. Johnson, Dec. 7, 1865, and J. G. Bennett to A. Johnson, Feb. 1, 1866, *ibid.*, LXXXII, LXXXV.
[5] Maj. R. P. L. Baber to A. Johnson, March 29, 1866, *ibid.*, XCI.

tion & the trading interests [6] of the country. They are far more dangerous than downright Copperheads." [7]

The question on which proponents of a strong Johnsonian organization did not agree, was whether the new movement should be a third party including some Democrats and some Radicals, or a reorganization within the Union Party. The Democrats, even unselfish, far-sighted ones who were willing that the Republicans should dominate the new organization, preferred a third party. To this end Dean Richmond, Dix, and Pierrepont consulted with Johnson and proffered their assistance.[8] But many Johnson Republicans like Raymond, Sherman, Seward, and Morton would have countenanced a Johnson party only if built up inside the Union organization. Faced with the difficulty of reconciling these two groups, Johnson hesitated, and did nothing.

A prime requisite of a successful political organization in the 'Sixties was control of the patronage. Civil service reform, as Julian says, was "in the distant future, and the attempt to inaugurate it would have been counted next to treasonable." Loyalty to party was "the best evidence of loyalty to the country" and of "fitness for civil position." [9] Federal office-holders were generally politicians of influence in the community. They were imbued with a sense of strict party loyalty. They had secured their offices for past services rendered to the party boss, and they hoped for future rewards for future service. However strongly they agreed with Johnson's policies, politicians could not afford to support him as long as his opponents controlled the plums of

[6] Men engaged in foreign commerce supported Johnson because a speedy restoration of the South would reduce the Radical tariff and increase their business.

[7] O. A. Brownson to C. Sumner, Jan. 2, 1866, Sumner MSS., LXXVI.

[8] J. A. Dix to A. Johnson, March 2, 1866, and J. Cochrane to A. Johnson, Jan. 23, 1866, Johnson MSS., LXXXIX, LXXXV.

[9] G. W. Julian, *Political Recollections*, 244.

office. However strenuously they objected to Johnson, politicians would have had to support him if he had made officeholding dependent upon loyalty to him.

When Johnson became president the Radicals were in possession of a goodly share of the offices. Appointments under Lincoln had been made with the purpose of securing unquestioned loyalty during a war. That meant that officeholders were often extremists.[10] Furthermore, fear of Democratic return to power inclined all actual incumbents to Radicalism.

The extent to which disloyalty to the administration infested all departments is indicated by Welles's difficulties with the navy-yards. As one of Lincoln's original cabinet, Welles had made the naval appointments himself. He had always been a Conservative. His department, if any, should have been free from Radical infection. Yet the navy-yards were a power for Radicalism that gave Welles constant concern. In 1865 before Welles could arrest them, assessments for campaign purposes amounting to $1052 were levied on the workmen of the Philadelphia Yard. Before hotly contested elections Radical yard-masters employed extra hands whose chief duty was party electioneering in the city.[11] Radical meetings were held in the yards. Welles's orders and threats had little effect. In October, 1866, he was still threatening with dismissal any master or foreman who used his position and patronage to oppose the administration, who coerced employees in politics, or who proscribed workmen for

10 The treasury agents, for instance, were nearly all Radicals chosen by Chase, who finally resigned chiefly because Lincoln refused to sanction his appointment of Radicals in New York when Radical opposition to Lincoln was at its height. See S. P. Chase to J. Cisco, July 1, 1864, Chase MSS., 2nd ser., III.

11 G. Welles to C. H. Bell, Comm. New York Navy-yard, Oct. 3, 1865, Welles MSS., "Letter-book." Similar letters indicate trouble in other yards. *Ibid.*, LXI, LXII, and "Letter-book."

desiring the full restoration of the Union.[12] In spite of Welles, the navy-yards were a factor in Radical victory.

Right here in Washington, Cochrane told Johnson, "are thousands in Office who are . . . rejoicing over every defeat you may sustain either before Congress or the people, and forming an immense Corps of Radical letter writers for the papers." [13] Administration men all the way from Dan Rice, the circus clown, to Henry Ward Beecher testified that the patronage was serving as an effective weapon against the President. Every day brought entreaties to reform the patronage in favor of friends of Johnson's policy. Some came from men themselves seeking position; but many came from wise friends of the administration who had no ax to grind. Welles,[14] and Parke Godwin [15]—in fact, nearly all of Johnson's personal friends—urged him to dismiss office-holders who were opposing his policy.

In May after a discussion in the *Herald* staff meeting, Phillips wrote, "Bennett . . . is firmly convinced that you cannot sustain yourself in any other way than by a bold, striking, and prompt action with the opponents of your administration. . . . His arguments are that the radicals are able to carry the timid and wavering conservatives with them because you are not decisive and bold enough in using the patronage in your hands against them and in favor of those who do support you. You 'are gone' he says unless you take the boldest and most decisive course, and thus rally all the conservatives to you." [16]

---

[12] G. Welles to C. H. Bell, Oct. 11, 1866, *ibid.*, "Letter-book."

[13] Oct., 1866, Johnson MSS., CV.

[14] E.g., Welles MS. Diary, Dec. 18, 1865—(II, 398).

[15] Godwin wrote, "It is particularly important that the federal offices be filled by men who comprehend your own ideal . . . Young men, not identified in any way with the old factions or cliques, but willing to do justice to all, accustomed to business, and capable of discerning and moulding the future, are the men now needed." Dec. 25, 1865, Johnson MSS., LXXXIII.

[16] W. B. Phillips to A. Johnson, May 20, 1866, *ibid.*, XCV.

As his parting admonition before sailing for Europe in December, Governor Morton wrote, "Were I in your place, I would not fail to employ every power and instrumentality in my hands to sustain my policy, and the friends who sustain it. While it is understood that members of Congress can oppose you, and in breaking down your policy break down your administration and yet control your patronage, you may expect to have opposition and to fail. The resolute wielding of your patronage in favor of your friends, *inside the Union party*, cannot fail to build you up with the people and disarm the Opposition in Congress." [17]

As the election approached, the gravity of Johnson's mistake became manifest. "Thousands of office-holders," declared Cochrane, "have been operating against you whose action would have been prevented if they had feared the loss of office." [18] A prominent lawyer of Troy, New York, protested, "You may rely upon it that the sound business men of our State are with you. But when the thousands of Postmasters and others holding office under the U. S., use their influence and means against us we can hardly expect in so close a vote to succeed. . . . I am quite sure that if the most of the political offices held under the U. S. Govt had during the past summer been filled by true *friends* instead of true enemies of your administration we should not have suffered the bad defeat which we have." [19]

Johnson's position was difficult at best. He had not grown up in the Northern party system, but had been superimposed upon it by chance. He did not control the key men. In fact, master politicians, bosses, and petty postmasters, all looked upon him as an intruder. It was, of course, hard to

17 Dec. 7, 1865, *ibid.*, LXXXII.
18 J. Cochrane to A. Johnson, Oct., 1866, *ibid.*, CV.
19 D. S. Seymour to A. Johnson, Nov. 8, 1866, *ibid.*, CV.

learn the true politics of a distant officer. Even where chance
removed the old incumbent, faction made wise appointments
difficult. But Johnson did nothing to meet the situation until
the fall of 1866 when it was too late. Meantime, the Radicals
used the full force of the President's own patronage against
him. Worse still, many of his supporters turned to the Radical cause in discouragement at seeing opponents of the President enjoying the political plums which should have been
their reward for loyal service.

* * * *

From all sides Johnson was importuned to remodel his
cabinet, at least to remove Stanton and Speed. When his
career was drawing to a close and he had time to ponder the
past, he wrote to his former private secretary: "I may have
erred in not carrying out Mr. Blair's request in putting into
my Cabinet Morton, Andrew, and Greeley. . . . I told Mr.
Blair that I wouldn't have Greeley on any account. . . . I
told him that Greeley was a sublime old child and would be
of no service to me. The others I thought well of at the time.
Andrew was great, and Morton was greater. . . . I do not
say I should have done so, or that I would do so had I my
career to go over again, for it would have been hard to have
put out Seward and Welles, who had served satisfactorily
under the greatest man of all. Morton would have been a
tower of strength, however, and so would Andrew. No senator would have dared to vote for my impeachment with
those two men in my Cabinet." [20]

Had Morton and Andrew been given portfolios, they
would not have secretly undermined Johnson's plans as did
Stanton. They would have given loyal support or resigned.

[20] A. Johnson to B. C. Truman, Aug. 3, 1868, *Century Magazine*, LXXXV
(1913), 438-439.

Both were originally Moderates. Morton's speech in September strengthened Johnson's cause. As late as February he still wanted a cabinet position.[21] Had he been actively at work, he would never in all probability have become a Radical. On the negro question he and Johnson agreed. On this Andrew, Massachusetts-bred, differed with them. But Andrew opposed the effort to penalize and incapacitate the natural Southern leaders.[22] His valedictory address as governor was condemned by both Sumner and Wilson. Andrew and Morton would have lent great strength to Johnson. Both were popular as no cabinet member was; both had great influence in the formation of popular opinion; both were sensitively in communication with popular moods; and both were men of action who could have led the aggressive campaign that the exigencies of the time demanded. Andrew and Morton are but examples of cabinet possibilities. Grant or Sherman would have brought strength to the War Office and prestige to the administration, though Johnson's greater need was for men whose political influence would have staved off the stampede of Moderates to the Radical ranks.

The anomaly of Johnson's position explains without making less ruinous his failure to act. He was the nominal head of a party of which he was not a member, and to whose machinery his enemies held the keys. In a country controlled by victorious Northerners, his Southern origin and training made his successful execution of any policy as impossible as it made his formation of a wise one feasible. Accident of war had thrown him into the vice-presidency, and a second

21 T. N. Stilwell to A. Johnson, Feb. 21, 1866, Johnson MSS., "Telegrams."

22 He urged "forebearance which discriminates those who are swept into the current of treason from those who are the wanton architects of ruin." J. A. Andrew, *Address of his Excellency to the Two Branches of the Legislature of Mass., Jan. 6, 1865*, 96-97.

chance into the executive chair at the head of a Northern party, in which men like Stevens and Sumner were his lieutenants, and New England abolitionists a power. His leadership of this party was obviously impossible. His mistake was to attempt it. In a contest of factions for supremacy in the Republican Party, Johnson did not have even a sporting chance. Yet he had the example of John Tyler's pitiable failure to deter him from a break with the party that had elected him. A stranger to the North, not knowing whom to trust and hence trusting no one fully, he hesitated, hesitated for months doing nothing—fatal months when the Radical campaign was successfully launched and carried far down the road to victory.

*   *   *   *

A party had stood ready made. But its natural leaders remained inactive while for six months Johnson merely defended a tiresomely immutable policy, leaving all aggression to the Radicals. Inactivity lost the Moderates much of the advantage of their original position. Finally, a sadly dwindled group of Johnson men did organize the Philadelphia Convention. Perhaps it was too late. Shortly before the Convention Doolittle wrote to his wife, "What is ahead in the political world just now we cannot certainly see. . . . My only fear is that the President has waited too long about making his cabinet a unit. It has demoralized our friends in all the States." [23] Randall and Dixon, however, were both sanguine,[24] and Doolittle soon became infected with the prevalent optimism.

It is not known who first had the idea of calling a national convention of conservatives; probably it was in many minds.

[23] June 20, 1866, State Hist. Soc. of Wis., *Proceedings* (1909), 291.
[24] S. J. Randall to A. Johnson, June 5, 1866, Johnson MSS., XCV; J. Dixon to G. Welles, July 21, 1866, Welles MSS., LXI.

Welles believed that he and Doolittle were responsible. In any case, Doolittle led the movement. He had early put out feelers, and undoubtedly had approached others than Welles. General Dix of New York, for instance, was consulted and invited to attend a conference in Washington. He suggested as a substitute Judge Pierrepont, whose "opinions reflect fairly those of the War Democrats." [25] Doolittle breakfasted with Welles,[26] and allowed him to feel he had suggested the convention. Together they went to the President, who fully acquiesced; indeed, it is likely that he had already been consulted. Doolittle agreed to draft the convention call. He wrote to his wife that "the Call cost . . . a great deal of thought and care." [27]

In preparation of the draft Doolittle conferred freely with the President, Browning, McCulloch, Seward, Welles, Cowan, Randall, Raymond, and the Blairs; [28] others like Judge Pierrepont were sounded. Raymond's sanction was difficult to win. As chairman of the National Committee of the National Union Party, he refused to support the convention if it was to form a new party. His final conversion indicates the infinite tact which the whole movement necessitated. Weed and Seward persuaded him that the convention would merely seek the election of Congressmen favorable to the admission of loyal representatives. Seward finally took him to call on Johnson, who said "he did not want any new party, nor did he want the Democratic party restored to power. He wanted Congress to restore the Union, and if those who favored this would take hold of it in the way . . . suggested, he felt sure the people would sustain them and that the next Congress

25 J. A. Dix to J. R. Doolittle, June 14, 1866, *Am. Historical Magazine* (*Americana*), IV, 331.
26 Welles MS. Diary, June 15, 1866—(II, 528).
27 July 1, 1866, State Hist. Soc. of Wis., *Proceedings* (1909), 291.
28 Welles MS. Diary, June 15-21, 1866—(II, 528-535).

would be overwhelmingly" on their side. After the interview Raymond recorded in his journal that "the President was very anxious to get a foothold in the South for the Conservative wing of the Union party—that he thought the Philadelphia Convention would lay the foundation for a *National* party, which would absorb the Democratic party of the North and West, and all of the Union party but the Radicals; and that the South would also join this new party, which would thus easily gain and hold the political ascendency." It seemed to Raymond "a desirable object—one which it was well worth any one's while to aid." [29] In this way he was won to the support of the movement which ruined him politically.

Those who backed the call fell into two groups. Some wished to make it an attack on the Fourteenth Amendment; others sought to avoid this issue lest they alienate at the beginning a large group whose minds were not made up. When a call was drafted with no mention of the Amendment,[30] Welles protested that failure to condemn the measure weakened the call. With Doolittle he went to see McCulloch about it, but that gentleman was out. After Doolittle left, Welles was worried,[31] and the next morning he called on the Blairs, who shared his misgivings although they had previously assured Doolittle of their entire approval. At Welles's request McCulloch called that evening, and agreed with his objections. Together they went to the President and spent an hour urging him to issue a Jacksonian appeal to the people declaring the Constitution in danger, or at least to

[29] Raymond's "Journal" in *Scribner's*, XX (1880), 277.
[30] Welles suspected Seward of responsibility for this omission in the call.
[31] Welles's diary is so amended through this portion that in the printed *Diary* Welles's suspicion of intrigue and predictions of failure for the milder form of the call appear stronger than they actually were. But he *did* distrust Seward and *was* troubled over the form the call assumed.

include in the call a denunciation of the Amendment. As usual Johnson appeared to agree, but did not commit himself except to say he thought the call too detailed.

The next day McCulloch and Welles importuned Colonel Cooper, the President's private secretary, to help them, and Cooper agreed. The second day Welles again pleaded with the President. On the succeeding day, June 21, Doolittle took tea with Welles, and they went together to a White House conference which discussed the draft call for three hours. Doolittle, Randall,[32] and some of Randall's friends from the National Union Johnson Club, feared that a pronouncement against the Amendment would drive many Conservative leaders over to the Radicals. Cowan, McCulloch, Browning, and Welles insisted upon a more aggressive call; gradually all but Welles were converted to Doolittle's draft. Welles went home gloomily fearing that without a definite program the convention would have no effect. The next day Weed came from New York to consult with the President on the proposed call.

In cabinet the proposition was not mentioned, as only Johnson and three of the cabinet were privy to the plans. While the Fourteenth Amendment and a Presidential message concerning it were thoroughly discussed, the Radical and doubtful members were given no hint of the pending convention summons.[33] The first proposal had been to have the cabinet officers sign the document, but with a divided cabinet this forcing of the issue was deemed inexpedient, and it was arranged that Randall, Doolittle, Browning, Cowan, Knap, and Fowler should sign it, and that Seward, Welles, and McCulloch should conceal their part in drawing it up,

32 Welles, probably unjustly, felt Randall was merely Seward's agent.
33 This account is from the Welles MS. Diary, June 18-22, 1866—(II, 531-536).

but later express their opinion in open letters to Doolittle.[34]
This would make the call appear to emanate from Republican leaders in Congress. Johnson's inability to secure cabinet discussion and support of this important administration measure demonstrates the weakness under which he labored.

On June 23 Doolittle, Cowan, Randall, Browning, Welles, McCulloch, and Seward met at the White House for consideration of the final draft.[35] After a paragraph-by-paragraph discussion, all approved. The call appeared in the papers of June 26.[36]

The next step was to gain the approval of leading Conservatives. The original plan of having Seward, McCulloch, and Welles write public letters of approval was broadened into one that would force the doubtful members of the cabinet to show their hands by adding their support to the movement or by openly acknowledging their Radical tenets and breaking with the administration. A letter was sent to every member of the cabinet. Strong, favorable answers came promptly from Seward, McCulloch, and Welles.[37] Dennison was absent in Ohio, but on his return, resigned, giving loyalty to the Republican Party as his honest reason. Speed and Harlan wrote letters of disapproval, and resigned.

Stanton made no reply to Doolittle's letter asking his opinion on the proposed amendment; in cabinet he reluctantly admitted, when cornered, that he opposed the convention. To the suggestion that he should have declared his opposition in an answer to Doolittle, he responded, "I did not choose to have Doolittle or any other little fellow draw an

---

[34] O. H. Browning to T. Ewing, June 26, 1866, Ewing MSS., XVIII.

[35] *Ibid.* Cf. the Welles account, MS. Diary, June 23, 1866—(II, 538).

[36] See, e.g., the *New York Times,* June 26, 1866.

[37] Doolittle's letter to Welles, dated July 10, 1866, is preserved in the Welles MSS., LXI. There, too, is the draft of Welles's answer, with penciled corrections, addressed first to Randall and then, with "Randall" scratched out, to Doolittle, first dated July 3 and then redated July 11.

answer from me." [38] Stanton had, however, prepared an answer, never sent and in his day unknown, wherein he condemned the whole movement. He wrote unequivocally:

"The within letter is returned to the person by whom it purports to be addressed to me, because I do not choose to recognize him as an organ of communication between the public and myself on any subject, and because moreover I am in favor of securing the civil rights to all citizens of the United States in the States lately in rebellion, am in favor of equalizing the representation in Congress so as to give the loyal States their due weight in the legislative branch of the Government, and am also in favor of repudiating the rebel debt, and of guaranteeing as sacred the national debt incurred to suppress the rebellion, and especially the obligations of the nation to its soldiers and their widows and orphans. These being the objects of the proposed amendments to the Federal Constitution adopted by Congress, I am in favor of those amendments. Understanding the object of the so called Philadelphia convention to be the organization of a party consisting mainly of those who carried on the rebellion against the Government, and undertook to destroy the national life by war, in the rebel States, and those in the northern States who sympathized with them, I do not approve the call of that convention. So far as the terms of the call and the purposes and objects of the Convention are designed to oppose the constitutional authority of Congress, I heartily condemn them." [39]

Yet Stanton remained in the cabinet.

Browning and Doolittle sought the public approval of other Conservative leaders. Publishable letters of approba-

[38] Welles MS. Diary, Aug. 7, 1866—(II, 573).
[39] July 16, 1866, Stanton MSS., XXX.

tion were requested from men like Dix, Ewing, Guthrie, and Judge Curtis.[40] Support of the Democrats was also necessary. How to win it without alienating Moderate Republican opinion was the problem. In a reorganized Union Party, or a new third party, the Democrats would have to be recognized; yet none but prominent War Democrats could safely be rewarded, and to give places to more than a few even of these, was dangerous. President Johnson, the Conservative Republicans, and moderate and wise Democrats like Dix and Richmond of New York and Burr of Connecticut, realized that the Democrats must be kept in the background and the prominent places held by members of the Union Party, since the Republicans would not vote for war-time Democrats nor for a party controlled by them.[41]

Democratic avidity for recognition by Johnson embarrassed him. Private expressions of whole-hearted approval in letters from leaders of the old Democracy were gratifying. But public demonstrations were disconcerting, for Johnson knew that every Democratic shout for him turned a Republican against him. Johnson knew, too, that many Democrats, often those who made the most noise, only joined the Moderate movement because they hoped to turn it into a Democratic movement.[42] Johnson's anterooms overflowed with

[40] O. H. Browning to Thomas Ewing, Sr., June 26, 1866, Ewing MSS., XVIII.

[41] McClellan, who ran against Lincoln in 1864, wrote, "I hope that the [Democratic] party & its leaders will not waste time and strength in regretting and striving to bring back what is inevitably past and gone . . . It often seems to me that the work to be done may perhaps be best accomplished by a new party which shall not have to contend against the prejudices which must ever exist against an old & active organization. I am sure that you will agree with me in thinking that what is to be desired is not the triumph of a party but the future prosperity of the country." G. B. McClellan to S. L. M. Barlow, June 3, 1866, McClellan MSS., XCII.

[42] E.g., Duff Green to A. Johnson, June 25, 1865, and S. L. M. Barlow to M. Blair, July 19, 1865, Johnson MSS., LXVIII, LXXI.

Democratic politicians who swore eternal loyalty in one breath, and sought an office in the next; his mails were burdened with their letters. In resisting importunities and connivances, Johnson showed persistent courage and sagacity. Replacing Radical office-holders with Democrats would have been more ruinous than leaving the Radicals undisturbed.

Many of the wiser Democratic leaders did recognize the necessity of keeping themselves in the background until the day when war feeling against the Democracy should have waned. "The Democrats," Burr wrote, "can endorse the call. . . . If [the Convention] can lay down a platform broad enough for Democrats to stand on . . . I see no reason why they may not compromise and unite in every Congressional District, and secure a Congress quite different from the present." "But," he insisted, "the Convention should be controlled by Conservative Republicans." [43] Democrats did endorse the call.[44] Arrangements were made for sending joint delegations separately chosen by Democrats and Moderate Republicans through their local organizations.

As time for the Convention drew near, Conservative hopes ran high. Enthusiasm was general. Even in Radical New England, Moderates were sanguine. From Connecticut, for example, came letters of encouragement not only from Senator Dixon and Babcock, but from Pratt who later went over to the Radicals, and Burr, the Democratic leader. These men all felt that the Convention would enable Moderates to carry the state overwhelmingly.[45] Doolittle, who had been touring the West, wrote, "The leading men, I mean not only Democrats but Republicans, are with us. . . . Things are

[43] A. E. Burr to G. Welles, July 8 and 24, 1866, Welles MSS., LXI.
[44] Even the most bitter Copperhead and self-centered office-seeker recognized that, temporarily at least, the only Democratic hope was Johnson's success against the Radicals.
[45] July 8, 1866, Johnson MSS., XCVII; Welles MSS., LXI.

Harper's Weekly, Sept. 29, 1866

THE ARM-IN-ARM CONVENTION

moving well. A very strong delegation will come from Wisconsin." [46] As the delegates gathered, Randall reported, "The Southern men are acting nobly and with a good sense which annoys the Radical Reporters here. . . . All are hopeful." [47] "Men never came together," wrote Browning, "in a better temper of mind. There seems to be complete unity and harmony of views and purposes." [48] The *New York Herald* predicted a sweeping victory for the party to be formed by the Convention, since the people would be behind it.[49]

The Radical press ridiculed, abused, and belittled the movement,[50] but this attitude merely emphasized Radical apprehensions of success; it did not dampen popular enthusiasm.

On August 14 the National Union Convention met in Philadelphia in a huge wigwam built for the purpose. All states, Southern and Northern, were represented. Each Congressional district sent two delegates, one Democrat and one Republican from states where both parties existed.

At the opening session the delegates from Masachusetts and South Carolina, led by General Couch and Governor Orr, came into the hall arm in arm.[51] Randall, who had just entered Johnson's cabinet, called the meeting to order; General Dix of New York was made temporary chairman. Senator Doolittle of Wisconsin became the permanent president; General Steedman of Ohio headed the committee on credentials, Montgomery Blair that on organization, Senator Cowan of Pennsylvania that on resolutions, and Senator

46 Aug. 8, 1866, Johnson MSS., XCIX.
47 A. W. Randall to A. Johnson, Aug. 12, 1866, *ibid.*, XCIX.
48 Aug. 13, 1866, *ibid.*, XCIX.
49 *New York Herald*, Aug. 12, 1866, *et. seq.*
50 E.g., James Russell Lowell in the *North Am. Rev.*, CIII, 520 ff.
51 *New York Tribune*, Aug. 15, 1866.

Reverdy Johnson of Maryland that formed to wait on the President. Henry J. Raymond of New York, the soon-to-be-deposed chairman of the National Union Party's National Committee, read the Address to the People of the United States. Robert C. Winthrop, Thomas Ewing, William C. Rives, and others who could not attend, wrote letters of approbation. Governor Orr of South Carolina and Alexander H. Stephens, former Vice-President of the Confederacy, made wise, conciliatory speeches which were enthusiastically received. The array of prominent men was imposing; but notable Moderates of a few months earlier were conspicuously absent—stumping for the Radicals: Morton of Indiana, John Sherman of Ohio, Trumbull of Illinois, ex-Governor Andrew of Massachusetts, men who in January would heartily have supported the movement.

At a big rally the night before the Convention assembled, Governor Orr of South Carolina delivered a masterful speech in which he declared that the doctrine of secession had been rejected by the decision of the War, and was therefore irrevocably renounced by Southerners. He insisted that the federal debt was the debt of the South as well as of the North, and that Southerners had no thought of repudiation. He described the destruction and distress in his section, and pronounced peace and the friendship of Northern capitalists to be the only hope of a broken South. Thus, he said, interest was added to principle to keep the South loyal. He insisted passionately that the South was loyal and ready to forget the past; that Southerners were sincere; that they loved "their common country" as much as did Northerners. He ended with an "eloquent appeal to all, of all sections and all parties whether Northern or Southern, whether whig, democrat, peace democrat, secessionist or anti-secessionist now that the close of the war [has] forever settled the vexed question of the last four years and vindicate[d] the integrity of the government to rally in its behalf" and to work unitedly to make real Webster's proclamation that "Liberty and Union [are] now and forever one and inseparable." [52] Orr's sincerity and evident loyalty to the Union impressed doubtful people throughout the North. "If it could be established," thought the *Cincinnati Commercial*, "that Governor Orr speaks the true sentiment of the Southern people, it would not take long to dispose of the complaint that they are not represented in Congress." [53] Former Provisional Governor Perry of South Carolina followed Orr with a telling speech which also had marked effect.[54]

From the first the Copperhead element had been a problem. Early in July Dix had written to Doolittle: "Our danger is that the men whom we do not want will get in to cover up their past political sins. This would be a most serious injury, and might imperil the whole movement." [55] The Copperheads saw a chance to rehabilitate their ruined fortunes, and both Wood and Vallandigham appeared as delegates. Wood graciously withdrew when he realized the strength of the opposition against him. Vallandigham stubbornly refused to retire; yet every prominent man in the movement felt that his participation would be fatal.[56] At the last minute, through infinite tact and adroit management, he was persuaded to withdraw without a scene. With his retirement

<hr/>

52 *New York Herald,* Aug. 14, 1866.
53 *Cincinnati Commercial,* Aug. 15, 1866.
54 *New York Herald,* Aug. 15, 1866.
55 July 10, 1866, *Am. Historical Magazine* (*Americana*), IV, 332.
56 From Vallandigham's own state Geiger wrote Johnson: The Conservatives "are hurt more by the prominence given Vallandigham than by all other causes—our people shrink from contact with him . . . The fellows [*sic*] doctrines *now* are not so bad, but his name is damnation. We were delighted that you refused to see him." Aug. 2, 1866, Johnson MSS., XCIX.

the one cloud that cast gloom over Philadelphia was blown away.

Dix's opening speech to the Convention was designed to arouse enthusiasm, and it succeeded. It contained three main thoughts: the urgency of electing a Congress that would restore the Union by granting to the South its right of representation; the indispensability of commercial and financial reforms as soon as the Union should be restored; and the certainty that the people would repudiate "ultraism" if only the issues were put clearly before them. Senator Doolittle's address appealed to old loyalties to a united country.[57]

The Declaration of Principles, adopted unanimously, expressed gratitude to Almighty God for restoring peace. It declared that the War had maintained the Constitution and the Union unaltered, and that neither Congress nor the General Government had any authority to deny the constitutional right of Congressional representation to any state. It urged the election of Congressmen who would admit all "loyal" representatives from the South. It reaffirmed the inability of a state to secede or to exclude any other state from the Union and the constitutional right of each state to decide for itself the qualifications for voting within its borders. It insisted that the Constitution could not be legally amended except with all the states voting in Congress and ratifying by legislatures. It denied any desire in the Southern States to restore slavery. It proclaimed, too, the invalidity of the rebel debts, the inviolability of a federal debt, and the right of freedmen to the same protection of person and property as afforded to whites. It urged government

[57] For a full report of the Convention see *The Proceedings of the National Union Convention held at Philadelphia, August 14, 1866*.

aid for federal soldiers and their families. Finally, it expressed a whole-hearted endorsement of Andrew Johnson.

Raymond's Address to the People was longer. He reiterated the claim that the War had in no way changed the Constitution or granted any new powers to Congress, and definitely repudiated the "conquered province" theory. He insisted that the only objects of the War had been attained—namely, the establishment of the indissolubility of the Union and the abolition of slavery. Then he argued the legal inability of Congress to exclude states from representation, and described the loyalty and good feeling in the South, where the results of the War were accepted without question. Indeed, he asserted that if Southern confidence and loyalty had in any way declined since the end of the War, the backsliding was directly attributable to the Congressional attack on the President's wise policy. Raymond concluded with a plea to the electors in each Congressional district to send to the new Congress only such men as would admit the Southern States to their right of representation and allow the country to return to its position as a sovereign nation, free to perfect its republican institutions.

Practically, the National Union Convention was a huge Johnson rally. From the time the delegates began to arrive, Philadelphia witnessed a tumult of enthusiasm. As the first convention in six years which had been truly national, the gathering was symbolic of the united country for which the people of both North and South longed. Confidence throughout the North was augmented by the character of the men sent from the South, by their moderation, and by their assurances that their fellow-Southerners were ready to accept the new order gladly, and to return in sincere loyalty to the Union. The psychological effect of the nationalism and harmony of the Convention worked as magic on the country. Here were Southerners and Northerners considering together the issues of the day and agreeing upon a platform of principles which indeed embraced all the measures that any Republicans save the extremists advocated—all, in fact, except the punitive clause of the Fourteenth Amendment, and the demand for negro suffrage or an alternative diminution of Southern representation. Guarantees of the federal debt and repudiation of their own, civil rights for the negro, and the nullity of secession, were here willingly granted by trustworthy Southerners, who declared that the South was glad to be rid of slavery and eager to return to loyalty. Could it be that the rest of the South was, after all, like these men?

The cheering and shouting of the wigwam meetings reverberated throughout the North. A wave of enthusiasm swept over the country which promised to carry Conservatives into Congress. Doolittle sounded the key-note of the Convention, an emotional one, when he declared: "If the people . . . could have seen—as we saw—Massachusetts and South Carolina, by their full delegations, coming arm in arm into this great Convention, if they could have seen this body, greater in numbers, and in weight of character and brain, than ever yet assembled on this Continent under one roof, melting to tears of joy and gratitude to witness this commingling, there could be no struggle at the polls in the coming elections." But he added more practically a warning, the full significance of which his auditors failed to grasp. "Unfortunately," he reminded the Convention, "the whole people of the Northern States do not witness what is now transpiring here; therefore, the greater work still rests upon us from this time until the election of the next Congress."

Leaders of politics and the non-Radical press joined in the enthusiasm.[58] Dix congratulated Johnson on the "cheering prospect." "The Convention," he declared, "is the most able, harmonious & enthusiastic body of men of such magnitude I have ever met in my long acquaintance with political affairs. I cannot be mistaken when I say it ensured the success of your patriotic and unwavering efforts to heal the breach between the two great sections of the Union." [59] The *Philadelphia Age* told its readers, "The action of this convention has consolidated and solidified the Union sentiment of the land, and its march will be magnificent and irresistible." [60] "The issue will now be the Philadelphia platform on the one side and universal negro suffrage on the other," said the *Herald*, which was confident of an overwhelming victory for the Conservatives.[61] Even the Radical *Springfield Republican* predicted: The stand of the Southerners at Philadelphia will "command respect among the people. It is in vain to assail it with ridicule and contempt. It will be found to be a reality, and no sham." [62] General optimism was reflected in a rapid rise of government securities.[63]

But in spite of its apparent success, the Philadelphia Convention had one fatal weakness. As a huge "pep session" it was eminently effective, but it did not form a party. Many of Johnson's friends realized the mistake. But men like Ray, quondam editor of the *Chicago Tribune*, Seward, Weed, Raymond, and Pratt of Connecticut, insisted upon organiz-

[58] The *Albany Argus, Bangor Times, Boston Commercial, Chicago Times, Detroit Free Press, Hartford Courant, Lafayette Journal* (Indiana), *Louisville Courier, New Haven Journal, Raleigh Sentinel,* and *Wilmington Journal,* foresaw success for the Convention movement.
[59] Aug. 16, 1866, Johnson MSS., C.
[60] *Philadelphia Age*, Aug. 17, 1866.
[61] *New York Herald*, Aug. 18, 1866.
[62] *Springfield Republican*, Aug. 17, 1866.
[63] *New York Herald*, Aug. 18, 1866.

ing a Conservative group within the old party. Their counsels, aided by political inertia, prevailed. The hope was to hold men who would not leave the Republican fold but who, like Raymond and Dennison, might be influential for moderation within it. The Philadelphia Conventioners, however, made a break with the party sufficient to cost Raymond his influence as a Republican, and Dennison refused to join the movement because it *looked* like a break with Republicanism. In August, a new party with party machinery, a party press, and party candidates in the election, might yet have been successful.

The delegates from the National Union Convention went home to their various Congressional districts full of enthusiasm. By a variety of methods they sought to secure the election of candidates who endorsed the Philadelphia platform. But no systematic campaign was launched. Sheer enthusiasm or righteousness of principle could not win an election without campaign tools. On August 17 the Philadelphia Convention was generally deemed eminently successful, but on that day the movement reached its peak. How signally it failed, and why, is the story of the campaign.

Chapter V

CLAPTRAP AND ISSUES

IN any campaign the issues which the politicians raise and questions which actually interest the public are apt to be confused. In 1866 they were inextricably entangled. Postwar excitement, dormant bitterness, and fear provided the Radicals with excellent raw material for a campaign of hysteria; hence most political speeches were largely claptrap. For the issues one must seek further. Important issues there were. But most of them were avoided because the Radicals regarded them as dangerous to their cause, and the Conservatives thought it futile to push them until the states were all back in the Union. On some questions opinion was hopelessly divided in both Radical and Conservative camps. The Radical campaign was waged to keep in power the party that had carried on the War and was still in the saddle in 1866. Conservatives sought to restore the Union in order to end the Radical monopoly of power and throw the government open to free competition of interests and sections, realizing full well that a return of the South would greatly improve their own chances of controlling the government. To these respective ends the leaders worked. Ultimate victory would depend upon the ebb and flow of a neutral popular opinion.

Popular opinion is at once the most potent and the most dependent of political forces; it can restrain or impel the most powerful of rulers; if roused, it overthrows governments; it can accomplish the seemingly impossible. But nevertheless it is dependent upon a complex multiplicity of delicate mechanisms. Theoretically, democracy is the panacea for all ills; the people, under ideal conditions, with all the facts truly before them, uninfluenced by prejudice, unmoved by passion, could perhaps be trusted in sagacity beyond any individual. The United States in 1866 was, however, not an abstract Utopia but a very real, average group of human beings; public opinion and democracy worked then as always, not in ideal abstract surroundings, but under the ordinary conditions of practical workaday human life. Public opinion in 1866 was dependent upon the usual unreliable channels of information: newspapers, preachers, politicians, selfish men with an ax to grind, sincere men with a reform to advocate, fearful men with chimerical dangers to prophesy, stubborn men with consistency to defend—prejudiced, conflicting, uninformed, opinionated sources of information. Public opinion was then as now, subject to its own inborn prejudices and sensitive to psychological influences, appeals to fear, to hate, to patriotism. It was influenced by defense of property and the status quo, and by attacks on privilege or invocation of economic dissatisfaction and unrest; it was affected by self-interest and opportunities for power or gain, and by feelings of generosity and magnanimity; it was above all subject to the rules of mob psychology, well known though yet unnamed. In 1866 all these factors played exaggerated rôles as they always do in the excitement of material and mental readjustment which follows war.

The people are never swayed by one interest alone; they

are rarely confronted by but one issue. A single issue may overbalance all others, but the others remain. It is dangerous to project the present into the past by interpreting that past through what appears, in the light of later unpredictable developments, to have been the paramount interest. Under the American system of elections it is usually impossible for the voters at the time, or historians in the future, to ascertain with any precision the determining interests. Party leaders have sought not to define, but to evade and conceal issues. Under the American two-party system it is always difficult for an individual to know how to vote wisely. Many voters adhere to principles because they bear the party label, instead of supporting the party because it will advance certain principles. But where an individual does try to think independently it is almost impossible to determine which man or which party will best advance the largest number of political interests of the voter. The thoughtful voter usually comes to the conclusion that neither party and neither candidate suits him, and votes the least objectionable ticket. The next man with like interests may under like conditions make a reverse decision. Popular votes in America, then, only exceptionally decide public questions, or show popular sentiment upon definite issues. Party loyalty, successful advertising, mob psychology, skilful creation of confidence or, more potent still, distrust, popular fears and passions—in short, psychological elements, efficient campaign machinery, and access to the public ear—play more significant rôles than do the merits of issues or party platforms.

It is in the light of these realities that the election of 1866 must be studied. Most historians and thoughtful public men now condemn the Radical program of reconstruction. Yet it was adopted. These men differ in analyzing the causes under-

lying the failure of the Johnson policy, but they generally
agree in assigning as chief among them the unreasonable
conduct of the South and the stubbornness and stupidity of
Johnson. While they condemn the man, many have come
to regard Johnson's policy as the most statesmanlike of any.
Some of his bitterest enemies lived to acknowledge this. Yet it
failed. To understand its failure and Radical success, comparative wisdom of policies and constitutional theories must
be thrown aside as inconsequential; other factors popularly
thought to be determining issues must be reduced to their
true 1866 proportions, and the methods and spirit of the
campaign must be studied. Reconstruction was decided not
through a consideration of the wisdom of various plans, but
by a skilful use of the tools of political campaigning.

The Radicals for one reason or another feared the return
of Southerners to participation in government. After a great
war, bitterness was natural. Men who had lost loved ones in
battle, did not look with pleasure upon the return to power
of the men who had slain them. Allowed to cool and tempered
by a return of friendly commercial and political intercourse,
this sentiment would soon have subsided, for magnanimity to
a vanquished foe is not difficult. In the West and in the
border communities, numerous relationships had bound
North and South before the War; between these sections
passions had fired more quickly, and conflict had raged more
violently than between the South and more distant New
England. But after all, reconciliation was easier between two
interrelated sections which knew each other's good qualities,
than between the South and a remote Northeast which condemned each other as inherently wicked, and hated each other
with the hate of long years of abolition controversy.

While resentment against Copperheads was most violent

in the West and border East, bitterness toward the South was cooling rapidly in non-abolitionist circles and, let alone, would gradually have died out. Abolitionists, however, had embraced as part of their creed belief in Southern wickedness, expressed in their definition of the Constitution as "a covenant with death and an agreement with hell." [1] Many New England teachers and preachers throughout the North continued with all sincerity to paint Southerners as disciples of the devil. Those who held this view of the South, opposed its return to participation in government.

To many, abolitionism had become a religion which made it a God-given duty, now that the slaves were free, to elevate them to civil and political equality with the white man. Many such "Niggerheads" knew nothing of the Southern negro, but they devoutly believed in their own theories; others of them actually worked with the negroes as missionaries and teachers, but like many reformers were blinded to practical difficulties by their own enthusiasm. Typical of these sincere "friends of the negro" was Charles Sumner.

Men did actually believe that if the "rebels" were allowed to regain political power, they would yet overturn the government. Many feared the return of "traitors" to offices from which loyal men would be displaced. But often such expressions of fear merely signified that a man dreaded to see good Republicans replaced by Democrats.

Many Northerners honestly saw in the Black Codes a Southern attempt to reënslave the black; others were interested in the negro chiefly because his vote would be a Republican one, and would counteract that of his white neighbor.

But a considerable group dreaded the return of Southerners to power not because they feared disaster to the

[1] Lindsay Swift, *William Lloyd Garrison*, 306.

nation, but because they foresaw in it injury to themselves, their section, or their class. For many years Southern statesmen had controlled the destinies of the country. Since the days when her own young-bloods had urged secession for New England, the industrial Northeast had been a "minority section." It was not powerless on questions where South and West divided, or where factors which bisected every community were concerned, but on such issues as the tariff or an agricultural or industrial dispute New England and the increasingly industrial Northeast were still a minority section. For thirty years Southerners or Northern "Doughfaces" had been supreme in the federal government. Now after a long and bloody war, a purely Northern party had conquered the South and won for itself and its section longsought power which was not lightly to be surrendered. Sheer love of power made many men hesitate before voluntarily relinquishing it by allowing Southerners to return to Congress. To politicians, whose chief function is to elect themselves and members of their party to office, retention of control seemed a sufficient cause for Radicalism, but this motive could not be publicly avowed.

For years before the War, the Northeast had been unable to get protection for industry. Then during the Civil War high taxes on industry had made necessary a high tariff, and, with the South out of the way and the North rather evenly divided, protectionists had managed to make the tariffs more than cover the taxes they supposedly offset. If the South were readmitted before this high tariff was permanently established, the protectionists would be overwhelmed.

Bondholders throughout the country feared, and were encouraged to fear, a repudiation of the debt through a return of Southern representatives. The South was traditionally opposed to national banks; hence, Eastern bankers and supporters of the new national banking system dreaded to see the South return. Hard money men, deflationists, business men who wished federal protection in the extension of their business into what they feared would be an inhospitable South, land speculators who sought confiscated lands, and new corporations that feared government regulation or sought government aid, shared this dread. The growing capital-owning group of the Northeast,[2] then, sought to keep the South out until through negro suffrage it could be brought under Northern control. The agricultural and debtor classes, on the other hand, would have welcomed Southern aid in Washington. Here was really in a new phase the familiar American struggle of East against West, old settled region against frontier, business against agriculture, city against country, "haves" against "have-nots," that made a civil war of the American Revolution, that turned Jeffersonians against Hamiltonians, Jacksonian Democrats against Whigs, and more recently farm bloc against Wall Street. This old antagonism and not a difference of opinion on the condition of Southerners, was what divided Conservatives and Radicals in 1866.

Radical leaders faced a perplexing problem. They were only a minority group. The two major issues motivating their campaign were their stand on various economic questions and their desire to secure the Republican Party in power. But the Radical leaders could not ask the people to support them merely because of their desire for power. Still less did they dare raise the economic questions. Indeed, they had to fight desperately against their being raised by

[2] Except the merchants.

the Conservatives, for on economic issues they would have
lost half their party.

On the reconstruction issue unconfused, the major portion
of the people originally supported Johnson;[3] hence, the
Radicals had to raise mere shibboleths. Had other Radicals
been as fair-minded, as public-spirited, and as tolerant as
Governor Andrew, Johnson's reputation would not have been
destroyed, and there would have been no split between Congress and the President. Andrew, though a negro suffragist,
deprecated the Radical tactics. "I am opposed to public
meetings," he said, "called in support of . . . any man,
leader or party. . . . Now, if one set of men get up meetings for Paul, another set will get up meetings for Apollos.
The result will be antagonism, not patriotism; and intensifying, and exaggerating the importance and value, of the
relatively unimportant, chance-utterances of individuals in
controversial moods; which ought if possible, to be forgotten.
. . . I, for one, desire not to encourage popular excitement,
most of all, not to aid in making any."[4] But in the creation
of this very situation which Andrew deplored, lay the Radicals' best hope of success.

The repudiation shibboleth was safe throughout the country. In the East economic issues could be insinuated into the
campaign, for Eastern supporters knew well the stand Radical leaders would take on them; in the West, when the Conservatives raised them, they were shouted down as non-
political and irrelevant. Talk of the return of rebels to power
conveyed a plain second meaning to the protectionist and to
the creditor, whereas it was taken at face value in the West.
If the South could be excluded, or admitted only with negro

3 *Supra,* 47-50.
4 J. A. Andrew to F. P. Blair, Sr., March 18, 1866, Johnson MSS., XCI.

suffrage, the new industrial order which the Northeast was developing, would be safe. Intentionally, then, the issues were befogged. Definite economic questions of importance confronted the country, issues on which a majority, even without the South, would have supported Johnson against the Radicals, issues which ten years later arose to plague the country. In 1866 these questions were pushed into the background, the South was kept out, and the Northeast succeeded in establishing minority government until the new industrial forces were strongly enough entrenched to withstand attacks.

Throughout the campaign constitutional arguments bulked large. It was a day when constitutional theories were required for all practice. But in our Anglo-Saxon world constitutional theories are derived from practice, not practice from theory. People were vitally interested in deciding whether the South should have its former place in the government or should be held in subjugation for a period of years, but they were not much interested in the theory of the right or wrong of either course, except as a justification in law for what they intended to do in practice. Lawyers and Congressmen, true to form, made lengthy speeches on matters of constitutionality, for this gave them an air of erudition, and satisfied the legalistic conscience of their constituents. Nevertheless constitutional discussions of the rights of the negro, the status of Southern states, the legal position of ex-rebels, and the powers of Congress and president determined nothing. They were pure shams.

We have already found [5] that the condition and temper of the South, especially in the light of biased fabrication or deceptive half-knowledge, proved a favorite topic of political

[5] *Supra,* chap. III, especially 64 ff. and 69 ff.

oratory in 1866. In a study of the issues this and the negro question and the Fourteenth Amendment must not be accepted at their campaign valuation. Other factors not recognized in the campaign literature as issues, must be considered because of their potential and actual importance. Politicians' tricks and machinery must be studied as the really determining factor. Claptrap and issues must be distinguished.

Chapter VI

RECONSTRUCTION *VERSUS* RESTORATION

IN his last public utterance, Lincoln had urged, "Let us all join in doing the acts necessary to restoring the proper practical relations between these [seceded] States and the Union." [1] "It is intended," said Thaddeus Stevens, "to revolutionize their principles and feelings . . . [to] work a radical reorganization in Southern institutions, habits, and manners." [2] In the distinction between the terms "restoration" and "reconstruction" lay the issue of 1866. Sumner honestly thought "Massachusetts could govern Georgia better than Georgia could govern herself." [3] Johnson believed that only the South could solve its problems. It was because Stevens and his Radical friends were victorious in the struggle of that year that we call the succeeding decade the "period of reconstruction" instead of what Lincoln and Johnson wanted to make it, an era of restoration.

Constitutional arguments loomed large in the discussions of the day. Restorationists argued ably that the states had a constitutional right to representation in spite of the War; reconstructionists found equally strong constitutional grounds for their exclusion. A states' rights theory, a

[1] *Complete Works of Abraham Lincoln* (Nicolay and Hay), XI, 88.
[2] Speech at Lancaster, Sept. 7, 1865, Stevens MSS., IV.
[3] Welles MS. Diary, Feb. 10, 1866—(II, 430-431).

theory of an indestructible union of indestructible states, a conquered province theory, a theory that the South had reverted to a territorial status, each had its ardent advocates. But for all of the heat and bombast of their enunciation, these constitutional arguments were mere justifications of practical ends. Except the men who made political capital out of them, few cared about constitutional niceties. What vitally concerned the whole country was the practicability and expediency of conflicting Southern programs.

Governmental policy should have depended upon the actual condition of affairs in the South, the temper of the people, their treatment of the negroes, and their readiness to resume responsibilities under the federal government. The complexity of Southern economic, social, and political conditions made it difficult at best to secure satisfying information. Only by perusal of a vast collection like the Johnson Manuscripts, can one fully comprehend the perplexity of the man who really sought facts.

Very few, however, sought to know the truth. While the ubiquitous Radical agent, as we have seen,[4] gathered every tale of crime and disorder, and every rumor of a tale of crime and disorder that could be gleaned in the wake of war to persuade voters that they needed Radical protection against an unrepentant South, the Democratic traveler, on the other hand, pictured a South that was universally tranquil, kind to negroes, and unquestionably loyal, if not eager to accept the results of defeat—since this would soonest bring Southerners back to help turn the Radicals out of power. But the Radical had a great advantage in that one case of violence or mistreatment of negroes counteracted in the popular imagination many instances of honest effort to

[4] *Supra,* 69 ff.

work with free negroes. "Unrepentant rebels" were more interesting than law-abiding citizens. Northerners were easily persuaded that the whole South was as bad as its most lawless element.   *   *   *   *

Several factors helped the Radical leaders in their task of persuading the country of Southern depravity. Prejudice was as important a factor in the distortion of the picture as conscious perversion. Provincialism of Northerners led them to misinterpret many conditions that were not dangerous but merely unfamiliar. The traveler's impressions usually corresponded to the ideas that he took South with him. His report of the negro's condition depended upon his attitude toward the negro, whether he viewed him as a full equal of the whites or bore a prejudice against him. If the Northerner had known the South before the War, he made allowance for Southern violence of language and excitability of temper; if not, he misjudged the South by taking its pyrotechnics seriously. Northerners, still extremely provincial in outlook, felt that a society fundamentally unlike their own must be inherently evil, and should be remodeled. Stevens,[5] masterful exponent of this doctrine, declared:

[5] Though Sumner defended Stevens against the charge, Rhodes believes part of Stevens's hatred of the South was traceable to vengeance for personal injury. "He never forgot a kindly act," says Rhodes, "but on the other hand was bitter and vindictive. During the Confederate invasion of 1863 his iron works near Chambersburg were destroyed; and common report had it that this act by which he was again reduced to poverty increased his virulence towards the South." J. F. Rhodes, *History of United States,* V, 544. A typical Southern analysis of Stevens is embodied in an amusing, perhaps justifiable, but extremely injudicious epistle. "Now, Thad," it runs, "I know you are a *rum* old chap and 'a good *hater*,' after Dr. Johnson's own heart; but I had no hand in the burning of your foundry and you must do me this little favor. Let me ask you a civil question. Which feeling is strongest and uppermost in your Abrahamic bosom, *love* of the *negro,* or *hatred* of the *white man* of the South? Tell me truly, do you care a farthing for the negro, but don't you *hate* the *white men* of the South till you can't rest? I will bet you a clean shirt (and lend you one to 'put up') that, after all your rhodomontade and hysterics over this dark subject, you never gave one dollar in charity to the poor

"The whole fabric of Southern society *must* be changed, and never can be done if this opportunity is lost. . . . How can republican institutions, free schools, free churches, free social intercourse exist in a mingled community of nabobs and serfs; of the owners of twenty thousand acre manors with lordly palaces, and the occupants of narrow huts inhabited by 'low white trash?' If the South is ever to be made a safe republic let her lands be cultivated by the toil of the owners or the free labor of intelligent citizens. This must be done even though it drives her nobility into exile. If they go, all the better. It will be hard to persuade the owner of ten thousand acres of land, who drives a coach and four, that he is not degraded by sitting at the same table, or in the same pew, with the embrowned and hard-handed farmer who has himself cultivated his own thriving homestead of 150 acres. [The country would be well rid of the] proud, bloated and defiant rebels . . . the foundations of their institutions, both political, municipal, and social, *must* be broken up and *relaid*, or all our blood and treasure have been spent in vain. This can only be done by treating and holding them as conquered people." [6]

Even James Russell Lowell insisted that the party of Northerners who had won the War were the "American people." "They are resolved," he told Southerners, "by God's grace, to Americanize you." A new "Union . . . of ideas, interests, and aspirations" was to be created until the South should become an "indistinguishable, compact, genuine portion of the United States." [7]

negro,—that Mr. Henry Wilson never gave ten cents, and that Mr. Charles Sumner never gave one cent, out of their sensitive pockets, for his benefit. Bet me, dear Thad, if you dare!" T. Powell of Halifax Co. Ho., Va., to T. Stevens, Feb. 22, 1866, Stevens MSS., VII.

   [6] Speech at Lancaster, Sept. 7, 1865, *ibid.*, IV.

   [7] *North Am. Rev.*, CII (January, 1866), 252; CII (April, 1866), 541; CIII (October, 1866), 531, 536-542.

The old abolition-born contempt for Southerners still led many good men to a sincere belief in the inherent wickedness of former owners of slaves, a righteous hatred of the whole South, and a determination to destroy Southern society. Abolitionism had preached Southern depravity as campaign propaganda, and the impress on many an abolitionist's heart was too deeply engraved to be erased. Without any real knowledge of that section, William Lloyd Garrison could write, "I know . . . that at the South the powers of hell are still strong and defiant, resolved upon doing whatever evil is possible, in the spirit of diabolical malignity. But, 'fore-warned, fore-armed.' By help of God, we will overcome the devices of the enemy, nor abate aught of heart or hope in any struggle we may yet be called upon to pass through." [8] What hope was there that Garrison's followers would ever see any good in the South?

War hatred warped many an honest man's judgment. A crowded Faneuil Hall meeting resolved: "The true doctrine of reconstruction is, that defeated rebels have no civil nor political rights, which loyal men are bound to respect, and that all loyal men, without regard to race or color, are entitled to equal rights as citizens." [9] Senator Chandler taught that the only rights Southern whites possessed were "the constitutional right to be hanged and the divine right to be damned." [10] "Traitors North and South have no rights that a negro is bound to respect," became an article of the Radical creed appalling to any one who knew the Southern negro. For "rebels" to seek to reorganize their state governments or restore their country to habitability was defiance; Southern recovery was a menace.

[8] W. L. Garrison to C. Sumner, Feb. 11, 1866, Sumner MSS., LXXVI.
[9] *Chicago Tribune*, June 1, 1866.
[10] *New York Herald*, Sept. 7, 1866.

Southern feeling toward Union and Confederate soldiers was misinterpreted. Not only were pride in Confederate heroes and honor for Confederate dead misconstrued into defiant disloyalty; many Northerners expected Southerners, if really loyal, to join in the denunciations of Southern military leaders and huzzah for Grant and Sherman. Southerners are persistently treasonous, wrote a Freedmen's Bureau friend of Stevens; "while they acknowledge themselves whipped and profess future loyalty . . . Confederate Generals are their heroes—Confederate bravery, and endurance under difficulties, their pride and boast—Confederate dead their Martyrs. . . . In all the stores of Richmond . . . I did not see the picture of a single Union General or Politician, but any number of Rebels. Why this difference? The former wouldn't sell. Passing along the street I saw a placard 'Concert for the benefit of Mrs. Stonewall Jackson.' I have since heard it realized some $350, and money at ten per cent a month. When Genl Lee's name was mentioned in the House of Delegates . . . it was received with cheers on all sides." [11]

For Southerners to elect to office their old leaders, all ex-rebels, was imprudent, stubbornly unreasonable, but most human. To expect them, on the other hand, to vote for Unionists as a test of loyalty, was about as reasonable as to have demanded that Sumner support Vallandigham or Fernando Wood. Southerners, moreover, often voted for ex-rebel leaders because of confidence in their ability to solve post-war problems, but by Radicals these votes were interpreted as convincing evidence of treason.

Above all, the South suffered in these years at the hands of men in whose eyes the Republican Party and the nation

[11] J. W. Sharp to T. Stevens, Jan. 17, 1866, Stevens MSS., VI.

were identical. To many, defeat of the Republican Party meant overthrow of the Constitution. The government's policy, complained one of Sumner's most prolific correspondents, "has been to use the military power merely for the purpose of defeating armed rebels, and not, as it should have been, for preserving and consolidating republicanism." [12] As experienced a man as ex-Secretary Speed claimed that the "rebels" were organized and planning a monarchy with Jeff Davis or Lee as king,[13] because they were opposing the Radicals politically in Kentucky. When analyzed, many of the "proofs" of Southern disloyalty turn out to be mere opposition to the Republican Party.

The South swarmed with Radical trouble-makers and nascent carpet-baggers who aroused resentment, and then interpreted it as perverse ill feeling. Freedmen's Bureau officers arrested men unjustifiably that they might appropriate the fines and forfeits.[14] Dishonest Treasury agents used the Confiscation Act as an excuse to rob Southerners of their cotton, and if the "rebels" protested, put them to such expense in regaining it, that the value of the cotton was wiped out.[15] Chase and his lieutenants organized the Florida blacks and non-resident whites to demand negro suffrage; rumor had it that if they would defy the white government as disloyal and establish their own, the Supreme Court would sustain them.[16] Radical leaders frequently excited the negroes, and organized assemblies of blacks. In March, 1866, Grant had to prevent a negro celebration organized by the

[12] J. W. Phelps to C. Sumner, May 3, 1865, Sumner MSS., LXXIII.
[13] J. Speed to E. Stanton, Aug. 4, 1866, Stanton MSS., XXX.
[14] Maj. Gen. J. B. Steedman and Brig. Gen. J. S. Fullerton to A. Johnson, June 14, 1866, Johnson MSS., XCVI.
[15] H. Marshall of New Haven to T. Stevens, Jan. 6, 1866, Stevens MSS., VI; H. M. Watterson to A. Johnson, July 8, 1865, Johnson MSS., LXX.
[16] H. Reed to M. Blair, June 26, 1865, *ibid.*, LXVIII.

Radicals which threatened disorder in Richmond.[17] Two days
before the New Orleans riot Radical leaders whom Sheridan
styled "political agitators and revolutionary men," organized in that city a negro mass meeting, at which incendiary
speeches were made, the negroes were called on to arm themselves, and Johnson was denounced.[18] The Secretary of the
Commonwealth of Virginia complained that the chief trouble
was "with those ill advised people who are endeavoring to
excite dissatisfaction amongst the freedmen, and to persuade
them to agitate for the right to vote, when the great question
with many of them, as well as the white people, is—how are
they to get bread?" [19] Radical agitators were the very ones
who most loudly denounced Southern disloyalty whenever a
Southerner complained of their machinations.

Garrisoning negro troops upon the South provoked many
of the outbursts of violence. General Thomas testified that
troubles between negro troops and whites were usually commenced by whites who could not endure the humiliation of
negro troops in their midst.[20] Colonel Parker at Vicksburg
conceded that less than half the number of white troops could
efficiently do all that the negro troops could and that the
colored troops were a trial to the white residents.[21] Grant
urged Stanton to muster out the colored troops as rapidly as
practicable.[22] Yet Schurz advocated garrisoning negroes
upon Southern whites, to impress upon them the negroes'
freedom. "There is nothing," he wrote, "that will make it

[17] U. S. Grant to Maj. Gen. Terry, March 29, 1866, Stanton MSS., XXX.
[18] P. H. Sheridan to U. S. Grant, Aug. 1, 1866, Johnson MSS., XCVIII;
A. Vorhees and A. Herron to A. Johnson, July 28, 1866, Stanton MSS.,
XXX.
[19] C. H. Lewis to A. Johnson, July 3, 1865, Johnson MSS., LXIX.
[20] Thomas had hoped not to have to use negro troops. G. H. Thomas to
A. Johnson, Sept. 9, 1865, *ibid.*, LXXVI.
[21] Jan. 27, 1866, *ibid.*, LXXXVI.
[22] Sept. 6, 1865, Stanton MSS., XXVIII.

more evident than the bodily presence of a negro with a musket on his shoulders." [23]

The Freedmen's Bureau was an important safeguard for negroes, but it was often an irritant to the whites and a source of misrepresentation. In response to many complaints from reliable sources, Johnson sent Generals Steedman and Fullerton to investigate the Bureau.[24] Steedman wrote back, "Our investigations have developed to my mind, clearly, that the Bureau officers, with a very few exceptions constitute a Radical close corporation, devoted to the defeat of the policy of your Administration. . . . Nearly all the Bureau officers are in correspondence with Radical Senators and Radical newspapers." [25] Former Brigadier General Tarbell after living in the South felt that Southerners had "well grounded complaints" against the Bureau.[26] Grant's aide, Comstock, thought that General Gregory of the Bureau, who was "well hated by the rebs," was "rather too harsh in talk with them." But the negroes were "doing well under him." [27] Governor Perry of South Carolina complained bitterly of the troops. "We are all quiet & hard at work," he declared. "The 'freed men & women' are behaving well & working well. There is no use whatever for any military force in the upper part of South Carolina. They are drinking, and behaving badly, both to whites & blacks. Fines are imposed on the humble people and pocketed. The soldiers are having frequent fights

[23] C. Schurz to A. Johnson, Aug. 29, 1865, Johnson MSS., LXXIV.

[24] The Johnson MSS. contain reports dispatched at various points along the route of the Generals. Before the Radicals and Steedman became open enemies, Horace Greeley had characterized Steedman as "one of the bravest and truest of our Union volunteers, and a capable, devoted patriot," and had recommended him for the War portfolio. Jan. 28, 1866, *ibid.*, LXXXV.

[25] Jackson, Miss., June 26, 1866, *ibid.*, XCVI.

[26] *Report of the Joint Committee on Reconstruction,* 39 Cong., 1 Sess., III, 156.

[27] C. B. Comstock MS. Diary, Galveston, Feb. 7, 1866.

with the citizens & negroes. The only disturbance we have is from the garrisons." [28] From Georgia, one young officer of the Bureau itself protested: "They are ordered to search houses and turn peaceable inhabitants out of their beds, women and men, for the purpose of hunting up a boy, who whipped a nigger in a street fight. We have been obliged to put soldiers in the houses of citizens, because their sons get into a drunken fight with a nigger, the men amongst the ladies of the family. I think I can see through the whole plot. It is a scheme to excite the citizens of Loudon Valley to attack us, in order to keep up the feeling against the South. In fact I have heard whispers of this kind; our presence, is intended to irritate the people and to cause grumbling against the government. Any speech or gesture of disrespect we have orders to report at once to Washington. So you see how apparent the diabolical scheme is. Can't you induce the President to have the troops recalled from here. They are only sent here to bully over unarmed men and women. I try to get on as well as I can, but it is fearfully disgusting." [29] Grant pointedly suggested to Stanton that officers "should be appointed who can act from facts and not always be guided by prejudice in favor of color." [30]

Indubitably the Bureau was necessary and gave satisfaction in many sections; [31] in others it was intolerable. Fullerton and Steedman explained the conflict in opinion about it

[28] B. F. Perry to A. Johnson, April 20, 1866, Johnson MSS., XCIII.
[29] July 25, 1866, *ibid.*, XCVIII.
[30] Aug. 30, 1865, Stanton MSS., XXVIII.
[31] McCarter tells of the Commandant's arduous labors in settling disputes, and concludes, "That Col Haughton in the performance of his almost hopeless task of reconciling these conflicting elements should occasionally lose his equanimity—was to be expected. But his general deportment was courteous, kind & conciliatory. He listened with patience & tried to do impartial Justice, but where the litigants had such opposite views of their several interests to give satisfaction was simply impossible." McCarter (of South Carolina) MS. Diary, II, 93.

when they said, "Faithful agents have been aided by the good-will of the citizens; incompetent and meddlesome ones have aroused bitterness and opposition." [32]

A propensity for boasting was another source of misunderstanding between Northern Radicals and the Southern people. The Southerner is noted for his pride, or false pride; he felt humiliated by his vanquishment. Hence in public places he often assumed an air of bravado to hide his consciousness of defeat. Southern men and women indulged in gasconade, to prove that they were not beaten but just gave up or that one Southerner was a match for a dozen Yankees. They enjoyed "putting the nigger in his place" by word or deed. Their bravado was intended to impress Northerners, and it did—but with unfortunate results. As serious evidence of unrepentant defiance, Reid described some Mississippi girls in a train who were volubly abusing the "Yankees" for the benefit of a Northern officer, and the delight of a drunken lad near by who asked him, "Didn't that Yankee officer look sheepish just now, when the gals was givin' it to him so hot?" [33]

Northern travelers, on their side, were braggarts who enjoyed worrying Southerners with radical ideas, threats of harsh treatment of the South, and talk of the punishment they would mete out to traitors. Above all, Northerners delighted in antagonizing Southerners by insistence on negro equality. Even men who did not favor it in the North, loudly advocated negro suffrage when on a Southern journey. General Hayes, "agreeable" though he was, wrote from Memphis, "The Rebel Officers are particularly interesting. I get on with them famously. I talk negro suffrage and our ex-

[32] Report to A. Johnson, June 14, 1866, Johnson MSS., XCVI.
[33] W. Reid, *After the War*, 442.

tremest radicalism to all of them. They dissent, but are polite and cordial." [34] As a counterpart to Southern talk on a train, Reid boasts, "The few Northerners on board" talked "Abolitionism enough to have astonished Wendell Phillips himself." [35] Yet he took seriously similar bluster which he heard from Southerners. Such exaggerated language on each side encouraged it on the other; and while each was aware of his own hyperbole, both Northerner and Southerner were misled into a false impression of one another by this mutual love of braggadocio.

To account for Radical success in convincing people that the South must be punished and remade is easier than to determine what true conditions in the South were. As in Germany just after the World War and in Soviet Russia, an impartial investigator, even when traveling through the country, found reliable information about the South difficult to get. Much that he learned was hearsay; more he heard second- or third-hand; only rarely did a traveler himself witness happenings which he related afterwards. Many "observers" had no other source of information than conversations on trains or formal interviews with men whose personal interest made their testimony useless. Official trips were heralded, and a proclaimed investigator saw only exhibits staged for his benefit. Reliable information was obtainable, but only with difficulty.

A few men earnestly sought to ascertain the truth. Johnson was one of these; his sources of information were numerous and varied. The *New York Herald* printed news and reports of all hues of opinion. General Grant, whose report, presented with Schurz's, was as favorable to the South as the

[34] C. R. Williams, *Rutherford B. Hayes,* I, 288.
[35] W. Reid, *op. cit.,* 342.

latter's was damaging, could not be accused of political bias, nor of Copperheadism, nor yet of lack of an opportunity to obtain facts, for while the specific trip on which his report was based was short, he had had many contacts with Southerners and with army officers detailed to actual duty in the South.

The truth was that a variety of conditions obtained. As in any community there were in the South good men and bad, wise and foolish, subservient and defiant. Many Southerners accepted the verdict of arms and were ready to return to loyal participation in government; others were inwardly docile but talked violently to ease fallen pride; some were bitterly defiant. In many sections former masters were remarkably successful in running their plantations with quondam slaves as well-satisfied wage-workers. In other regions the planter, while honestly trying to meet new labor conditions, met disaster because of the irresponsibility, ignorance, and laziness of the negro. In still other districts the planter, stubbornly refusing to try the new system, was seeking to impose terms upon the negro that meant peonage, if not slavery. Some negro house servants and town laborers were intelligent, capable, thrifty; most plantation negroes were densely ignorant not only of reading and writing but of the meaning of morals, the family, ordinary honesty, and even free labor itself.

To generalize upon either the white or the negro was to pervert the truth. A young friend of Sumner's startled that senator with this outburst: "I would that you could spend a week incognito in the field of my daily life and work. . . . Constant contact with the minutiae of this mixed life . . . makes me suspicious of *generalizations*, and very careful of making them. That which is true in one District may not be true of another. . . . I am wearied with the general theories of political newspapers, based on 'the statement of a most intelligent gentleman in the cars,' or . . . an 'intelligent contraband.' After six months of intimate association I have determined on the startling proposition that a man is not necessarily a saint because black, nor a devil, because white, and vice versa. The problem of freed labor, has many difficult points for solution & neither blacks or whites are sole causes of the difficulty." [36]

Many of Johnson's informants painted gloomy pictures of a South that needed complete reconstruction. President Cochran of the Second National Bank of New Orleans felt certain that, "save in the large cities, northern men could not remain after the withdrawal of military power, and that the negroes would be far worse off than before the war." [37]

General Baird thought "if martial law & troops were withdrawn that the northern men in the South and the negroes would band for defense & that a second Kansas war would extend over the South." [38] Negroes, Comstock testified, "distrust their old masters who are rarely able or willing to pay them weekly or monthly. Whites fear negro risings—both sides wish troops to remain." "There is much bitter feeling still at the south," he concluded, "but no idea of hostility. . . . The government will have to exercise some control over the South for a year to come to secure the

---

[36] J. C. Beecher, an officer of the Freedmen's Bureau at Summerville, S. C., for whom Sumner had secured an appointment as brigadier general. Oct. 25, 1865, Sumner MSS., LXXIV.

[37] C. B. Comstock to Rawlins, Feb. 1, 1866, Johnson MSS., LXXXVI. Canby and Sheridan believed this, too. Yet Sheridan thought that "if Northern men [were] protected by martial law & the presence of troops . . . in a short time all questions [would] be settled without trouble." And Canby thought "loyal representatives should be admitted to Congress." C. B. Comstock MS. Diary, New Orleans, Jan. 30 and Feb. 2, 1866. Canby thought feeling worse than at the close of the War.

[38] *Ibid.*, New Orleans, Feb. 2, 1866.

best treatment of the negro. . . . Keeping their members out of Congress till they have done everything necessary to secure the negro's well being, is the best way." [39]

General Beckwith found feeling "very bitter," and thought "officers could not stay if martial law were withdrawn." [40] Grant's aide, Comstock, recorded in Charleston: "Feeling of citizens apparently bad. Howards brother tells me the feeling between white[s] and negroes is bad, the negroes having no trust in the whites and the latter fearing a rising. As we rode through the city I saw several who called themselves ladies make faces at the Yankee officers with us. It is useless to say they are only women—they express openly what their husbands & brothers feel but do not show." [41]

General Baird reported that "feeling in Nov. & Oct. was very bad, that officers were insulted at St. Charles, that officers wives at St. Charles table . . . were not waited on and that on remonstrance being made were told they were not desired there as it might affect the custom of the house." But in February he found Southerners' conduct "more moderate" because they had learned "that power was not yet in their hands." [42] In December, 1865, ex-Governor Holden told in discouragement of the machinations of rebel malcontents in North Carolina. "The true Union men," he explained, "were so oppressed under Confederate rule, and so cowed by the charge incessantly made that they were traitors, that they seem not to have entirely recovered their manhood, and hence . . . these malcontents are not denounced and exposed as they should be." [43] By August he was despairing. "I have been silent . . . for many months," he wrote, "in the

[39] *Ibid.*, Raleigh, N. C., Nov. 29, 1865, and Washington, Dec. 12, 1865.
[40] *Ibid.*, New Orleans, Feb. 2, 1866.
[41] *Ibid.*, Charleston, Dec. 1, 1865.
[42] *Ibid.*, New Orleans, Feb. 2, 1865.
[43] Dec. 6, 1865, Johnson MSS., LXXXII.

hope that our leaders . . . would prove themselves loyal, and would aid in good faith in carrying out your plan. But I have lost all hope." [44]

The district-attorney at Mobile reported the fitting out of an old blockade runner to carry a cargo of negroes to Cuba.[45] "The colored man," exclaimed Glavis of the Bureau, "has apparently no rights which this N. C. chivalry feels called upon to respect; floggings, unjust arrests by so-called Home-Guard, of colored persons are of daily occurrence." [46]

Mark Howard of Hartford wrote that he had "mingled with and felt the pulse of all classes, and found little real friendship for the Gov't, tho' a general disposition to submit to that force which could not be successfully met." [47] On another trip in November he found the subdued feeling of the past summer replaced by bitterness and defiance. Planters were combining against negroes. Politicians were ready to do anything to get back into power.[48] After a month in the South, Chase was convinced that the negro must have the ballot for his protection.[49] Whitelaw Reid, correspondent of the *Cincinnati Gazette* who accompanied Chase in June, 1865, and then went back unofficially for six months more, concluded that Southern loyalty was but enforced submission to a powerful government, and that the

[44] Aug. 1, 1866, *ibid.*, XCVIII.

[45] May 7, 1866, *ibid.*, "Telegrams." His information was second-hand and never substantiated.

[46] Nov. 1, 1865, Sumner MSS., LXXV.

[47] M. Howard to G. Welles, July 27, 1865, Welles MSS., LIX.

[48] Nov. 13 and Dec. 2, 1865, *ibid.*, LX.

[49] Chase was undoubtedly sincere, but went South so imbued with the idea of converting Southerners to his ideas that it is questionable whether he really learned anything of their attitude. Reid (*op. cit.*, 315) says, "Whoever approached the Chief-Justice or his party, was likely to have some special motive for doing so, either of courtesy or interest. Naturally, whatever did not comport with that motive was glossed over or kept out of sight."

negroes must have the suffrage, although they were "not
such material as, under ordinary circumstances, one would
choose for the duties of American citizenship." [50] Schurz in
his oft-quoted report agreed that the "loyalty of the . . .
southern people consists in submission to necessity," and
that the negro was amply fitted for the ballot and must
have it since he was now regarded, not as "the property of
the individual master," but as "the slave of society." [51]
Chase, Schurz, and Reid were reliable observers

*　　*　　*　　*

A preponderance of trustworthy opinion expressed to
Johnson was sanguine about Southern conditions. At the
same time that he sent Schurz, Johnson also dispatched Harvey M. Watterson, father of the subsequently famous Louisville journalist. Watterson found Southerners ready to be
loyal to the Union and fair to the negro. He praised Governors Holden, Sharkey, Johnson, and Parsons, and Generals
Palmer, Swayne, Steedman, and Tillson for the successful
work they were doing.[52] McCulloch believed that if a "free
conference" between leading Northerners and "some of the
representatives of the Southern States" could be arranged,
"some plan of restoration might be agreed upon." [53]

Southerners like Wade Hampton, ex-Governor Parsons of
Alabama, Howell Cobb, Alexander H. Stephens, and even
the former abolitionist, Daniel Goodloe of North Carolina,

[50] Yet much of his evidence would convert the modern reader to Johnson's policy. *Ibid.* The wealth of detailed description, the journalistic ability of the author, and the nature and thoroughness of his observations
make this account valuable even today.

[51] C. Schurz, *Report,* 45. For a discussion of the bias of Schurz's report
see *supra,* 70-73.

[52] Series of letters to Johnson, Johnson MSS., LVI-LXXX.

[53] He wrote Senator Wilson to urge him to confer with Gov. Parsons of
Alabama on the subject. March 12, 1866, H. Wilson MSS.

insisted that the South was loyal, and was trying to work out
its problems in justice to both whites and blacks.[54] These men
condemned Southern agitators, but felt that most disturbances were after all not political.[55] They pointed out that
Southern society was chaotic. Until Johnson reëstablished
them, the courts were not sitting; state governments did not
exist; the revenue officers and post offices were not functioning. "On the way to their homes," McCarter exclaimed,
"many of which had been utterly desolated—it was not surprising they should take from the Commissary & Quarter-
master every thing they could find belonging to the Government—& when public property could no longer be found
the lawless soldiers seized on the horses & mules of citizens
who they chose to think had more than their fair share.
All quiet & order loving citizens now began to perceive the
absolute necessity of having an efficient government of some
kind: & many an honest Secessionist who hated the very
name of Yankee began to wish for the presence of a Yankee
garrison to protect them from the violence of our own lawless population."[56] Military government and the Freedmen's
Bureau preserved comparative peace and order, but neither
could be omnipresent, and neither had the sanction of the

[54] H. K. Beale, "Decision of Reconstruction," 248—MS. dissertation for
the Ph.D. degree at Harvard, now in Widener Library. McCarter, a Northerner living in Columbia, S. C., certified to the truth of this: "When the
first effects of this severe blow upon our State pride began to wear off,
the attention of our leading men was turned to the best and quickest way
of returning to the old Union. A few leading Secessionists were for
abandoning the State Government entirely to the conquerors, & sullenly
await the fate allotted to us: others recognizing the real conditions of our
affairs were for honestly accepting the new status in which we found ourselves & by heartily cooperating with the federal authorities resume the
control of the State." McCarter MS. Diary, II, 93.

[55] *Massachusetts and South Carolina. Correspondence between John
Quincy Adams and Wade Hampton . . .* ; Speech of Parsons in the *New
York Herald*, Sept. 18, 1866; H. Cobb to Gen. J. H. Wilson, June 14, 1865,
Johnson MSS., LXVII; A. H. Stephens to A. Johnson, May 10, 1866, *ibid.*,
XCIV; D. R. Goodloe to C. Sumner, Sept. 11, 1865, Sumner MSS., LXXIV.

[56] McCarter MS. Diary, II, 92-93.

people. The trouble was not that Southerners were defiantly lawless, but that all the criminal elements that exist in any community were free, in the absence of organized government, to indulge their instincts without restraint.

While most Northern soldiers, business men, and missionaries in the South were led by private grievance or interest to defame the South, some even of these reported favorably of Southern conditions.[57] Symonds who was in business in New Orleans found "the cotton factors & huge planters who [were] losing control of . . . business" the only bitter classes.[58] Major General Gordon Granger repeatedly sent encouraging reports to Johnson, and then in the midst of the campaign published a plea for restoration and the better understanding that more frequent intercourse would breed.[59] In similar letters and a published report Ben Truman expressed faith in the loyalty and dependability of returned rebel soldiers; he explained that most of the reported bravado emanated from politicians and demagogues who had to defend their "records"; he insisted that most of the ill feeling toward Northerners was social and understandable; he was certain that the negro problem would be solved satisfactorily, since in spite of the inherent Southern attitude toward negroes which critics failed to understand, the treatment of negroes was increasingly good.[60] Generals Fullerton and Steedman after thorough investigation affirmed this judgment in their report.[61] General Humphreys,

[57] The Johnson MSS. abound in examples of both kinds.

[58] C. B. Comstock MS. Diary, Jan. 30, 1866.

[59] See Johnson MSS. His report was published in the *New York Herald,* Aug. 28, 1866.

[60] Johnson MSS., LXXXIV-XCII. Truman's report was printed in pamphlet form as *The Condition of the South.*

[61] *New York Herald,* Aug. 10, 1866. Other generals such as Andrews in Alabama (May 11, 1865, Johnson MSS., LXII), Wager Swayne (*New York Herald,* Dec. 24, 1866), Canby (Comstock MS. Diary, Feb. 2, 1866), Schofield (May 18, 1865, Johnson MSS., LXII), and J. H. Wilson (June 15,

who was in New Orleans to repair the "levees if he [could] get funds," took "a very favorable view of affairs." Along the Mississippi he found "no bitterness," but reported the planters "ready & willing to do what is desired." [62]

While Grant's aide, Comstock, as already cited, reported unfavorable conditions in parts of the South, he more frequently saw hopeful signs. In Charleston where he dined with Gov. Aiken, Gov. Orr, Dr. Mackay, and Judge Magrath, he wrote, "Magrath is only a few days out of Ft Pulaski & the imprisonment has apparently done him good, for now (I dont doubt—honestly) he admits & accepts all the results of the war & is perfectly willing to make the most of the present & future. In other words as the rebel officers say 'he is whipped.' " [63] Later on meeting Lieutenant General Gordon who commanded the left wing of Lee's army at its surrender, Comstock commented, "He was formerly I should judge very bitter—is very earnest—but entirely 'reconstructed,' & thinks the war will prove a blessing to the South." [64] Former Brigadier General Tarbell, after four months in the South, felt complete confidence in the loyalty of the more intelligent whites, their friendliness toward the North, and their fairness to negroes.[65]

Most important of all, both Grant and Sherman felt the South was loyal and urged its speedy restoration. Sheridan, later a convert to Radicalism, wrote Johnson in November, 1865, "There are without doubt many malcontents in the State of Louisiana and much bitterness but this bitterness

1865, *ibid.*, LXVII, and July 6, 1865, W. T. Sherman MSS., XVII), in Georgia, and Sharp of the Freedmen's Bureau in Virginia (Feb. 9, 1866, Stevens MSS., VI), depicted encouraging conditions in the South.

[62] C. B. Comstock MS. Diary, Jan. 31, 1866.

[63] *Ibid.*, Dec. 2, 1865.

[64] *Ibid.*, Augusta, Ga., Dec. 5, 1865.

[65] *Report of the Joint Committee on Reconstruction*, 39 Cong., 1 Sess., III, 155-157.

is all that is left for these people, there is no power of resistance left, the country is impoverished and the probability is
that in two or three years there will be almost a total transfer
of landed property, the North will own every Railroad,
every steamboat, every large mercantile establishment and
everything which requires capital to carry it on; in fact
Mr. President I consider the South now Northernized. The
slave is free and the whole world cannot again enslave him,
and with these facts staring us in the face we can well afford
to be lenient to this last annoyance, impotent ill feeling." [66]

*   *   *   *

Whether the Southern situation was what it should have
been and whether restoration or reconstruction was the wiser
policy were two somewhat different questions. Those who
were satisfied with the Southern attitude favored restoration,
of course. But many who admitted the gravity of Southern
problems, also maintained the efficacy of restoration as the
remedy. Everybody who knew the South conceded that military control could not suddenly be withdrawn from it. Johnson had no thought of removing the troops until justice and
order could be maintained without them. But whereas Johnson did want gradually to remove them as soon as it became
safe, Radicals urged that the military grip be tightened. In
what was indubitably a subtle rebuke, Governor Andrew of
Massachusetts wrote Sumner, "We must cultivate all there
is of possible good in the Southern people themselves. The
educated most enlightened and superior persons of the South
have a strong tendency *now* towards the right side. They see
a new order of society, to which they must conform. They
have learned very rapidly these last five years. We may win,

[66] Johnson MSS., LXXXI. In February he was still sanguine. Comstock
MS. Diary, Jan. 30 and Feb. 1, 1866.

instruct and help them to do right, if we try. . . . The right
position for *New England* is one of friendliness, not of antagonism." [67]

Henry Ward Beecher, Senator Dixon of Connecticut,
Thomas Ewing of Ohio, Grant, Sherman, and other prominent Union generals, President Lincoln before he died, Secretaries Welles, McCulloch, and Seward, Henry J. Raymond, and scores of other influential men urged conciliation and speedy restoration. Grant wrote to his wife from
North Carolina in May, 1865, "The suffering that must
exist in the South the next year, . . . will be beyond conception. People who talk of further retaliation and punishment, except of the political leaders, either do not conceive
of the suffering endured already or they are heartless and
unfeeling and wish to stay at home out of danger while the
punishment is being inflicted." [68] "No matter what change
we may desire in the feelings & thoughts of people South,"
wrote General Sherman to his senator brother, "we can not
accomplish it by Force. Nor can we afford to maintain there
an army large enough to hold them in subjugation. All we
can or should attempt is to give them rope to develop in an
honest way if possible, keeping [?] in reserve enough Military Power to check any excesses if they attempt any. But
I know they will not attempt any, and you may look for outbreaks in Ohio quicker than in Georgia or Mississippi. You
hardly can realize how completely the country has been
devastated or how completely humbled the man of the South
is." [69] McCulloch preferred to suspend taxes for years
"rather than to undertake to collect them by men not identified with the taxpayers in sympathy or in interest." "The

[67] Nov. 21, 1865, Sumner MSS., LXXV.
[68] Quoted in A. Badeau, *Grant in Peace*, 31.
[69] Sept. 21, 1865, W. T. Sherman MSS., XVII.

rebellion," he said, "grew out of an antagonism of opinion between the people of the free and slave states, the legitimate result of a difference of institutions. With the abolition of slavery, all real differences of opinion, and all serious causes of estrangement, ought rapidly to disappear. It will be a calamity, the extent of which cannot now be estimated, both to this nation and to the cause of civil liberty throughout the world, if, instead of looking towards reconciliation and harmony, the action of the government shall tend to harden and intensify a sectionalism between the Northern and Southern States." [70]

The President's own ideas are ably expressed in a proclamation of April 2, 1866. "It is . . . a fundamental principle of government," he said, "that people who have revolted and who have been overcome and subdued, must either be dealt with so as to induce them voluntarily to become friends, or else they must be held by absolute military power, or devastated, so as to prevent them from ever again doing harm as enemies, which last named policy is abhorrent to humanity and freedom." Military force, he added, is "contrary to the genius and spirit of our free institutions, and exhaustive of the national resources." [71] "The idea," he exclaimed, "of muzzling the press and tying the tongues of the people of the South, after the manner of the suspicious tyrants and the Holy Inquisition of the Old World. . . . A

[70] H. McCulloch to Senate and H. of Rep., March 19, 1866, McCulloch MSS., II.

[71] E. McPherson, *Political Manual* (1866), 15-16. Cf. Ewing's suggestions to his son, Tom, for a speech the latter was to make: "States and Nations have been conquered by force, but never so governed. Conquering nations have always found it necessary to adopt one of two expedients, cut off with the sword and reduce to slavery the conquered people or incorporate them into the conquering State and give the people the privilege of Citizens or Subjects . . . People may be driven to desperation by what they conceive cruelty, insult, and injustice but no degree of forbearance kindness and oblivion of past errors can ever make rebellion again acceptable to the crushed and ruined South." Sept. 12, 1866, Ewing MSS., XVIII.

people should be allowed to grumble who have suffered so much, and they would be unworthy the name of men if they did not respect the brave officers who have suffered with them, and honor the memory of their gallant dead who sleep on a hundred battle fields around their homes." [72]

Whatever the unbiased verdict on Southern conditions may have been, it did not interest Radical leaders. Their task was to convince the Northern people that to readmit the South to Congress without thorough-going reconstruction of their society, would be dangerous. The South abounded in diversified evidence to support any program. To the men who sought facts, stories, rumors, that would damage the South and Johnson's policy, and arouse the Northern voter to a sense of danger, the South offered rich rewards for even a short trip. Not on facts, but on carefully gathered propaganda, was the Southern issue in the campaign fought.

[72] *Boston Evening Commercial,* July 21, 1866.

Chapter VII

NEGRO SUFFRAGE

N EGRO suffrage occupied an anomalous position among campaign issues. Extremists like Sumner, Stevens, Wade, Chase, Schurz, and Chandler were from the first determined to secure it. But to many Northerners it was unthinkable. The Radical minority depended for support upon moderate voters who would have scurried to the Conservative fold, had negro suffrage been suggested for the North. To secure it in the South without alienating Northern followers required delicate handling.

One small group of Radicals favored negro suffrage *per se*. The old abolitionist group revamped its program and renewed its campaign, merely substituting complete equality of races for abolition. These men in New England and among New Englanders and Germans in the West, believed in negro suffrage from principle.

Others who did not sanction it, but who hated Southerners, advocated it for the South as a means of punishing a defeated enemy. The very fact that negro equality was abhorrent to Southern whites made these men support it to humiliate the "haughty Southerner." But the same reasoning made equality of race in the North intolerable. Still others favored negro suffrage because they were convinced that only through the ballot would the negro be able to defend his rights.

For a more numerous group of Radicals, expediency was the motive that urged negro suffrage.[1] The negro vote would be admittedly ignorant and hence easily controlled from the North. Locally it would be anti-white; nationally it would be Radical. Hence it would offset the white vote of the South. After all, disfranchisement and disqualification for office .were only temporary expedients, even though guaranteed in a constitutional amendment. The problem was to insure themselves permanently against a white South, solid, not against the government, but against the extremes of Radicalism. Only a small minority of whites would support them. Minority rule could be sustained only by force furnished from the North. But all Radicals realized that some day Northern soldiers would have to be withdrawn and the Southern States admitted to a share in the government. The Radical leaders knew that however much they talked of reconstructing the Southern whites, and however long they succeeded in governing them by military power, the rule of force was no cure but an aggravation of Southern opposition to Radicals. The only permanent guarantee of Radical tenure of power was to give the negro the vote, and thereby to *create* in the South a pro-Radical party.

As early as May, 1864, Boutwell had urged negro suffrage in the rebellious states as the only way of keeping down the old dominant class.[2] B. Gratz Brown said there was

---

[1] Even Sumner did not hesitate to exploit this motive. E.g., *Cong. Globe*, 39 Cong., 1 Sess., 675, 685. General Sherman believed "the whole idea of giving votes to the negroes [was] to create just that many votes to be used by others for political uses." J. F. Rhodes, *op. cit.*, V, 525. He told his wife that he did not approve a scheme "whereby politicians may manufacture just so much more pliable electioneering material." *Home Letters of General Sherman*, 353.

[2] *Cong. Globe*, 38 Cong., 1 Sess., 2104.

no other way to secure what the Radicals had gained. "The Radical sentiment of the country will have to make itself known & felt," he declared, "and control not only the President but the Administration also. Otherwise we are thrown back on half a century of warfare." [3] Senator Howard wanted "all the security possible for the future" with "colored suffrage . . . in the inventory of assets; whatever the *northern* people may do to their *own blacks*." [4] General Brisbin wrote from Arkansas to warn Stevens that unless he kept the South out until negro suffrage was established there, the South "by the aid of their Copperhead friends in the North" would control Congress.[5] Winter Davis demanded negro suffrage as the only guarantee that "the *friends* & not *the enemies* of the government" would "continue to govern it." "However ignorant," he said, the negroes "know enough to be on the side of the Government: & the intelligence of the master has not yet taught him that wisdom." [6] In June, 1865, he urged Sumner to force it through Congress. "The mere rejection of members & Senators," he insisted, "will not answer: for that will merely carry the question before the people into the election—& you will *certainly* be beaten." [7] Just after Congress opened he wrote again, "Though it is *now* impossible to moot negro suffrage with success; yet if *Cong* do its duty & the Republicans *then* require it of the *rebel* States, I will undertake it in Md—*if* we can get the administration off our backs. The registry law which *excludes* the *Secesh*, will give us a grand

---

[3] B. G. Brown to C. Sumner, Sept. 12, 1865, Sumner MSS., LXXIV.

[4] J. M. Howard to C. Sumner, Nov. 12, 1865, *ibid.*, LXXV.

[5] Dec. 29, 1865, Stevens MSS., V.

[6] "I think [negro suffrage] offers not a question of abstract right but of pure political dynamics. It is a public necessity—the only alternative to the loss of all the fruits of the war." H. W. Davis to Whom It May Concern, May 27, 1865, McPherson MSS., V.

[7] June 20, 1865, Sumner MSS., LXXIII.

hold on their friends & enable us to *compel* the removal of *all* disabilities, as the condition of restoring the disfranchised rebels—which then can be *safely done:* for 30,000 negro votes will balance 8,000 rebel votes!" [8]

In June, 1865, Welles recorded in his diary: "A great party demonstration is being made for negro suffrage. . . . It is evident that intense partisanship instead of philanthropy is the root of the movement. When pressed by arguments which they cannot refute, they turn and say if the negro is not allowed to vote, the Democrats will get control of the government in each of the seceding or rebellious States, and in conjunction with the Democrats of the Free States they will get the ascendency in our political affairs. It is curious to witness the bitterness and intolerance of the philanthropists in this matter." [9]

A few Southerners did desire votes for negroes. But they were either fanatics, or self-seekers who through manipulation of the negro electorate hoped to win political plums for themselves. Many of them were political chameleons who had won the contempt of their neighbors during the War as Copperheads had in the North. Unionist populations there were in sections of the South like East Tennessee. But Johnson represented this element; like the "poor whites," they hated the negro as did no planter. In Confederate eyes Southern "Unionists" had been "traitors," but they did have the merit of having stood manfully by the Union. The Southern "Radical" was usually a political renegade and social outcast, who was loyal to nothing. These nascent scalawags had

[8] Dec. 5, 1865, *ibid.*, LXXV.

[9] Welles MS. Diary, June 27, 1865—(II, 324). Boutwell called on McCulloch to convert him to negro suffrage for the sake of "the unity of the Republican party." G. S. Boutwell to H. McCulloch, July 1, 1865, McCulloch MSS., II. In July Reid urged McCulloch not to commit himself against it, because "before Congress meets, the pressure from the North will be such as no Administration can resist." July 9, 1865, *ibid.*, II.

no constituencies; their only hope was to create black ones. In offering a negro suffrage resolution in the Radical Philadelphia Convention, Hill of Virginia pointed out, "Without it, the Unionists of the South are in a minority; . . . with it, they are a strong majority." [10] Brownlow stated frankly, "I find here at the North you do not need, and many of you do not want, negro suffrage. We are not so. We want the loyal negroes to help us vote down the disloyal traitors and white people." [11] All agreed that most of the whites of the South would oppose giving the negro the ballot. Winter Davis testified, "The loyal are as much against it as the rebel leaders." [12]

* * * *

The opposition of many Northerners to the negro's voting was based upon fear of his ignorance. Even Johnson would have agreed to a qualified suffrage based upon educational and property tests. Many, indeed, who wished to see the civil rights of the colored man fully protected, steadily opposed giving him the ballot.[13] David D. Field, an eminent New York jurist, expressed a general sentiment when he said, "The elective franchise is not a natural right, but a political trust. . . . Because the blacks have fought for the country, that does not necessarily give them the right to govern it. . . . It is a curious feature of the Freedmen's Bill . . . that it took the blacks under the protection of the Federal

[10] *The Southern Loyalists' Convention (The Tribune Tracts,* No. 2), 13.
[11] Speech in New York, *New York Herald,* Sept. 12, 1866.
[12] H. W. Davis to Whom It May Concern, May 27, 1865, McPherson MSS., V. McCulloch believed the negro could not be enfranchised without violence, and that it would require "a strong military force in every county" to protect him in voting. "Can the nation stand the expense, and can our republican institutions stand the strain of continued military rule?" he asked Sumner. Aug. 15, 1865, McCulloch MSS., II.
[13] E.g., Welles (MS. Diary, May 9, 1865—[II, 302]) ; and Sherman (W. T. Sherman, *Home Letters,* 353) who wrote his wife, "The negroes don't want to vote. They want to work and enjoy property, and they are no friends of the Negro who seek to complicate him with new prejudices."

Government, as if they were not able to take care of themselves, while the same persons who urged . . . the measure are the most clamorous to give this same dependent population a large share in the Government of the country." [14] General Howard of the Freedmen's Bureau "hoped that it might be limited at least by an educational qualification." "The gross ignorance," he said, "of the mass of colored soldiers rendered them especial objects of . . . extortion and fraud." He favored negro suffrage under an educational qualification, and hoped the Bureau would be maintained to educate the negro.[15] "A people who are just emerging from the barbarism of slavery," Morton told the Indiana Legislature, "are not qualified to become a part of our political system, and take part not only in Government of themselves and their neighbors, but of the whole United States. So far from believing that negro suffrage is a remedy for all our national ills, I doubt whether it is a remedy for any, and rather believe that its enforcement by Congress would be more likely to subject the negro to a merciless persecution, than to confer upon him any substantial benefit." [16] Major General Sickles of the Freedmen's Bureau in Charleston declared, "Mr. Sumner would not be in such a hurry to confer negro suffrage, if he could see the plantation negroes and thus comprehend how hopelessly they lack capacity for political franchises." [17]

The greatest obstacle to negro suffrage was the Northern prejudice against the negro, which Radicals and Conservatives shared. Many who thought negro suffrage for the

[14] *Mass Meeting of the Citizens of New York, Feb. 22, 1866,* 9-10.
[15] Oliver O. Howard, *Autobiography,* II, 293, 317-318.
[16] Gov. Morton to A. Johnson, Nov. 12, 1865, Johnson MSS., LXXXI.
[17] D. E. Sickles to E. M. Stanton, July 19, 1866, Stanton MSS., XXX. Sherman agreed entirely with this. W. T. Sherman to J. Sherman, Jan. 19, 1866, W. T. Sherman MSS., XVIII.

South a necessary safeguard against white disloyalty and treachery, would have sooner risked the Southern danger than faced the hazard of encouraging blacks to move into their own communities by offering them civil equality and the ballot. Especially through the half of the Old Northwest originally peopled by Southerners was dislike of the negro intense.

Lincoln, himself from the Northwest, understood this antipathy. He realized that only the psychological effect of the firing on Sumter had united against the South Northwesterns of Southern stock and abolitionists whom they hated. Lincoln showed his acute comprehension of the widespread prejudice against negroes, when he insisted on keeping the main issue the preservation of the Union in spite of Radical pressure for emancipation. His constituents in the Northwest would never have fought a war for the negro. No more would they in 1866 adopt a reconstruction policy whose end was equality of races. To preserve the Union against "unrepentant rebels" they would go a long way. But only very gradually could they be brought to overcome their repugnance for the negro sufficiently to view the Radical suffrage program with equanimity. The fact that the War did free the slaves and that five years later the negro suffrage amendment was ratified, had obscured the keenness of Northern racial prejudice before Radical "education" had done its work.

From all over the North warnings came to Radical leaders not to inject negro suffrage into the campaign. Grosvenor of the *New Haven Journal and Courier* warned Sumner that the aversion of soldiers who had known the negro in the South would render futile any effort to establish negro suf-

frage in Connecticut.[18] Ohio politicians predicted that on the
negro suffrage issue the Radicals would be beaten by one
hundred thousand votes in that state alone.[19] General Ord
wrote from Michigan that the soldiers would "vote almost to
a man against such a proceeding." [20] Senator Trumbull's
friends warned him that the election was already lost if this
were to be an issue.[21] Morton fought desperately to suppress
it, as he knew it would wreck the campaign in Indiana, and
Julian, strong negro suffragist that he was, averred that
Morton expressed the sentiment of "the great body of Republicans." Even many of Julian's old anti-slavery friends
shared the prejudice against the negro.[22] According to
Dana, a negro suffrage amendment could not have been carried in any Western state except perhaps Iowa and Minnesota.[23] Even Thad Stevens recognized the color prejudice to
the extent of evading the subject in his key-note speech at
Lancaster, Pennsylvania, in September, 1865.[24] Eli Thayer,
stout abolitionist and negro suffragist that he was, expressed
alarm lest Southern conditions force the negro to leave.
"If they come North where they can vote," he warned,
"they will be worse off, for we do not want them & would not
endure them." [25]

Northern feeling was further indicated by the movement
for foreign colonization of the negroes. Lincoln had urged
this solution. It was favored by McCulloch and by Johnson

[18] Sept. 5, 1865, Sumner MSS., LXXIV.
[19] Johnson MSS., LXXXV, LXXXVI, LXXXVIII.
[20] Gen. Ord to W. T. Sherman, Jan. 27, 1866, W. T. Sherman MSS.,
XVIII. He urged Sherman, Sheridan, and Thomas to state the truth
about negroes, especially to men like Fessenden and Morrill. He thought
agitation of the question would sooner endanger than insure Republican
retention of power.
[21] Trumbull MSS., LXIV, LXVI, LXVII.
[22] George W. Julian, *Political Recollections,* 303, 263.
[23] C. A. Dana to C. Sumner, Sept. 1, 1865, Sumner MSS., LXXIV.
[24] Stevens MSS., IV.
[25] Eli Thayer to A. Johnson, March 17, 1866, Johnson MSS., XCI.

himself.[26] To sound others out on segregation, Johnson sent out an agent who found men in all parts of the North interested in it.[27]

More tellingly still did Northern treatment of negroes indicate the feeling toward them. A negro servant who had accompanied Jewett's niece to New York was refused admission to Jersey City and New York hotels, and finally found a place to sleep at three in the morning only through the "hospitality of a sensible up-town gentleman." [28] In New York a black Union soldier was not allowed to ride in the street-cars, and Greeley told Mrs. Whipple he was obliged to give up his effort "to pilot . . . a most respectable colored clergyman" through that city.[29] In Wisconsin a black woman was injured by the rough handling of two brakemen who ejected her from the train.[30] Instances like this were rare principally because of the paucity of blacks in the North.

Some Northern states, moreover, had "black laws" on their statute books as late as 1865 and 1866, discriminating against negroes, and attempting to keep them out of the state. In Maryland Radicals tried in 1866 to pass a law allowing negroes to testify; they sought to repeal the old apprentice law and to remove other disabilities of slavery days. Yet not one of these measures was carried in a legislature that had a decided Union Party majority in the Senate, and a two-thirds majority in the House.[31]

[26] H. McCulloch to C. Sumner, Aug. 22, 1865, Sumner MSS., LXXIV. Governor Cox of Ohio and Boutwell of Massachusetts favored setting aside Georgia, South Carolina, and Florida as negro states. Geo. H. Porter, *Ohio Politics during the Civil War,* 211; *Cong. Globe,* 38 Cong., 1 Sess., 2104. Boutwell deemed this fit punishment for the whites of these states whom he never wished to see reënter the Union.

[27] J. Mitchell (Comm. of Emigration under Lincoln) to A. Johnson, Nov. 21, 1865, Johnson MSS., LXXXI.

[28] W. C. Jewett to C. Sumner, Feb. 19, 1866, Sumner MSS., LXXVII.

[29] April 13, 1865, Greeley MSS.

[30] *Janesville Gazette,* reprinted in the *Chicago Tribune,* June 1, 1866.

[31] W. Daniel to C. Sumner, Feb. 13, 1866, Sumner MSS., LXXVI.

In 1866 and long thereafter, the Illinois law which required education for apprentices contained a proviso "that if such minor be a negro or mulatto, it shall not be necessary to require that he or she shall be taught to write, or the knowledge of arithmetic." [32] Long after the Emancipation Proclamation,[33] Illinois had a law concerning "Negroes, Mulattoes, and Indians," that required every free negro in the state to possess a certificate of freedom and file a one thousand dollar bond with the county clerk, or be hired to labor for a year.[34] Another law forbade a negro or mulatto "to give evidence in favor or against any white person." [35] Illinois had a severe fugitive slave law,[36] and only in February, 1865, had she repealed "An Act to Prevent the Immigration of Free Negroes into this State," which provided that any free negro who entered the state should be fined fifty dollars, and on failure to pay, sold to the man who would pay the fine for the shortest period of labor, and that on payment of his fine or completion of his term of service, the negro should leave the state in ten days or suffer a second, double fine; in each case the accuser got half of the fine.[37] As late as 1862 in a referendum which rejected the rest of the new constitution, the section excluding negroes from the state was accepted by a two to one vote, and became part of the old state constitution. A section proposing negro suffrage for Illinois was rejected by a six to one vote.[38]

Indiana was one of the states that ratified the Thirteenth Amendment. Yet the vote in the Indiana House was 56-29; [39]

[32] *Revised Statutes for the State of Illinois* (1845), chap. VI, sec. 11.
[33] None of the following Illinois laws was repealed until Feb. 7, 1865.
[34] *Ibid.*, chap. LXXIV.
[35] *Ibid.*, chap. XXX, sec. 16.
[36] *Ibid.*, chap. LXXIV.
[37] *Illinois Session Laws* (1853), 57.
[38] *Tribune Almanac* (1863), 59.
[39] *Indiana House Journal* (1865), 396.

and in the Senate a change of one vote would have defeated the Amendment, for the vote stood 26-24.[40] In December, 1865, the Legislature for the first time granted negroes the right to give testimony in the courts.[41] But at the same session a bill to provide tax-supported common schools for negroes was defeated, because it would encourage too many negroes to enter the state. A similar law failed in 1867. Furthermore, the Legislature of November, 1865, failed by a vote of 22-22 in the Senate to repeal the portion of the Indiana constitution which still forbade free negroes to enter the state.[42]

In 1865 the people of Connecticut voted down a negro suffrage amendment to the state constitution by 33,489 to 27,217. Wisconsin voters rejected a similar measure by 55,591 to 46,588. In 1867 Ohioans defeated an amendment which sought to extend suffrage to negroes and disfranchise disloyalists. Analysis of the vote shows that twelve counties which cast Republican majorities for the governorship voted against the amendment. The popular majority of 38,353 for rejection is significant just a year after an Ohio majority had helped establish Radical rule in the South.[43] In 1912, fifty years after Ohio voted to impose negro suffrage on the South, another amendment to strike out the word "white" from her own constitution was rejected by a popular majority of 22,958.[44]

Within the Radical ranks, however, arose a struggle between the extremists and the moderates. Some of the Radical leaders openly advocated negro suffrage; others favored it,

---

[40] *Indiana Senate Journal* (1865), 315.
[41] *Indiana Session Laws, Special* (1865), LVI.
[42] Indiana Legislature's *Brevier Report, Special* (1865), 164.
[43] *Tribune Almanac* (1866), 53, 57; *ibid.* (1868), 45.
[44] C. B. Galbreath, "The Vote on the Ohio Constitution," the *Independent*, LXXIII (December, 1912), 1408.

but saw the folly of losing all by advancing too rapidly for
the mass of the voters. Still others opposed it because of the
unfitness of the negro, or their own anti-negro prejudice.
The simultaneous meeting in Philadelphia of a Southern
Loyalists' Convention [45] and a conclave of Northern Radicals brought a party crisis in early September. At first a
joint meeting was planned, but the Northerners finally remained aloof, partly because they wanted the Southerners
to appear independent of any influence of Northern Radicals, and partly because the Northerners themselves wanted
to be free to repudiate any rash acts of the Southerners on
negro suffrage that might injure them in the election. The
border state delegates joined the Southerners. In fact, James
Speed, recently in Johnson's cabinet, became permanent
president of the Convention. Some of the Northern leaders
participated to the extent of accepting seats on the platform. The border state delegates, who as representatives of
"poor whites" and Unionists disliked the negro, tried to
eliminate him from the discussion. Northern Radicals tried
to persuade the Southern delegates to treat Fred Douglass
and other negroes as Vallandigham and Wood were treated
in the August Convention of Conservatives; the negroes they
urged to "withhold their claims to seats for expediency's
sake." [46] Morton personally pleaded with Tilton to persuade
the negroes quietly to withdraw.[47] Some white delegates declared they would not attend if the negroes were admitted.
Negroes did receive seats. But in the convention proceedings
they were almost entirely ignored. When Crane of Louisiana
asked to have a letter from an absent negro delegate read,

[45] *The Southern Loyalists' Convention* (*The Tribune Tracts, No. 2*)
gives the proceedings of the Convention.
[46] *New York Herald*, Sept. 3, 1866.
[47] G. W. Julian, *Political Recollections*, 303.

it was "sent to the chair but was not read." A motion to ask
Fred Douglass to sit on the platform was ignored.[48] An
effort to add Douglass's name to the committee that was to
tour the North precipitated an uproar. Loud applause mingled with cries of "No, no!" "Do you want to ruin us?" "It
will never do." Douglass did accompany the committee,
however.

During the sessions of the Convention a group of Northern governors met in secret conclave.[49] Governor Yates of
Illinois told them he was personally favorable to negro suffrage and thought the people might be brought to it, but
that it must be kept out of the present election and the Fourteenth Amendment be retained as the Radical platform.
Lieutenant Governor Bross of Illinois, Governor Crapo of
Michigan, ex-Governors Dutton and Buckingham of Connecticut, and ex-Governor Newell of New Jersey all agreed
that negro suffrage would be a fatal issue. Governor Cony of
Maine expressed the sentiment of many extreme Radicals
when he said, "I am in favor of negro suffrage as much as
any man in the country, and if the question was submitted
to the people of my State, the answer would be 'yes' . . . I
believe that the negro at the South is better fitted to vote
than the most accomplished rebel from the Potomac to the
Rio Grande; but I don't believe in making negro suffrage
an issue now. Our great object now is to secure the next
Congress. If we don't get that, then all is lost; if we do get
it, then all is safe. Therefore I am opposed to any changing
of the issue." Morton unconditionally opposed negro suffrage *per se*, and testified that his constituents did, too. In

48 *New York Herald*, Sept. 5, 1866.
49 A *Herald* reporter was inadvertently admitted. When his presence
was discovered Morton moved that the meeting be secret, and he was
ejected. But the next day he published the discussion up to the time
of his ejection. *Ibid.*, Sept. 5, 1866.

fact he had not planned to go to Philadelphia until he learned how negroes were to be featured in the Convention there. Then he hurried eastward to wield his personal influence against it. The Northerners agreed to await the outcome of the Southerners' Convention, and then to endorse their program if no mention were made of negro suffrage, but to adjourn in silence if the Southerners persisted.

The test came toward the close of the fourth day when the Committee on Unreconstructed States sought to submit a report known to include a recommendation of negro suffrage. The border state delegates tried to force an adjournment *sine die*. In an excited speech Hamilton abused them for trying to block the wishes of the Convention when they were only there through courtesy anyway. It was hard to persuade men whose only constituents were blacks to side-track negro suffrage. The adjournment was overruled. Then all but fifteen of the border state men left the Convention and went home. Chairman Speed withdrew rather than face the issue. The next morning, with Botts in the chair, the Southern delegates and the remaining fifteen border state men considered the report. Botts tried to prevent its acceptance by substituting for it a series of resolutions which omitted the negro suffrage clause. But he was overridden and left the chair, while the Southern delegates accepted the committee report 80-8.

Had this second Philadelphia convention been reported in the same newspapers in the spirit in which the earlier one was described, it would have lost the Radicals thousands of votes. But Radical papers which had ridiculed the orderly, dignified gathering in August, eulogized and dignified the September convention beyond recognition. Democratic papers reversed both pictures. Moderate papers were rare.

The *Nation*, which had condemned the Philadelphia National Union Convention and was at the moment vigorously denouncing the President's conduct on his Western tour, remained discreetly silent, publishing not one comment on a Radical gathering which it could only have condemned. Other Radical papers were not so honest.

* * * *

The only safe argument for negro suffrage, and a powerful one for Radical reconstruction, was the claim that the negroes would never be safe unless protected by the ballot. Northern military force, or organized colored suffrage exercised under Radical tutelage, must stand between the blacks and Southern whites who hated them, said the extremists.

The Conservatives admitted the difficulty of racial readjustment that the sudden change from slave to free labor had necessitated. But, said ex-Governor Seymour of New York, the Southerner is far better fitted to solve the problem than are functionaries of the Freedmen's Bureau whose office depends upon its not being solved. The South must ultimately settle the matter, for amendments and military force cannot forever stand over the blacks. What the negroes most need is the friendship of Southern whites.[50] They "will find work enough," said Johnson, "and . . . probably better remuneration than any other class of agricultural laborers in the country. The competition of capitalists and land owners will insure good treatment and good pay from the planters. That there will be much disorder is to be expected; but there will be no more than there would be at the North were the number of black laborers sufficiently numerous to enter into serious rivalry with the white laborers." [51]

[50] Speech at Cooper Institute, *New York Herald,* Oct. 31, 1866.
[51] *Boston Evening Commercial,* July 21, 1866.

To comprehend the Southern problem one must recall that the South had been devastated by invading armies, that much of its wealth had been destroyed, that its government was not functioning, and that its economic and social systems had been shaken to their foundations. Into this chaos four million negroes were suddenly turned loose without land, money, education, means of livelihood, or experience beyond that of a five-year-old child. The problem was much more than a racial one. It combined the difficulties of the most ignorant labor with those of the sudden economic disaster of a whole people, and adjustment to a system of labor new to both blacks and whites.[52]

Northerners usually judged the Southern negro by the free blacks of the North or the house servants of the South. The plantation hands were different beings. These negroes were not only illiterate; they had no conception of the func-

[52] An unbiased observer's description of the troubles of a conscientious Freedmen's Bureau officer illustrates the difficulty of the situation. "The new system of hiring services of negroes by the planter," wrote McCarter, "& the amount of wages to be paid whether in coin or kind now required the whole attention of the commandant. & he was involved in a continual round of complaint from both parties each claiming his aid to settle their disputes. It was soon evident this breaking up—& reorganization of our system of labour was no easy matter—from morning till night the time of the commandant was taken up—ordering, advising, entreating, threatening, the parties hoping they would conform with alactrity to the new order of things. It was easy to see some coertion was necessary to compel the negroes to work—& some even stronger coertion to prevent the master from imposing on his former slave. In some instances there was a sincere desire on the part of the Master, to accommodate himself to the new order of things & try the experiment fairly whether free labour might not even be more profitable than the old arrangement. In other cases the hopelessness of the undertaking seemed to paralyse all exertion & both parties were sullen & discontented. The negro fond of change & interpreting freedom to mean absence of labour could not comprehend his obligation to perform his contract—& violated it whenever he saw fit: at his convenience. While the master accustomed to arbitrary rule, would some times forget that according to the new military law whipping could no longer be tolerated. Some cases of violence were brought before Col H by the negroes— but more appeals were made by their former masters to the court that his negroes would not work." McCarter MS. Diary, II, 93.

tion of money, or the meaning of terms like government, morality, suffrage, or even free labor. With the ways of the world beyond their own plantation many of them had had no experience. "The truth is," McCulloch reminded Sumner, "the great mass of [them] are, at the present time, unconscious of what self-ownership means. They are indolent, sensual, and to the last degree, ignorant, and there is, it seems to me, an absolute necessity that they should be educated before becoming voters." [53]

Negro naïveté was pitiable. Freedom was a new toy; what it meant they did not know. But they left homes, families, and work to flock to the cities to enjoy it.[54] In the congested, impoverished towns of the South this concentration of negroes brought crime, immorality, and mortality astounding in extent. These uncontrolled masses of moneyless, foodless, homeless, moraless negroes were indeed a menace. A New Jersey minister who had lived in the South wrote, "New England would sooner reach the judgment of common sense touching re-construction, if 100,000 colored troops could be a few months quartered in the principal towns of Maine, Massachusetts, and Vermont; or if 500,000 of the helpless

[53] Aug. 15, 1865, McCulloch MSS., II. Schofield wrote Grant: "They can neither read nor write; they have no knowledge whatever of law or government; they do not even know the meaning of the freedom that has been given them." J. F. Rhodes, *op. cit.*, V, 525.

[54] McCarter tells us: "In many cases the slaves deserted their homes without a word—leaving the household drudgery to be performed by delicate ladies—who had never cooked a meal or washed a garment & this two [*sic*] without taking leave of their former owners who had perhaps been uniformly kind to them. In a great many cases this conduct was a great relief to the owner whose property having been destroyed by the war, & the fire—he no longer had the means of providing them food— In many of the families of the more wealthy citizens of Columbia you might count 30 or 40 Servants whose only employment was in waiting on their owners & on each other. To be rid of the necessity of providing daily bread for all these surplus mouths was certainly a blessing—& yet the parting was disagreeable even painful to both parties." McCarter MS. Diary, II, 95-98.

old blacks of the South could be indiscriminately scattered through those six New England states." [55]

Southerners faced the situation with despair. The negro's labor they had to have. They expressed willingness to experiment with free labor. But they were firmly convinced "that the negro was worthless except under the lash." "The poor, shiftless creatures will never be able to support themselves in freedom," Southerners told Reid.[56] "The Northern People do not understand managing 'Sambo,'" wrote a Memphis owner of slaves worth $100,000, to explain why the Freedmen's Bureau was doing "Sambo" no lasting good.[57]

Northern protagonists of the negro, who would have been aghast at the suggestion that Northern property ought to have been divided with their own laborers, insisted that the negroes should be given part of the old plantations.

"Forty acres and a mule" by Christmas became the Northern-bred expectation of the negro who could not comprehend that he would not be cared for in freedom as in slavery.[58] "There is no doubt," wrote the Radical Governor of Texas, "but that many of them, really believed, that about Christmas, they would be furnished with homes, and whatever else they might need. This was calculated to disincline them to

[55] M. R. Watkinson (a loser by rebel confiscation acts) to A. Johnson, Aug. 31, 1866, Johnson MSS., LXXV.

[56] W. Reid, *After the War*, 33.

[57] C. D. McLean to A. Johnson, June 29, 1865, Johnson MSS., LXIX.

[58] McCarter relates, "In many cases the Servant . . . seemed to think he had an interest in all his former masters property, that he could live in his house, eat his food—cook with his fuel & work with his tools—& yet feel no obligation to work for his former owner—as compensation. In one case, a gentleman was discussing with his Servant the means of his making a living, when the man with a most pardonable innocence exclaimed—'Why master you know, I can haul wood to town & sell it'—'But' said the master 'where are you going to get wood?' 'Take it from our place'; but it was no longer *our* place in the eyes of the master; & the poor fellow was made to comprehend that the interests of master & servant were no longer identical—The [wood] belonged to the master & he told his man to touch it at his peril." McCarter MS. Diary, II, 95-98.

hire, to labor for fair wages, and I had reason to fear that midwinter, would find them without homes or food, and that they would be compelled to go to stealing, to preserve life."[59] Neither Howell Cobb [60] nor his son's overseer [61] could make the negro work. Comstock reported from New Orleans, "I saw very few [negroes] as I came down the river, especially on the coast, and was told by the planters that they could not be depended on and could not even be got to come to the plantations." [62] General Beckwith said New Orleans swarmed with negroes who would "work for a day & then stop." He thought the army should run the Freedmen's Bureau and "make negroes work." [63] Reid found most of them earning nothing at all, but gaining "a precarious support by picking up occasional jobs, and by a pretty general system of pilfering." [64] Yet the South was paralyzed for want of labor.

The land-distribution phantasy, slavery-bred irresponsibility, and inability to comprehend the meaning of free labor, combined to make the negro undependable for steady employment, even when he worked at all. As soon as he had a pocketful of small change, he departed at the busiest season to " 'joy his freedom" until hunger forced him back to labor.

[59] Gov. Hamilton to A. Johnson, Nov. 27, 1865, Johnson MSS., LXXXI. Negro credulity is illustrated by the letter of a Mississippi friend of General Sherman. "The freedmen are ineradicably filled with the idea that the government is to divide the land among them about Christmas, and so will not make engagements to work beyond that time. Agents of the Freedmen's Bureau address them to disabuse them, but they will listen and then say, 'This ain't no yankee. He is a Southern man in disguise.' General Howard addressed them. The troops being out they knew this was genuine, but soon they had a story that he had been bribed." Dec. 2, 1865, W. T. Sherman MSS., XVII. In Virginia and North Carolina Comstock found the negroes unwilling to make contracts for this same reason. MS. Diary, Nov. 29, 1865.

[60] H. Cobb to his wife, December, 1866, Am. Hist. Assoc., *Annual Report* (1911), II, 684.

[61] J. D. Collins to J. A. Cobb, July 31, 1865, *ibid.*, 665.

[62] C. B. Comstock to Rawlins, Feb. 3, 1866, Johnson MSS., LXXXVI.

[63] C. B. Comstock MS. Diary, Feb. 2, 1866.

[64] W. Reid, *op. cit.*, 334-335.

Or for some whimsical reason he packed up on a moment's notice, broke his contract, and changed to a new employer, often losing by the shift. Even Reid admitted the blacks' inability to care for themselves. "Negroes need to be taught," he said, "just as slaves of any race or color would need to be taught—that liberty means, not idleness, but merely work for themselves instead of work for others; and that, in any event, it means always work. To teach them this, do not gather them in colonies at military posts, and feed them on Government rations; but throw them in the water and have them learn to swim by finding the necessity of swimming. . . . It must be the first care of the authorities to diminish the charity, and leave the negroes, just as it would leave the white men—to take care of themselves." [65]

On the whole Southerners were trying to find a *modus vivendi* tolerable to both blacks and whites.[66] "We are willing and desirous to retain our negro population, to treat them kindly, employ them at fair wages, and secure them amply in life, liberty and property," declared Governor Bramlette of Kentucky; "but we are not willing to take with them a 'Freedman's Bureau' which places a Northern fanatic as Overseer over white & black, and over the Government and Civil Authorities of the State." [67] Freedmen's Bureau officers

[65] *Ibid.*, 18.

[66] "Let neither master nor servant be judged harshly," urged McCarter. "Each had been placed in trying circumstances: From being the acknowledged superior & arbiter of negroes the owner was reduced by a stroke of the pen to a political equality with his former slave. The slave as suddenly was elevated in theory to a level with his former master. And there were found plenty of white men who preached to them the honied words of 'liberty—equality—fraternity.' These theorists told them it was degrading to wait on their former owners. That they must on all occasions assert 'the dignity of their new position,' & resent with indignation any assumption of authority by their former masters. As may be expected such a condition of things led to collisions between the races." McCarter MS. Diary, II, 95-98.

[67] Governor Bramlette to A. Johnson, Feb. 12, 1866, Johnson MSS., LXXXVI.

themselves reported that intelligent Southerners were gradually of their own accord giving the negro civil rights; that outrages upon negroes were the exception, not the rule, and often exaggerated or not true; that the negroes' own ignorance was usually responsible when they failed to get justice in the courts; that in business they were fairly treated; [68] that "all people of good character [were] inclined to do them justice"; and that those who do "wish to defraud them are persons who have, for years, been regarded as *tricky* in their relations with neighbors of their own color." [69] Major General Wood of the Bureau in Mississippi reported prompt punishment of offenders against negroes in every case of outrage where he had laid the case before the state authorities. "The policy," he explained, "of leaving all infractions of the public peace and safety to the civil authorities, has given increased confidence." [70] Browning, later a cabinet officer, expressed the Conservative point of view when he said, "One great industrial and social system cannot be disrupted and overthrown and another substituted for it in a day. Time and patience are necessary to accomplish the work. The South is the congenial climate of the colored people. They need employment and the planters need labor. Their interests are interwoven. They will both soon understand this, and be brought together upon terms that are fair and just." [71]

Vicious slave-holders there were who purposed to retain the old system under new names. The Black Codes were partly the work of these men, but they were primarily honest attempts to eliminate lawlessness and save the economic

---

[68] General Tillson and Brig. Gen. Lewis, *New York Herald*, Sept. 4, Oct. 13, 1866.

[69] J. W. Sharp to T. Stevens, Feb. 9, 1866, Stevens MSS., VI.

[70] Report published in the *New York Herald*, Oct. 25, 1866.

[71] O. H. Browning to J. C. Cox of Quincy, Ill., April 21, 1866, *Speeches of Hon. Edgar Cowan . . . Jas. R. Doolittle . . . Letter of Hon. O. H. Browning of Illinois . . . (National Union Club Documents)*, 22.

situation by forcing the negro to work. Gradually as crime decreased and the labor situation improved, fair-minded whites began to lessen the severity of the Codes. In Mississippi where the Code remained harshest, planters soon found it difficult to get negroes to come into their state to work. Besides, the North had apprentice and vagrancy laws, too. Illinois had apprentice laws for whites that read strangely like the much abused Black Codes.[72] The Illinois vagrancy law for whites provided that a man able to support himself but not doing so and found loitering, might be sold to the highest bidder for four months' service.[73] In view of the perplexity of the problem, the Black Codes seemed to many to be explicable, justifiable.[74] By March, 1866, most Southern states had statutes granting the negroes the right to hold and inherit property, to sue and be sued, to make and enforce contracts, and to bear witness in all cases where one or both parties were black.

Perhaps the Southerners would gradually have evolved a wise system, just to whites and blacks alike; many were honestly experimenting. Perhaps the vicious element would have established a new peonage; some stubborn ex-masters were attempting it. Which type of Southern employer would succeed, no one in 1866 could tell. Few cared to know. Extreme Radicals wanted negro suffrage; outrages against the

---

[72] *Revised Statutes of the State of Illinois* (1845), VI.

[73] *Ibid.,* XXX, sec. 138.

[74] Lincoln had foreseen the necessity of "Black Codes," and had promised in advance not to interfere with them as long as they recognized permanent freedom and provided for education of the negroes. J. D. Richardson, *Messages and Papers of the Presidents,* VI, 417. Dunning pronounced this legislation "a conscientious and straightforward attempt to bring some sort of order out of the social and economic chaos . . . faithful on the whole to the actual conditions with which it had to deal." "The greatest fault of the Southern law-makers," he says, "was, not that their procedure was unwise *per se,* but that . . . they failed adequately to consider and be guided by the prejudices of their conquerors." Wm. A. Dunning, *Reconstruction, Political and Economic,* 57-59.

negroes, and an exaggeration of cruel codes would reconcile Northerners to it. The Democrats wished the South restored; fair treatment of the negro would make it possible. Each side gathered exceptional cases that served its purpose. Ultimately the Radicals brought a reluctant country to negro suffrage.

In the election, however, negro suffrage and social equality, while preached by extremist leaders, were not officially sanctioned by the Radical Party. In the Northwest they were definitely disclaimed. Radicals who favored negro suffrage could afford to wait as long as the South was not readmitted; those who opposed it, could be reassured by the claim that the Fourteenth Amendment was the election platform. Consequently, negro suffrage remained a vague issue, ominously present, but shunned. No one clearly knew whether in supporting the Radical ticket he was voting for or against it; many firmly believed they were not sanctioning it. But the extremists could by pointing back to their speeches, claim that the election had endorsed negro suffrage.

Chapter VIII

THE FOURTEENTH AMENDMENT

OFFICIAL Republican historians and the Rhodes school of reputable historians tell us that the great issue of the 1866 campaign was a choice between Johnson's policy and the Fourteenth Amendment, that had Johnson and the South accepted the few "reasonable guarantees" of the Amendment, the seceded states would have been readmitted without the years of hardship under negro and army domination.[1] This simple analysis served Radical campaign purposes, but it ignores the facts. To understand the true rôle of the Amendment one must know its origin.[2]

For months the Joint Committee of Fifteen postponed formulating definite terms of readmission, while it "educated" people and gathered evidence. As early as January plans were discussed in committee, but none was presented to Congress until April 30. Upon terms of admission, as upon the tractability of the South, opinion varied hopelessly; no two exactly agreed. Notable among the proposals were Stewart's and Owen's. Stewart suggested immediate restoration, national protection of civil rights, universal suffrage,

[1] See, e.g., the *Life and Services of Gen. U. S. Grant,* prepared by the National Republican Committee.

[2] An able account of the work of the Committee of Fifteen and of the many proposals made in it, is presented in Benjamin B. Kendrick's study, *The Journal of the Joint Committee of Fifteen on Reconstruction.*

and universal amnesty.[3] Robert Dale Owen's plan embodied
repudiation of the rebel debt, civil rights, a diminution
of Southern representation until 1876 if negroes were deprived of the ballot and thereafter universal suffrage, immediate restoration, and universal amnesty except for the
disqualification for office of military and naval officers, cabinet members, and Congressmen who resigned to enter the
Confederate service. Both plans were rejected, partly because Republican leaders opposed, or favoring feared the
injection of negro suffrage into the campaign; partly because Radicals opposed any plan that, by granting amnesty
and restoration, endangered Radical control of the South.[4]

When finally the Committee's proposals appeared, there
were six: four really distinct amendments presented as one,
and two bills.[5] The first section forbade a state to "make or
enforce any law which shall abridge the privileges and im-
munities of citizens of the United States," [6] or to "deprive
any person of life, liberty, or property, without due process
of law," or to "deny to any person within its jurisdiction the
equal protection of the laws." The second section settled the
dispute over Southern representation by a compromise which
provided that "Representatives shall be apportioned among
the several States . . . according to their respective numbers, counting the whole number of persons excluding Indians not taxed," but that whenever "the elective franchise"
is denied to any of the "male citizens" who are twenty-one
years of age, "except for participation in rebellion or other
crime, the basis of representation shall be reduced" in the

[3] *Cong. Globe,* 39 Cong., 1 Sess., 1906.
[4] *Journal of the Committee of Fifteen,* 83 ff., 295 ff., and Robert Dale
Owen, "Political Results from the Varioloid," *Atlantic Monthly,* XXXV
(1875), 660.
[5] *Cong. Globe,* 39 Cong., 1 Sess., 2265, 2286.
[6] The definition of citizenship was added later. *Ibid.,* 2897.

proportion which the number of such male citizens shall bear to the whole number of male citizens twenty-one years of age in the state. The third section punished the South by excluding "from the right to vote for Representatives in Congress and for electors for President and Vice-President" until July 4, 1870, "all persons who voluntarily adhered to the late insurrection, giving it aid and comfort." The fourth section repudiated claims for compensation for slaves, and for debts "incurred in aid of insurrection or of war against the United States." [7] These four distinct proposals the Committee lumped into one amendment, bound together by a fifth clause empowering Congress to enact enforcing legislation.

The first bill provided for the restoration of a state to the Union as soon as the Amendment had become a part of the Constitution of the United States, provided the state in question had ratified the Amendment and incorporated its provisions into the state laws and constitution. In the second, certain high officials and army officers of the Confederate government and certain former officials of the United States who betrayed their posts by giving aid to the rebellion, were declared ineligible for federal office.

When the composite amendment reached the more moderate Senate after passage in the House, the punitive section proved a stumbling block. Opposed to its harshness were enough Republicans of milder principles to endanger all four articles. Consequently, to please a group of moderate Republicans, a new provision was substituted, still punitive but supposedly more reasonable in that it affected a smaller class than did the original third section, though a much larger class than did the original disqualifying bill. The new section permanently excluded from office all who had held

[7] The guarantee of the federal debt was added later. *Ibid.*, 2941.

any office, civil or military, federal or state, however petty, which required an oath of allegiance to the United States, and who had subsequently given aid or comfort to the rebellion. With this change incorporated the Amendment passed the Senate, and the House under protest accepted the modification.[8]

*   *   *   *

To understand the later campaign the four parts of the Amendment must be considered separately. The last one was generally acceptable to Conservatives and Radicals alike. Among Johnson's own three requirements of the Southern States, had been repudiation of debts incurred in the rebellion. The South repudiated her debt and shouldered part of the North's—not eagerly of course, but unquestioningly as a natural result of defeat. Thought of repudiating Northern obligations was entertained only in the ingenious campaign manufactories of the Radicals, and in the brains of fanatic Copperheads and a few irreconcilable Southerners. It would have been impossible anyway since, unlike a political question or an economic one like the tariff, a Southern attempt to escape payment would have rallied Conservatives and Democrats as well as Radicals to the defense of justice, national honor, and their pocketbooks. The debt amendment raised no question of principle, only doubt whether the constitutional action was necessary. To reassure timid minds or to secure a guarantee of recognition of the Southern representatives, Johnson and the South would have accepted it.

To the second section more objection was raised. Every one felt the need of readjustment so that the abolition of slavery would not, through the automatic extinction of the three-fifths rule, merely increase per capita representation of the South. This would be patently unfair to the North, and yet

[8] *Ibid.,* 2770, 2869, 2897-2902, 2914-2921, 2938-2941, 3144-3149.

no remedy was easily determinable. Extreme Radicals would have met the problem by giving the negro the ballot, and controlling his vote, thereby removing the objection to counting him for representation. But this could only be safely done by constitutional amendment, and many Northerners, Radicals and Conservatives alike, considered this remedy as bad as over-representation of Southerners. Some Radicals would have favored negro suffrage for the South alone, but objected to an amendment because that would also apply to the North. Some would have approved of qualified negro suffrage by state action, but opposed national meddling in the state's sphere. A proposal palatable to many Northerners was to base representation on voters, and then let the states determine who those voters should be.

The second section of the Amendment was a compromise. It provided representation according to numbers, but specified that if any group, such as negroes, were denied the vote in any state, the representation of that state should be cut in proportion to the number thus disfranchised. In practice it would cut Southern representation to a white basis, and then offer increased power in Congress as an inducement for states to grant negro suffrage. This satisfied those who merely wished to cut down Southern representation, and it left the franchise for the states to determine. But many Conservatives opposed making so vital a change while several states had no voice in the matter. Others objected because it looked like a first step toward negro suffrage in the South. Extreme Radicals were dissatisfied because they wanted to impose full negro suffrage.

In January Johnson had proposed an amendment basing representation upon voters, and taxation upon wealth,[9] and

---

[9] *National Intelligencer,* Jan. 29, 1866. Also May 28, 1866, Johnson MSS., XCV.

at one time this plan had been advocated by Moderates now become Radicals. Johnson also favored state laws extending the suffrage to negroes of property and education, and to those who had served in the army. He and other Conservatives objected to votes for ignorant negroes before they could be qualified to use them intelligently. He considered national action unwise in any case. But reduction of Southern representation if the negro was not to vote, was popular; the Amendment really left the suffrage question to the states. The Conservatives might therefore have accepted this section, too, as the price of readmission of the Southern States.

With the principle of the first section of the Amendment, Johnson himself, and many, though not all, of the Conservatives agreed. In Northern states the negro was usually granted the civil rights that the Amendment sought to guarantee. In Southern states he was gradually being accorded most of them,[10] as the Black Codes were relaxed and modified. It was not, then, a desire to deny the negro civil rights that aroused opposition to this clause, but objection to protecting those rights by federal action. Conservatives felt that justice to the negro would be surer and more permanent if it came from the states themselves than if it were imposed by federal legislation or amendment. Transferring the protection of personal rights from the states to the federal government involved a fundamental change of our constitutional system that many were not prepared to make.[11] Still, with more difficulty, Conservatives might have agreed even to this, if doing so would have insured the restoration of the excluded states.

The third provision was the critical one. It looks innocent

[10] Edward McPherson, *Political Manual* (1866), 29-44.
[11] See *infra,* chap. IX.

when described as merely preventing the leaders of rebellion
from returning to power, or debarring from office rebels who
by violating their oaths of office under the United States had
rendered themselves perjurers and betrayers of trust as well
as traitors.[12] Actually, this clause of the Amendment made
ineligible for office nearly the whole class of men to whom
the South had always looked for leadership.

Fully to comprehend what it meant to Southerners one
must forget for the nonce that a reversal of the situation was
impossible because the North had won and because the
Northern was a "righteous cause," and must then consider
how Northerners would have reacted to a demand that they
repudiate, never to trust again, Lincoln, Grant, Sumner,
Stevens, and even moderate men like Senators Doolittle and
Reverdy Johnson, even all minor state and federal officers of
all nuances of opinion, except the Copperheads who had in
every way blocked the War. If a Northerner can imagine
this, he may know what the South faced emotionally. Nor
does this tell the whole story, for in the South the leader-
producing class was not, as in the North, the whole community, but a small part thereof. In Southern society the
planters had dominated, had held the offices, and had constituted what might be called a ruling class. The poor white
element was scarcely better fitted to rule, and but little more
productive of leaders, than were the freed negroes. In the
non-slave-holding up-country communities was a more virile
stock, but even there the men of natural ability were either
included in the prohibition, or else by supporting the Union
cause had lost the confidence of Southerners. To embrace in
the debarment, as the Amendment did, all who had held an
office however insignificant, even that of constable or justice

12 Thus Senator Chandler explained it. *New York Herald,* Oct. 30, 1866.

of the peace, was to leave the South leaderless. This might have served the Radical purpose by reducing the South to impotence, by filling its offices, both state and federal, with men of no ability, influence, or power, men in whom the South had no faith, men who could never figure in national affairs. But to the South this clause made the Amendment unthinkable. Southerners might readily have agreed to the debt clause, they might have accepted the citizenship section and the cut in representation, and they might have granted a qualified negro suffrage. But to agree to disbar from office all the men whom they trusted as leaders was impossible. The thought made them desperate.[13]

Northern Conservatives realized what this punitive clause meant to the South. In complaining against the test oath McCulloch declared: "I am well satisfied that it will be difficult, if not impossible to find competent men at the South to fill the revenue offices, who can qualify under the statute. . . . In the progress of the rebellion very few persons of character and intelligence in most of these States failed, in some way or other, to participate in the hostilities, or to connect themselves with the insurgent government."[14] For this same reason he opposed the Amendment, as did General Sherman who wrote, "The poor whites and negroes of the South have not the intelligence to fill the offices of governors, clerks, judges, etc., and for some time the machinery of State Govts must be controlled by the same class of whites as went

[13] In its ably written "Address to the Soldiers and Sailors of the Union," the Cleveland Convention pointed out that this one clause necessarily and justly killed the whole Amendment. *Ibid.*, Sept. 17 and 19, 1866.

[14] He added, "It is true that there are still some applicants for office in Southern states who present what they call 'a clean record for loyalty,' but, with rare exceptions, they are persons who would have been able to present an equally fair record for place under the confederate government if the rebellion had been a success, or persons lacking the qualifications which are needed in revenue positions." H. McCulloch to Senate and House of Representatives, March 19, 1866, McCulloch MSS., II.

into the Rebellion against us." [15] In time, leaders might grow up out of the lower strata of society, as Johnson had before the War, or as "Pitchfork" Tillman, and Vardaman rose in the 'Nineties, or Heflin and McKellar in our own day, from a "shirt-sleeves democracy." But that was a gradual, a then unforeseen, development.

Personal reasons would have led some men in Johnson's position to favor a measure which meant ruin for the Southern leaders who had fought him politically and ostracized him socially. But as a Southerner Johnson knew the calamity that incapacitation of all leaders of opinion would wreak. Furthermore, he and many Northerners, even some Radicals, realized that to attain a true peace the surest method was to allow the natural leaders of opinion to work out a reasonable solution of their problems and convert the people to it, that, properly handled, these leaders could be useful to the North. Conservatives might have accepted the other three principles of the Amendment, but to them this punitive clause was intolerable. Some thoughtful Radicals agreed with them in opposition to it.[16]

Radical leaders must have comprehended the significance of the clause. Conservatives charged them with putting it in as a joker to insure the rejection of the Amendment by the South,[17] and thereby make it possible to force more advanced measures upon the country. Hoffman, the Democratic candidate for the New York governorship, declared to the people of Elmira: "This radical Congress knew as well as you know

[15] W. T. Sherman to J. Sherman, Aug. 18, 1865, W. T. Sherman MSS., XVII.

[16] The *Nation* (II [April 19, 1866], 486) urged full negro suffrage and negro rights, but opposed the exclusion of either a small or a large group of white leaders from office.

[17] E.g., Raymond thought it "inserted for the express purpose of preventing the adoption . . . of any of the amendments." *Cong. Globe,* 39 Cong., 1 Sess., 2503.

that there is no people on the face of the earth who would ever consent to a constitutional amendment which would proscribe their own brothers, fathers and friends—the men with whom they had labored and suffered." [18] The Radicals frankly did not like the Amendment; it was too moderate. Yet they dared not at the time propose a more extreme measure.

They did also refuse to allow the four proposals to be considered separately, but insisted on lumping them into one to be taken or rejected as a whole,[19] presumably because part of the four amendments would have been accepted and part rejected, if considered independently. In the campaign they stressed the three parts to which alone the South and the Conservatives might have agreed, and ignored or minimized the significance of the punitive section which they brushed aside as merely "the exclusion from office of a few of those who had been most prominent in rebellion." [20] Then they abused the Conservatives, Johnson, and the South for opposing repudiation of the rebel indebtedness and guarantee of the federal debt; for denying the negro civil rights; and for demanding over-representation for Southern whites—unjust though these accusations were. Including the unacceptable punitive clause gave the Radicals the much sought chance to place the Conservatives before the people in the false light of opposing *all* the principles of the Amendment. And they played this card well. Thus in his key-note speech, Stevens declared that the Amendment "changes the base of representation in Congress, so that the vote of a white man in the North will be equal to the vote of a white man in the South;

[18] *New York Herald,* Sept. 29, 1866.
[19] *Cong. Globe,* 39 Cong., 1 Sess., 2463 ff., 2991, 3040.
[20] Republican National Committee, *Life and Services of Gen. U. S. Grant,* 129.

now a white man's vote in the rebel States counts nearly as much as two white men's votes in the free States. This amendment meets with the violent opposition of the President." [21] This was good campaign talk; but the men who made such assertions knew them to be untrue.

Conservatives felt that the Amendment was a Radical step toward more extreme ends. The South joined them in refusing to believe that the Radicals were sincere, or that they would restore the South if it did ratify. Stevens and Sumner openly urged negro suffrage; both admitted to Owen in 1866 that it was simply lack of a majority that kept them from establishing it then.[22] The bill guaranteeing restoration to the South in return for ratification, after repeated postponement, was finally tabled and allowed to die in both Houses. In the Senate Sumner attempted to amend it on May 29, by making negro suffrage an additional prerequisite of restoration.[23] Stevens, Kelley, and other Radicals tried the same thing in the House.[24] Stevens, in fact, proposed a substitute bill that embodied most of the ideas of the later reconstruction acts save actual military rule.[25] After being spasmodically debated until June 20,[26] and called up once more July 20, the guarantee bill was finally tabled in the House, too.[27] The Radicals who opposed it, did so on the ground that the South must not be readmitted until negro suffrage had given the "Union Party" assured control of the coun-

21 Sept. 4, 1866, Stevens MSS., VIII. See also the misrepresentation in the restatement of this campaign cry by the Republican National Committee in *op. cit.*, 129.

22 *Atlantic Monthly*, XXXV (1875), 663, 665.

23 *Cong. Globe*, 39 Cong., 1 Sess., 2869.

24 June 11, 1866, *ibid.*, 3090.

25 The *Nation*, II (June 5, 1866), 712. On July 25 Stevens again brought up his substitute bill, but the House, afraid of it before elections, tabled it. *Cong. Globe*, 39 Cong., 1 Sess., 4157.

26 *Ibid.*, 3303.

27 *Ibid.*, 3981.

try.[28] Campaign expediency led them to table it instead of voting against it. So little thought had the Radicals of passing the guarantee measure that three months after its presentation, and many weeks after the passage of the Amendment, it had not even been printed, and Le Blond could complain that no one had had a chance to consider it.[29]

The Radical *Independent* came out boldly for negro suffrage, denouncing the National Committee for not having the courage to take its stand upon that ground. "We know personally," it said, "every prominent member of Congress, and we know that the leaders do not mean to admit the unadmitted States on the mere adoption of the amendment. Moreover, we know personally the leading radicals . . . outside of Congress, and we know that they have no intention of making the amendment the final measure of admission." [30] At the Radical Soldiers' Convention at Pittsburgh, Butler asserted that after the Amendment was ratified, further steps might be required.[31] Perhaps a confidential letter of White of the *Chicago Tribune* to Trumbull best shows how the Radicals regarded the Amendment. "The Senate Reconstruction scheme," said White, "is an improvement on the original report, & regarded as a politicians' dodge rather than the work of statesmen, it has considerable merit. I have no doubt we can carry Illinois with it, though you must not be disappointed if you find Republicans rather lukewarm throughout the campaign." [32] Immediately after the introduction of the Amendment to Congress, Senator Dixon pointedly remarked, "It is hardly worth while to discuss the

28 *Ibid.,* May, June, and July. See also B. B. Kendrick, *op. cit.,* chap. VII.
29 *Cong. Globe,* 39 Cong., 1 Sess., 3981.
30 Reprinted in the *New York Herald,* Oct. 2, 1866.
31 *Ibid.,* Sept. 27, 1866.
32 May 31, 1866, Trumbull MSS., LXVI.

merits of the measures which to be valid must be accepted by communities which are sure to reject them." But as a test he did offer a substitute resolution, which read, "That the interests of peace and the interests of the Union require the admission of every State to its share in public legislation whenever it presents itself, not only in an attitude of loyalty and harmony, but in the persons of representatives whose loyalty cannot be questioned under any constitutional or legal test." [33] This was ignored, and in spite of it the Radicals kept on insisting that he and Johnson demanded the relinquishment of the government into traitors' hands.

*　　*　　*　　*

In states whose Radicalism was not of the extreme variety, doubt of the finality of the Amendment became a danger. Moderate Radicals of Indiana, Illinois, Ohio, New York, and Connecticut urged the adoption of the guarantee bill, as necessary to their success in the fall elections; unless Congress pledged its word to admit the South upon a definite plan, they argued, many voters would swing to the definite Johnson proposal. Medill, sanguine in May, was worried in July and wrote Trumbull and Washburne in despair. "After sitting three-quarters of a year," he cried, "it will not do to adjourn without agreeing on some plan. Don't you see the fix it leaves us in? We can't stand on nothing. If Congress can provide no plan the people will accept Johnson's. The amendment amounts to nothing as a plan unless you pass an enabling act declaring that upon its ratification the outside states may come in. The mass of our party actually suppose that such is the fact now,—that the amendment does constitute the congressional terms of admission, and they are cordially supporting it with that understanding. But what will

[33] May 2, 1866, *Cong. Globe,* 39 Cong., 1 Sess., 2332.

they say a few days or weeks hence when they find themselves
fooled and learn to their chagrin and astonishment that after
all, Congress has proposed no terms of admission to the
South, and that the amendment means nothing; that its ratification by a Southern State confers on it no benefit and
opens not the door for its admission? This blunder must be
cured or the cops will turn our flank and rear and completely
rout us at the polls." [34] In the admission of Tennessee the
Radicals found a means, without binding themselves to anything, of making the people believe that the Amendment was
an offer of terms of admission. Medill, like the others, seized
eagerly upon this chance.[35] Then through the campaign,
though they knew better, many "honest" Radicals persuaded
the people that the Congressional plan contained a pledge of
admission. Had not Tennessee been admitted as soon as she
ratified? If they had failed to convince the people on this
point, they would have lost the election.

Many Moderates voted the Radical ticket because they
approved the comparatively moderate terms of the Amendment and accepted Radical assurances that the South would
be readmitted upon ratification. Other Moderates, who did
not really approve, supported the Radicals because the
South appeared stubborn in its refusal to agree to "reasonable" terms. Others acquiesced in the Fourteenth Amendment and the Radical ticket because they saw in them a
chance to forestall more extreme measures which they dis-
approved. Thousands of voters, then, supported the Radicals because they believed the Amendment to be the Radical

[34] July 17, 1866, Trumbull MSS., LXVIII; July 17, 1866, Washburne
MSS., LII.
[35] On hearing of Tennessee's ratification, he and Horace White wired,
"We think that Tennessee ought to be admitted instantly. Show this to
Judge Trumbull and such members as you choose." H. White and J. Medill
to S. Colfax, July 20, 1866, Trumbull MSS., LXVIII.

terms of readmission of the South. Radicals were glad to encourage this belief.

But the Stevens and Sumner class of Radicals never admitted the finality of the Amendment. While they loudly proclaimed that the Fourteenth Amendment was the issue, they killed the promissory bill and in the campaign refused to commit themselves to readmitting Southern states upon their acceptance of the Amendment.[36] Then as soon as they had won the election, supposedly upon the terms expressed in the Amendment, they began to ignore the Amendment completely. All thought of readmission was abandoned and preparations for military rule of the South began.

The election, then, really decided nothing in regard to the Amendment. Many who cast Radical votes believed they were presenting final terms to the South. Others regarded the Amendment as just another milepost on the road to negro suffrage, subjugation of the South, and the final enthronement of the Northeast in power. Many neither knew nor cared whether the Fourteenth Amendment was wise or bad, final or temporary, for thousands of people were decided by other issues. The position of the Amendment was vague at best. Of what the nation thought of the Amendment *per se*, the election revealed nothing.

[36] After careful studies of the period Kendrick (*op. cit.,* chap. VII) and David M. Dewitt (*The Impeachment and Trial of Andrew Johnson,* 109-110) agree that the Radicals never had any intention that the Amendment should be ratified, nor if it had been, that the South should be readmitted; they both declare the Amendment merely a Radical election trick. The *New York Herald* maintained this thesis until after the September elections.

Chapter IX

PARLIAMENTARY CENTRALIZATION OR FEDERAL CHECKS AND BALANCES?

O UT of a maze of constitutional argument that was mere embroidery for more practical desires, there stands one fundamental constitutional issue that in importance outranks the whole reconstruction question. The years following the Civil War witnessed a Radical attempt, and failure, to remodel the very form of our government into a parliamentary system. Had this plan of the Radicals succeeded, it would share with reconstruction the attention of historians of the later 'Sixties. As it is, the importance of the question in 1866 has been almost forgotten. The Radical movement was twofold; it sought to concentrate power in the national government, substituting high centralization for our existing constitutional system; and it then hoped to locate that centralized authority in an omnipotent Congress to which executive and courts should be subordinate. To argue the respective merits of parliamentary government and a government by checks and balances, of a centralized state and a federated nation, is beside the point. But it is of great importance to recognize that this conflict of constitutional systems developed in 1866.

Ever since Lincoln's inauguration, extremists had chafed

under the restraint of a President who would not move as
rapidly as the left wing of his party. They had wanted to
rush into the War in 1861, and he had held them back; they
had urged immediate emancipation, and he had checked their
enthusiasm until the Emancipation Proclamation could be
safely issued; they had then wanted to extend the process to
all the states, and he had refused until it could be done by
the slow method of constitutional amendment. They had
urged harshness in the treatment of rebels, and he had
taught forbearance; they had advocated government by military power in the reclaimed sections of the South, and he had
set about restoring normal conditions as speedily as possible.
Then came Johnson, whom the restless Radicals thought they
could carry with them to extremes, or brush aside.

In 1866 the Radical managers controlled the votes, if not
the opinions, of an overwhelming majority in Congress; the
South lay prostrate in their grasp. Chief Justice Chase expressed a general Radical conviction when he announced
"that the war had changed the government, and that the
powers of the government were essentially different from
what they were before the war." [1] Only two obstacles blocked
their path to complete power in the country—the President
and possibly the Supreme Court. Event after event height-
ened the Radical exasperation. If only Johnson could have
been removed or rendered powerless, Congress would have
been as omnipotent as the English Parliament. More than
mere verbiage lay back of Stevens's outburst that had Johnson's suggestion of an amendment been made centuries ago
"to Parliament by a British King, it would have cost him

[1] When told this by Chase, Bartley thought it was "one of the peculiarities
of the Chief Justice." "I did not realize," he said, "that any serious attempt would be made to carry into practical operation such an idea untill
I fully understood the effect of the position taken by Congress." T. W.
Bartley to W. T. Sherman, Oct. 27, 1866, W. T. Sherman MSS., XX.

his head." [2] Stevens had the Parliament as well as the King in mind in the parallel. With the weak-spirited Foster in Johnson's place,[3] Congress would have been indeed supreme, and the president would have become not an English prime minister but an English king, a mere figure-head for an omnipotent legislature.

All through the campaign of 1866, a few of the most extreme Radicals talked of impeachment, but only a few; most of them realized that public opinion was not ready for it. Therefore they bided their time. They knew that if the elections gave them a large majority, many things would be possible whose serious advocacy would injure them in the campaign. Their grievance against Johnson was that he made the executive a check on the dominant party in Congress when complete power was almost in their grasp. According to Sumner's theory, Congress had "plenary powers, the Executive none, on reestablishing the Union." [4] Loring believed legislatures were and always had been the important part of government—"the great creative power, and the great popular defender." [5] Stevens epitomized the doctrine when he said, "Congress is the sovereign power, because the people speak through them; and Andrew Johnson must learn that he is your servant and that as Congress shall order he must obey. There is no escape from it. God forbid that he should have one tittle of power except what he derives through Congress and the constitution. This is the whole question." [6]

[2] Jan. 31, 1866, *Cong. Globe,* 39 Cong., 1 Sess., 536.

[3] As president pro tem. of the Senate, Foster would have succeeded to the presidency if Johnson had been removed.

[4] Welles MS. Diary, Dec. 8, 1865—(II, 393).

[5] *Speech of Hon. George B. Loring upon the Resolutions on the State of the Union Delivered in the Massachusetts House of Representatives, March 12, 1866,* 11.

[6] Speech at Lancaster, *New York Herald,* Sept. 29, 1866.

Johnson, on the other hand, regarded himself as the protector of the people against a usurping Congress. He compared himself to the old Roman tribune of the people who stood at the door of the Senate, "so that, when that body ventured on oppressive acts, he was clothed with power to say '*Veto*,' 'I forbid.'" "Your President," he declared, "is now the Tribune of the people, and, thank God, I am, and I intend to assert the power which the people have placed in me." "Tyranny and despotism," he believed with Jefferson, "can be exercised by many more rigorously, more vigorously, and more severely than by one." [7] Johnson felt it his high duty to protect the checks and balances of the Constitution against revolutionary changes, the people against the tyranny of a partisan omnipotence in Congress.

Had the impeachment succeeded, instead of failing by one vote, the fundamental principle of separation of powers would have been swept away; the president and the courts would have sunk to a position of subordinate departments whose sole function was to execute the decrees of an all-powerful Congress. Had the Radicals succeeded in ousting Johnson because he did not agree with the dominant party in Congress, the Supreme Court would soon have been similarly incapacitated, and neither would again have dared to oppose the will of the legislature. Congress, and not the Constitution, would have been supreme.

Radical theory made Congress paramount not only to the president, but to the Constitution. The "unconstitutional" acts for which the Radicals denounced Johnson were often so characterized merely because contrary to the Congressional will. For the Constitution itself they had little

[7] "President Johnson's Speech on the Occasion of the Soldier's and Sailor's Serenade," April 18, 1866, Johnson MSS., XCIII.

respect. Sumner revered parts of the Declaration of Independence, but on him the Constitution was no check. Because it countenanced slavery, it had lost the respect of the abolitionist group who now formed an important part of the extremist party. The phrase, "A league with death and a covenant with hell," had expressed the feeling of some of them toward it; four years of exercise of war powers had accustomed them to a stretching of it, until many had actually come to consider it changeable, like the English constitution, by simple legislative enactment. Sumner opposed a civil rights or negro suffrage amendment as unnecessary, since Congress had, he claimed, full power to enact both. In his mind specific phrases of the Constitution embodied not what the framers intended them to mean but what was demanded by the "best interest of society," as Congress controlled by him and his Radical friends interpreted that best interest. To the Declaration of Independence, which in matters of "human rights" he considered more important than the Constitution, all statutes must conform.[8] During the session of 1865-66 he kept trying to establish negro suffrage by mere act of Congress,[9] in accordance with his theory that whatever was required for the national safety (or thought by Radicals to be so required), was constitutional.[10]

* * * *

A second phase of the Radical constitutional change was minimization of state functions in government. Since before the origin of our constitutional system, the relation of state and federal government has been a fertile subject of dispute. The old state sovereignty party was a power in America

[8] Jan. 31, 1872, *Cong. Globe,* 42 Cong., 2 Sess., 728.
[9] See bills presented Dec. 4, 1865, *ibid.,* 39 Cong., 1 Sess., 2; Feb. 2, 1866, *ibid.,* 592; Feb. 6, 1866, *ibid.,* 674.
[10] *Ibid.,* 673 ff.

right down to the Civil War. That conflict settled indisputably the question of secession and nullification; but states' rights was merely recast into a new mold. Since that war, the struggle has continued between the partisans of centralist and state control of the minutiae of government. On such questions as control of corporations, aid to corporations, internal commerce, education, child labor, prohibition, woman suffrage, economic regulations, and many phases of police power, from the Civil War to the present moment, the country has been divided between advocates of national control and a strong state action party. In his message of December, 1925, President Coolidge warned against too great centralization, and declared society in "much more danger from encumbering the National Government beyond its wisdom to comprehend, or its ability to administer, than from leaving the local communities to bear their own burdens and remedy their own evils." [11] Here is the old question of 1866. Coolidge agrees with Johnson. A long series of Supreme Court decisions has drawn a compromise line across the field of police power and that of commerce. Child labor, prohibition, and woman suffrage were decided in favor of state action, so that only by constitutional amendment could the nation regulate them. In many other matters the dispute has been settled arbitrarily one way or the other, or a compromise has been effected. The dual federal system has been modified and defined, but retained through it all. Immediately after the Civil War, however, this struggle in its new phase reached a crisis.

During the War the central government had from necessity acted in high-handed fashion. To win the War the states acquiesced in temporary infringement of their rights. Then

[11] Dec. 8, 1925, *ibid.*, 69 Cong., 1 Sess., 457.

when peace came, the Radicals sought to rule the country from Washington as they had fought the War from Washington. The Northern states stood a necessary obstacle in the way of obliteration of state lines. But as long as centralization worked to its advantage, the party in control in Northern states did not seriously object. In establishing their rule in the South, Radicals rode roughshod over the theory of state action. Their program provided for central authority in fields where the state's prerogative had never been questioned, even by opponents of states' rights. They attempted to bring ownership of land, procedure in state courts, qualifications for suffrage, poor laws, state elections, education,[12] and all manner of police regulations into the realm of national control. Stevens, like Sumner, expressed contempt for the Constitution whenever it stood in the way of complete centralization.[13]

Greater centralization was intended to serve another purpose. Complaints of businesses, particularly railroads, against regulations and restraints imposed upon them by state legislatures, were beginning to pour into Washington. The new industrialists wanted protection for the future in the special privilege and enormous profits that they could secure only in disregard of the interests and welfare of a public that could not always be ignored while it controlled state legislatures. Though this was not generally discussed, some of the framers and supporters of the Fourteenth Amendment undoubtedly hoped to make it, as it later became, a national bulwark of business against state regulation. In arguing the case of San Mateo *vs.* the Southern

---

[12] They tried to establish a national bureau of education, which the *Nation* (II [Jan. 18, 1866], 71) advocated. *Cong. Globe,* 39 Cong., 1 Sess.; 835; 39 Cong., 2 Sess., 1842 *et seq.*

[13] G. Welles, "Lincoln and Johnson," the *Galaxy,* XIII (1872), 669.

Pacific Railroad [14] in 1882, Conkling who had been a member of the Committee of Fifteen claimed that the Amendment was intended to provide corporations with "congressional and administrative protection against invidious and discriminating state and local taxes . . . and oppressive and ruinous rules . . . applied under state laws." The Radicals of 1866 had "intrenched" in the Constitution, Conkling testified, a rule "to curb the many who would do to the few as they would not have the few do to them." [15] In short, corporations were to be protected by Congress against regulation or interference by states. Open avowal of this motive would have defeated the Amendment. Though they dared not attack him on this ground, the hatred of Andrew Johnson by Radical Congressmen, representing as they did the business interests thus to be protected, was partly based upon his known opposition to their desire to raise business above regulation by states. For the future of industrial America Johnson's championship of public interest and the common man was far more dangerous than any Southern policy he might conceive.

Under the full operation of Radical theory, the states would have been deprived of their police powers. Some extremists even talked obliteration of state lines.[16] To be sure, the purpose, so far as it was openly avowed, was simply to impose upon all the states for the sake of the negro the local regulations and systems already in force in negrophile Northern states. But the principle of centralization would thereby have been established, and then if the time had come when a majority of the nation had chosen to impose their

[14] 116 *U. S.*, 138.
[15] Conkling produced the journal of the Committee, hitherto unpublished, to prove his point. His testimony is quoted in B. B. Kendrick, *Journal of the Joint Committee of Fifteen*, 28-36.
[16] E.g., W. Sigerson, Aug. 18, 1865, Sumner MSS., LXXIV.

views upon a minority section of the North, no barrier would have stood in the way. The time has come; the situation is reversed; and one center of 1866 Radicalism—New England—is today firmly defending the principle of state action against the imposition upon her of the will of the rest of the country on taxation that hurts her, on regulation of manufacturing, on national aid to improvements which do not benefit New England but for which she pays heavily, on prohibition, and on the very national bureau of education which she once strongly advocated. Had New England's leaders in Congress succeeded in the 'Sixties in substituting a centralized national government for our federal system, New England would today have no defense against Western, Southern, and radical attack. But in 1866 when centralization would have served her sectional interests, she led in a movement to make the national government all-powerful in the country as she hoped to make Congress omnipotent in that centralized government, thereby removing all the obstacles to the speedy and unhampered enactment into law of the "popular will" which she intended to keep identical with her sectional will.

*   *   *   *

Conservative men opposed changes that would break down the checks on the rashness and tyranny which they feared an omnipotent Congress would practise. Much of the old frontier dread of too much government remained; to many the greatest advantage of our system of government was the difficulty of action that the various checks and balances imposed upon it. The very year 1866 seemed to prove the value of the system, for had Johnson and the Supreme Court not stood in the way, there were no lengths to which Congress would not have gone. All believers in a written Constitution were aroused by the boldness with which Sumner declared that laws of Congress would serve as well as constitutional amendments. The old states' rights forces sprang vigorously to the South's defense.

Part of the opposition to Radical measures came from men who objected on the ground of the unconstitutionality of Congressional action. "The position assumed by Congress," wrote a Cincinnati friend of General Sherman, "is a virtual abrogation of the government we had before the war, & an attempt by mere politicians to make a new government through usurpation for the manifest purposes of sheer partisan supremacy, without an appeal in the legitimate [way] made to the people of the several states, as the original source of power." [17] In his own state, Trumbull encountered opposition to his Freedmen's Bureau and Civil Rights bills. "Do you really believe," wrote one of his constituents, "that Congress has under the constitution authority to create such a power and exercise it by the national agents *in the States.* If so then the National Government may usurp all the municipal powers of the States, and take charge of every personal right of every person in the U. S. and make a consolidated Government at once." [18] Bingham of Ohio opposed the Civil Rights Bill and voted to uphold its veto, because he thought it unconstitutional, but he approved what it sought to do and in the Joint Committee of Fifteen sponsored the measure that would protect by constitutional amendment these civil rights, which he did not believe Congress had the power to protect by mere legislation. [19]

[17] G. W. Bartley to W. T. Sherman, Oct. 27, 1866, W. T. Sherman MSS., XX.

[18] M. McConnell to L. Trumbull, Jan. 7, 1866, Trumbull MSS., LXIII.

[19] *Cong. Globe,* 39 Cong., 1 Sess., 1290 ff., 1861; B. B. Kendrick, *op. cit.,* 213-220; H. E. Flack, *Adoption of the Fourteenth Amendment, passim.*

But most of the opponents of Radicalism objected to centralization itself, and opposed it only less vigorously if it were to be brought about by constitutional amendment than if by illegal legislation. Browning wrote, "One of the greatest perils which threatens us now is the tendency to centralization, the absorption of the rights of the States, and the concentration of all power in the General Government. When that shall be accomplished, if ever, the days of the Republic are numbered." [20]

In his widely read letter to the Cleveland Convention, Beecher declared, "The federal government is unfit to exercise minor police and local government, and will inevitably blunder when it attempts it. . . . To oblige the central authority to govern half the territory of the Union by federal civil officers and by the army, is a policy not only uncongenial to our ideas and principles, but pre-eminently dangerous to the spirit of our government. However humane the ends sought and the motive, it is, in fact, a course of instruction preparing our government to be despotic and familiarizing the people to a stretch of authority which can never be other than dangerous to liberty." [21] In spite of Johnson's patent faults, he said, he respected him because he had "jealously resisted a centralization of power in the federal government," and had "sought to dignify and secure a true State rights." [22]

The first section of the Fourteenth Amendment gave con-

[20] *Speeches of Hon. Edgar Cowan . . . Jas. R. Doolittle . . . Letter of Hon. O. H. Browning of Illinois . . . (National Union Club Documents)*, 20.

[21] *New York Herald*, Sept. 2, 1866.

[22] *Ibid.*, Sept. 10, 1866. The Radical Parke Godwin of the *New York Evening Post* wrote Sumner that he could not agree with the Senator's Worcester speech. "Now that the war is ended," he declared, "we must not run into an overshadowing and crushing Centralism. That is our danger of dangers." Sept. 18, 1865, Sumner MSS., LXXIV. His editorial column defended constitutionalism and local self-government.

stitutional sanction to this very centralization of government, and it was for that reason that Conservatives opposed it.[23] In fact, many of the Radical proposals Johnson men opposed only because the federal instead of the state government was to carry them out. Full negro suffrage they would have opposed however granted; the punitive clause of the Amendment they could not approve; but other Radical policies proposed in 1866 they would have supported in state legislatures. Back of Johnson's opposition to the bills he vetoed and to the Amendment, was the realization that if once Congressional omnipotence were established, nothing in the federal government nor in the sanctity of states could restrain the Radical Congress. To men who sensed the danger of ultra-centralism, Johnson seemed the defender of the American system of government. Field said, "The maintenance of the Constitution . . . is of more value to the people of this country than the rise or fall of any party, or the success or failure of any measure. In the present unhappy differences between Congress and the President, the latter, in obedience to his sense of constitutional duty, declines the vast patronage and power, civil and military, which the former would give him. We honor him for this. We believe the whole country will do as much. It knows no man has suffered more, or struggled harder for his convictions." [24]

Welles pointed out that Lincoln's and Johnson's constitutional views were identical. "The real and true cause," said Welles, "of assault and persecution [of Johnson] was the fearless and unswerving fidelity of the President to the Constitution, . . . his opposition to central Congressional usurpation, and his maintenance of the rights of the states

[23] See, e.g., Browning's letter cited above.
[24] "Address of Hon. David D. Field," *Mass Meeting of the Citizens of New York, Feb. 22, 1866,* 11.

and of the Executive Department, against legislative aggression." Welles described the reconstruction struggle as a conflict "carried on by a fragment of Congress that arrogated to itself authority to exclude States and people from their constitutional right of representation, against an Executive striving under infinite embarrassments to preserve State, Federal and Popular rights." [25] In the end Johnson's opposition prevented, whether for good or evil, a fundamental change in the form of our government. This he did accomplish, though he ruined himself in the process and lost in the more immediate reconstruction quarrel.[26]

In over-emphasizing this stand against centralization, Johnson unwittingly committed a tactical error. There was dawning unperceived, a new era which had already begun to affect the point of view of the Northwest toward government. In the days of Jefferson and Jackson, frontiersmen had opposed government interference, and had believed that no government was the best government. In those days the Northwest could always be counted upon to oppose centralization. But in that section in 1866, the old frontier individualism was giving way to a new factor—the need of government aid and government interference. Many new enterprises had sprung up during the Civil War in the older portions of the Northwest—notably manufacturing, building of railroads, and wool-growing—which were looking to the government for protection through the tariff or acts of bounty. On the other hand, a cry was beginning to be raised for government protection against the predatory tendencies and price discriminations of both railroads and grain elevators.

[25] G. Welles, "Lincoln and Johnson," the *Galaxy*, XIII (1872), 664.
[26] Ultimately the Supreme Court upheld Johnson's views by declaring the Civil Rights bills unconstitutional even *after* the enactment of the Fourteenth Amendment. Civil Rights Cases, 109 *U. S.*, 3.

An age had dawned when Western farmers would look to the government for protection against big business, and for aid in their periods of depression. In 1866 times were good, the pinch was not yet great enough to make the cry audible, but the point of view toward government was changing. Had Johnson made his Chicago trip ten years earlier, he would have aroused enthusiasm. Had he based his policy on economic issues, he might have stirred the Northwest to its depths. Had he even appealed to the Western feeling of magnanimity or of fair play, or had he sought to spread over the land a true picture of the South, he might have gained support, though not so certainly. But Johnson did not know the Northwest. He merely iterated and reiterated his plea for states' rights and decentralization of government, and met complete indifference. People of the Northwest were too constantly migrating to have any state pride, and new factors were turning them from individualists into supporters of a strong central government. To fail to sense this, and thus to miss his opportunity on other issues on his Western trip, was perhaps Johnson's most fatal error.

Chapter **X**

ECONOMIC ISSUES

AS important as the Southern question in determining reconstruction measures were various economic issues. If Southern economic interests had coincided with those of the rising industrial groups of the North, there would have been no Radical reconstruction. The real danger from "a return of rebels to power" was not overthrow of the Union, but ousting of the new industrial forces from control in Washington through a renewed union of Southern planters and Western farmers. In an alignment on the new industrial questions, the Radicals would have been outnumbered even in the North. If Johnson had staked his fortunes on them instead of on the indeterminable condition of a remote South, his chances of success would have risen. Economic policies did figure in the struggle to a greater extent than has been recognized, but in handling them the Radicals, with an initial handicap, superbly outgeneraled the Johnson men.

I. GOVERNMENT FINANCE

Congress had been spending money lavishly. The squandering of the national revenues through extravagance and corruption for which this and the following decade became notorious, would have been a powerful weapon against the Radicals could the electorate have been fully aroused. Specific expenditures of the Thirty-ninth Congress, already controlled by Radicals, did arouse criticism.

The Freedmen's Bureau, however necessary, was expensive; and reorganization under the act passed over Johnson's veto, added to the original cost.[1] "We are groaning," complained a Democratic farmer of Illinois, "under burdensome taxation. If the policy of Stephens and Sumner are [sic] carried out, involving additional expenditure of millions if not hundreds of millions in unnecessarily large armies of soldiers and armies of politicians under the Freedmens bureau bill piling taxes still higher upon the people, it will end in repudiation of the whole government debt. The money can not be raised by the people." [2] Men who questioned the value of the Bureau, and many who approved its work, protested over the expense of maintaining it indefinitely.[3]

Complaint was made against the proposed Bureau of Education on the same ground. The benefits would devolve chiefly upon negroes of the South, and not many Northerners were sufficiently interested in the ex-slave to delight in paying extra federal taxes for his education. Many objected even to the cost of educating the few negroes in their

[1] General Fullerton of the Bureau, after carefully estimating costs, had reported to Johnson that the new law could not be administered for less than $20,000,000 annually. Feb. 12, 1866, Johnson MSS., LXXXVI. This was one of the reasons for Johnson's veto.

[2] C. Dement to A. Johnson, Feb. 19, 1866, ibid., LXXXVII.

[3] Locy of Illinois expressed a common Northern feeling when he declared, "Together with the sacrifices which I have made I have also borne cheerfully, the taxation, necessary to an earnest prosecution of the war, to a successful termination—but I am unwilling to be taxed for the support of the negro. His freedom has cost us enough & if the abolition leaders believe what they said before the war, to wit,—that the Negro was capable of exercising all the rights of freedmen, among which preeminently was the idea that he could maintain & support himself & those dependent upon him, I say let them stand or fall by their favorite dogma now." Feb. 25, 1866, ibid., LXXXVIII.

own state. Opposition to the Mexican loan centered about its expense, as many deemed it a mere gift. Bounty legislation was opposed because it raised taxes without proportionate benefit to the ex-soldiers,[4] although many who objected to other expenditures did favor this one extravagance.[5] Their financing of the War could have been added to the score against the Radicals, as graft, profiteering, and inefficiency had run riot.[6] Government grants to planters of the lower Mississippi to help rebuild the levees, funding the debt by methods which would reap rich profits for Jay Cooke, squandering of vast national resources under the Montana land scheme, and princely grants to the Northern Pacific Railroad were all attacked as raids on the Treasury.

The most discussed extravagance was a "salary grab" comparable to the more famous one of Grant's day. Near the close of the session Congressmen voted to increase their own pay from three thousand to five thousand dollars. A presidential veto was certain. To avoid it, Congress fastened the salary clause to a necessary and just bounty equalization law. Johnson chose to accept the obnoxious rider rather than to kill the bill. In this way Congressmen got a sixty-six per cent increase in salary, but aroused a storm of criticism. They had already encountered bitterness among the soldiers for refusing to pass a new bounty bill. Now even the equalization law was made distasteful by the salary rider. Radicals soon saw their mistake. Menager of Gallipolis wrote Sher-

[4] McCulloch reminded Commissioner Wells that the bounty legislation would mean borrowing two hundred to two hundred fifty million dollars. McCulloch asked whether the country could stand it. Wells doubted it. The *Tribune* thought it could not. *New York Semi-Weekly Tribune,* May 4, 1866.

[5] Either as a source of personal profit, or as a form of "patriotism."

[6] According to the *Herald* (Aug. 1, 1866) the Radicals admitted that "their party would have been broken to pieces . . . by its financial errors" had not the quarrel with Johnson diverted popular attention to reconstruction.

man: Congress must "modify that Law—particularly since the executive's 'swing in the circle' denouncing the 'Radical Congress' and ridiculing them for giving the soldiers 'only $100.' " [7] Democrats began to speak of Congress as the one that "at its first session voted Four Thousand dollars extra pay to its members but failed to make any provision for the payment of bounties to the soldiers." [8] Johnson struck a popular note when he combined a protest against the "salary grab" with a plea for the bounty. But he failed to make his criticism of Congress part of a constructive financial reform, instead of a mere excuse for added vituperation against Radicals.

Retrenchment would have been a cry popular with taxpayers all over the country.[9] The *Herald* took it up; its editors pleaded with Johnson privately [10] as well as editorially to force this issue into the campaign. The Radicals, said that paper, "think that they can raise enough noise about negro riots, restoration and other side topics to keep the financial question out of the coming canvass and carry all the Northern States. But they forget that every voter is a taxpayer." [11] The *Herald* calculated the cost of "reckless squandering of the public treasure" at $250,000,000. "Look at

---

[7] Nov. 5, 1866, John Sherman MSS., CVII. Even from Radical Massachusetts came protests. Reynolds of Monson wrote Stevens, "I was sorry to see that you voted to increase the pay of your Congressmen. It has been, next to president Johnson & my *policy,* the topic of political conversation." Oct. 14, 1866, Stevens MSS., VIII.

[8] T. I. Turner to E. B. Washburne, Sept. 21, 1866, Washburne MSS., XCVI.

[9] Victor S. Clark (*History of Manufactures in the United States, 1607-1928,* II, 56) estimates the per capita tax of 1866 at $16.04 in currency or $11.46 in gold, "probably the heaviest at that time paid in the world."

[10] Johnson's staff friend Phillips assured him that the "reckless and corrupt legislation of Congress" was a point on which the Radicals were vulnerable, since "nothing touches the people more sensibly than to show them how their money is being wasted." Aug. 7, 1866, Johnson MSS., XCIX.

[11] *New York Herald,* Aug. 1, 1866.

the enormous·Congressional jobs," it urged, "in every one of
which the ear-marks of a private or partisan plundering
scheme are discernible." [12] "If . . . any respectable party
will go into the next elections upon the platform of retrenchment, . . . and a thorough change of the present corrupt
. . . Congress, success will follow. Such a platform would
beat all the negro platforms the radicals can construct." [13]
From Ohio Johnson's friend Campbell urged a campaign for
"retrenchment and reform." [14] Ray [15] wrote Trumbull, "You
all in Washington must remember that the excitement of the
great contest is dying out, and that commercial and industrial enterprises and pursuits are engaging a large part of
public attention. The times are hard; money is close; taxes
are heavy; all forms of industry here in the West are heavily
burdened; and in the struggle to pay debts and live, people
are more mindful of themselves than of any of the fine
philanthropic schemes that look to making Sambo a voter,
juror, and office holder." In this period of corruption and
wasting of public money,[16] Johnson's scrupulous honesty was
dangerous to men who were profiting by pork-barrel legislation and Crédit Mobilier scandals. His opposition made
the grafters his enemies, and he failed to organize the general

[12] Freedmen's Bureau job, $7,000,000; "useless extravagance of the na-
tional bank system," $30,000,000 a year; Mexican loan, $30,000,000 to $50,-
000,000; Montana scheme, "intended to filch from the national domain a
vast tract of valuable gold and silver," $20,000,000; debt funding by
"financial monopolists and political empyrics," $35,000,000 to $40,000,000;
Education Bureau, $5,000,000; increased revenue, $8,000,000; Mississippi
and Yazoo rivers project, $40,000,000 to $50,000,000; proposed tariff,
"pilfering $30,000,000 to $40,000,000 from the pockets of the people";
grants to railroad corporations, amount indeterminable. *Ibid.*, July 16
and 26, 1866.

[13] *Ibid.*, July 2, 1866.

[14] Aug. 21, 1865, Johnson MSS., LXXIV.

[15] Former editor of the *Chicago Tribune,* Feb. 7, 1866, Trumbull MSS.,
LXIII.

[16] General Sherman wrote his wife, "Washington is as corrupt as Hell,
made so by the looseness and extravagance of war." W. T. Sherman, *Home
Letters,* 351-352.

protest of ordinary taxpayers against the Radicals by advertising their extravagances and promising that Conservatives would institute economies.

* * * *

Taxation was a vital question. The War was over, but the war taxes continued. On his return in May from consultation with some of the leading bankers in Chicago, the president of the National Bank of Galena wrote Washburne, "The subject of taxation is the all absorbing one at present. Some of the largest stockholders declare they will close, & I think we shall *all* be forced to do so. If Congress fails to relieve us . . . what is to become of the country?" [17] "The local taxes," wrote a Chicago friend of Trumbull, "added to the national are becoming grievous. The farmers by the ceasing of the war have lost their great customer, and prices of agricultural products, I believe will soon fall off, and then there will be a general howl. The democrats are waiting and watching for this, and are expecting to turn it to account; and I fear their hopes have good foundation . . . taxation is the terror of the day." [18]

But many more agreed upon the necessity of reduction than upon the incidence of the remaining taxes. A Philadelphia correspondent of Washburne had a simple solution: "Reduce the revenue Tax and increase the duty on Iron and the Country is safe. We can then defy Uncle Andy and the Devil." [19] The trouble was that each special interest saw prosperity for the country in cancellation of the tax upon its own article and related ones and retention of other taxes to

[17] May 18, 1866, Washburne MSS., XIX. See also J. D. Platt to E. B. W., Dec. 31, 1866, *ibid.*, XVIII.
[18] April 24, 1866, Trumbull MSS., LXV.
[19] J. P. Verree to E. Washburne, April 12, 1866, Washburne MSS., XCVI.

pay the debt. Factory owners wanted the tariff raised and revenue taxes on manufactures repealed. Monied men wanted the income and luxury taxes repealed and the necessary burdens distributed as widely as possible, so that all the people, and not just the wealthy, would contribute. Debtors, agriculturalists, Westerners, on the other hand, urged taxation of luxuries,[20] incomes, and national banks, and exemption of the necessities of life. The Western farmer felt himself particularly ill-used. He bore heavy local taxes, and he felt he also bore the manufacturer's tax in the form of an increased price which the tariff forced the consumer to pay. This seemed particularly unfair because the farmer sold, whether in Europe or America, without the benefit of a compensatory tariff to keep his produce up to the general American price level. Therefore he demanded reduction of taxes that fell on the people and retention of those on wealth. Underneath reconstruction controversies, then, seethed this age-old dispute between those who had and those who had not.

Suggestions for transferring the tax to Southern products raised another sectional issue. Because of its commercial interest in Southern prosperity, the West clamored against such proposals. McFarlan, Straight, & Co., commission merchants of Cincinnati and New Orleans, protested that the American sugar industry would be completely wiped out by the tax upon it. "Crush out the agricultural interests of any portion of the South," Straight wrote Sumner, "and the freedmen are beggars. . . . We are advancing to planters, —former Slave holders, who could not cultivate their plantations without our help, who cheerfully listen to our advice, in regard to the treatment of their laborers, paying them

[20] E.g., J. D. Platt to E. B. Washburne urging him to "tax whisky . . . tobacco & cigars, & other luxuries" instead of industry, Dec. 31, 1866, *ibid.*, XVIII.

promptly and well, and, who are becoming models for all the surrounding country. Please hold up our hands by doing them justice." [21] An Illinois farmer wrote Senators Trumbull, Yates, and Morgan, "In the interest of the Western farmers and of the Eastern manufacturers a liberal encouragement should be given to the cultivation of the rich soil of the South. Where are we Western farmers to find Market for our corn, oats, flour, pork, horses & mules if the cultivation of a large partition [sic] of the Southern States are to be abandoned, on account of the heavy tax imposed on their productions." [22]

Many of the Radicals who were not making cotton goods, particularly the woolen manufacturers, thought the best way to ease the tax burden was to tax Southern cotton heavily. But this, like the sugar tax, raised opposition in the Northwest. "There are thousands of your old soldiers," wrote Buell to Sherman, "who lost money by serving throughout the whole war, and who have invested their all in this country hoping thereby to make a little money." [23] Others who felt that a prosperous South would bring prosperity to the North opposed the cotton levy. "By placing this atrocious tax upon cotton," the *Herald* protested, "Congress not only cripples our own resources, but encourages cotton growing in rival countries. In reality the radicals have accorded protection in favor of foreign cotton growers and against those of our country to the amount of twenty-five millions per annum. The loyal people of the North, being the principal consumers, have to bear this enormous burden." [24] Besides, in the collection of the tax from the producer, carpet-bag offi-

---

[21] Feb. 15, 1866, Stevens MSS., VI.
[22] March 27, 1866, Trumbull MSS., LXIV.
[23] March 28, 1866, W. T. Sherman MSS., XVIII.
[24] *New York Herald*, Aug. 5, 1866.

cials practised notorious corruption. Conditions became so intolerable that Johnson finally wired orders to governors and generals in the South not to collect the tax at all. "All cotton transactions," he declared, "cause more difficulty and expense than profit. . . . The people are oppressed greatly now and they are little able to bear it in this transition State." [25] Yet the Radicals actually increased this tax.

In January, 1866, the Revenue Commission headed by Special Commissioner Wells, rendered a report [26] that is unique in a period of haphazard legislation typified by the tariff bill of 1866 and partisan investigations whose technique the work of the Joint Committee of Fifteen precedented. The Commission spent seven months in painstaking investigation, and then presented a report that was a landmark in government finance. The Commission was composed neither of Radicals seeking party ends, nor of sectionalists attempting to enrich their homeland and punish another's, nor yet of "business men" seeking practical prosperity for their class; its members were economists attempting to render impartial justice to all sections and classes in a well-ordered piece of legislation. In essence the report said:

"A system of taxation . . . so diffuse as the present one necessarily entails a system of duplication of taxes, which in turn leads to an undue enhancement of prices, a decrease both of production and consumption, and consequently of wealth, a restriction of exportations and of foreign commerce, and a large increase in the machinery and expense of the revenue collection." The present diffuseness of taxation maintains high prices, "and were the price of gold and of

[25] A. Johnson to Gov. J. M. Wells and A. Johnson to Gen. J. S. Fullerton, Nov. 1, 1865, Johnson MSS., "Telegrams."
[26] "Report of the United States Revenue Commission," *House Ex. Docs.*, 39 Cong., 1 Sess., ser. no. 1255, doc. no. 34.

the national currency made at once to approximate, and the present revenue system to continue unchanged, it would be impossible for the prices of most products of manufacturing industry to return to anything like their former level." The present system of taxation "violates all the fundamental principles of taxation, inasmuch as the taxes are neither definite in amount, equal in application, nor convenient of collection." The Commission therefore recommends "the abolition or speedy reduction of all taxes which tend to check development, and the retention of all those which, like the income tax, falls chiefly upon realized wealth."

The Commission presented a revenue bill to Congress.[27] It proposed repeal of the tax on all raw products except cotton, and reduction of the tax on manufactures, but retention of the excise on incomes and corporations, and the stamp taxes which few felt. It recommended the installation of a merit system for revenue officers and an adjustment of excise and tariff. In short, the bill purposed to relieve the common people, lift the burden from necessities, remove all impedimenta to the development of the country, tax wealth, and reform the apportionment and efficiency of collection of taxes until the government could secure the largest revenue possible with the least burden. The *Nation*, though Radical, highly recommended the report.[28] Because he feared what the politicians would do with his recommendations, David Wells, declaring that he had spent more hours than any one else in the country had minutes on this subject, wrote Stevens, "May I not ask of you, one of the acknowledged leaders of public opinion in the country, that my recommendations . . . shall be considered fairly & candidly; and if I am *right*, am I not

---

[27] For an analysis of the bill see H. K. Beale, "The Decision of Reconstruction," MS. dissertation, 387 ff.
[28] The *Nation*, II (Feb. 8, 1866), 167.

entitled to your support? On the other hand, if I am wrong, & you can demolish my evidence & arguments, no pride of opinion will prevent my abandoning my former position." [29]

But though experts could recommend, politicians had to enact, a law. Congress pretended to accept the report, and then proceeded to emasculate it by amendments that discarded most of the experts' recommendations. Tariff readjustment had no chance in Radical legislation. Civil service reform was opposed by politicians of all parties, since Radicals knew the patronage to be one of their strongest weapons against Johnson, and Democrats could scarcely wait until the day when they should regain control of it and be able to turn it against the Radicals. By the time Congress had passed the bill, the experts could not have recognized it.

Once the principle of reduction was admitted, all the special interests began to clamor for reduction on their particular products. The result was a mongrel bill that favored the manufacturers, but gave little relief to the poorer classes. Had it been accompanied by a correlative reduction of the tariff, the people would have benefited through reduced prices. With the war tariff retained, prices remained unaffected, and the revenue bill reductions looked like added profits for manufacturers.[30] This incongruous tax legislation while the country was groaning under war taxes in peace times, offered the anti-Congressional party a handle of attack that would have been effective in the campaign. In

[29] Feb. 2, 1866, Stevens MSS., VI.
[30] The *New York Herald* (Aug. 1, 1866) pointed out "that the tax on the speculating interest in Wall Street is reduced, and that on such necessary articles to every family as cotton it is increased . . . A careful analysis of the bill will show that the tax on articles of luxury has been reduced, and power given to monopolies to collect their tax of the people, while the necessaries of life are taxed according to the old rate." To prove this the *Herald* printed (Aug. 28, 1866) a comparative list of tax rates under the old and new laws.

these matters Johnson, who heartily approved Wells's recommendations, sympathized with the "have-nots." He had always opposed a tariff and favored taxation of the wealthy. He persistently opposed the corruption and special favors of the tax laws of this period. These views as much as his reconstruction policy aroused the resentment of the Republican politicians and the interests favored by them.

* * * *

Contraction of the currency was already a subject of heated controversy, though the opposition to it had not yet gained the momentum necessary to the launching of a political party. Still, most of the factors that in subsequent years underlay Greenbackism, the Granger movement, Populism, Progressivism, and the Farm Bloc were at work in 1866. It is significant that it was while in retirement on his farm from May of 1866 to the following May that Kelley in conversation with his Minnesota friends worked out the details of the Granger organization suggested to him by what he saw on a Southern trip early in 1866. Therefore, while the first Grange was not organized until 1867, its need was based on conditions of 1866.[31] Had the South been back in the Union, similar economic conditions would have united the Northwest and the South in advocacy of an inflated currency. Realization of this fact was one of the reasons for Radical determination to keep the South out of the Union.

During the War greenbacks had been issued, and then had rapidly depreciated in value. Greenbacks and bank notes together had driven gold out of circulation. Furthermore, an unfavorable foreign trade balance had for several years been draining the country of gold. People had consequently

[31] Oliver H. Kelley, *Origin and Progress of the Order of the Patrons of Husbandry in the United States*, 13 ff.

come to depend upon the inflated paper money which was all the ordinary man ever saw, and to regard gold as a noxious monopoly of the rich.

The price of gold in greenbacks had soared during the War until at the top price in July, 1864, one hundred gold dollars were worth two hundred eighty-five dollars in greenbacks. By March, 1866, the premium on gold had toppled to only $25. But then the quarrel between Johnson and Congress, the Overend-Gurney panic in England, and uncertainty over contraction sent it upward again to a June premium of $67.75. By the end of the year, the premium had again dropped to $31.25.[32] This fluctuation was obviously bad for the country. The government was faced with the problem of stabilizing the money-market. Economists, the government, and the creditor class were united in certainty that the country must be rid of inflation, though they differed upon the means.

Great numbers of voters, however, desired continued inflation. Westerners were generally inflationists, since the wealth of the country was centered in the Northeast and the debtor classes were predominant in the West. Debtors, of course, wished to pay their obligations in as cheap a medium as possible. Besides, many felt that the surest aid to prosperity was to print more and cheaper money. This, they said, would raise the prices of their produce, stimulate business, and by breaking the money monopoly of the wealthy give every one plenty of currency. In a letter to Fessenden, Richardson of Canaan, New Hampshire, described the situation he found on a lecture tour through the West. The "Laboring & Producing classes" were in distress because, as a result of "the

[32] W. C. Mitchell, *Gold, Prices, and Wages under the Greenback Standard*, 4-15.

scarcity of money, . . . property would not pay debts without a ruinous sacrifice." A particularly bad condition obtained among "the virtuous, & respectable class of small Farmers, and mechanics, who were commencing life with dear families around them; and were under the necessity of commencing, in part, on credit. Hundreds of thousands of such families, after struggling, with an agony, for years, in paying costs & high rates of interest, have been made wretched, & ruined in property & in hope, because money was so hoarded up that common country real Estate would not pay debts without a ruinous Sacrifice." "But," Richardson reported, "since the large issue of Green-Backs, as a Lawful Tender[,] Great Prosperity was produced extensively through that class which had formerly not been able to pay their debts, & educate their families, even by the hardest struggle, but often had been wretched, and almost ruined. . . . The very numerous respectable class that I have been speaking of, all through from the Bay of Fundy to the Mississippi, say that the Green-Back currency made so plenty, has been far the greatest blessing in the form of currency that they have ever known, or heard of in the world. Labor and everything else would sell for a good price and it is their earnest wish that influential men, who regard the good of the millions of people would do all they possibly can to have the laws made such that instead of withdrawing the Green-Back currency more shall be thrown into circulation; so much more is now needed since many parts of the South are now being opened to business enterprise." [33]

Few political leaders were inflationists in this full sense

[33] "It is necessary," he believed, "that a currency, which will pay debts should be plenty; one which the wealthy classes cannot, or will not get, & hoard up, so as to depreciate the value of country real estate, etc. & make it impossible for those in debt to get money, and pay their debts without ruin." Feb. 5, 1867, Fessenden MSS.

of the word, though plenty of their followers were. But many of the leaders, with great numbers of non-debtor voters did oppose contraction under the conditions that existed in 1866, though they acknowledged the evils of inflation. They argued that economic readjustment would be difficult in any case, and that to withdraw thousands of dollars of currency from circulation would merely add to the distress. They did not wish either to increase or decrease the amount of money in circulation. Even that inveterate Radical, George L. Stearns of Boston, feared a panic would result from contraction. He urged the Treasury merely to gather the specie of the country unto itself "as a guarantee for the stability of the Public Debt," until with the restoration of government credit, the greenbacks would stabilize themselves at par.[34] The quarrel of these men with the contractionists was really a difference of judgment over the amount of money that would adequately meet the needs of the people. They were actuated not by the debtor impulse to secure partial repudiation through inflation, but by a real economic pressure for more money than had been available before the Civil War. They felt that the new, expanding industrial system required a larger amount of currency to meet its ordinary needs than had the older pre-war order.

In the face of much popular opposition, Congress passed a contraction measure called a "loan bill," authorizing the Secretary of the Treasury to dispose of bonds "to such an amount, in such manner, and at such rates as he may think advisable, for lawful money of the United States, or for any Treasury notes . . . or other representatives of value." Morrill and his contractionist friends had wanted to leave unlimited power to the Secretary, but so strong was the

[34] G. L. Stearns to A. Johnson, Nov. 21, 1865, Johnson MSS., LXXXI.

opposition even among Radicals, that they had to accept a compromise proviso: "That of United States notes not more than ten millions of dollars. may be retired and cancelled within six months from the passage of this act, and thereafter not more than four million dollars in any one month." [35]

Even in the East the bill faced bitter opposition. A Brooklyn correspondent of Stevens wrote, "If the House would send two or three members . . . to . . . New York to ascertain the state of trade . . . they would soon understand why it is that the trade is at a stand still. The fact is our currency and our circulation are in a very precarious position. They will not bear tinkering with at all. . . . Let the Secretary exercise with great caution the withdrawing process or as sure as his name is McCullough he will swamp the business men of the country, the Banks, the Nation *and the party!*" [36] Stevens's Lancaster friend, Patterson, wrote, "If you, Congress, do not do something to restrain McCulloch . . . he will crush the business of the whole Country to death—deprive us of more than half our present Internal Revenue, and play the devil generally. Why under the circumstances, twelve or fifteen years will be a short time to bring about specie payments." [37] Lewis of Philadelphia asked Stevens: "Do you see how perniciously these Treasury threats of contracting the currency are operating on the national industry? Mechanics, Manufacturers, etc., all pausing, and many almost stopping their factories, & discharging many of their hands, lest the measure of value be suddenly so changed as to entail heavy loss on them. . . . The farmers in Illinois holding meetings to thank God for former small crops, and make agreements to till less land in

[35] March 23, 1866, *Cong. Globe,* 39 Cong., 1 Sess., 971, 1614.
[36] March 23, 1866, Stevens MSS., VII.
[37] March 21, 1866, *ibid.,* VII.

the present year. These are significant facts, while landlords of the free trade foreign City of New York are putting up the rents of stores to sell British & German goods in, from $15,000 to $40,000 a year." [38] "Why should we," asked the *Herald*, benefit a few fundholders and rich men at the cost of the industrious millions? . . . The currency will gradually approximate the specie standard through natural laws, through the wonderful growth of the country and development of our vast resources." [39] Eastern farmers protested.[40] Eastern merchants, and even some of the manufacturers who feared that a diminution of the currency in the pockets of the people would cut sales, joined the opposition.[41]

But from the West came the loudest outcry. "You can hardly conceive," the head of a Chicago firm wrote Trumbull, "what a feeling of despondency has settled down again upon Manufacturers and business men. . . . Scarcely a business man we have conversed with, feels that the Contraction policy should be enforced at present." [42] It would bring "a perfect panic and a general failure," wrote a constituent of Sherman; "we must keep the ball in motion until we can have the products of the soil in good supply, and that will regulate Exchange and Gold, and *nothing else will do it*." [43] But the most interesting opposition came from Sherman himself, the later financial mentor of Congress. "The amount of

[38] Feb. 8, 1866, *ibid.*, VI.

[39] *New York Herald*, Sept. 10, 1866.

[40] E.g., the *Herald* of Norristown, Pennsylvania, Jan. 13, 1866, Stevens MSS., VI; and Pike of Maine in the House, *Cong. Globe*, 39 Cong., 1 Sess., 1455.

[41] McManus, an iron manufacturer of Reading, protested to Stevens: "In the name of all that is good why don't we let well enough alone," and "go on encourage industry . . . It is a fallacy that we have too much money in circulation; if we had, interest would not be from 7 to 9 per cent." Jan. 2, 1866, Stevens MSS., VI.

[42] E. W. Blatchford to L. Trumbull, Feb. 25, 1867, Trumbull MSS., LXX.

[43] Z. Street to J. Sherman, May 25, 1866, John Sherman MSS.

legal tenders now outstanding," he insisted, "is not too much for the present condition of the country. I expect to come back to specie payments and I expect to see gold approach the level and standard of our paper money, without any material reduction of our currency. . . . The mere amount of legal tender outstanding does not fix the rate of gold. That is the result of the restored confidence of the people of this country and of all nations in the credit of the United States. . . . I would make no opposition to the bill, no opposition to the vast power to sell bonds, . . . if the Secretary would not in this way undertake to carry out . . . a contraction of the currency. . . . That is what I am afraid of." [44] Sherman expressed general Ohio sentiment in voting against the bill.

The vote on the modified contraction of the loan bill is interesting.[45] It passed the House 83-53, but of the 83 ayes, 48 came from the Northeast, and only 33 from the Northwest, while of the nays 20 were from the Northeast, and 32 from the Northwest. The Northeast voted 48-20 for the bill.[46] The West [47] voted 33-32 for the bill but Ohio opposed it 5-11, Michigan 1-4, and Iowa 1-4, while Kansas and Missouri were tied, and McCulloch's own state approved it only 4-3. In the Senate the count was 32-7; the Northeastern vote, 18-0; the Northwestern, 9-7. The East favored contraction; the West was divided, or opposed to it.[48]

Subsequent events appear to have justified the opposition plan of maintaining in circulation the number of greenbacks

---

[44] *Cong. Globe*, 39 Cong., 1 Sess., 1850.

[45] *Ibid.*, 39 Cong., 1 Sess., 1614, 1854.

[46] In fact, Rhode Island voting 0-1, Maryland, 1-3, and West Virginia, 1-1, were the only states of the Northeast not strongly for it.

[47] Exclusive of the "Far West" which voted 2-1 for the bill.

[48] This vote does not tell the whole story of opposition, for reluctant aye votes were won by incorporating into the bill a necessary refunding provision.

then outstanding. Popular protest forced the repeal of the loan bill in 1868. Then slowly the cancelled greenbacks were reissued to continue in circulation to this day. It is possible that the expanded industry and wealth of the country, and the requirements of the new industrial age that had dawned, necessitated a larger stock of money than had sufficed in the very different era before the Civil War.[49]

Secretary of the Treasury McCulloch, an Indiana banker, was a leading contractionist. His position was succinctly stated in a letter to Boston friends.[50] "Our present prosperity," he wrote, "is rather apparent than real, . . . we are measuring values by a false standard, . . . we are, in fact, exposed to all the dangers which attend an inflated currency, which diminishes labor—the true source of national wealth—and stimulates speculation and extravagance which lead invariably to thriftlessness and demoralization. Before the country becomes again really prosperous, the specie standard must be restored, prices reduced, industry stimulated, the products of the country increased, the balance of trade between the United States and other nations cease to be against us." New England heartily agreed. The *Boston Daily Advertiser* declared: "When the country understands that the policy of reduction and resumption is fairly determined upon, it will adjust its business to that end, and will prepare itself definitely for a return to the specie standard by a curtailment of extravagances which for some months past have been plunging us into debt, and raising an interest against resumption which in the first half of the last year was scarcely heard of or suspected to exist." [51]

[49] In any case the circulating medium of the country by 1920 was $56 per capita instead of $22 as in 1866.
[50] *Boston Daily Advertiser*, Aug. 21, 1866.
[51] *Ibid.*, March 26, 1866.

Johnson himself leaned to the inflationist view. His sympathies led him to align himself with the poorer people, and to suspect the financial interests. In 1868 when McCulloch prepared a veto message for the bill repealing the contraction law, Johnson refused to use it,[52] and allowed the bill to become a law. But in the earlier part of his administration he abided by the advice of his Secretary of the Treasury, and refrained from interference in favor of the inflationists.

McCulloch's stand required courage. Soon after his speech in Fort Wayne announcing his contraction policy, an Indiana banker who approved warned him, "The clamorous will howl, and the quiet will beg, and pray, little less than nerves of iron controlled by calm and cool judgment, will be adequate to the task, which seems imposed on you." [53] His New York agent Forbes wrote him, "*Whenever* you move towards constriction the army of Debtors which always exceeds five times that of Creditors will cry out, 'Stop a little!' *Not yet—wait!*—& then the timid honest ones like Greeley will re-echo. Even men sound in theory, who have been led into expansion —will find some reason for your waiting till *they* have got out." [54] McCulloch's position was economically sound but politically injudicious. Had the administration favored inflation, or had it even taken a stand on Sherman's middle-of-the-road views, opposing both further inflation and contraction, the deflationist demands of Morrill and other leading Radicals could have been used to organize a powerful political opposition to them that would have split the Radical Party.   *   *   *   *

[52] The unused veto message is in the Johnson MSS., XCII.

[53] G. C. Clark, Pres. of Rushville Nat. Bank, to H. McCulloch, Nov. 14, 1865, McCulloch MSS., II.

[54] "You want to have the steps toward resumption gradual so as to divide the loss of our depreciated currency over as many hands as possible. If you had the power today I don't believe you would dare to use it strongly . . . it would raise a tremendous outcry." Sept. 8, 1865, *ibid.*, II.

A quarrel between bondholders and non-bondholders over the payment of the principal and interest of the national debt assumed the proportions of a political issue. Many of the bonds had been bought with depreciated greenbacks worth from forty to sixty cents on the dollar. The stipulations for repayment varied, but many of the bonds provided that interest and principal should be paid in "lawful money." Poor men contended that to pay the bonds in gold would mean paying a huge premium to bondholders. Bondowners maintained that not to do so would be a violation of government faith, since the bonds could not have been sold at par even in the depreciated greenbacks, had it not been tacitly promised that they would be redeemed in gold.

Nation-wide protests against payment in gold poured in from the debtor class. "Administrative or legislative action to force the purchasing power of the currency one-third," protested the farmers of Pennsylvania, "would add a like value to Government securities (many of which were purchased when gold was above $2.50) and to the interest derived therefrom, (which would be equal to 15 per cent with currency at par), and would settle a debt upon us and our posterity whose value would be $4,500,000,000 for $3,000,-000,000 paid in. This would be a splendid condition of affairs for capitalists and bond holders, foreign and domestic; but it would be gross injustice to the people, who have suffered so much. . . . The plainest dictates of common sense, and national honor, justice, harmony and safety, would seem to require that an enormous debt contracted to preserve the national existence should be liquidated with a currency of the same value as that with which it was created. Relative value between debt and its payment would then be uniform; no wrong would be committed upon debtor or creditor." [55] Blatchford, of a Chicago firm bearing his name, wrote Trumbull assuring him that "all are equally firm in the conviction that the Compound Interest notes should be redeemed in *plain legal* tender because they have got to go into Bank Reserves any way and we feel that the Banks are making money enough without drawing interest on their Reserves." [56]

To the demand for repayment in greenbacks was added a popular cry for taxation of bonds, at least of those issued for refunding. Debtors resented the fact that the wealth of bondholders escaped its portion of taxation, of which the burden was made heavier by the necessity of paying interest and principal upon these very bonds which escaped. The *Herald* printed among a set of "pertinent questions by soldiers to a Radical member of Congress," the query: "Do you endorse the law that exempts the bondholder from paying taxes on said bonds, while we boys have to pay the taxes, at least our portion, after serving to put down the rebellion, while you bondholders remained at home enjoying ease and comfort?" [57] It was a question that many ex-soldiers, especially in the West, were raising. Ross of Illinois introduced a resolution into the House that no more government bonds should be issued unless they were subject to taxation; but it was tabled by a vote of 61-36.[58]

The necessity of refunding the debt was generally recog-

[55] Communication to the *Norristown Herald* of Pa., Jan. 13, 1866, Stevens MSS., VI. Ohio's veteran politician, Ewing, wrote similarly to McCulloch: "The public debt is now $3,000,000,000 equal to $2,000,000,000 in gold. The funds received did not bear a higher relative value when the debt was contracted; so the U. S. in fact borrowed no more than $2,000,-000,000 in gold, and is not now under any obligations moral or financial to bring gold to par and thus enhance the debt $1,000,000,000. For the U. S. would thus pay over to capitalists one thousand millions more than was borrowed of them." June 30, 1866, Ewing MSS., "Letter-book."

[56] Feb. 25, 1867, Trumbull MSS., LXIX.

[57] *New York Herald,* Sept. 5, 1866.

[58] *Cong. Globe,* 39 Cong., 2 Sess., 151.

nized. But the method was disputed. Debtors insisted that the new bonds be payable in greenbacks and taxable. Others protested vigorously against the employment of Jay Cooke in the refunding.[59] The popular imagination exaggerated the profit he would make. Always suspicious of financiers, farmers and Westerners looked upon the funding proposal as a scheme to milk the taxpayers to pay Jay Cooke handsomely for services which the government could perform for itself.

In their Northern campaign for control of the South, the Radicals capitalized their position with bondholders. Thousands supported the Radicals as the party that would secure and enhance the value of their government securities. The Conservatives failed to organize the opposition of thousands of others who looked with suspicion on a party that used the government for the service of bondholders.

* * * *

Around the new national banks centered continual controversy. A strong tradition of opposition to the idea of a national bank remained from Jackson's day. The new banks were different, but they bore the onus of the popular distrust of the "monied monster" of the 'Thirties. In truth the new banks *were* a potent influence; they were intended to be. They aroused Western opposition by intensifying the concentration of financial control in the Northeast—in New York, Philadelphia, and Boston. Endowed with greater resources than the old state banks, they wielded great power. "Business" stood solidly behind them as it had behind the Bank of Jackson's day, and urged their extension. These new national banks it was that later helped Big Business in the extraordinary financing of the last years of the cen-

[59] E.g., *New York Herald,* July 23, 1866.

tury. Small banks, Western state banks, debtors, hated them as early as 1866 for their very stabilizing activity, and for their apparent favoring of Easterners and business men. Even in the East some opposition to the new system was raised. Both Bennett and Phillips of the *Herald* were persuaded that "the system of National Banks is a fraud upon the country, a gross monopoly, and dangerous." [60] L. R. Flanigen of the *Philadelphia Daily News* wrote, "The Radical power is the monied power of the country, and the National Banks constitute the most important element of that power. The dividends which they earn and declare are without precedant, and those who controll them are lavish of their contributions to partisan purposes." [61]

Opposition was raised to the government's patronizing of national banks. Use of the vast resources of the government would simply add to the danger of the money power. Within the cabinet Welles protested against McCulloch's depositing government money in national banks. "I have never believed," he declared, "that the funds of the government should, under any pretext whatever, be used for business purposes." [62] The banks' power to issue currency was particularly resented. By June, 1866, circulation of national bank notes had reached $281,479,908, almost three-fourths as much as the $400,619,206 in greenbacks. [63] But the two were on a different basis. Greenbacks had no other backing than the willingness and ability of the government to redeem after it had met all other obligations. Bank notes were guaranteed by government bonds. National banks were allowed to

---

[60] W. B. Phillips to A. Johnson, July 1, 1866, Johnson MSS., XCVII. In the *Herald* they repeatedly expressed these sentiments.
[61] Sept. 21, 1866, Johnson MSS., CII.
[62] G. Welles to H. McCulloch, May 17, 1866, Welles MSS., "Letter-book," XII.
[63] *Statistical Abstract* (1878), 14.

deposit United States bonds in the national treasury as security, and then issue bank notes for ninety per cent of their value. In this way the banks drew interest on their capital invested in bonds, and at the same time used ninety per cent of it in the form of bank notes. Opponents of the system argued that this was paying the banks to perform the government's function of issuing currency. In transmitting an anti-bank resolution of a farmers' convention in Illinois, Locy protested against McCulloch's plan of withdrawing greenbacks and substituting national bank notes. "The interest upon the Bonds standing behind the circulation wd be about $60,000,000 annually," he wrote, "which the producing interests (for they at last bear all these burdens) have to pay into the coffers of these so constituted National Banks and for what? That is the question which the people want answered. These very banks are today making in the money of trade from 15 to 40 per cent upon the capital invested—I ask is this not a centralizing power to be dreaded?" [64] Even Francis Bowen, the Harvard economist, in a Lowell Institute lecture attacked the national banks as expensive to the government. "The National Bank Act," he declared, "actually offers any holders of national securities who choose to come together as a banking association, that on condition of leaving this sum on deposit, they shall receive as a free gift an amount of currency equal to 90 per cent. of their stock, on which the government will pay them the full market rate of interest." [65]

The National Bank Act provided the means of withdrawing the notes from circulation. A bank placed on deposit in the Treasury "lawful money" of the amount of the bank

[64] G. H. Locy to A. Johnson, Feb. 25, 1866, Johnson MSS., LXXXVIII.
[65] *Boston Daily Advertiser*, Feb. 21, 1866.

note issue; the bonds were then turned back to the bank, and the United States assumed liability for the bank's notes, and gradually, as they became soiled and worn, withdrew them from circulation. Meantime the Treasury did not hold the "lawful money" paid by the bank to redeem its currency, but used that as part of its quick assets. Consequently, after the United States assumed responsibility, bank notes were on exactly the same basis as greenbacks, guaranteed by nothing but the credit of the government. It was pointed out that if all the banks redeemed their notes through this process at the same time, the result would be the same as withdrawing the bank notes and issuing a like amount in greenbacks in their stead. This is what inflationists and opponents of the national banks wished to require by legislation. They pointed out that if then the "lawful money" deposited, instead of being added to the quick assets, were used to redeem the bonds held by the banks, the government could save the interest money, and by issuing greenbacks in their place as the bank notes came in for redemption could maintain the same amount of currency as the combined bank notes and greenbacks totaled. At one blow this would deprive the banks of profits at taxpayers' expense, redeem the bonds, and increase greenbacks, the money of the people. The *Herald* advocated this plan, and pointed out that if then the government would reserve the gold that was constantly coming into the Treasury from the customs, the business community would feel assured of the ability of the government to redeem paper in specie if demanded, and the country would be saved from distress of inflation and scarcity of circulating medium, alike, without being oppressed by a "dangerous moneyed power." [66] If a simple statement of this

[66] *New York Herald*, Sept. 17, 1866.

plan is spread before the people in a presidential message, wrote W. D. Bartlett, "they will take care—prompted by self-interest—to compel Congress to provide some practical measure to carry it into effect." [67]

Early in the session which opened in December, 1866, Ross, an Illinois Democrat, introduced a resolution "to inquire into the expediency of withdrawing the national bank currency and winding up the national banks and furnishing the country . . . with greenbacks, or other currency of similar character." It was tabled, 87-58. Then Harding, also of Illinois, proposed a resolution prohibiting the diminution of the number of greenbacks, and declaring that it was to "the interest of the whole people of the United States that the Government should issue all bills intended and designed to circulate as money," and that issues of currency by banks or corporations should be discouraged. This, too, was tabled. But the vote, 94-60, is illuminating. Of the 94 votes for tabling, 54 were Northeastern and only 36 Northwestern. The East voted 54-12 against considering Harding's resolution; the West, 41-36 for consideration. [68]

There were, of course, advantages in the national bank currency system that business men recognized, but the anti-bank forces could not see them. From the point of view of hard money men, the plan for abolishing national bank notes was simply an inflationist scheme to double the issue of greenbacks. The opponents of the bank retorted that if necessary the government could itself hold the bonds to back the extra issue of greenbacks, and pay itself the interest. The whole proposition was further made unpalatable to hard money men because it involved redeeming the bonds in "law-

[67] Nov. 30, 1865, Johnson MSS., LXXXII.
[68] Cong. Globe, 39 Cong., 2 Sess., 49.

ful money" instead of in the gold demanded by bondholders. But if "lawful money" was sufficient for the banks to pay the government in regaining their deposited bonds, anti-bank men could not see why the same money should not suffice when the government redeemed the bonds from the banks that owned them. So the controversy ran on.

Johnson's own opinions were stated when he finally broke his silent acquiescence in his Secretary's views, and expressed his own on currency and banks in his last annual message. The amount which the government obtained, he said, "was in real money three or four hundred per cent less than the obligations which it issued in return. It can not be denied that we are paying an extravagant percentage for the use of the money borrowed, which was paper currency, greatly depreciated below the value of coin. This fact is made apparent when we consider that bondholders receive from the Treasury upon each dollar they own in Government securities 6 per cent in gold, which is nearly or quite equal to 9 per cent in currency; that the bonds are then converted into capital for the national banks, upon which those institutions issue their circulation, bearing 6 per cent interest; and that they are exempt from taxation by the Government and the States, and thereby enhanced 2 per cent in the hands of the holders. We thus have an aggregate of 17 per cent which may be received upon each dollar by the owners of Government securities. . . . Our national credit should be sacredly observed, but in making provision for our creditors we should not forget what is due the masses of the people. It may be assumed that the holders of our securities have already received upon their bonds a larger amount than their original investment, measured by a gold standard. Upon this statement of facts it would seem but just and equitable that

the 6 per cent interest now paid by the Government should
be applied to the reduction of the principal in semi-annual
installments, which in sixteen years and eight months would
liquidate the entire national debt." [69] But Johnson maintained silence during 1866, waiting until the South should be
restored before he turned to other matters.

II. BIG BUSINESS

Another phase of economic unrest was the growing popular dislike of railroads, monopolies, and the methods of
nascent "big business," that in the latter part of the century
was to call down upon itself denunciations and regulatory
acts until its activities were in a degree limited. By 1866 a
new industrial age, that era of extraordinary expansion and
development that has made present-day America, had begun.
But the average man could not foresee the new order; had
he been gifted with prophecy, it might have made his opposition to the forerunners of Big Business the more determined.

For several years before the Civil War, inventions, railroad building, growth and expansion of population, and the
opening up of untold natural resources, had been preparing
the way. But it was the demands of four years of war upon
industry and agriculture that gave the immediate stimulus
to the industrialism which has dominated American history
ever since Hayes's removal of Northern troops from the
South discharged "reconstruction" from the leading rôle on
our stage of national affairs. The age of business did not, of
course, spring Athena-like into being with the relegation of
reconstruction to unimportance. The process was a gradual
evolution from the war days in the early 'Sixties to the end

[69] J. D. Richardson, *Messages and Papers of the Presidents,* VI, 678.

of the century. Economic problems had been present in 1866 which were forgotten during years of reconstruction excitement, and not recalled until they had attained huge proportions.

Before the Civil War, the United States, and in particular newly-settled regions, had been dominated by an individualism and freedom from restraint, a daring initiative, and a buoyant optimism that would have been impossible in an older country. The qualities of the industrial and financial geniuses who led industry to the extraordinary developments of the new age were part and parcel of the same youthful spirit of adventure that had dominated the frontier for centuries. Initiative in a man inspired respect, and, under the rules of free competition and equal opportunity, stimulated activity in neighbors eager to emulate his success. But initiative and freedom from restraint in a corporation with wealth and government influence behind it, aroused hatred among individualists of Western communities, whose fortunes its power and wealth controlled as government never had been able to control them. Competition might be free among individuals of a new community, or among corporations and great financial wizards of the approaching era, but ordinary individuals and corporations could never exist together both unrestrained. Either corporations would control men, or men through their government would succeed in restraining corporations. The former frontiersman, then, came to be the bitterest enemy of his own individualistic spirit when manifested in a powerful corporation. The excesses of Big Business were eventually to transform the West's hatred of restraint into a demand for governmental restraint of the more powerful business pioneers who were controlling individual men. The Westerner gradually developed from the most extreme individualist of the country into the most persistent advocate of regulation and control.

In 1866 the transition period had just begun. The Northwest was still a new country, still dominantly agricultural. It had the frontier's love of free competition, but also its hatred of monopoly and Big Business. A few years later the Old Northwest was to be the center of agrarian efforts to destroy encroaching industrialism by regulatory acts. Many years later this Old Northwest was itself to be the home of a great industrial system, thoroughly conservative and economically orthodox. But in 1866 Big Business was just beginning to creep in, and railroads were still free from all restraints. Petroleum companies were getting their start in western Pennsylvania, Ohio, and Indiana. Big mining concerns of the Great Lakes iron country were beginning to open up the wealth of that region. The Chicago stockyards were being organized. Cleveland and Toledo and Pittsburgh were laying the foundations of a great steel industry. Lumber interests of Michigan and Wisconsin were beginning to dominate whole counties. Western railroads were competing for huge grants of valuable lands, and older roads were still operating under the motto: "The public be damned." Unless pecuniarily interested, Westerners were suspicious of these new enterprises. * * * *

The railroads, especially, were the butt of denunciation and righteous indignation. During the two decades preceding the Civil War, Westerners had not been able to secure railroads fast enough. Farmers had mortgaged their farms, and towns and counties had issued bonds, to buy stocks encouraging railroad construction. The people never realized any profits on their investments; many men lost their farms, towns paid extra taxes to meet their railroad indebtedness, and firms failed because of debts thus contracted. The railroads were reorganized under financing that voided earlier claims on the companies, and men who had suffered financial ruin to bring the railroad into the region, saw rehabilitated roads making large profits for outsiders from high rates levied on the sufferers from early mismanagement.

After the Civil War, railroads ceased all thought of service to the community, and assumed the attitude that they were above any kind of control. Railroad employees were pointedly rude to passengers; the officers burdened whole communities with excessive rates, charging all the traffic would bear. If competition kept charges reasonable between main points, way-stations which were dependent upon one railroad had to pay exorbitantly, more than was charged for much longer hauls from one railroad center to another. Towns near which the roads owned sections of land were especially favored. Railroads and grain elevators combined to take every possible advantage of the farmers who had to employ them. In 1865 corn was being burned for fuel in parts of the West because a bumper crop, low price of corn, and high freight rates made it cheaper to burn corn than to sell it and buy fuel.[70] Specific grievances, then, combined with the inherent Western dislike of big corporations, led the agricultural West to seek regulation of railroads.

Farmers' conventions in Illinois, Wisconsin, Minnesota, and Ohio joined in the cry.[71] In January, 1865, Brown of

[70] C. C. Royce to E. B. Washburne, Dec. 10, 1865, Washburne MSS., L.
[71] The resolutions of a northern Illinois meeting are typical:

"WHEREAS, Under the present system of railroad combinations and other freight monopolies, the farmer and producer has no redress, and is, by the inadequate means of transportation, compelled to give two-thirds of his crop to get the other one-third to market; and,

"WHEREAS, We regard the present system of transportation as little less than a semi-legalized system of plunder, by which a combination

Winnebago County introduced a regulatory act in the Illinois Legislature, and the supervisors of his county required each candidate for office to pledge support of it. At Springfield an anti-monopoly league was formed whose platform embraced "restrictions on railroad combinations, uniformity of freight rates, a three-cent passenger fare, and an annual report of expenditures and receipts of each road." [72] In January, 1866, several counties sent delegates to Sterling for a meeting of "farmers and all others interested in finding some cheaper way than over the Rail Roads to market for the products of this country." [73] At Morris a convention was held in December, 1866, "to derive practical measures to bring the railroad Cos. to a sense of justice." [74] In Amboy was a strong Laboring Men's Association ready to support any party that would protect "the rights of the laboring and producing part of the country, against Monied Monopolies." [75] Washburne led a fight in Illinois against railroad monopolies. A speech he made at Morris in November, 1865,

of capitalists are rearing immense fortunes upon the ruins of the producing interests of the Northwest; therefore,

"*Resolved,* That the extortionate charges of the railroads generally of the State of Illinois, and their frequent unjust discrimination between places, their combinations with warehousemen, and the system of grain inspections as now practiced in Chicago, one, each and all are so unjust and oppressive, as to force upon the people the seeking of appropriate remedies; and, as we know of no adequate remedy for the present wrongs, or security against future oppression, but legislation, we must turn our attention to the law making power, and demand such appropriate and efficient legislation as will remedy these evils, and thus teach corporations and unholy combinations that the sovereign people have rights which they are bound to respect,

"*Resolved,* That in order to carry these principles into practical effect, we hereby pledge ourselves to cooperate with the people throughout the State in electing a Legislature pledged to the same." James Parton, *Manual for the Instruction of "Rings," Railroad and Political,* 70.

[72] A. C. Cole, *Era of the Civil War* (*Centennial History of Illinois,* III), 358.

[73] D. Richards to E. B. Washburne, Dec. 25, 1865, Washburne MSS., XVI.

[74] W. Birney to E. B. W., Dec. 3, 1866, *ibid.,* XIX.

[75] A. Kinyon to E. B. W., Sept. 10, 1866, *ibid.,* XIX.

won him great popularity.[76] The *Chicago Tribune* sent one of its best reporters to "make a big thing of it," and agreed to "go any length in fighting all these extortionists." [77] When Washburne carried his attack to the floors of Congress where the Illinois Central was seeking favor,[78] that road threatened him with personal ruin.[79] The monopolies subsidized the press,[80] and in the end were so powerful in the legislative halls that the protestants accomplished nothing. Various canals were projected in attempts to break the rail monopoly.[81] Rumors were afloat of a great combination of railroads, elevators, steamboat lines, and express companies of the upper Mississippi region. The railroads' refusal to answer a questionnaire which Chicago merchants addressed to them, was regarded as confirmation of the rumor.[82] In February, 1866, the Chicago Board of Trade and the Chicago Mercantile Association compiled a list of grievances expressed in "the various public meetings that [had] recently been held through the country." [83]

[76] See, e.g., S. D. Atkins to E. B. W., Dec. 6, 1865, C. U. Worthington of the *Sterling Gazette* to E. B. W., Dec. 6, 1865, C. C. Royce to E. B. W., Dec. 10, 1865, *ibid.*, L; J. A. Noonan to E. B. W., March 15, 1866, *ibid.*, XIX.

[77] H. White to E. B. W., Nov. 18, 1865, *ibid.*, LI.

[78] *Cong. Globe*, 39 Cong., 1 Sess., 1194.

[79] H. White to E. B. W., April 30, 1866, Washburne MSS., LIII.

[80] S. G. Patrick to E. B. W., March 21, 1866, *ibid.*, LIII.

[81] Illinois felt particularly bitter over the boosting of freight rates when the outbreak of the War closed the Mississippi, cutting off water competition. A state-wide movement was launched for the building of a ship canal between Chicago and Rock Island on the Mississippi. *Chicago Tribune*, Jan. 6, 1866, *et seq.*

[82] A. C. Cole, *op. cit.*, 357-358.

[83] "First, irregular and incorrect inspection of grain in bulk at Chicago, and the tampering with and mixing of grain by warehousemen; Second, extravagant and arbitrary rates of storage adopted by warehousemen; Third, incorrectness of weighing bulk grain at Chicago, and large losses sustained by inferior shippers by alleged shortage on their shipping weights; Fourth, arbitrary rules of railway companies in compelling the delivery of bulk grain to certain elevators, and the lack of notice to consignees of the arrival of shipments; Fifth, alleged complicity on the part of railroad officials with the management of grain elevators; Sixth, the consolidation of certain railroad lines, which, it is claimed, works injuriously

The Ohio Agricultural Convention passed resolutions declaring that "combinations of carriers, for the purposes of maintaining or increasing rates for transportation of property . . . are oppressive to producers and consumers, and should be prohibited by law." [84] In a speech urging the resolutions, Millikin declared: "How completely the farmer's interests are under the control of the railroad combinations . . . [is] fully understood. . . . The demands of the carrier have to be met *nolens volens*. . . . And thus millions of bushels of wheat are thereby depreciated in value 5½ cents per bushel. . . . Surely there ought to be limitation to the capricious action of men, who are really not held accountable to the public for their conduct. . . . The extent to which unjust combinations have damaged the character of railroads, or dishonorably extorted money from the public is beyond computation. One thing, however, is certain, that if half that has been sworn to by apparently truthful and competent men can be confided in, then more is true than has been even suspected." [85] Stockdale likewise protested: "If the stock shipper is not protected better the business will be ruined. . . . Our stock dealers will buy hogs and cattle under contract, when they can secure contracts in the East; but when the day of shipment arrives, the railroad monopolists will raise the price of freight enough to ruin the dealer. And this is done every year, so that we have to drive our stock overland to Philadelphia, at such a cost that we could

and oppressively upon the interest of the community; Seventh, combinations between railroad companies and steamboat lines, which are claimed to create monopolies, and by high rates of transportation, inflict unnecessary burdens upon those who are obliged to patronize those lines; Eighth, excessively high rates for travel and transportation by the various railway lines leading westward from Chicago." J. Parton, *op. cit.*, 67.

[84] Ohio State Board of Agriculture, *Twenty-first Annual Report* (1866), 48 ff.

[85] *Ibid.*, 68.

not afford to continue the business. This Convention should call upon the Legislature of Ohio to establish some uniform rate of charges, and break down these railroad monopolies; require them to establish such a rate in July as they will live up to in December. Another thing: Why should freight from central Ohio to Baltimore, be more than it is from Chicago to Baltimore. . . . I know of farmers who lived in Fairfield county, Ohio, who moved West because they could ship their stock 1000 miles from that section cheaper than we could 500 miles. . . . Last year I wanted to ship some grain east. I found I could get corn here for 40 cents per bushel; but on inquiring into the freight business, I found it would cost two dollars to ship to an eastern market. . . . Eastern capitalists control our railroads, and require them to charge what they please. Will the Legislature of Ohio lay supinely on their backs and let these railroad monopolists' rob our farmers of what would be remunerative prices for their products? I am proud to say that we, the farmers of Ohio, own three-fourths of the property in the State, and have a right to the protection which our Legislature can afford." [86]

A steamboat magnate named Davidson sought a monopoly of trade on the upper Mississippi but was vigorously attacked by the *St. Paul Pioneer*, Democratic organ of the region. To silence it, Davidson bought the paper. Popular indignation broke out in an anti-monopoly convention at St. Paul, February 7, 1866. Twenty-eight Minnesota and four Wisconsin counties participated. Resolutions against monopolies were adopted, but no action was taken on the practicability of financing an independent company, as no one wished to furnish the money. Hence the convention came to

[86] Ohio State Board of Agriculture, *Twenty-first Annual Report* (1866), 70-71.

nought, and after the Radical victory of 1866, Davidson felt safe in reselling the *Pioneer* to the Democrats.[87]

Realization of Western discontent and unrest penetrated as far as Sumner's state, where a Boston paper told its readers, "The enormous railroad, canal, and lake charges on grain . . . have fully aroused the people of the Northwest . . . and they are now giving every emphatic expression to their determination to submit no longer to the exactions of the transportation companies." [88]

Many Easterners were themselves seeking regulation of railroads, not because of unfair rates, but because of the methods of business organization employed. "The truth is," wrote the *Herald*, "our railroad companies are mere stock gambling concerns, and neither the lives and comfort of the traveling public nor keeping up the value of their property by repairs give them a moment's thought." [89] The *Herald* vociferated against the unscrupulous stock manipulations out of which the directors made personal wealth at public expense. "Unless it is stopped in some way it will ruin the railroad interests of this country. No capitalist will be willing to intrust his money in any such enterprise; for he will not know at what moment this shuttlecock operation of the directors in Wall street will destroy his property, and make his stock worthless. . . . If the Legislatures have not the power [to correct the evils], then let Congress take hold of

[87] L. B. Shippee, "Steamboating on the Upper Mississippi after the Civil War," *Miss. Valley Hist. Rev.,* VI, 474-487.

[88] "It costs three bushels of corn to send one to market a distance of one hundred miles; one hundred bushels to get a pair of boots; one thousand bushels to get a suit of clothes; and two tons of corn for a ton of coal. A farmer of Waterloo, Iowa, was actually brought five dollars in debt by a shipment of barley to Chicago . . . Iowa grain shippers complain that their wheat is 'doctored' by the Chicago warehousemen, by which the price of their best wheat is reduced to that of the mixed qualities shipped East." J. Parton, *op. cit.,* 66.

[89] *New York Herald,* July 13, 1866.

it." By December the *Herald* had been won to actual government management of railroads and telegraph lines "as public
institutions, for the benefit of the Commonwealth." [90] The
Nation agreed that government regulation was legitimate,
and advocated a law making accidents so expensive that the
roads would be forced to provide safety devices.[91] In its
Financial Circular of May, 1866, Jerome, Briggs, and Company attacked the railroads vigorously. These brokers contended that the fall in prices of railroad securities that had
been in the highest favor was caused by "the well grounded
distrust as to the condition and management of our roads." [92]

* * * *

In the fall of 1866 James Parton published an anti-monopoly pamphlet of eighty-three pages, called a *Manual for
the Instruction of "Rings," Railroad and Political.* The
booklet contained a detailed account of the "history of the
grand Chicago and North Western 'Ring' and the secret of
its success in placing an over-issue of twenty millions, with
a margin of three millions in three years." It was a startling
exposé of the way in which Tilden and Ogden, by fleecing
stockholders and patrons, had built up a huge monopoly in
the West, and had secured to themselves great wealth and
vast political power. The book was cleverly written in the
form of directions to others who wished successfully to create
"rings." It told what to do and what not to do in evading the
law, buying courts and legislatures, and duping stockholders. Parton proved himself a worthy forerunner of the
most successful muck-rakers of Roosevelt's day. If a small
part of what he recounted was true—and probably most of

90 *Ibid.*, July 19, Dec. 10, 1866.
91 The *Nation*, II (Jan. 4, 1866), 8.
92 J. Parton, *op. cit.*, 82. See also H. K. Beale, "The Decision of Reconstruction," 442.

it was—the book furnished damning evidence against Tilden, Ogden, and the Chicago and North Western Railroad. Its revelations, had they reached popular circulation, would have caused an uprising in the West against monopolies and railroads that would have swept into power any party that had adopted an anti-monopoly slogan. Tilden was a Democrat, but neither party had a corner on monopolists, and in general the Radical Party represented Big Business, railroads, manufacturers, and monopolists to the popular mind, if not in fact. But the powers which the booklet condemned controlled the courts and Tilden secured an order for its suppression.[93] It remains merely as a curio, one of the interesting might-have-beens, but it clearly evidences the popular feeling against monopolies.

The national banks were most bitterly attacked as "a dangerous monopoly, controlling all the labor and products of labor, the markets and commercial affairs of the country, placing, in fact, all the industrial interests of the country in the hands of grasping capitalists." Their "power of forestalling and controlling the markets and business of the country," said the *Herald*, is a real menace. "The farmers of the West, the planters of the South, and the business of the country everywhere are at their mercy. . . . We complain of high prices, and justly; but the cause of these high prices is neither the premium on gold nor the difference between gold and currency, but the monopoly and influence of the national banks. . . . The capital which the government literally gives them enables them to forestall the markets, keep up high prices and oppress the people." [94]

[93] A few copies escaped confiscation and during the Hayes-Tilden campaign the booklet was reprinted from one of these by the Illinois Republican State Committee.
[94] *New York Herald*, Dec. 12 and July 1, 1866.

Johnson had the same dislike of monopoly and Big Business that dominated Western farmers. Indeed, his hatred of monopoly was greater than his very strong states' rights theories, as was indicated in his attitude toward the Camden and Amboy Railroad. New Jersey granted this railroad a monopoly of all traffic across the state and then taxed the railroad so that all freight and passengers that passed from New York to Philadelphia, from New England to the national capital, had to pay a camouflaged tax to the State of New Jersey. In Maryland the same situation obtained with the Baltimore and Ohio road, which had a state-given monopoly. Together these monopolies had cost interstate commerce $1,948,513.62.[95] Lincoln had objected, but had seen no remedy that did not violate states' rights. Johnson had similar respect for the prerogative of a state. But since his hatred of monopoly was greater, he sought to charter a national airline railroad between New York and Philadelphia in competition with the state monopoly; a bill to this end passed the House, but was blocked in the Senate by the closure of the session—and by the "money of the monopolies."[96]

In his first annual message Johnson urged the use of the commerce power of Congress to prevent railroad monopolies. He declared, "Monopolies, perpetuities, and class legislation are contrary to the genius of free government. . . . Wherever monopoly attains a foothold, it is sure to be a source of danger, discord, and trouble. . . . The Government is subordinate to the people; but, as the agent and representative of the people, it must be held superior to monopolies, which in themselves ought never to be granted, and which, where

[95] S. F. Barr to T. Stevens, Jan. 6, 1866, Stevens MSS., VI.
[96] *New York Herald*, July 29, 1866.

they exist, must be subordinate and yield to the Government." [97] These views were as dangerous to business interests as speedy restoration. In fact, the probability of Southern agrarians' joining the President in blasting the hopes of incipient monopolists was one factor that made admission of Southerners to Congress dangerous. Yet a great anti-monopoly movement was awaiting a national leader.[98] Johnson failed to organize it, and federal regulation of interstate commerce and combinations in restraint of trade had to wait another twenty years.

*   *   *   *

As President, Johnson did strenuously oppose the entry of Big Business into the new lands of the West. All his life he had fought for the small pioneer farmer, until the Homestead Act in 1862 finally crowned his labors with success. Now he had no intention of seeing the actual settler deprived of his hard-won rights by the rapacity of great corporations and land speculators. He therefore consistently opposed the granting of public land to railroads and insisted that it be reserved for homesteaders.

The Radicals favored full exploitation of the national resources. They wanted to open the mineral lands to sale and settlement. This would produce, they estimated, five hundred million dollars of gold and silver; and, by reducing the speculative value of gold, would deprive the Democrats of political capital.[99] Furthermore, many leading Radicals and their constituents were interested in the new corporations that hoped to make fortunes through exploitation of natural

[97] J. D. Richardson, *op. cit.*, VI, 361-362.
[98] The *Nation* (II [Jan. 4, 1866], 8) pointed out that even Congress on December 11 had approved government regulation of railroads.
[99] According to Conkling of Cincinnati, Harlan, Dennison, Chase, John Sherman, and Julian advocated this plan. E. Conkling to A. Johnson, Oct. 14, 1865, Johnson MSS., LXXIX.

resources which a generous government granted to its friends.

Johnson men in Arizona, for instance, complained that the Radicals controlled the legislature of the Territory, and used "their personal and official influence to prevent the election of any and every man they thought could not be used to promote their sordid and selfish ends." By this means they secured laws giving them special privileges, and a perfect monopoly of all railroad and telegraph lines to be built, and all mines and public lands to be developed, in the Territory.[1] "Millions of the best lands in the West," complained Goodwin of Indianapolis to Sumner, "are held by speculators in the east, driving the actual settler further away and making schools, and churches and roads and other essentials of civilization very expensive if not impossible in some neighborhoods."[2]

One of the land-speculating companies was the Connecticut Emigrant Society. In violation of the treaty with the Cherokees, Secretary Harlan as one of his last official acts before resigning to join the Radicals, sold 800,000 acres of Cherokee reserve lands in Kansas to this company for $800,-000 on the installment plan. Johnson objected strenuously, and Stanbery, after he replaced Speed in the attorney-generalship, declared that the sale was "illegal and ought to be ignored."[3]

In his opposition to large government grants to corporations, Johnson was adamant. In 1865 some Eastern financiers organized a second Pacific railroad company. Their hope was to get a bill through Congress separating the Eastern Division of the Union Pacific, known as the Kansas Route, from the main company, by allowing it to build independently westward instead of joining the main line at the

[1] J. Howard to A. Johnson, Jan. 20, 1866, *ibid.*, LXXXIV.
[2] F. A. Goodwin to C. Sumner, Oct. 5, 1865, Sumner MSS., LXXIV.
[3] *New York Herald*, Oct. 7, 1866.

hundredth meridian. Stevens was closely associated with these men. In the summer of 1865 he and President Scott of the Pennsylvania Railroad conferred at Bedford, and Stevens explained his views of the new organization. After that a number of Stevens's Pennsylvania friends acquired an interest in the enterprise. In November Scott wrote Stevens that the matter could be managed to satisfy him, and urged that Congress be prevented from taking adverse action until Scott could see Stevens and fully explain the new sound basis of the project by which, "with reasonable encouragement from Congress," they could get the new western road.[4] Finally, under Stevens's ægis the proposed bill was introduced into Congress.

The Union Pacific had been regarded as a semi-official undertaking, and many felt that the large grants to that road were justifiable only because connection with the Pacific coast was so urgently needed by the whole nation. Besides, five government directors made the first continental line a quasi-public concern. John A. Dix, president of the Union Pacific, with personal interest added to Democratic conviction, protested vigorously against the proposed grants, as did the five government directors. In June Dix sent a long formal argument probably intended to help in preparing a veto message.[5] The government directors pointed out that the proposed bill inaugurated a new policy in granting

---

[4] Nov. 30, 1865, Stevens MSS., V.

[5] "We have gone on in good faith and expended five or six millions of dollars in the confidence that the acts of Congress authorizing the work would not be so amended as to create a competition injurious to the enterprise, to the commercial interests of the country, and to the investments of private capital, which those acts may be considered as having . . . invited by the Government aid they promised. This aid will be greatly impaired if the Kansas and Sioux City lines are allowed to cut loose from us, and divert into other channels, the means and the traffic necessary to complete and sustain the principal work, the greatest one undertaken by any country, and one which will need all its available resources." J. A. Dix to E. D. Morgan, April 14, 1866, Johnson MSS., XCIII; J. A. D. to A. J., June 29, 1866, ibid., XCVI.

aid to a line that was not a public necessity but an enterprise for private gain. "The effect will be that Congress and the public authorities will be besieged for new grants of land and subsidies of public money," under the pledge implied in this bill.[6] Johnson as always opposed using the public domain for aid to corporations whose end was private profit, but he did not need to resort to a veto as the project died in Congress.

During this same two years a more pretentious undertaking, the Northern Pacific Railroad, was being organized. Stevens again was deeply interested. Just before the opening of Congress in December, 1865, Putnam wrote that he would like to consult again with Stevens's friends with whom he had already discussed the project. "I feel particularly anxious," he wrote Stevens, "that you should be Chairman of the Pacific Railroad Committee and that you shall have good men on the Committee with you." A few days later he again expressed anxiety and "earnestly and respectfully" asked Stevens "to look out for the interests of the Northern Pacific Railroad in the construction of the Committee." After repeated consultation Stevens suggested to the promoters a plan that would secure their land grant before Congress adjourned.[7] During the discussion of the bill, the group that had sponsored the Homestead Act opposed it bitterly. "The friends in Congress of the project to build a Northern Pacific Railroad," said the *Herald*, "are the coolest personages, we warrant, that can be found this hot weather. Not satisfied with grants of land by Congress in aid of the undertaking, grants that are not only extravagant

6 C. F. Shuman to J. Harlan, June 30, 1866, *ibid.*, XCVII.
7 J. Putnam to T. Stevens, Dec. 2 and 7, 1865, Stevens MSS., V; E. Conkling to T. S., June 11, 1866, A. W. Morse to T. S., June 20, 1866, and J. Perham to T. S., July 19, 1866, *ibid.*, VIII.

but profligate, they now ask from the government a loan of a hundred millions of dollars upon bonds, the security for which is the very lands Congress has granted them." [8] In the final rush, the measure got lost, and Johnson did not face the necessity of vetoing it until the next session when Radical omnipotence had made vetoes so futile that he had ceased to impose them.

In the spring of 1866 the Radicals in Congress passed "an Act to enable the New York and Montana Iron Mining and Manufacturing Company to purchase a certain amount of the public lands not now in market." The bill provided that this company might at any time within a year preëmpt two tracts of land not exceeding twenty sections in all, three of which could be lands containing iron ore and coal, and the remainder timber lands. The company might even choose Indian lands, save what was within a reservation. The price was fixed at $1.25 an acre, though by previous laws mineral lands had been reserved from sale, and coal tracts sold at a minimum of $20 an acre and only in limited amounts. Johnson vetoed the bill because it set at naught the principle of the Homestead Act. That law had sought to prevent the "abuses of speculation or monopoly," and to secure to each individual an independent farm. Hence it had made "actual residence and cultivation . . . indispensable conditions" to land grants. Johnson objected that this new bill reversed the policy of the government, and threw open its mineral and coal resources to unlimited exploitation for private gain. He cited Magna Charta as proof that landholding by corporations had always been "regarded as in derogation of public policy and common right," and quoted the Supreme Court to show that preëmption was a special "privilege"

[8] *New York Herald*, July 16, 1866.

justified only by the necessity of aiding the "poor" settler. "Many thousand pioneers," argued the President, "have turned their steps to the western territories, seeking . . . homesteads to be acquired by sturdy industry under the pre-emption laws. On their arrival they should not find the timbered lands and the tracts containing iron ore and coal already surveyed and claimed by corporate companies, favored by the special legislation of Congress. . . . In view of the strong temptation to monopolize the public lands, with the pernicious results, it would seem at least of doubtful expediency to lift corporations above all competition with actual settlers, by authorizing them to become purchasers of public lands . . . for any purpose, and particularly when clothed with the special benefits of this bill. . . . This bill is but the precursor of a system of land distribution to a privileged class, unequal, unjust, and which ought not to receive the sanction of the general government." [9] Congress sustained the President's veto. A little later, however, the same proposition appeared under a slightly different form, this time as an "Act erecting the territory of Montana into a surveying district and for other purposes." Johnson vetoed this, too.[10] Again Congress sustained his veto.

In rejecting the first of this pair of bills, Johnson had enunciated a principle which was to be heard again under Roosevelt, and yet again in the 1924 oil scandals. "The public domain," he declared, "is a national trust, set apart and

[9] *Sen. Ex. Docs.,* 39 Cong., 1 Sess., ser. no. 1238, doc. no. 50. See also Stanton MSS., XXX.

[10] This time because it bestowed "a large monopoly of public land without adequate consideration"; conferred "a right and privilege in quantity equivalent to seventy-two pre-emption rights"; introduced "a dangerous system of privileges to private trading corporations"; and was "an unjust discrimination in favor of traders and speculators, against individual settlers and pioneers, who are seeking homes and improving our western Territories." *House Ex. Docs.,* 39 Cong., 1 Sess., ser. no. 1267, doc. no. 156. Also Stanton MSS., XXX.

held for the general welfare upon principles of equal justice, and not to be bestowed as a special privilege upon a favored class." These two vetoes of Johnson's were popular in the West of 1866, though they won Johnson the enmity of the whole tribe of Radical politicians who were seeking profit through exploitation of public wealth. They stamp Johnson as one of the first great conservators of our national resources.

III. THE TARIFF

Most important of the economic issues was the tariff. During short intervals prior to 1846 customs duties had been high, but from that year until the Civil War, Northeastern manufacturers had been living under a mere revenue tariff in which a combined South and West steadily refused to grant them "protection." [11] It was only the departure of Southern senators that enabled industry to gain a protective schedule in the Morrill tariff of 1861. During the War, however, rates were raised again and again. In fact, the general acts of 1862 and 1864 completely reversed our national tariff policy.

Several factors combined to secure extraordinary war rates. The enormous cost of war necessitated high taxes, and higher customs duties provided a less unpopular means of augmenting revenues than direct taxation. Taxes on industry also became necessary, and then customs rates were raised to offset the excise that domestic manufacturers were paying, in order that they might continue to compete with foreign rivals on a pre-war basis. Honest protectionists who had been an ineffective minority before the War saw a chance

[11] For a history of our tariff see Frank W. Taussig, *Tariff History of the United States,* and Ida M. Tarbell, *The Tariff in Our Times.*

to build the tariff barrier higher and higher.[12] Unscrupulous men utilized the opportunity to obtain special favors and to increase at public expense their already large war profits. In the extravagance of war-time, added protection was easily obtained. Besides, both specific and ad valorem duties were levied, and falling prices at the close of the War further increased the protection afforded by specific duties. The most sanguine protectionist could scarcely have hoped to retain these war-time rates after the return of peace.

The War ended. War taxes on industry were repealed. Unless a new policy of protection such as the country had never experienced was to be inaugurated, customs duties should have been reduced proportionately as Congress removed the taxes which they had been established to offset. Protectionists were convinced that not only the compensatory war rates but the newly acquired protection would be repealed unless Southerners could be kept out of Congress. The South *was* excluded for several years, and, by means of negro suffrage and Northern military force, was kept Republican and hence protectionist for many years more. Thus the compensatory war duties were retained, providing hitherto undreamed-of protection, by a process which Commissioner Wells pronounced "only equivalent to legislating a bounty into the pockets of the producers." [13]

The reconstruction period ushered in a new economic era, an industrial age whose business has been based upon highly protective duties. High import taxes did not cause the economic development; that would have come anyway. But they molded its course. Finally, after the new industrial system had depended for years upon a war tariff never repealed, that war tariff ceased to be such, and became an integral part

[12] Republicans had bid for their support by including a tariff plank in the platform of 1861.

[13] Special Commissioner of the Revenue, *Report for 1868*, 23.

of the new economic order. Had the rates been reduced in 1866 and succeeding years, as they must have been had Johnson's policy of Southern restoration succeeded, the industrial development of the country would have been different—equally great, but different.

During the War profiteers had been active; legitimate business had enjoyed enormous profits. Government expenditures had been lavish and unquestioning. High prices had been easily attainable during scarcity which augmented demands of war and the tariff had combined to create. Quantity of production rather than quality or efficiency had been the desideratum of business. Manufacturers had become accustomed to extravagant methods and large and easy profits. Through the purchase of new and expensive equipment, plants had been expanded beyond any possible peacetime demand. Notwithstanding uncertainties, business expansion continued even after the War, until by 1866 "current production was already gaining noticeably upon consumption." [14] Cutting off the extra protection of the war period would have forced manufacturers back to efficient methods and normal production. It would have ruined some; it would have meant temporary depression for all during a period of readjustment. But it would have established the new industrial America upon the non-protective basis operative in the days before the War. Probably little serious opposition would have been met in retaining the extra protection secured during the War. Manufacturers, however, not only maintained the tariff rates at the heights to which war taxes on industry forced them, thus increasing protection as war taxes were abolished, but they actually tried to raise them.

*   *   *   *

[14] Victor S. Clark, *History of Manufactures in the United States, 1607-1928*, II, 58.

Northeastern Radicals were the leading protectionists. An underlying cause of their Radicalism was dread of the tariff reduction which they felt a combined West and South would force through Congress if the Southern members were seated.[15] In the Northeast, danger to the tariff was an effective argument against Johnson's policy. For instance, Brewer of Newport wrote Sumner: "In a selfish point of view, free suffrage to the Blacks is desirable. Without their support, Southerners will certainly again unite,—and there is too much reason to fear successfully, with the 'Democrats' of the North, and the long train of evils sure to follow their rule is fearful to contemplate . . . a great reduction of the Tariff doing away with its protective feature—perhaps Free Trade to culminate with Repudiation, . . . and how sweet & complete will be the revenge of the former if they can ruin the North by Free-Trade & repudiation."[16]

Governor Andrew of Massachusetts warned against the Southern desire "to impose a greatly reduced duty on European manufacturers . . . with the intent to disintegrate the free States, to break down American manufactures, discourage skilled, intelligent labor, and reduce the laboring classes, by measures alike audacious and insidious, to the dependence held by the slave-power appropriate for the masses of men."[17]

Conway, that rabid Kansas anti-slavery leader who was living in Richmond at the close of the War, was so discour-

[15] It was almost universally assumed that Southerners, if readmitted, would vote almost solidly against protection. The question arises whether the old Whig support for a tariff could not have been revived in the South. Upon investigation I agree with contemporary Northerners that Southerners would have opposed protection after as before the War. See H. K. Beale, "The Tariff and Reconstruction," *Am. Hist. Rev.*, XXXV (January, 1930), 277-278.

[16] July 7, 1865, Sumner MSS., LXXIV.

[17] J. A. Andrew, *Address of His Excellency to the Two Branches of the Legislature of Massachusetts, Jan. 6, 1865*, 95.

aged over the prospect of the South's coming back to power "through a Northern alliance—say for free trade or anti-protection," that he thought Sumner had made a mistake in not recognizing separate Southern nationality.[18]

The *Tribune* thought that reconstruction of the South and restoration of the Union must be based upon Southern support of the tariff, if that could be won. Allowing the South to return without proper tariff guarantees would be dangerous, for "a blended Copperhead and Rebel ascendency, thickly veneered with office-holding and office-seeking Unionism, could not help . . . disturbing the safeguards of National Industry." [19] The American Free Trade League it dubbed Democratic, depending on Copperheads for votes, and hence disloyal.[20] Caution was necessary lest the *Tribune*, widely read as it was, alienate anti-tariff Republicans in the West. Yet even the *Tribune* wrote, "In the . . . traitorous section of Northern politics, it is consistent for Americans to advocate and plot with foreigners British Free Trade. The cotton planters were educated by Calhoun to the policy of keeping the Yankees from manufacturing, and confining them to raising cheap food for their slaves. The failure of their Rebellion has not softened the temper of this education. The reconstructed South would vote solid to destroy the wealth-producing industry of the Loyal States. And their unprincipled slaves in the 'copper mines' would lick their shoes while they voted with them." [21]

Northeastern Radicals were determined never to allow the South to reënter the Union as long as their tariff schemes might be thereby endangered. Wendell Phillips insisted that

18 M. F. Conway to C. Sumner, Jan. 16, 1866, Sumner MSS., LXXVI.
19 *New York Semi-Weekly Tribune*, Feb. 23, April 20, Oct. 5, 1866.
20 *Ibid.*, Feb. 6, 1866.
21 *Ibid.*, April 3, 1866.

Southerners should not be readmitted until the North had succeeded in making over the "South in its likeness, till South Carolina [gravitated] by natural tendency to New England," [22] or as Governor Seymour paraphrased it, "until their ideas of business, industry, money making, spindles and looms were in accord with those of Massachusetts." [23] But this tariff question required cautious handling. The *Commercial and Financial Chronicle* of New York reminded Easterners that it was "an extraordinary thing . . . that in a country which is ruled by a perpetual recurrence to the will of the people, the large measure of protection which American manufactures have received should ever have been accorded to them." It warned them that "the utmost judgment is required to avoid pushing a given advantage so far as to unite an overwhelming reaction." "It cannot certainly be the purpose of the Manufacturing States," the *Chronicle* said, "to provoke . . . a consolidation [of South and West] which should it ever be effected, would rapidly and irresistibly revolutionize our whole commercial system; and it is therefore important that the Manufacturing States themselves should take timely warning of the perils which they are certain to incur by an over-large desire on the part of their representatives, to push the principle of protection beyond the limits at which it has been fixed for some years past. . . . The practical control of our political affairs is destined at no distant date to pass into the hands of the Western people. When the *Southern States* shall return to their position in the Union as coequal participators . . . agricultural interests . . . especially when combined with commercial interests, will be entirely irresistible." [24] Western sensibilities

22 Speech at Cooper Institute, *New York Tribune*, Oct. 26, 1866.
23 Speech at Cooper Institute, *New York Herald*, Oct. 31, 1866.
24 *Commercial and Financial Chronicle*, III (July 7, 1866), 3.

made it unwise for their speakers or a journal like the *Tribune* too openly to avow this motive for Radicalism.[25] But they did not need to avow it. When orators and newspapers spoke of danger to the Union in a return of Southerners to Washington, protectionists understood full well that tariff reduction was an important element in that danger.

Changing gold premiums and resulting fluctuations in prices influenced political opinion. Speculation in gold aroused repeated protest from business men. The Government occasionally intervened to stabilize the price of gold, as when in May, 1866, it sold gold in quantity to counteract the effect of the Overend-Gurney panic upon the American market.[26] But the Government's currency policy was not fully determined; expansion and contraction, together with the uncertainty of government credit, kept prices unstable. Besides, the constant floating of loans abroad caused incessant price movements in international commodities. Contemporaries knew that fluctuating premiums on gold affected international trade prices, and consequently the profits of men who sold in competition with imported goods. For this reason, the *Tribune* urged a resumption of specie payments

[25] Individual Conservatives did realize it existed. For example, in analyzing the election the *Memphis Commercial and Argus* (Nov. 8, 1866) explained, "With these appeals to the ignorant and fanatical was the still stronger element of associated wealth in the immense capital invested in manufactures, whose power to extort hundreds of millions of dollars annually from the people . . . through the iniquitous provisions of a protective tariff depends upon the perpetuation of radical ascendency." But Radicals kept it out of the public discussion.

[26] New York bankers agreed at that time that "the sales of Gold made by the Treasury . . . had the effect of preventing a much greater advance in the premium on Gold" which would have caused many failures. E. D. Morgan & Co. wrote, "The want of Importers for the payment of Duties, and the sudden demand for Export consequent on the financial disturbances in England, could not have otherwise been supplied, and we believe much good in a financial point of view will be the result of our large exports of Gold at this juncture." E. D. Morgan & Co. to H. H. Van Dyck, L. A. von Hoffman to A. Speyers, and E. O. Read to P. M. Myers, May 30, 1866, McCulloch MSS., III.

to reduce nominal values and thereby decrease imports.[27] Manufacturers generally sought contraction of the currency along with an increase of tariff rates. Farmers, too, complained, and after all, it was they who suffered most from the fluctuating prices. Manufacturers, who depended mainly upon the home market, did have the tariff to protect them, whereas farmers had to compete in the world market. Modern theories of international prices substantiate the instinctive belief of farmer and manufacturer that gold premiums, international trade conditions, and domestic prices were related,[28] and help to explain the political importance of the tariff to the manufacturer, and of reduction of the tariff to the farmer who needed to offset in a lower price for what he bought, the low price that international price tendencies dictated for what he sold.

Several factors played into the manufacturers' hands. For one thing, Radicals succeeded in imbuing people with the idea that the tariff must be kept high to pay the war debt. Many, therefore, who in principle opposed protection and in practice suffered from it, resigned themselves to it as inevitable, and merely tried to secure for themselves some of its benefits. On this ground, for example, Jones urged Ohio farmers to present a "consistent and solid front" in demanding as much protection for the farm as for the factory.[29] At just this time the expiration of a Canadian reciprocity treaty made protection against the Canadian wheat-grower possible, and dulled the edge of the farmer's opposition to protection.[30] Industrialists were glad to placate the farmer with duties on foodstuffs, as the amount imported was negligible

[27] *New York Semi-Weekly Tribune,* May 22, June 5, and June 22, 1866.
[28] See H. K. Beale in *Am. Hist. Rev.,* XXXV (January, 1930), 281-283.
[29] Speech at the Agricultural Convention, Ohio State Board of Agriculture, *Twenty-first Annual Report* (1866), 77.
[30] See H. K. Beale in *Am. Hist. Rev.,* XXXV (January, 1930), 292.

and neither manufacturer nor farmer was much affected. The farmer much preferred no protection for any one, but if there had to be a tariff, he would be more content if he could feel that he, too, benefited.

The wool-grower, too, was in a peculiar situation.[31] During the War sheep-raising had increased enormously in all the Western states, and especially in Ohio and Michigan.[32] Most farmers, indeed, sold a little wool. The War shut off the American cotton supply, and wool had to be used instead. Simultaneously the army began to demand great quantities of woolen clothes and blankets. Prices on raw wool rose sixty-seven per cent. Wool-growers began to picture years of prosperity ahead. Even under normal conditions it would be long before the South could adjust itself and the negro to free labor; if the Radicals succeeded it would be still longer.[33] Western optimism was boundless. Farmer-like, the Western wool-grower figured prices in inflated currency values and exaggerated the profitableness of his occupation. Like every one else, he expanded his business unreasonably. Wool was now to be king. Unfortunately, the causes of the boom were largely psychological.

As a matter of hard fact, only the tremendous demand of

[31] For an able treatise see Chester W. Wright, *Wool-Growing and the Tariff*, 156-207.

[32] The number of sheep in the loyal states, excluding the Far West, rose from 15,390,346 in 1860 to 35,822,185 in 1867. Ohio alone had 7,159,177; New York, 5,373,005; Michigan, 4,028,767. *U. S. Census* (1860), "Agriculture," CXX; "Report of the Commissioner of Agriculture for the Year 1866," *House Ex. Docs.*, 39 Cong., ser. no. 1297, doc. no. 107, 67.

[33] "It does not seem probable," rejoiced one Ohioan, "that the cotton crop can reach its former figures for many years to come. Though the freedmen should prove models of industry, it is not possible that their labor can be directed so much in one channel as heretofore. They will have a thousand new objects of pursuit, and whether all of them are conducive to happiness or no, they will equally interfere with the production of cotton." N. S. Townshend, "Address to the Ohio Wool Growers Convention," Ohio State Board of Agriculture, *Twentieth Annual Report* (1865), 341.

the War had saved American wool-growers from ruin in an unfavorable world market. The shortage of cotton was exaggerated. In 1861 the London markets were overstocked with it. Besides, great increases in the production of Indian and South American cotton enabled London to get fifty per cent of her normal supply, in spite of the Southern blockade, at lower prices than she paid for the wool substitute. Consequently, it was not until 1864 that the world market seriously felt the shortage of cotton. Meantime, foreign production of wool had increased until without the American increment, the wool supply was commensurate with the increased demand.[34] When the inflated currency values are reduced to gold equivalents it becomes evident that extraordinary war conditions merely a little more than maintained at its old level a wool price that would otherwise have fallen precipitantly.[35]

A few sheep-farmers did have premonitions of danger. For a short time after the War, prices of both wool and sheep actually increased, but by 1866 a reaction foretold trouble. Randall cautioned Ohio sheep-raisers that with the end of the War would come a flood of cotton, competition from foreign wool, and a cessation of demand that would cause depression.[36] In 1866 the Ohio Board of Agriculture warned against the over-production of sheep, and advocated a

[34] In five years world production increased 26%; the average annual increase during the Civil War was three times that of the previous decade. C. W. Wright, op. cit., 164-165.

[35] When compared with the low prices of July, 1861, the peak prices of October, 1864, dazzled the sheep-raiser, but the advance of 171%, 217%, and 355%, respectively, on Ohio fine, medium, and coarse washed wool, figured in currency prices, dwindles to 31%, 53%, and 110%, when reduced to gold prices. The boasted 67% increase in the average price of wool for the period 1862-65 over that for 1852-61, when reduced to a gold equivalent, shrinks to 5%. Ibid., 156-160.

[36] H. S. Randall, Address to Ohio Wool-Growers, Jan. 6, 1864, Ohio State Board of Agriculture, Eighteenth Annual Report (1863), 343-353.

change from wool-growing to the production of mutton.[37] Even optimists who saw no danger, and anti-tariff men who opposed protection in principle, were eager to gain the extra profits that a wool item in an inevitable tariff would give them.[38] Increasing interest in organized action prompted the formation in 1866 of state wool-growers' associations in several of the Western states, and the holding of a National Wool-Growers' Convention at Cleveland.[39] As early as 1863, President Randall of the New York Wool-Growers' Association had told Ohio sheep-raisers that they were not profiting from a tariff that was making manufacturers rich.[40] If only

[37] "Sheep," Ohio State Board of Agriculture, *Twenty-first Annual Report* (1866), "Essays," 189.

[38] President Garland of the Illinois Wool-Growers' Association wrote Trumbull in anxiety over the wool clause in the proposed tariff. "Illinois can't get along," he wrote, "on corn & wheat, & wool is fast taking a prominence in our annual productions—& if fostered only by the small help the bill proposes . . . would be of vast importance to the West. Will not the Senate in whatever tariff bill it does pass in Dec. retain or make better still the wool clause? Unless we get some definite knowledge upon this, our present clip of wool (now ready for market) will pass into the hands of the manufacturers at a reduced price." July 14, 1866, Trumbull MSS., LXVIII. "Thousands of wool-growers," Meade of Vermont wrote Fessenden, "are looking to Congress . . . with inexpressible anxiety" for the enactment of a wool duty. "A great amount of money has been expended in Sheep improvements and if our late hopes of friendly legislation are realized much more will be . . . But I regard it as certain that, in hopeless competition with the cheap and comparatively valueless wools of Africa and South America, thousands referred to will be compelled to sacrifice investments already made and turn to other pursuits." Jan. 3, 1867, Fessenden MSS.

[39] C. L. Miller, Attitude of the Northwest toward the Tariff (unpublished M. A. thesis at the University of Chicago), 13. Typical of the action of these associations were the resolutions of a Central Illinois Convention: "WHEREAS, . . . The wool-raising interest of the country is laboring under disadvantages and difficulties seriously affecting its prosperity, and in fact threatening its ruin, the Central Illinois Wool-Growers' Association adopted the following resolutions: *Resolved,* That it is the duty of our Congressmen to see that we have sufficient protection against the low prices of foreign wool. *Resolved,* That while we are willing that the important woolen manufacturing interest . . . shall receive all the protection . . . necessary to render it prosperous, we firmly insist that the wool-growing interest is equally important and is entitled to equal protection." *Illinois State Journal,* March 21, 1866.

[40] Jan. 6, 1864, Ohio State Board of Agriculture, *Eighteenth Annual Report* (1863), 349-350. Wright shows that this was true. *Op. cit.,* 166-171.

sheep-farmers could coöperate with woolen manufacturers to shut out foreign competition, Townshend urged, the wool industry would grow without bounds.[41] Commissioners of statistics and boards of agriculture began to report that prosperity for sheep-owners had always accompanied high tariffs, and depression, low ones. Jones admitted in a speech in the Ohio Agricultural Convention that their Wool-Growers' Association was "but a combination to put up the price of wool" by seeking a tariff.[42] Urgency was needed, since prices of wool and sheep were falling alarmingly between 1865 and 1868,[43] in spite of Western optimism and the growing flocks of sheep—partly because of the latter, in fact. Only the Wool and Woolens Act of 1867 prevented a terrific crash.

Eastern Radicals were shrewd enough to turn this wool situation to their own advantage. In the fall of 1864, the National Association of Wool Manufacturers was formed under the guiding spirit of John L. Hayes, who became secretary and chief lobbyist. This was the first great business interest to organize; one of its chief purposes was to secure favorable tariff legislation. Hayes felt the South would inevitably oppose protection when she returned. He knew the anti-tariff feeling of the West. He saw that the East alone could never save protection. At the first meeting of the Association he struck to the heart of the problem. "There can be no reliance," he said, "upon a permanent friendly legislation

[41] "Address to the Ohio Wool Growers Convention" cited above.

[42] Ohio Agricultural Convention, *Proceedings* (1866), 72.

[43] The average price of sheep fell from $3.50 per head to $1.90 during this period. In 1866 every county had boasted at least one $1,000 ram; in 1867 many good Marinos sold for one or two dollars, some for 60 cents. Wool fell from an average of 61 cents in 1866 to 51 in 1867, and to 45 in 1868. A great slaughter of sheep at enormous loss resulted. U. S. Department of Agriculture, "Special Report on the History and Present Condition of the Sheep Industry of the United States," *House Misc. Docs.*, 52 Cong., 2 Sess., ser. no. 3124, doc. no. 105, 555-561.

for both interests unless the wool growers are satisfied. Our object is not to reach Congress but to convince the farmers of the West, who will inevitably control the legislation of this country, of the absolute identity of our interests." [44]

At Hayes's suggestion, a joint meeting of wool manufacturers and wool-growers assembled at Syracuse, New York, in December, 1865.[45] There Hayes convinced the sheep-raisers, as he had already persuaded the manufacturers, that the future prosperity of both interests depended upon their united demand for a high tariff on both wool and woolens. The convention agreed upon the principle that wool should have high protection and woolens a duty sufficiently higher to allow the manufacturers to pay the extra price for wool that the tariff would create, and still have protection on their woolens. Then in a struggle between the two interests over the apportionment of protection, Hayes and his better-organized manufacturers managed to secure a duty on woolens that covered the proposed duty on wool, the old duty on woolens, and new protection all combined. Both interests did finally agree, and then in coöperation pushed their schedule to final success.[46]

Through a well-organized lobby, the wool men wrote their Syracuse schedule into the tariff bill of 1866. Wool manufacturers worked gladly with other protective interests as long as the general tariff seemed likely to pass. But Hayes realized

---

[44] John L. Hayes, *Speech before the First Annual Meeting of the National Association of Wool Growers, Sept. 6, 1865,* 63.

[45] See *Report of the Proceedings of the Convention of Delegates from the National Association of Wool Manufacturers and from the Several Organizations of the Wool Growers of the United States, at Syracuse, New York, Dec. 13, 1865.*

[46] *Joint Report of the Executive Committee of the National Association of Wool Manufacturers, and the Executive Committee of the National Wool-Growers' Association, Addressed to the United States Revenue Commission, Feb. 9, 1866.* The *New York Semi-Weekly Tribune* (June 22, 1866) saw and urged the wisdom of this union between wool-growers and manufacturers.

that the Western farmer would more willingly support a wool item alone, than a general tariff. In fact, he claimed that the tariff bill of 1866 was carried in the House "mainly through the popularity of the wool and woolens sections." [47] Consequently, he had the wool and woolens schedule of the Syracuse meeting introduced as a separate bill,[48] and the House passed it.[49] On the Senate table it was allowed to lie until the general bill failed in 1867, when it was called up by John Sherman to become the Wool and Woolens Act of that year.[50] Though this wool lobby served both growers and manufacturers, it was the latter who supported it. In fact, Hayes says that "no agent of the wool-growers being present, facts and arguments in favor of increased duties on wool were supplied, even to the representatives of the wool-growing districts of the West." [51] Johnson's veto was feared, but careful management won his signature.[52]

This lobby of the National Association of Wool Manufacturers played a significant part in the election. In spite of the Conservative failure to capitalize it, the tariff question would have injured the Radical cause, had not this clever manœuver won the support of the Western wool-grower. Sheep-owners still opposed protection in the abstract, but they accepted this particular tariff because it promised to aid them personally.[53]

[47] "The Senators," he tells us, "most influential in effecting the postponement have distinctly admitted that their opposition had no reference to the sections relating to wool and woolens." J. L. Hayes, *Second Annual Report of National Association of Wool Manufacturers, Oct. 3, 1866,* 14.

[48] July 23, 1866, *Cong. Globe,* 39 Cong., 1 Sess., 4046.

[49] July 27, 1866, *ibid.,* 4253.

[50] March 1 and 2, 1867, *ibid.,* 39 Cong., 2 Sess., 1925, 1958.

[51] J. L. Hayes, *Report of Second Annual Meeting of National Association of Wool Manufacturers, Oct. 3, 1866,* 14.

[52] J. L. Hayes, *Third Annual Report of the National Association of Wool Manufacturers, Oct. 2, 1867,* 5.

[53] H. S. Randall voiced a general sentiment when he declared: "I have never been friendly to the enactment of high tariffs for the purpose of

An incipient manufacturing industry was rapidly developing in the West,[54] especially in Ohio and Michigan.[55] The most important growth took place in iron production. Factories and mills were springing up in many new centers.[56] At the same time a great mining region was being exploited. In quick succession, the rich Lake Superior mines were opened up; the canal at the Sault was completed; Jacob Reese demonstrated to doubters that Superior ore could be

protecting industry. But the exigencies of our government will, in future, demand a high tariff for revenue purposes only; and in adjusting the degree of incidental protection which it must necessarily afford to American industry, we have a right to demand—1st, That the woolen interest shall be protected equally with other interests of no greater importance; and, 2d, That the producer of wool shall be protected equally with the manufacturer of wool." Address to Ohio Wool-Growers cited above.

54 The *Tribune* recognized this fact. It pointed, for example, to the establishment of a second woolen mill and plans for a cotton mill in Minneapolis and to new factories in Lawrence, Kansas, and other places in the West, and hoped that this might make a tariff seem profitable to the West. *New York Semi-Weekly Tribune*, Feb. 13, June 22, 1866. For the development of Western manufacturing, see V. S. Clark, *op. cit.*, II, 54-153.

55 Before the War the chief Western manufacturing centers were Pittsburgh, Cincinnati, Louisville, and St. Louis. Isaac Lippincott, *History of Manufactures in the Ohio Valley to the Year 1860*, 192. By 1866 Cleveland, Toledo, Detroit, and the surrounding counties were becoming industrial regions, though the process was slow. In Lucas County, Ohio, for example, because of the growing importance of Toledo, the capital invested in manufactories grew from $855,445 in 1860 to $3,172,155 in 1870, an increase of 270%; the number of establishments increased 21%; the number of hands employed, 75%; the amount of wages paid, 166%; and the value of the manufactured product, 177%. Ohio Secretary of State, *Annual Report* (1881), 906. For Michigan the total output of manufactures grew from $33,068,071 in 1860 to $124,122,191 in 1870, a gain of 275%. *Statistics of the State of Michigan* (1860), 315; *ibid.*, (1870), 626.

56 By 1868 Cleveland boasted 14 rolling mills, 200 puddling furnaces, and, not including rails, spikes, nuts, bolts, and horseshoes, a daily capacity of 400 tons. Ohio Secretary of State, *Statistical Report* (1869), 217. When the Bessemer plant was built in Cleveland, that city produced all its machinery. Alexander L. Holley, *Bessemer Process and Works in the United States*, 35-36. Ohio's output of pig iron increased astoundingly. It was reported to be 50,704 tons in 1863; 62,536 in 1864; 63,991 in 1865; 81,790 in 1866; and 167,591 tons in 1867. The Secretary of State pointed out that these figures were entirely too low, probably because they were the tax assessor's. But if specifically useless, relatively viewed these figures are significant, especially the more than 100% increase in 1867. Ohio Secretary of State, *Statistical Report* (1872), 221-222. In 1860 Michigan manufactured a negligible amount of iron; in 1870 her product was valued at $3,646,129. *Statistics of the State of Michigan* (1870), 626.

successfully used; a steam railway was built to the mines;[57] the Cleveland Company built the first pocket system of ore-loading docks in the world; then war demands brought the Michigan mines into relation with the market; and during the War the Bessemer process was imported from England to be first used at Wyandotte, Michigan.[58] A great boom followed. The Cleveland and Johnson companies paid their first dividends in 1862. In 1863 Peter White, the great pioneer of the iron country, made a fortune. By 1866 the output of the mines, like the production of new Western mills, had grown to promising proportions.[59] Here were the beginnings of America's great steel industry. Even in Boston the significance of the simultaneity of the opening of the Lake Superior mines and the introduction of the Bessemer process was recognized. "Before many years," wrote a correspondent to the *Boston Daily Advertiser*, "enormous quantities of steel rails will be produced in the Western iron districts of this country," for the ore there is superior to that of England.[60]

The West was developing other manufacturing interests, too. Indeed, several of the members of the National Association of Wool Manufacturers were Westerners.[61] Besides,

[57] The old strap railway with its mule teams had carried 35 tons a day from the Cleveland mines; the new one carried 1200.

[58] Of the first seven Bessemer mills Wyandotte and Cleveland each had one. A. L. Holley, *op. cit.,* 37, 12.

[59] Shipments through the self-dumping ore dock at Escanaba, Mich., tell the story of growth: 31,072 tons were shipped in 1865; 116,868 in 1866; 196,831 in 1867. In 1863 three Michigan mines shipped 200,000 tons; in 1866 nine shipped 300,000; and in 1867 the same nine shipped 468,000. This account of Michigan mining is taken from Henry R. Mussey, *Combination in the Mining Industry,* 52-61, and Ralph D. Williams, *The Honorable Peter White,* 133-174.

[60] *Boston Daily Advertiser,* Supplement, April 5, 1866. Indeed, Holley tells us (*op. cit.,* 35-36) that by 1868 "railway supplies for the West and Northwest, and lake and manufacturing machinery [were] already furnished largely by the various iron works in the [Cleveland] region."

[61] Massachusetts had seventy-nine members, Connecticut thirty-two, New York thirty-seven, and Pennsylvania twenty-one, but Indiana had one member, Ohio three, and Michigan with four had as many members as Vermont and one less than half as many as Rhode Island. J. L. Hayes, *Address*

Lake Superior copper miners distressed by temporary depression,[62] Ohio and New York salt miners who were suffering from the competition of new Michigan mines, the Michigan men themselves,[63] and a large lumbering interest in Michigan [64] all desired protection.

Hope of industrial growth, then, silenced opposition to the Radicals in sections of the Northwest that their tariff hopes would normally have antagonized. Alone neither wool nor manufacturing, mines nor lumber, was important; together they were a potent factor. At best, however, these factors could only weaken Western opposition to protection. They could not suppress it.

* * * *

In spite of these special conditions and the Radical claim that the tariff was not an issue, vigorous protests against the Radical tariff policy poured in from the West.[65] During the War the country had acquiesced in the tariff as necessary to secure victory.[66] Even during the War, however, Democratic

before the National Association of Wool Manufacturers, Sept. 6, 1865, 75-80. In fact, by 1870 Michigan had fifty-four woolen factories with an annual output worth $1,138,172. *Statistics of the State of Michigan* (1870), 626.

[62] "Previous to 1860," Commissioner Wells explained, "about one half of the product . . . was exported to France and Germany; now [1866] the proprietors of these mines represent that their whole investments are threatened with destruction, through failure to secure even the home market." D. A. Wells, *Report* (1866), 29-30.

[63] The opening of Kalamazoo mines forced Thomas Ewing, for example, to dispose of his Ohio mines, since his Michigan competitors could use plentiful charcoal where he had to buy coal. His only hope was a tariff shutting out foreign salt that would enable all American producers to sell profitably. T. Ewing to W. L. Savage and others, July 24, Aug. 27, 1865; T. E. to J. Sherman, April 2, 1866, Ewing MSS., "Letter-book."

[64] Between 1860 and 1870 the value of lumber annually produced in Michigan rose from $6,891,769 to $33,356,986, an increase of 384%. *Statistics for the State of Michigan* (1860), 315; (1870), 417.

[65] See C. L. Miller, *op. cit.* Miller points out that the tariff made the East richer at the expense of the West; that by shutting out foreign goods it removed the only means Europe had for buying Western agricultural products; and that the duty on iron doubled the cost of building railroads desired by the West, and thereby increased freight rates.

[66] Miller says that during the War "a concerted opposition" to the tariff "was thwarted by three factors: . . . the dread of the stigmatic 'Copper-

strength in Indiana had been in part due to dislike of the "Yankee tariff" and the feeling, voiced by leaders like Hendricks, that New England was getting rich out of the War at the expense of Western farmers.[67] New England had retaliated with the cry of "Copperheadism."[68] But with peace Indiana renewed her protests. In Ohio Thomas Ewing, who had been a protectionist before the War, felt that no business which had not been able to establish itself under the high war rates ought to be encouraged. He was certain that no party could safely advocate higher rates for the "overburdened community" to pay.[69] Grimes of Iowa was rapidly being driven into "free trade" by the "high pressure for an extreme and almost prohibitory tariff."[70] Washburne of Illinois opposed protection and predicted that the tariff would "resume its old importance" and again "divide parties."[71] Senator Trumbull opposed the Radical tariff. Burchard, an Illinois legislator and future Republican Congressman, wrote, "Educated a protectionist, since 1847 a constant reader of the *New York Tribune,* all my proclivities and sympathies have been toward that school. But during the past summer, considering what is for the interest of the people of Illinois and the Western agricultural States, every examination drives me farther and farther from my early views. . . . Upon every pound of iron used, the farmer

head,' . . . the need of revenue," and "a belief on the part of the agricultural interests of the West that they were enjoying a period of great prosperity."

[67] James A. Woodburn, "Party Politics in Indiana during the Civil War," Am. Hist. Assoc., *Annual Report* (1902), I, 238-239.

[68] Thus was S. S. Cox's temerity in opposing the tariff rewarded. *Cong. Globe,* 38 Cong., 1 Sess., 2681.

[69] T. Ewing to E. J. Williams, Sept. 6, 1865, Ewing MSS., "Letter-book."

[70] Welles MS. Diary, June 27, 1865—(II, 542). He voted against the tariff.

[71] H. C. Burchard to E. B. Washburne, Nov. 16, 1865, Washburne MSS., XCIII.

must pay a bonus. . . . He must sell, or pay the price of one bushel of oats, *to pay the extra cost imposed by the tariff,* when he has a horse shod. . . . Illinois must be an agricultural state . . . 50,000,000 bushels of wheat— shipped as grain or flour—from Chicago annually is not to decrease. Let us get in exchange for it as cheaply as we can the products of other regions, and if the English Importer will sell us in New York more Iron or other commodities for it than the manufacturers of the Eastern States, let us buy of him." [72] Western opposition began to organize in the spring of 1866 in agricultural associations and Johnson clubs.[73]

The powerful *Chicago Tribune,* a vigorously Radical organ, opposed the protection that Eastern manufacturers were seeking. "We tell these gentlemen," it wrote, "that they are traveling to destruction as fast as they can go. They are cutting open the goose to get all the golden eggs at once. They are legislating the government funds into their pockets too rapidly for the permanence of the system." Again it wrote, "The increased rates of duties (except possibly on wool) are wholly unnecessary and unjustifiable, and if adopted, will work injury to revenue and to public interest. The present tariff is high enough . . . on increase one man would make his thousands while 50 would lose their hundreds." "The new tariff Bill . . . is a financial monstrosity. . . . Turn which way we will, a new mountain of taxation arises before us, taxation avowedly not to put money in the National Treasury but to keep it out." "Western members . . . are in favor of a tariff that will yield the largest amount of revenue and at the same time afford adequate

[72] *Ibid.*
[73] E.g., the Johnson Club of Nevada City, Mo., resolved that the tariff was oppressive to the West, the South, and the poor man. June 7, 1866, Johnson MSS., XCV.

protection to American manufacturers. . . . The Eastern members are clamoring for a prohibitory tariff that will cut off all importations and reduce the revenue from imports from forty to seventy millions of dollars per annum. This is the issue." [74]

Horace White, editor of the *Tribune* and a leading Radical, denounced the Internal Revenue Commission. "They propose," he wrote, "to give the American manufacturer a bounty of five cents per pound for exporting . . . to be paid by you & me. Then they propose to put a tariff of five cents a pound on all imported cotton goods which tariff, you & I & all consumers have to pay. But it does not end here, for this five cents a pound tariff will operate to raise the price of all domestic cotton goods five cents a pound in addition to the five cents tax on raw cotton, & of this extra five cents the Government will get nothing, while the people will be paying it all the time. Have we killed King Cotton and set up King Sheeting?" [75] Charles Ray, former editor of the *Tribune*, wrote Trumbull, "We are being consumed by the good of New England & Pennsylvania. If matters are not regulated and on a fairer and juster principle, the West will be badly injured before five years have elapsed. When will men see that legislative interference in trade as in religion or morals is always mischievous? . . . The Protectionists are very bitter, as all men are whose profits are threatened, and very powerful as all men are who have great amounts of money and are willing to use it. . . . The remedy for the Evils of which I complain will not be found until the process of robbing by law becomes plain to the farmers whose money is now so profusely poured into the capacious pockets of the manufacturer." [76]

[74] *Chicago Tribune*, June 22, 26, 28, and July 3, 1866.
[75] H. White to E. B. Washburne, Jan. 30, 1866, Washburne MSS., LIII.
[76] Feb. 2, 1866, Trumbull MSS., LXIII.

These men were regular Republicans. Western Democrats, of course, were vehement in their denunciation of Radical protection. "The new tariff bill," said the *Chicago Times*, "is so plainly a scheme for plundering the people that prominent republican newspapers allege that it can only be carried by bribery. . . . It will pass because the manufacturers and jobbers will use their money liberally and because New England for whose benefit the bill is . . . framed controls Congress." [77]

In some quarters in the East opposition to the tariff was manifest. Maine ship-builders, for instance, blamed the tariff for the decline in their trade.[78] Laborers and merchants opposed protection, as did a group of influential leaders and newspapers who were free-traders from principle.[79] Democrats opposed the tariff as a matter of course.

* * * *

Northeastern Radicals, however, struggled for increased protection. Blaine and Stevens each tried to secure combined protection for cotton mills and punishment for Southerners, by repealing the constitutional prohibition of export taxes in order to keep cotton in the country by levying a tax upon its exportation.[80] But both efforts failed. In 1866, however, a new tariff bill proposed augmented duties. Each protected interest cried out for special favors. Advocates of a return to purely revenue rates attacked each increase. But by com-

[77] *Chicago Times*, June 29, 1866.
[78] V. S. Clark, *op. cit.*, II, 92.
[79] E.g., Godwin, Godkin, Bennett, Bryant, Lieber, Cyrus Field, J. A. Roosevelt, Pratt of Connecticut, the newly formed Free Trade League, the New York Chamber of Commerce, and the *New York Evening Post*, the *Herald,* and the *Nation*. See H. K. Beale in the *Am. Hist. Rev.*, XXXV (January, 1930), 288-289.
[80] March 24, 1864, *Cong. Globe*, 38 Cong., 1 Sess., 1261; March 2, 1865, *ibid.*, 38 Cong., 2 Sess., 1313; Dec. 5, 1865, *ibid.*, 39 Cong., 1 Sess., 10. Governor Andrew of Massachusetts strongly advocated a moderate export tax on cotton. *Address to the Two Branches of the Legislature of Massachusetts, Jan. 6, 1865,* 94.

bining to help each other, the interested members managed to get their respective demands incorporated into a thoroughly incongruous bill that passed the House, but was tabled in the Senate until after the fall elections.

When in the next session the Senators turned to further consideration of the measure, Secretary McCulloch recommended to them an alternative bill prepared by David A. Wells, Special Commissioner of the Revenue. This Wells draft approached the problem in an entirely new spirit. It reduced the duties on certain raw materials such as lumber, coal, flax, hemp, and scrap-iron. It equalized the inconsistencies in the existing Act of 1864. It left duties on manufactured goods at the old rates or very slightly lowered them. Reform, not reduction, was its principle.[81] After a long debate the Senate adopted this Wells proposal as an amendment to the House bill. In the House it was again subjected to attack by protectionists. But the end of the short session was near, and if the protected interests could not get the House bill, they were willing to accept the Wells offer, since even this provided high protection. Therefore, under the lead of Morrill and Stevens, they rallied to its support. Western Republicans, however, refused to support protection even under party pressure. To pass the bill before March 4, Morrill moved a suspension of the rules. On the test vote he secured a majority of 106-64, but not the necessary two-thirds.[82] He urged the bill as the best they could get. Garfield begged members of the Union Party not to "consent to aid our enemies in tying the hands of the House." [83] But Western

[81] *Sen. Ex. Docs.*, 39 Cong., 2 Sess., ser. no. 1276, doc. no. 2. Also F. W. Taussig, *Tariff History of the United States*, 175-178.

[82] *Cong. Globe*, 39 Cong., 2 Sess., 1658.

[83] "I ask them," he said, "whether they will now precipitate a division by using the power in their hands to-day in connection with our political enemies to defeat a measure which a very large majority of their friends desire?" *Ibid.*, 39 Cong., 2 Sess., 1657.

distaste for protection was stronger than party loyalty. Two amendments were adopted, favorable to wool and food-stuffs, as a bid for Western support. Then Stevens again moved a suspension of the rules. But even the powerful whip of Stevens failed. The vote, 102-69, was less favorable than before.[84] With the end of the session both the extravagant House bill and the more reasonable Wells proposal died.

The votes on these tariff bills are significant. They indicate strong anti-tariff sentiment in the West, except in Ohio and Michigan where wool-growing and nascent industry counteracted normal Western antipathy. They show the Northeast strongly favorable to higher duties but the Eastern border states evenly divided or opposed. On the Wool and Woolens Bill, on the other hand, the West was overwhelmingly favorable, whereas the Northeast was only lukewarm. The Radicals carried each vote by a safe majority. In each case, however, the measure would have been defeated had the Southerners been back in Congress voting solidly against protection, as it was feared they would if uncontrolled from the North. A solid Southern vote combined with the negative one actually cast, could have defeated protection under any of the plans of apportionment—under full representation counting all negroes, under the old three-fifths rule, or under the Fourteenth Amendment scheme of counting only whites.[85] An analysis of the votes is given in the table on the following page. These votes explain Radical success in suppressing the tariff issue; they indicate what a powerful campaign issue against the Radicals the tariff would have been for the Conservatives, and one reason for

---

[84] *Ibid.*, 39 Cong., 2 Sess., 1659.
[85] The conjectural votes are compiled from tables prepared by Roscoe Conkling to show the apportionment of representatives under the various plans. *Ibid.*, 39 Cong., 1 Sess., 357.

	House Vote[1] on Tariff Bill of 1866		House Vote[2] on Stevens's Motion to Suspend the Rules for Vote on Tariff of 1867		Senate Vote[3] on Tariff of 1867	
	Aye	Nay	Aye	Nay	Aye	Nay
Actual Vote with South Excluded	95	52	102	69	27	10
Possible Vote with South Voting under Full Representation for Negro	95	122	102	130	27	30
Possible Vote with South Voting under Old ⅗ Rule	95	113	102	122	27	30
Possible Vote with South Voting under 14th Amendment with No Negroes Counted	95	100	102	110	27	30

VOTE BY SECTIONS

	Total[5]		Northeast[6]		New England, New York, and Pennsylvania		Other Northeastern States[7]		Northwest[8]		Northwest without Ohio and Michigan		Ohio and Michigan		Far West[9]	
	Aye	Nay	Aye	Nay	Aye	Nay	Aye	Nay	Aye	Nay	Aye	Nay	Aye	Nay	Aye	Nay
House Vote on Tariff Bill of 1866	95	52	63	13	58	5[10]	5	8	28	39	9	36[10]	19	3	4	0
House Vote on Stevens's Motion to Suspend the Rules for Vote on Tariff of 1867	102	69	64	22	58	15	6	7	31	41	12	37	19	4	5	0
Senate Vote on Tariff Bill of 1867	27	10	16	0[11]	11	0	5	0	7	8	3	8[11]	4	0	4	0
Senate Vote[4] on Wool and Woolens Act of 1867	31	12	12	7	8	4[12]	4	3	14	3[12]	10	3			4	1

[1] July 10, 1866, *Cong. Globe,* 39 Cong., 1 Sess., 3725.
[2] Feb. 28, 1867, *ibid.,* 39 Cong., 2 Sess., 1659.

Radical determination not to let the Southerners return.

Radicals fully realized the importance of the tariff issue and the strength of Western opposition to protection. This was why they feared the political consequences of the Tariff Bill of 1866. Horace White, for example, wrote to Senator Trumbull, "Would it not be well to get that fatal tariff bill postponed, smothered, or in some way put out of sight when it comes to the Senate? There is absolutely no difference of opinion about it here—protectionists & free traders both agreeing in considering it a bill of abominations. The only class who favor it . . . have stocks of goods on hand—a very small class numerically. Mr. Medill, the oracle of the Protectionists in the West has written the most pressing letters to his fellow Protectionists in the House telling them that the bill must be killed, or both Protectionism & Republicanism will be killed in Indiana, Illinois, & Iowa. I have written as strongly as possible on this subject to Senators Fessenden & Wilson." [86]

The Radicals handled the situation admirably. In the East the tariff was plainly a stake in the election. In the West it was dodged as irrelevant. When Radical Senators awoke to its dangerous potentialities in the election, they quickly tabled the tariff bill. The *Herald* said it "died of party apprehension," because in the Northwest "even the Radicals" had begun to understand that what "is clear

[86] July 5, 1866, Trumbull MSS., LXVIII.

---

[3] Jan. 31, 1867, *ibid.*, 39 Cong., 2 Sess., 931.

[4] March 2, 1867, *ibid.*, 39 Cong., 2 Sess., 1958. House vote not recorded.

[5] The discrepancies in these totals on the second, third, and fourth votes are accounted for by Tennessee's vote of 2-6, 0-2, and 1-1, respectively.

[6] "Northeast" is here used to include New England, New York, New Jersey, Pennsylvania, West Virginia, Maryland, and Delaware.

[7] New Jersey, Delaware, Maryland and West Virginia.

[8] "Northwest" is used to include the five states of the Old Northwest, Minnesota, Iowa, and the Western border states of Kentucky, Missouri, and Kansas.

[9] "Far West" embraced Oregon with many New England settlers, California, and the Radical war-baby, Nevada, admitted to give the Radicals two senators.

[10] Not a vote was cast against the Tariff of 1866 from all New England, and not a vote for it from Delaware, Indiana, or Illinois.

[11] In the Senate not a New England vote was cast against the Bill, and not a vote for it from Indiana, Iowa, Kansas, Kentucky, and Missouri.

[12] Both Massachusetts senators, Buckalew of Pennsylvania, and Sprague of Rhode Island, opposed the Wool and Woolens Bill. The only three negative votes of the Northwest came from Indiana, Kentucky, and Missouri.

profit in the way of tariff protections to the New England and Pennsylvania manufacturers and importers with heavy stocks on hand, is dead loss to the great West." [87] The *Tribune* said Sumner and four others killed it because they were tired of hearing New England denounced as selfish in her demands for protection.[88] According to Hayes, "The postponement of the bill . . . by votes of Senators known to be generally favorable to a protective policy, was undoubtedly due to national considerations believed to be more important than any industrial necessities." [89] Some of the strongest protectionists urged tabling a measure that gave the highest protection the country had ever seen. The bill might have failed. What Radical leaders feared was its *passage* just before the election. On this issue a veto could not have been sustained, and the passage of the bill would have provided Conservatives with a weapon ready made.[90]

Johnson's shrewdest supporters tried to emphasize the tariff factor. Ex-Governor Seymour, for instance, told his Cooper Institute audience: The House bill "will fall heavily upon the commercial and farming interests of our country. It will harm this great city. It will lengthen the hours of labor, and will scant the food and clothing of the poor; but who hears of this amid the howlings of sectional rage? . . . This question of tariffs and taxation, and not the negro

[87] *New York Herald*, July 13 and 14, 1866.
[88] *New York Semi-Weekly Tribune*, July 13, 1866. Patterson blamed weakness of knee of "those Massachusetts Senators—the ungrateful scamps." D. W. Patterson to T. Stevens, Dec. 10, 1866, Stevens MSS., VIII.
[89] J. L. Hayes, *Second Annual Report of the National Association of Wool Manufacturers*, 14.
[90] Burchard wrote Washburne when he heard it was tabled: "The west and the Republican party owe you a large debt of gratitude for your resolute resistance to the passage of the Tariff Bill. . . . A Presidential veto of that Bill would have atoned with very many of our western people for the previous exercise of that prerogative and Congress would have lost the sympathy and respect now entertained for it by the large majority of the northern people." July 14, 1866, Washburne MSS., XCIII.

question keeps our country divided. . . . The men of New York were called upon to keep out the Southern members, because if they were admitted they would vote to uphold our commercial greatness and the interests of Western agricultural states." [91] Johnson's political training made him instinctively oppose protection. Had he or the Philadelphia Convention vigorously attacked it, and launched in the West a campaign of repeated public iteration that a desire to maintain the protective system was an important factor in Radical opposition to Johnson's Southern policy, the Radicals would have found themselves facing a hopeless dilemma. The Eastern wing of that party could not have defended protection without alienating Western followers. Yet not to have defended it would have been to relinquish before the fight the choicest fruit of victory. In spite of the special factors which sugar-coated the pill of protection for some Westerners, in spite of all that the Radicals could do to minimize its importance, a tariff issue would have split the Radical Party, and won many converts to Conservatism. Johnson's silence allowed the Radicals to use the tariff tacitly but effectively in the East, and to avoid it in the West where it was generally unpopular.

*　　*　　*　　*

In these economic questions lay potentially powerful election issues. Some of Johnson's advisers recognized their significance, and urged the President to stress them in the campaign. Phillips of the *Herald* wrote begging him to make war on the national banks. Both Phillips and Bennett thought the banks a question of "such magnitude that it [would] enter more prominently into political affairs . . . than the old United States Bank did." Bennett thought that Johnson

[91] *New York Herald*, Oct. 31, 1866.

could win the election by using this issue to "wake up the people." [92] Chase thought the currency problem second in importance only to "Freedom of labor." [93] Bowen, the Harvard economist, wrote Sumner that there was no question in which the people were more interested than in finance.[94] Ex-Governor Seymour protested because "while there is danger that the paper bubble is to be blown up until it bursts, and throw our whole system of debt, banking and currency into ruin, the public thought is . . . taken up with schemes to fasten a despotic and military government upon the people of the South." [95] Seymour wanted to divert attention from the South to debt, banks, and currency. He believed the tariff, too, a vital question. McCulloch urged Johnson to make an issue of it.[96] Repeatedly did the *New York Herald*, one of Johnson's staunchest supporters, urge the President to utilize these economic factors in the campaign.

Johnson personally leaned toward the position of these opponents of the economic tenets of Northeastern Radi-

[92] W. B. Phillips to A. Johnson, July 1, 1866, Johnson MSS., XCVII.

[93] S. P. Chase to J. W. Schuckers, July 7, 1865, Chase MSS., 2nd series, III.

[94] April 5, 1866, Sumner MSS., LXXVII.

[95] "Not only," he said, "is the public debt, which pays nothing to the support of government, held mainly in one corner of our country, but the banks, which have a right to make the currency for all the States, are placed and owned in a large degree by the Eastern and Middle States. Not only our debt but our currency is sectionalized" so that profits of the bank circulation go largely "to these three New England States [Massachusetts, Rhode Island, and Connecticut]. The number and wealth of the people of the great States thus left with little or no means of getting currency except as borrowed from more favored section, make this a glaring evil. . . . They will demand, with a strong show of reason, that they shall be put upon an equal footing with the Northeastern section of the Union. And this will be done by an increase of paper money, for the debtor and the speculative interests will always control Congressional action." Speech at Cooper Institute, *New York Herald,* Oct. 31, 1866.

[96] Toombs looking back years afterward felt that the tariff should have been the leading issue against the Radicals. "The West," he said, "is as ready for it as the South, from the enormous amount of her exports of her grain and hog-products, and is, always has been, and always [will] be the most valuable ally of sound principles." R. Toombs to A. H. Stephens, March 25, 1880, Amer. Hist. Assoc., *Annual Report* (1911), II, 739.

calism. As the father of the Homestead Law he opposed parceling out the public domain to corporations before the homesteaders could settle it. By training and instinct he was an enemy of bondholders, national banks, monopolies, and a protective tariff. Had he, then, followed his bent and launched into the campaign an attack upon the economic views of the Eastern wing of the Radical Party, had he used his "Swing 'round the Circle" to arouse the West upon this subject, he could have marshalled all the latent discontent of the West to his support, and could have split the Radical Party at one blow.

Johnson's failure to do this was a fatal error in political judgment. In an interview with a Boston journalist he explained his action. He declared that nothing could be "safely and permanently done in regard to restoring the currency, diminishing taxation and establishing the prosperity of the country on a sound and enduring basis until representatives from all the States [were] present in Congress." [97] He failed to see that an attempt to solve these other issues would bring success to his Southern policy by dividing its enemies. His attitude enabled Radicals to relegate all of these dangerous economic issues to a position of irrelevance.

[97] *Boston Evening Commercial,* July 21, 1866.

Chapter XI

THE CAMPAIGN

VICTORY was not won through the popularity or soundness of Radical tenets on important issues, but by skilful generalship that succeeded in shunning issues. Originally, popular opinion was antagonistic both to the Southern program and to the economic interests of the Radical leaders. Yet the Radicals won because neither Southern policy nor these potentially powerful economic factors decided the election. It was masterful campaign management, a clever use of claptrap, and vituperation against the "Copperheadism" of all friends of the South, that determined our Southern policy.   *   *   *   *   *

In organizing their forces, the Radical managers utilized several powerful centers of influence. One of these was the foreign element among the voters. Germans and Scandinavians had generally settled on farms in New England's portion of the Northwest, and were Radicals anyway.[1] But

---

[1] Even before the War they had been anti-Southern for several reasons: they hated slavery; many who had come to America through a love of liberty disliked the aristocracy of the South; Southerners had won the enmity of foreigners by opposing immigration from a fear that it would endanger the slave system and, by filling up the great Northwest, overpower the South; many of the Germans had been political agitators driven from their own land for radical ideas who easily became extremists in this country. E.g., see George M. Stephenson, "Nativism in the Forties and Fifties," *Miss. Valley Hist. Rev.*, IX, 185. Even in the East, Germans were

the Irish living in crowded cities were predominantly Democratic. In winning their vote, circumstances aided the Radicals. At just this time the Fenian movement in America reached its height. On June 1 American Fenians executed an armed attack upon Canada. It proved a fiasco. O'Neill at the head of eight hundred enthusiasts crossed the Niagara and captured Fort Erie. But the next day many deserted; the rest were routed by the Canadians and surrendered to the United States warship *Michigan*.

While the "raid" looked like an idle threat, Johnson hesitated, but when the Fenians actually crossed the border, he took strenuous measures to enforce our neutrality, arrested some of the leaders, and seized the Fenian arms. He undoubtedly acted wisely and with dignity. He made clear our neutrality, and under trial maintained friendly relations with England. Anglo-American relations were strained at this period by Northern bitterness over England's dubious attitude during the War, and by delicate problems like our claims against England for her violations of neutrality, her claims against us arising out of the Trent affair, and the old quarrel over fisheries. Hot-headed Americans wanted to rush into war, and chafed under Seward's and Johnson's caution. Irish-American hatred of England added to the impatience. Johnson maintained friendly relations with England in the

apt to be Radicals. E.g., see "Resolutions of the German National Club of Hoboken," Johnson MSS., XC, and E. Vorster to C. Sumner, Oct. 5, 1865, Sumner MSS., LXXIV. There were exceptions, however, and some Germans did support Johnson, e.g., Magnus Gross, editor of the *Staats Zeitung*, who shouted, "Down with intolerance and fanaticism," at a German meeting in Union Square, New York (*New York Herald*, Sept. 18, 1866); a "German Democratic Union Party" which endorsed the Philadelphia Convention at a meeting in New York (*ibid.*, Aug. 23, 1866); and Dorsheimer of Buffalo, who, on the intercession of Welles and Blair, was retained in the collectorship because he was influential against "the machinations of Schurz" (F. P. Blair to A. Johnson, March 1, 1866, Johnson MSS., LXXXIX, and P. Dorsheimer to G. Welles, Sept. 25, 1866, Welles MSS., LXII).

full knowledge that it was weakening his chances in the election.

The Fenians felt aggrieved at the Government's attitude toward their Canadian escapade and its refusal to release prisoners taken in suppressing the raid, at the failure of American consuls in Ireland to maintain the "rights" of naturalized Americans who returned to Ireland to make trouble, and at the illiberal attitude of Adams in England.[2] The Radicals encouraged this dissatisfaction, and ingratiated themselves with the Fenians. They made Johnson's enforcement of neutrality an issue against him. Shortly before Congress adjourned, they adopted a resolution requesting the President "to urge upon the Canadian authorities and also the British Government the release of the Fenian prisoners recently captured in Canada," and another urging Johnson "to cause the prosecution instituted in the United States courts to be discontinued."[3] In the cabinet Speed, soon openly to avow Radicalism, aggravated the situation by issuing an offensively worded preliminary to the proclamation in spite of Johnson's objection to it—meddling which Welles thought part of a Radical trick to alienate Irish votes from Johnson.[4] When Radical leaders learned after midnight the day before adjournment that the Fenians wanted the Fair Building which Congress had already given to a committee of women for the benefit of the Soldiers' and Sailors' Orphan Home, they hastened to please the Fenians by passing a bill in the small hours of the morning giving them the hall in spite of the earlier grant. Prominent Radicals improved the occasion with flattering speeches framed to win Irish votes.[5]

[2] *New York Herald,* Sept. 19, 1866.
[3] *Cong. Globe,* 39 Con., 1 Sess., 4047-4048.
[4] Welles MS. Diary, June 7, 1866—(II, 524).
[5] *New York Herald,* July 29, 1866. *Cong. Globe,* 39 Cong., 1 Sess., 4274, 4293-4298. Lowell, though a Radical, expressed "disgust at the demagogism which courted the Fenians." *North Am. Rev.,* CIII (October, 1866), 546.

In Chicago where the Irish vote was particularly important, the Radicals staged a large Irish picnic which Governor
Oglesby, Speaker Colfax, and General Logan attended. "In
the rebellion," Oglesby told the huzzahing Irish, "the
English tried to divide us, and every rebel found shelter
under Queen Victoria's petticoat. Now the Englishmen are
on their knees begging. What do you find Andrew Johnson
doing? He has taken the rebel side, and is in perfect accord
with the British. Johnson is now the friend of the English
government, and he and his party have always got your
votes. If you keep doing this you will never deserve to be
anything more than dirt pickers for Johnson. He encouraged
you until you got across the border, and then he obeyed the
British government and was against you." Oglesby emphatically declared that his sympathies were with the Fenians in
their efforts to free their native land. Had he been president
he would not have interfered with the Fenian invasion of
Canada. "Go on," he urged, "and assert the rights of Ireland." Colfax and Logan each contributed a pro-Fenian
speech denouncing Johnson and England.[6] Down-state
Logan and Washburne were catering to the Fenian vote.[7]

How many Irish votes the Radicals won is unknown. The
Irish were not all Fenians, and the Fenian leaders themselves
were divided. Many Irish supported Johnson.[8] The Conserv-

6 *New York Herald*, Aug. 16, 1866.

7 C. C. Royce to E. B. Washburne, Sept. 1, 1866, Washburne MSS., LIII;
A. Kinyon to E. B. W., Sept. 10, 1866, *ibid.*, XIX.

8 E.g., on July 29 a meeting of Irishmen was called "in view of the
unscrupulous efforts which the leaders of the radical party are making
to entice the Irish citizens of the United States from the path of duty in
the present crisis in the affairs of our beloved country." Its purpose was "to
repudiate the unnatural alliance so treacherously sought and to proclaim
their unswerving adherence to the reconstruction policy of President Johnson." On August 1 a similar meeting of Irishmen in Washington adopted
resolutions denouncing the Radicals and endorsing the President. Later in
the month General Sweeny, an officer of the Fenian organization, issued
an address to all Fenians deprecating the Radical efforts to draw Fenians
into politics. "Those," he declared, "who would attempt to traffic in the
sacred impulses of Irish hearts deserve, and should receive, the scorn and

atives, however, considered the situation serious. In September Tilden urged Johnson to release the arms and material taken from the Fenians; "opponents of the administration," he reported, "are using such demagogical arts to take from it the votes of the Irish, that no pretext should be given them which clear duty does not compel." [9] Senator Dixon wrote, "Cant something be devised proper in itself which will appease them? . . . We certainly lost many of their votes in Maine & should today in this state. There is no doubt of this. I think we shall feel it in Pennsylvania & New York." Again, "A very earnest & successful effort on the part of the President to procure the pardon of the Fenians now under sentence of death in Canada is all important"; without it the election is lost.[10] In September Johnson did order the dismissal of the cases pending against the Fenians, and restored the seized arms to the owners. Yet the Radicals undoubtedly won many Irish votes.

*   *   *   *

No man in the country enjoyed greater prestige and respect at this time than did General Grant. The Radicals eagerly sought to win him away from the Conservative cause. They failed in this because Grant was one of the staunchest supporters of the Conservative Southern policy which he had helped to mold, because Grant dreaded political turmoil, because even after he lost respect for the person he honored the office of the President, because an inbred loyalty

detestation of all true men." *New York Herald*, July 29, Aug. 2, Aug. 20, 1866. The *Universe*, Catholic organ of Philadelphia, and its editor, Spellissy, supported Johnson and the Philadelphia Convention. J. M. Spellissy to G. F. Train, Aug. 10, 1866, Johnson MSS., XCIX; J. M. S. to A. Johnson, Aug. 4, 1866, *ibid.*, XCVIII. The Boston *Pilot*, the most powerful Catholic organ in the country, and its editor, Donahue, strongly advocated Johnson's policy. A. H. Dorsey to A. Johnson, Aug. 6, 1866, *ibid.*, XCIX.

    9 Sept. 21, 1866, *ibid.*, CII.
    10 J. Dixon to G. Welles, Sept. 29, Oct. 27, 1866, Welles MSS., LXII.

to a superior officer restrained him, and because his adviser, Rawlins, felt it was not time for him to throw off the mask of indifference and enter the political arena. When they could not win him to open opposition to Johnson, the Radicals sedulously worked to create the impression that Grant was disgusted with the President and opposed to his policy, remaining silent merely out of a sense of soldierly duty. When Grant appeared with Johnson at the reception of the committee from the Philadelphia Convention, the Radicals declared he did so only in obedience to explicit orders.[11] Early in July their press reported that Grant had "expressed his preference for the Congressional Reconstruction policy." [12] The hope proved false, but the rumor persisted.

The Radicals were seriously worried all through the campaign over Grant's position. His friend Washburne was besieged with admonitions to prevent his aiding Conservatives with the prestige of his approval.[13] Early in September the *Tribune* was perplexed.[14] A week later White found the public mind in so "feverish a condition" concerning Grant that he published a special dispatch giving what reassuring facts he could.[15]

Repeatedly Grant's Radical friends sought to dissuade him from accompanying the President to Chicago.[16] Unsuccessful in this, they informed the public that he went only under compulsion. Logan asserted in a speech at Galena during the progress of the tour that he knew Grant intimately, and that Grant held sound Radical views, and remained silent only because he dreaded becoming embroiled in poli-

11 They were nevertheless worried over the episode. J. D. Defrees to E. B. Washburne, Aug. 23, 1866, Washburne MSS., XIX.
12 J. H. Wilson to E. B. W., July 5, 1866, *ibid.*, LII.
13 *Ibid.*, XVII, XIX, LIII.
14 *Chicago Tribune*, Sept. 7, 1866.
15 H. White to E. B. W., Sept. 14, 1866, Washburne MSS., LIII.
16 For evidence see Washburne MSS., XIX and Trumbull MSS., LXIX.

tics; but that rebels and Copperheads were using his silence
to discredit him with Union men.[17] After the first of Johnson's encounters with a hostile crowd, Grant left the party
at Cleveland and went with Rawlins by boat to Detroit. The
Radical press shouted with glee, and gave out that the General had separated from the party out of disgust at Johnson's "drunken display" in Cleveland.[18] At the Southern
Loyalists' Convention then sitting in Philadelphia, the secretary read a telegram announcing Grant's and Farragut's
desertion of the President; this dispatch "created the wildest
enthusiasm, the entire Convention rising and waving their
hats, and giving three cheers for Grant and Farragut." [19]
Unfortunately, Grant soon rejoined the Presidential party.
But that made little difference as the Radicals had so successfully circulated the report that it was currently believed
that the General did abandon Johnson. Even contemporary
biographers believed and repeated the story. "The people
were humiliated and ashamed," says Coolidge. "Grant seized
the earliest opportunity to plead sickness, quit the party,
and return to Washington." [20] "Finally," says Badeau, "his
disgust was so great that he became half unwell, and pleading illness left the party and returned to Washington in
advance of the President." [21] General Wilson wrote, "Grant
also soon became disgusted with the undignified exhibition
the President was making of himself, and took leave of the
party at Buffalo, going with Rawlins by lake steamer to
Detroit. They rejoined Johnson at Chicago and accompanied the party to St. Louis, where they finally left it,
ostensibly for the purpose of visiting Grant's father near

17 *New York Herald*, Sept. 4, 1866.
18 *Supra*, 13-15; *infra*, 362 ff.
19 *The Southern Loyalists' Convention* (*Tribune Tracts*, No. 2), 13.
20 Louis A. Coolidge, *U. S. Grant*, 239.
21 Adam Badeau, *Grant in Peace*, 39.

Cincinnati, but really because, as Grant expressed it, he did not 'care to accompany a man who was deliberately digging his own grave.' " [22] Church described the Grant-Johnson relationship thus: "An ambitious and intriguing politician, Johnson was much more than a match for the single-minded soldier in artfulness and craft. By various subtle methods he sought to entangle the General in his controversies with Congress." [23]

The fact is that Grant was a friend of the President personally and a whole-hearted supporter of his Southern policy. At first he thought Johnson too harsh in his desire to administer a few exemplary punishments to "leaders of rebellion." He counseled clemency in all cases, prevented Lee's arrest, endorsed his application for pardon, and was undoubtedly instrumental in softening Johnson's policy. Until the election of 1866, General and President remained close friends; Grant was a trusted and willing adviser; he even attended cabinet meetings from time to time. In Welles's diary there is no mention of Grant's unfriendliness. Contemporary documents prove only the fact that the Radicals were trying to convince the public of an estrangement, and meantime to create one if possible. Johnson himself testified to their intimacy and to his dependence upon Grant's judgment.[24]

In spite of almost universal belief that he did, and supplications of his Radical friends that he should, Grant did not leave the Presidential party on the Chicago tour except for two brief, easily explicable separations, after each of which he rejoined Johnson. In an unprinted portion of Welles's

[22] James H. Wilson, *Life of John A. Rawlins,* 330.
[23] Wm. C. Church, *Ulysses S. Grant,* 347.
[24] A. Johnson to B. Truman, Aug. 3, 1866, *Century Magazine,* LXXXV (1913), 439.

diary is recorded the real cause of the first absence, ascribed
by Radicals to disgust with Johnson's drunkenness. "Grant,"
confides Welles to his diary, "left the party at Cleveland and
went by steamer to Detroit. He had abstained from liquor,
until our arrival in Buffalo. Thence through the day until
we reached Cleveland he became garrulous and stupidly com-
municative to Mrs. F. [arragut] as she afterward informed
me, and was with Surgeon Gen Buvois put on board the
steamer for Detroit both of them intoxicated." [25] From St.
Louis Grant hurried on to Ohio where he visited his father
and then rejoined the Presidential party in Cincinnati. The
day that Grant spent waiting for Johnson was made unpleasant by attempts to lionize him. At night he slipped off
alone to the theater to avoid the crowds, but was discovered
there by Radicals who sought to stage a demonstration. He
forbade it and told them he was annoyed at their evident
attempt to offend the President, but he promised that, in
company with the President, he would be glad to see them
the next day.[26] A letter of Rawlins, Grant's personal adviser
who accompanied him on this trip, to his wife, establishes
the friendliness of Grant's relations with Johnson and the
fact that Grant did not go with the President under compulsion. "The ovations to the President," wrote Rawlins,
"have been very fine all the way from Washington here. The
one in New York perhaps has never been excelled in this
country. General Grant and Admiral Farragut came in for
a large share of the cheering, I assure you. And I am now
more than ever glad that the General concluded to accom-

[25] Welles MS. Diary, Sept. 17, 1866. This is particularly reliable because
Welles was an admirer of Grant and remained his friend even after the
quarrel between Grant and Johnson.

[26] The account in the *New York Herald* (Sept. 13, 1866), agrees with the
special dispatch in the *Chicago Tribune* (Sept. 14, 1866), which White published to counteract reports that Grant had made a speech in support of
Johnson.

pany the President, for it will do Grant good, whatever may be his aspirations in the future, and fix him in the confidence of Mr. Johnson, enabling him to fix up the army as it should be, and exert such influence as will be of benefit to the country." [27]

Late in October Johnson and Seward planned a mission to Mexico to hasten French evacuation, and tried to persuade Grant to accompany Minister Campbell. Johnson talked the matter over with Grant twice, and Grant considered accepting. But "on further and full reflection," he begged to be excused from "diplomatic service" for which he was "not fitted either by education or taste." [28] Two days later in a cabinet meeting which Grant attended, the President repeated the request. Then through Stanton he sent orders for Grant to go; [29] again Grant respectfully yet firmly declined, pleading ignorance of diplomacy and the need of reorganizing the army. [30] The Radicals insisted that this was a trick to get Grant out of the way that Johnson might use the army against Congress. Stanton told Grant that this was the purpose. [31] Comstock recorded in his diary that Grant believed it, but ascribed the desire to be rid of Grant to the belief that he now opposed the Presidential policy. [32] When Sherman accepted the Mexican mission, he enigmatically wrote his brother, "I had to make this trip to escape a worse duty and to save another person from a Complication that should be avoided. I am determined to keep out of politics—even quasi political offices." [33] Grant's implicit faith in Sherman, who would have commanded the army during his absence in Mex-

[27] J. H. Wilson, *op. cit.*, 334.
[28] U. S. Grant to A. Johnson, Oct. 21, 1866, Johnson MSS., CIV.
[29] A. Johnson to E. M. Stanton, Oct. 26, 1866, *ibid.*, CIV.
[30] U. S. Grant to E. M. Stanton, Oct. 27, 1866, *ibid.*, CIV.
[31] C. B. Comstock MS. Diary, Jan. 23, 1867.
[32] *Ibid.*, Oct. 23, 1866.
[33] Nov. 11, 1866, W. T. Sherman MSS., XX.

ico, makes it incredible that he seriously apprehended use of the army for purposes of intrigue if he accepted the mission. He did want to remain to reorganize the army. Comstock suggests what was probably the determining factor with a man already aspiring to the Presidency, when he records, "If the General were to go & the negotiations fail, it could not fail to damage him, while if he did anything Seward whom he dislikes thoroughly could either overrule or appropriate the credit." [34] Whatever Grant's or Johnson's motives, the Mexican episode was used just before election to convince voters that Grant was in open opposition to a President who was plotting the use of the army against Congress.

Grant had a shrewd political adviser in the person of his chief of staff, John A. Rawlins. How much political ambition Grant himself had in these days is uncertain, but even in 1866 Rawlins was managing Grant's actions with an eye to the presidency. Grant himself was no politician. Rawlins was wise enough to see that his safest policy was to follow his own inclination and abstain from speech-making or other political activity. Consequently, Grant was exhibited all over the country and acquired a reputation of great wisdom and dignity through determined silence in a period when those who spoke displayed neither. Garland says Grant admitted presidential aspirations as early as March, 1866, but thought he was too young. He thinks that by fall Rawlins, Babcock, and other politicians on Grant's staff had implanted in him the idea that he was "the irresistible choice for the Presidency at the end of Johnson's term." [35] Wilson thinks that by September Rawlins was convinced "that Johnson could not be renominated, and that Grant's chances for the succession would be injured by further identification

[34] C. B. Comstock MS. Diary, Oct. 23, 1866.
[35] H. Garland, *U. S. Grant,* 347.

with Johnson or his policy." [36] In any case, as soon as Johnson's defeat was certain, Rawlins's attitude changed and the friendship between Grant and Johnson cooled.[37] In October Grant finally broke silence sufficiently to write privately to Hyllis and others assurances which Illinois Radicals considered "bully" and certain to put him in the Presidency in 1868.[38]

Near the end of his term Johnson privately wrote his former secretary, "Grant was untrue. He meant well for the first two years, and much that I did that was denounced was through his advice. He was the strongest man of all in the support of my policy for a long while, and did the best he could for nearly two years by strengthening my hands against the adversaries of constitutional government. But Grant saw the Radical handwriting on the wall, and heeded it. I did not see it, or, if seeing it, did not heed it. Grant did the proper thing to save Grant, but it pretty near ruined me. I might have done the same thing under the same circumstances." [39] Here Johnson probably explains the whole relationship. Had Grant given Johnson his unquestionable verbal support, Johnson's cause would have gained greatly, but Grant might have lost the presidency and gone down with Johnson to a perhaps inevitable defeat. The false picture that Grant's silence enabled them to paint won the Radicals many votes. 　　*　　*　　*　　*

Politicians were easily won to the Radical fold by the fear of losing office and power. Every political leader who was not

[36] J. H. Wilson, *op. cit.*, 330.

[37] Porter wrote Wilson that the "'swing around the circle' completely cured Rawlins of his sympathy" for Johnson, and won him to support of the Amendment. J. H. Wilson to E. B. Washburne, Oct. 13, 1866, Washburne MSS., LIII.

[38] J. E. Smith to E. B. W., Oct. 16, 1866, *ibid.*, XIX.

[39] A. Johnson to B. Truman, Aug. 3, 1868, *Century Magazine*, LXXXV (1913), 439.

willing to come out openly for Johnson, from the senator
in Washington down to the ward boss, realized that unless
the Radicals won he was doomed. With the South still excluded, principles and issues could be fought out within the
party after the election; but if the election were lost, party
politicians would be turned permanently out of power, and
offices, career, and principles would all go down together to
ruin. Only by winning the election of 1866 and keeping the
South out or making it Radical, could this minority party
remain in power.

Conservative leaders realized the effectiveness of this
motive, and tried to turn it against the Radical politicians.
George Dallas told the people of Pennsylvania that the Radicals were determined to have "no Union until conditions
unknown to our constitution, and having for their sole object
the continuance of party ascendency, shall have been accepted." [40] Senator Dixon assured the Connecticut Constitutional Union Convention that "the purpose of the radicals"
was "the saving of the republican party rather than the
restoration of the Union." [41] The "faction in power here,"
said Cowan, "tasting the sweets of power . . . tell you that
these people [the Southerners] are unfit to come in; and
why? Because, come in as they may, there can be no reconciliation or union between them and this faction. . . . What
then is to be done? Usurp, grasp power yourselves, remodel
the Constitution, remodel the laws, so that the few, not the
many, can hold on to power. . . . That is exactly what it
means. Are you afraid the Democrats will get the power?
. . . That is disunion." [42] In August, 1865, Blair had

[40] Speech at Ashland, Pa., *New York Herald*, Sept. 29, 1866.
[41] *Ibid.*, Aug. 2, 1866.
[42] May 11, 1866, *Speeches of Hon. Edgar Cowan . . . Doolittle . . . Mc-
Culloch . . . (National Union Club Documents)*, 9. Also *Cong. Globe*, 39
Cong., 1 Sess., 2559.

warned Johnson against the "New England junto" that wanted to rule the country.[43] "Not a single emotion of solicitude for the welfare of the black race," averred the *Detroit Free Press*, "animated the feelings or action of the Radicals in Congress. . . . Their action has been dictated by what they thought was policy, in their anxiety to perpetuate the rule of their party." [44] In condemning the Radical lust for power, Henry Ward Beecher wrote the Cleveland Convention, "It is said that, if admitted to Congress, the Southern Senators and Representatives will coalesce with Northern democrats and rule the country. Is this nation, then, to remain dismembered, to serve the ends of parties? Have we learned no wisdom by the history of the past ten years, in which just this course of sacrificing the nation to the exigencies of parties plunged us into rebellion and war?" [45]

Neither the chiding of Beecher nor the accusing speeches of Conservative senators could move politicians in danger of being turned out of power. While Lincoln yet lived, Beckwith of Boston had written Sumner, "Better let La., Ark., & Tenn., all wait for years than let in a single State or man not permanently reliable for the support of the right policy." [46] Another Bostonian wrote Stanton, "We have them now under a control which we must not lose, even if we hold them as military dependencies." [47] In the days before his conversion, Stewart of Nevada revealed the argument that was being used with him when he protested, "Are we willing to prolong the restoration of the Union and risk the experiment of taxation without representation for fear that the

[43] Aug. 1, 1865, Johnson MSS., LXXII.
[44] March 15, 1866, quoted in Harriette M. Dilla, *The Politics of Michigan, 1865-1878*, 51.
[45] *New York Herald*, Sept. 2, 1866.
[46] Jan. 28, 1865, Sumner MSS., LXXII.
[47] H. Woodman to E. Stanton, April 24, 1865, Stanton MSS., XXVI.

application of the rule, that the voice of the majority is law, shall drive us from power?" [48] "Seward," the *Chicago Tribune* warned its readers, "wants to open the doors of Congress and let in twenty-two whitewashed rebels, which will secure Mr. Johnson a working majority of Copperheads." [49] Medill of that paper protested to McCulloch that Johnson's policy "if persisted in, will split our party and turn the administration of the country over to the copperheads." "Have you reflected," he asked, "on the consequences of rushing 75 or 80 ex-rebel votes into the House of Repr. and 20 ex-rebel Senators?" [50] Wade opposed Johnson's course because it meant "consigning the great Union, or Republican party, bound, hand and foot, to the tender mercies of the rebels we have so lately conquered in the field, and their Copperhead allies of the North." "To admit the States on Mr. Johnson's plan," he wrote Sumner, "is voluntarily, with our eyes open, to surrender our political rights into the hands and keeping of those traitors we have just conquered. . . . It is nothing less than political suicide." [51] In planning their campaign, Winter Davis told Sumner that the campaign must be based, "not on the rights of the negro—nor the general requirements of justice & humanity—they are vague generalities that solve nothing—but on the direct & practical consequences of allowing the rebel States to go into exclusive control of the men who led or the men who

[48] Dec. 21, 1865, *Cong. Globe,* 39 Cong., 1 Sess., 111.

[49] *Chicago Tribune,* June 5, 1865.

[50] June 23, 1865, McCulloch MSS., II. McPherson said if the doctrine of state indestructibility be true, there will be one hundred "rebels" in the next Congress "who will affiliate with their friends from the North, and control that body, . . . and we shall be where we were before the war commenced. They may and probably will defeat every measure for the future safety of the republic." "Paper on Reconstruction," McPherson MSS., V.

[51] July 29, 1865, *ibid.,* LXXIV.

followed in the rebellion—for us equally fatal." [52] "I am weak enough," wrote Senator Howard, "to prefer my *friends* tho' black to my *enemies* tho' white. It is not to be denied that we have few friends in the rebel states but the blacks." [53] He wrote frankly to Sumner, "We don't want [the Southerners] back now. . . . We have the power without them to do all that is requisite, & it seems to me we are children & almost fools to run the risk of losing it by introducing enemies into Congress, who will be sure to vote against us & for rebel interests. Is such blindness & improvidence worthy of our fathers—of us?" [54]

In later years that shrewd political observer Colonel McClure summarized the situation in 1866. "The question of political control," he maintained, "was then, as ever, before and since, paramount. . . . In a little time it became evident to the Republicans that Republican control in the South could be maintained only by universal suffrage and disfranchising the great mass of the property owners in those states." [55] A contemporary issue of the *London Times* epitomized the reconstruction controversy in one sentence: "After years of adversity the Radicals have gained the supremacy, and they are reluctant to part with it—and very naturally, if their own interests alone are considered." [56]

* * * *

The Radicals succeeded in controlling almost the entire Republican press. Several factors made this possible. In the first place, the War had forced editors to take sides for or

[52] June 20, 1865, *ibid.*, LXXIII. What Davis feared was a union of rebels and Copperheads "into an irresistible power which must wrest the government from the hands of those who have saved it." H. W. Davis to Whom It May Concern, May 27, 1865, McPherson MSS., V.
[53] J. M. Howard to C. Sumner, July 26, 1865, Sumner MSS., LXXIV.
[54] June 22, 1865, *ibid.*, LXXIII.
[55] Alexander K. McClure, *Recollections of Half a Century*, 302-303.
[56] Aug. 31, 1866.

against the government. Supporting the government during war time meant propagating views that would win the war. Hatred of the enemy was one of these views; only through hate could people be brought to desire the South's defeat sufficiently to persist in a dreary struggle. Even a newspaper editor could only hate Southerners if he implicitly believed in their wickedness. Many editors were convinced of it from the beginning. The others soon persuaded themselves by the dogmatism that successful war journalism required of them. War editors who had worked themselves and their readers into a frenzy over phantom Southerners, inevitably sought harsher treatment for them after the War than did a soldier like Grant who had come to know and respect them in flesh and blood as men very like himself. The probability was, then, that a war editor would incline to Radicalism in reconstruction.

Furthermore, the newspaper editor was dependent upon advertising and party patronage for financial support. Radical manufacturers, business houses, and other large advertisers boycotted Johnson papers. Worse still, government patronage was denied the latter for the Radicals controlled its disbursement. The Department of War, which did the largest amount of advertising, and the Departments of Justice and the Interior, were headed by Radicals; the others were infected with anti-Johnson subordinates. From Stanton down, Radical officials made certain that only the Radical press received advertising. Many reports came to Johnson of administration journals that could get no patronage and of Radical sheets that displayed government printing and denunciations of the President side by side.[57] In that

[57] E.g., McClernand complained that the *Illinois State Journal* was the "recipient of a lucrative patronage dispensed by the Executive Departments" whereas the *Illinois State Register*, a staunch Johnson supporter,

"very black radical city," Philadelphia, the *Universe* suffered so much in loss of advertising because it loyally supported Johnson,[58] that the President intervened on its behalf and ordered his subordinates to advertise in it.[59] The departments merely ignored the Executive's order, and a month later Spellissy, the editor, complained: "The War Department Quartermasters have advertisements every week: but we never hear from them." [60] Pease was certain that many of the Connecticut papers "would act right were it not for fear of pecuniary loss." [61] *Frazier's Magazine* asserted that Raymond's *New York Times* and "several other leading journals" were "compelled, on pain of financial ruin, . . . to relinquish the support of the President." [62] Newspapers could not pay bills with the gratitude of Johnson or with satisfaction that they had defended a just cause.

Republican editors had learned to look, when seeking favors and political guidance, to the men who had been most influential during the War. The men trusted during the War were those whose loyalty was most unquestionable, and they, in turn, except for the close advisers of Lincoln whom he could know personally, were apt to be the most vociferously anti-Southern. These men whose favor news-

received no other recompense than the "encouragement" of "conscious duty.". Feb. 24, 1866, Johnson MSS., LXXXIX. A. Smith of Boston protested, "Strange as it may seem—yet such is the fact—while the Radical papers of this city are accusing you, daily,—not only of Treason & other high crimes—but are holding you up to the *ridicule* & contempt of mankind, there may be seen—side by side with such articles—fifty dollar advertisements by United States officers of your appointment." July 23, 1866, *ibid.*, XCVII, and April 19, 1866, *ibid.*, XCIII. See also Samuel Stern's complaint on behalf of the *New Yorker Abend Zeitung* and the *New Yorker Democrat*, April 4, 1866, Johnson MSS., XCII.

58 J. M. Spellissy to A. Johnson, Nov. 5, 1866, *ibid.*, CV.
59 A. Johnson to Secretaries of State, Treasury, etc., Oct. 1, 1866, *ibid.*, "Letter-book."
60 J. M. Spellissy to A. Johnson, Nov. 5, 1866, *ibid.*, CV.
61 L. E. Pease to G. Welles, July 23, 1866, Welles MSS., LXI.
62 *Frazier's Magazine*, LXXV (1867), 243.

papers sought were now generally Radicals. A strictly partisan press, then, was almost universally Radical, if Republican,[63] and orthodoxly Democratic, if not. Independent papers that might have supported Johnson were rare.

The lack of widely read newspapers in which to propagate his views was one of the great causes of Johnson's defeat. Conservatives sought desperately to secure a few. The Democratic journals generally backed Johnson, but it was not Democrats that the Conservatives needed to reach. Their success depended upon their ability to convert conservative, moderate, and doubtful Republicans. A few sheets like the independent but erratic *New York Herald*,[64] the well-meaning but weak-kneed *Times,* and the friendly but impotent *National Intelligencer* were the best support the Philadelphia Conventioners could find. In March Truman had urged upon Johnson the need of a national organ to take the place of the *National Intelligencer* which was useless to the government because of its "old fogy" style and "bad" antecedents; he felt "a great administration paper" in Washington would meet with certain success.[65] From Connecticut Senator Dixon

[63] When the *Tribune* refused to give publicity to his favorable report on the South, a friend on the staff wrote Truman to express personal regret and to explain, "We can't afford to see any good in [Johnson] or his policy." J. R. Young to B. Truman, May 12, 1866, *Century Magazine,* LXXXV (1913), 440.

[64] W. B. Phillips, one of its editors, explained to Johnson the inner workings of *Herald* policy. In announcing the *Herald's* desire to bring Grant prominently forward as a candidate for the presidency in 1868, he wrote, "There is something sentimental, new, and striking in the idea, which is always in keeping with the manner of conducting the *Herald.* By and by another course may be taken." Feb. 23, 1866, Johnson MSS., LXXXVII. Later he told of the disposition of the younger Mr. Bennett, "who is self-willed and not very steady or comprehensive in his views," to waver in his support of Johnson. He added, "I do not think the *Herald* will oppose your conservative policy under any circumstances, though it is true it sometimes makes extraordinary somersaults, but it is strongly inclined to take a new start." June 3, 1866, *ibid.,* XCV. Levermore throws light on the tactics of the *Herald* and the elder Bennett in "The Rise of Metropolitan Journalism," *Am. Hist. Rev.,* VI (April, 1901), 446-465.

[65] March 24, 1866, Johnson MSS., XCI.

wrote Johnson, "We greatly need a Newspaper as we have now no conservative organ. If I had the control of this important office, I could by its aid, start a daily paper of vast influence. . . . Public opinion is now benighted.—Your views and policy are misrepresented and misunderstood, and we have no means of reply, except the Democratic papers which reach few Republicans." [66] Pease wrote, "Were it not that the Republican press are all most a unit in opposing President Johnson's policy and throw their influence in favour of the radicalism of Congress, he would obtain a large per cent of the party support and votes." [67] In the fall of 1865 Doolittle had assured Johnson that two-thirds of the Republicans were for him, but that the "noisy and clamorous" Radicals had "got control of many newspapers who follow the lead of the *Chicago Tribune*." [68]

Only a few periodicals were favored with a wide circulation and influence. Of these the most powerful were the Radical *New York Tribune*,[69] which through its own circulation and reprints in local papers whose political mentor it was, reached Republican households throughout the North, the *New York Herald*,[69] whose politics was indeterminable, and the thoroughly Radical *Chicago Tribune*,[70] whose circulation already included several states. Two great weeklies boasted a nation-wide subscription list, *Harper's Weekly*, representing orthodox Radicalism, and the newly established *Nation*, usually intelligently liberal, but on reconstruction, Radical.

Most newspapers of the day were local sheets. Unlike their degenerate successors with "boilerplate" copy and

[66] Sept. 17, 1866, *ibid.*, CI.
[67] L. E. Pease to G. Welles, July 23, 1866, Welles MSS., LXI.
[68] Sept. 23, 1865, Johnson MSS., LXXVII.
[69] Daily and semi-weekly.
[70] Daily and tri-weekly.

"patent insides," the small journals of 1866 were a determining factor in the life and thought of most American communities. The local editor was a man of importance. He wrote his own editorials; he did his own thinking. Often he was politically experienced; he was always highly respected by his fellow-citizens. His opinion was sought and followed. Because of the rôle the local paper played in the community life, able men were attracted to the editorships, and often the editorials of a rural paper were strikingly well written.

But however ably edited a paper might be, its sources of information were indirect and unreliable. Modern methods of news dispatching were unknown. The Associated Press, just sixteen years old, served only a few city dailies. Not many papers could afford their own representatives, even in Washington. Most editors had to depend upon sources of information that were cheap or free, and hence undependable. They gleaned their news from scattered chance dispatches, from the columns of the few great journals, from pamphlets circulated for campaign purposes, and from rumor. At best such sources were untrustworthy.

The widely published story of Johnson's plot to overthrow Congress provides a good example. On October 11 the *Philadelphia Ledger*, a large city journal, printed a verbatim copy of a list of questions submitted by Johnson to Attorney-General Stanbery on the constitutionality of the actual Congress. Reports had been rife all summer of Johnson's scheme to use the army to overthrow Congress and to set up in its place a new body composed of Southerners and Copperheads. These questions were widely printed as proof of this plot. Had the charge been less damaging, it would have passed unquestioned, as did thousands of falsely "authentic" news reports. But the gravity of the charge led

Harper's Weekly, Nov. 3, 1866

CONGRESS OVERTHROWN! RADICALS BEHEADED! LONG LIVE KING ANDY!!!

to an investigation.[71] Because the proprietor of the Ledger, George W. Childs, felt his reputation was at stake, he gave Johnson full coöperation in tracing the report to its source. The Ledger had received the dispatch from J. A. Abbot, Childs's agent in New York. It had come to Abbot carefully prepared in the hand of his regular correspondent in Washington, Henry M. Flint. Abbot explained that this was the normal channel for news, and that Flint was an old and trusted agent. When first interrogated, Flint wired back, "I believe it is [perfectly authentic], but am not absolutely certain; some questions were certainly propounded on the subject." Finally under pressure, Flint admitted that he had phrased the questions himself and then sent them as a verbatim copy of Johnson's. He had based the questions upon information "derived from two persons" whose names he was under promise never to reveal. Both men worked in his office. Though he sometimes "found them to be mistaken on certain points," neither one had ever deceived him "by false information." "In this case," Flint explained, "neither one of them knew that the other had told me anything about this matter. From one of them I learned that the President had recently stated to an intimate friend 'that he had never made any hasty or unconsidered statements about the constitutionality or legality of the present Congress, or about the right of the Southern States to representation, and that all that he had said he intended to abide by, and that the Radical leaders of Congress seemed disposed to carry matters with a high hand next winter but that unquestionably the Constitution confered certain powers upon him, . . . which he would not shrink from performing, but that he

[71] Full correspondence between Flint, McKean, Abbot, Childs, and Johnson, is preserved in the Johnson MSS., CIII.

would take no step . . . without consulting his constitutional legal adviser and would be governed by his advice.' From the other I learned that a paper had been seen in the Attorney Generals office, but by accident and only for a moment, purporting to have come from the Executive Office. . . . No information was furnished me in regard to the exact or particular phraseology of the questions. . . . It seemed to me perfectly natural that the President should seek counsel of his constitutional legal adviser, on so grave a subject, especially when the leaders of the Rump were boldly proclaiming their intention to depose and imprison him." In short, Flint wrote out some questions that the President might under the circumstances have sent to Stanbery, and forwarded them through the regular news channels as a verbatim copy of actual questions.

Well might McKean declare, "Flint's letter . . . throws no more light on the subject. His whole story seems to be built up of inferences, and whether the two clerks are real persons or not, he has been guilty of gross deception." McKean further told Johnson, "I know considerable of this man's history, and I beg to renew my assurance to you that if trusted by you in any way he will make mischief for you as he has for us." Yet Flint, the trusted correspondent of the *Ledger*, never saw any reason why the printing of the questions was not a normal and justifiable proceeding. The subsequent denial of the false report was never widely circulated. Every reader of every small paper reprinting the story, believed it. Subsequently, historians repeated it. After all, the questions were as reliable and well authenticated as any editor deemed necessary, or as any editor, no matter how scrupulous, could have secured. Dependent upon rumors as it was, the country was putty in the hands of Radical propaganda-mongers.

False reports were common. In April Morton "publicly contradicted as false and untrue" a widely published report of an interview between him and the President which sought to belittle Johnson.[72] Most misquoted politicians were not as honorable as Morton in denying, merely because they were untrue, stories that served their purposes.

At the time of Johnson's tour, rural papers in the West quoted an interview in which Grant was credited with telling a *Chicago Tribune* reporter that "neither Mr. Seward nor any other person could commit him to any set of political principles,—that he was annoyed at the successive attempts which had been made by Seward and others to announce to the people along the road that his political views were in harmony with those of Mr. Johnson." The General was reported as denying that he attended the reception of the committee from the Philadelphia Convention voluntarily, and as saying, "I was there at the request of the President, and all attempts to attach a political significance to my presence are unwarranted and impertinent." [73] The story was unfounded but widely circulated, and, like all false reports, made an impression that many denials could not counteract.

Another factor that militated against accuracy of information was the partisanship of both reader and editor. The average voter was more orthodox than he is today. He read a strict party paper. A vague rumor sponsored by his own party was believed as gospel, and far outweighed a well-authenticated fact published by the opposing party's organ.

[72] O. P. Morton to A. Johnson, April 18, 1866, Johnson MSS., "Telegrams."
[73] "General Grant's Position," *Hendricks County Union* (Indiana), Sept. 20, 1866.

In the absence of an abundance of newspapers and magazines of diverse opinions, the reader was forced to depend for
information and ideas upon the limited media of a party
paper and political speakers. With no competition for news
to force publication of information and discussion of issues
that politicians wished to suppress, a party press could regulate the news it fed its public to suit its political tenets. An
unsophisticated public was easily satisfied with simple devices
that are made impossible today by the wide circulation of
independent dailies, and such non-partisan, if conservative,
periodicals as the *Saturday Evening Post* and *Literary
Digest*.

Practically all domestic news was political, and subjects
which today are treated as news in the news column were
then discussed in the manner of editorial critiques, though
still in the news column. Whether describing a debate in Congress, a political speech, social festivities in the Capital, or
happenings in the South, news stories were no indifferent
statement of fact, but a curious interweaving of fact and
comment thereon, highly colored by the particular views of
the editor. The leading articles were convincingly, often
charmingly, written, but the impression conveyed, if not the
fact itself, was frequently erroneous.

An example of a front-page news story on the passage of
the Civil Rights Bill over the Presidential veto will suggest
how voters were made Radicals. The *Hendricks County
Union* wrote:

"The battle opened early in the Senate. Lane, of Kansas,
presented a resolution based upon the President's letter to
Governor Sharkey, and made it the occasion of a bitter personal attack upon Mr. Wade, in vindication of the President. It was the speech of a demagogue, couched in the

language of a bully, and delivered in a manner which would
disgrace the stump. It was but an occasion to make known
the fact that he had sold himself to Mr. Johnson, and he announced this by declaring that he should henceforth follow
the President wherever he led. . . . To this attack Senator
Wade replied in a speech which brought out all the lion in
him. He met the Senator from Kansas on a field of his own
choosing, and completely foiled him. Several other Senators,
by questions, placed this political trickster in the light he
deserved to have cast upon him. All this time the interest
was increasing—the morning hour had expired—the regular
order was announced, and yet this sharp and cutting debate
went on; the President suffering severely both from the
scathing reviews of his course by Mr. Wade, and the weak,
ill-advised and intemperate defense of Mr. Lane. . . . To
the infinite disgust of everybody, Mr. Davis rose. It was a
terrible infliction, but something which is certain to come
whenever any measure distasteful to rebels is likely to pass.
. . . Senator Saulsbury followed in a speech, which, for
plainness, treasonable sentiments, and villainy, was never
surpassed when, in 1860, the plotters of rebellion stood on
this floor and denounced the North. He asserted that the
gallant sons of Delaware would never allow this law to be
executed, that its passage was the virtual reinauguration of
civil war; and with this he threatened the Senate. His style,
and language, and sentiments could not have been exceeded
by any one who stood on the floor of the Richmond cabal in
the height of the rebellion. The floor was crowded, the lights
showed every countenance in the chamber. Those in the lob-
bies had crowded up to the outer circle of desks, and these
with all others in the chamber stood with set lips and flashing
eyes fixed on the frenzied speaker. When he had finished,

there was a moment's silence, and Governor Yates rose, and said quietly, but very firmly, 'Mr. President: Let every Senator who loves his country and desires to serve her, serve her now.' The effect was thrilling; all eyes were turned on Senator Morgan, and though his countenance could not be read, all seemed to feel that he would never vote with men who thus plainly avowed their wishes and their purposes. All felt that Doolittle was gone; that even this could not move him. . . . Contempt was written in unmistakable lines upon hundreds of faces as Lane, of Kansas, answered 'No,' and sealed his sale. Then McDougal responded No,' and every face was turned upon Morgan, every breath was suspended, and every heart was still, as his name rang out on that quiet, and his firm 'Aye' came in answer to the call. Then that assembly, as if striving to cast off the great weight of silence, broke out into hearty applause. There were clapping of hands on all sides, and murmured thanks and manifestations of deep gratitude. It was as if every heart had spoken a fervent 'Thank God!' . . . 'On this question the ayes are 33, and the noes are 15, so the bill has passed.' At this announcement there was a universal shout, long continued and earnest. All efforts to check the applause were unavailing, and so that shout rang on. . . . It was a shout of deliverance, the rallying cry of freemen, the rejoicing of brave men, fighting in a noble cause; and though Senators did not join in it, their hearts responded.—None who saw and heard it all will ever forget it. Its record can never pass from American history." [74]

In this vein thousands of papers told the story of a vote that was carried by the illegal expulsion of one senator, the plighted pair of a second, and the refusal of the Senate to

[74] The *Hendricks County Union,* April 19, 1866.

wait one day until a third who was extremely ill could be carried to Washington.[75] "News items" like this were the only source of information of thousands of voters. Newspaper editors were not necessarily unscrupulous; they were merely the victims of party bias and an inadequate and unreliable system of collecting information.

The press, though unreliable, was very powerful in the 'Sixties. Before concentrated hurry and commotion in business and social life, high speed, mass production, and efficiency came to dominate a restless American world, men had leisure to read and ponder over what they read. In an age before the theater was known to more than a few in the largest cities; before the cinema or the Rotary Club had made its advent; before numerous and cheap books and popular magazines were available; when the large and time-consuming Sunday edition was unknown; when the local Y.M.C.A., the swimming beaches and municipal pools, recreation parks, and that peculiar time-killer, golf, were yet undreamed of; when dancing and cards were rare in respectable communities; in a day when automobiles and the radio were mere poetic fancies—political and religious discussion provided the chief diversion of men who knew nothing more exciting than reading the local paper and then arguing about its ideas in the post office, corner saloon, barber shop, or grocery. Politics was then an important factor in life. Politics centered in the local newspaper and its editor.

"Our people are very much governed by the papers they read," wrote Pease of Connecticut. "Those who read the New York Independent, Tribune, and Philadelphia Press,

[75] *Supra*, 88-90.

are the most violent and radical." [76] Campbell assured Johnson: In Ohio "your most bitter foes" are the readers of the "'New York Independent,' General Howard's paper 'the Right Way,' and similar precious sheets of the same stripe that are being circulated by your post masters and Revenue officers all over the country." [77] From St. Louis General Sherman testified, "Much of the ill feeling here as elsewhere is caused by the inflamed language of the partisan Press and of stump orators, who are irrepressable." [78] "Juries and Civil courts," he declared, enforce laws "only . . . according to the higher law of the County Newspaper." [79] Basing their ideas on scant and unreliable information from party-prejudiced sources, newspaper editors became a great power for good or evil. It was these editors and their papers that the Radical minority in the Republican Party controlled.

Two powerful weapons of ridicule were at the disposal of the journalists of 1866: the humor of David R. Locke and the drawings of Thomas Nast. Under the *nom de plume*, Petroleum V. Nasby, Locke regaled the public with devastating descriptions of Johnson and his followers. His wit played through a series of letters on politics that later appeared in pamphlet form under such titles as "Divers views, opinions, and prophecies of yoors trooly Petroleum V. Nasby," "Andy's trip to the West, together with a life of its hero," and "Swingin round the cirkle." Nasby's travesties reached and influenced men as did no serious critique of the President.

Thomas Nast had begun sketching war pictures for *Harper's Weekly* in 1862. His first cartoon was drawn in 1863

[76] L. E. Pease to G. Welles, July 23, 1866, Welles MSS., LXI.
[77] L. D. Campbell to A. Johnson, April 25, 1866, Johnson MSS., XCIV.
[78] W. T. Sherman to A. Johnson, Aug. 9, 1866, *ibid.*, XCIX.
[79] W. T. Sherman to J. Sherman, April 11, 1866, W. T. Sherman MSS., XIX.

at the expense of General Butler and the *London Times*.
By the end of the War his cartoons were famous. But it was
Andrew Johnson that first provided him with an ideal subject for ridicule. Now Johnson was pictured as Iago trying
to persuade the negro that he was his friend; now as a snake
charmer blowing on a flute labeled "constitution" while a
huge copperhead encircled a struggling black man before
him; now as King Andrew enthroned in crown and scepter,
looking on while Seward directed the beheading of Greeley,
Beecher, Sumner, and other prominent Radicals; and again
as Nero sitting in the "amphitheatrum Johnsonianum" in
New Orleans, holding the Constitution while rebel gladiators
destroyed negroes huddled about the American flag. Welles
and Seward were usually at hand officiating while Stanton's
spectacled eyes managed to express disapproval. Locke and
Nast first combined forces in the production of "Swingin
round the cirkle," a masterpiece of burlesque. Through the
medium of *Harper's*, Nast's drawings reached hundreds of
thousands of voters. Nasby's pamphlets ran speedily through
many editions.

        *   *   *   *

The pulpit like the party newspaper spoke with authority to an attentive public. In a day when churchly religion was, like politics, a major factor in human life, the
preacher spoke peremptorily, and often unreasoningly. The
function of the church was to regulate life toward the salvation of souls. But since politics was an important part of
life, preachers provided political as well as spiritual guidance, and many of them believed Radical political tenets were
as necessary to salvation of the soul as was belief in hell-fire
and eternal damnation. The preacher often lacked the ability
and political acumen that characterized the newspaper ed-

itor, but his position and his enthusiasm redeemed any mental deficiencies.

Republican preachers often outdid the politicians in Radicalism.[80] From their pulpits they read political tracts in the guise of religion.[81] Many advocated negro suffrage.[82] The pastor of Tremont Temple in Boston declared, "Andrew Johnson belongs to the Strata of Society from which Southern Serfs were reared. He can stand opposition beating & kicking, but not the praise of Southern born Aristocrats. It is on this rock if any he will flounder. Let him know that the Southern Aristocrat is unchanged since his wife was insulted & his life was endangered & he will come to the help of the loyal & the true." [83] The Radical Party was pictured as that of respectability and piety. "There are always in this country," wrote the *Christian Examiner*, "powerful elements to which such a party as the President has started may effectively appeal. The 'unwashed' democracy, who hate Godliness and cleanliness with equal cordiality, and who form the scum of our great cities, are always ready for any measures which they instinctively know to be offensive to high-toned, moral, and philanthropic men. They properly regard the Republican party as led by the piety and worth of this nation, by the people who detest grog-shops and sabbath-breaking and gambling-saloons and dance-houses; and that is enough to make it odious to them; and their personal enemy." [84] Of course, no God-fearing, respectable churchgoer wished to be included in this God-hating "scum."

[80] Henry Ward Beecher was an exception.
[81] E.g., *New York Herald,* Oct. 8, 1866.
[82] E.g., E. Beecher to H. W. Beecher, *Chicago Tribune,* Sept. 26, 1866; Dr. Cheever's sermon, *New York Herald,* Nov. 19, 1866; and almost any of W. Phillips's "speeches."
[83] J. D. Fulton to C. Sumner, Dec. 27, 1865, Sumner MSS., LXXV.
[84] *Christian Examiner,* LXXXI (November, 1866), 407.

So firmly did Edward Beecher believe in the satanic intent of Southerners that he publicly answered his brother's epistle to the Cleveland Convention. He opposed restoration without accompanying rebel disfranchisement and negro suffrage, because he sincerely believed that to readmit Southerners to power would "neither tranquilize society, nor benefit the freedman, but tend to disorganize the nation, enslave the freedmen, and plunge us into another civil war." How could there be a good Southerner? "What good reason have you," he asked his brother, "to trust in the generosity and magnanimity of slavery-begotten aristocracies?"[85] At the Southern Loyalists' Convention, Mr. Newman opened one session with a prayer to God to "deliver us from the rule of bad men, especially from him who through satanic agency has been raised to authority over us"; then waxing eloquent, he shouted, "Great God, interpose, and in making bare Thine arm for vengeance, save us from his infamous and ruinous policy."[86] "The devil is in the people of the South," cried that preacher-governor, Brownlow, "and in the man at the White House (in) particular. If you are to have another war I want a finger in that pie. I want your army to come in three divisions. The first to kill, the second to burn, the third to survey the land into small parcels and give it to those who are loyal in the North."[87] Brownlow was a "Christian" minister, feted and entertained by respectable Radicals on an extensive Northern tour.

Lawyers, too, were often extremists. The tirades of Wendell Phillips as he stumped the country for Radicalism, his accusations, his abusive language, his hate, could be excused only as the ravings of a bigot.

[85] E. Beecher to H. W. Beecher, *Chicago Tribune,* Sept. 26, 1866.
[86] *New York Herald,* Sept. 6, 1866.
[87] *Ibid.,* Sept. 11, 1866.

Especially bitter were the missionary clergy who had gone South to minister to the negroes. They had made themselves unwelcome in the South by preaching not only negro suffrage but full social equality of blacks and whites. Then they vented their spleen against unhospitable Southerners by returning North, or sending letters, to relate tales of Southern depravity.[88]

To understand these Radical preachers, one must remember their abolitionist past. Many of the leaders of the abolition movement had been New England ministers or ministers of New England extraction in the Northwest. To them abolitionism had been a religious duty to extirpate sin. Slave-holders had been sinners against God, totally lost disciples of the Devil. During the Civil War, as always in war, preachers had been good recruiting agents. At its end slavery was abolished, but not their belief in the wickedness of the South. It was natural to carry this feeling of years of religious war against slavery into a religious crusade to crush an iniquitous Southern race beyond hope of recovery.

Albert Smith of Boston warned Johnson: "The Presidential campaign for 1868 was opened by several of the clergy of the city . . . by the most low & vulgar abuse of *yourself* & your policy.—The campaign of 1860 was opened in the same disgraceful manner—nearly every pulpit in the State being desecrated by vile political harangues on the Sabbath. —Mr. Lincoln owed his election more to these 'Men of God' (or the D...l) than to any other single cause."[89] The ministerial attitude was, to be sure, scarcely Christian, but it was fervidly religious, a revival of the animus of the inquisition.

88 The Southerners boldly say, wrote Walker from Trenton, New Jersey, that "they will give the colored people *Hell* as soon as the troops are withdrawn." W. E. Walker to C. Sumner, Dec. 11, 1865, Sumner MSS., LXXV.
89 July 17, 1866, Johnson MSS., XCVII.

Not to understand this spirit is to fail to understand an important element in Radical success; for religious fervor in opposition to the South, and pious belief in the godliness of the Radical cause, made many Radicals.

*　*　*　*

Success for the Radicals depended upon their ability to arouse the passions of the voters. Appeals to fear were important campaign tactics. Among these the bogy of repudiation was one of the most serviceable, since thousands of voters owned bonds. Not only banks and financiers, but ordinary men with small savings in East and West alike, had acquired with their bonds a special interest in the validity of the national debt. The Radicals carefully circulated rumors that if Johnson's plan of restoration of the Southern states were followed, these government securities would be worthless. It was widely believed that the first act of returned Southern Congressmen would be to repudiate the federal debt and if possible validate that of the Confederates, and that Northern Democrats were only too eager to join forces with them for this purpose. "Viewed as a practical matter," asked the *Nation*, "what would be the effect upon Government securities of the immediate admission to Congress of 58 Southern Representatives and 22 Senators, nearly all of whom could be counted on as determined repudiationists? . . . It would hardly be a safe thing for the national credit to have such a body of men in Congress, reinforced as they would probably be, by a considerable number of Northern men ready to go for at least qualified repudiation." [90] Winter Davis declared: The Johnson plan "will instantly change the balance of political power in the United States . . . None of the white population of the Southern States is interested

[90] The *Nation*, II (Jan. 11, 1866), 36.

in paying the public debt or imposing taxes to meet its interest. They hold none of it. It was created to subjugate them to the laws. It has been consumed in their overthrow. It is to be paid in great part out of their substance. It has annihilated their public debt. It has filled the land with ostracised officers, with wounded soldiers, with an odious free negro population, lately their slaves, & still under their political control. If the whites be restored to political power, their representatives are interested in repudiating that public debt, in refusing to pay its interest, in restoring their officers to the Army & Navy, in placing their wounded in the pension roll, in indemnifying their friends for losses by war or confiscation or forced tax sales." [91] After its autumnal somersault the *Herald*, which had hitherto scoffed at the idea of repudiation as a bugbear, began to insist that security in advance in the form of the Fourteenth Amendment was a "practical view of the matter, which every man of business [could] readily comprehend." "Herein," it continued, "lies the secret of the astounding popular strength of this restoration plan of Congress . . . No man who has a fifty dollar government bond salted down would trust its redemption to the chances of the casting vote in Congress of a Southerner who has lost his thousands in Confederate scrip." [92]

In defense of his Radicalism, Calvin Day of Hartford wrote Welles, "I do not believe there is a single district in the whole south in which a man could be elected to Congress on the issue of taxing the south to pay the interest & principle of our national debt. It would require much more love for our institutions than has been exhibited anywhere in the

[91] H. W. Davis to Whom It May Concern, May 27, 1865, McPherson MSS., V.
[92] *New York Herald*, Sept. 30, 1866.

'Conquered States,' . . . to levy taxes to pay a debt—contracted for their subjugation and how long think you would it take the party at the North who were in entire sympathy with those in the rebellion to join them in this further effort to disgrace & destroy our beloved nation." [93] If we let the South return, wrote a Radical publicity agent, we then face "the unpleasant dilemma of having either to pay the rebel debt or borrow the rebel theory and secede from the very Union we have restored by conquering the rebels . . . I think I could easily convince any man, who does not allow his prejudices to stand in the way of his interests, that it will probably make a difference of at least $1,000,000,000 in the development of the national debt, whether we reconstruct on the basis of loyal white and black votes, or on white votes exclusively, and that he can better afford to give the Government at least one-quarter of his estate than have it try the latter experiment." [94] Thaddeus Stevens repeatedly reiterated repudiation rumors. "Under 'restoration,'" he threatened in his key-note speech, "every rebel State will send rebels to Congress; and they, with their allies in the North, will control Congress and occupy the White House. Then . . . our public debt will be repudiated or the rebel National debt will be added to ours, and the people will be crushed beneath heavy burdens." [95]

How many of the propagators of the repudiation terror

[93] Feb. 26, 1866, Welles MSS., LX.

[94] Elizur Wright's "Letter to the *Boston Daily Advertiser*," published by Geo. L. Stearns with other speeches and letters of like purport in pamphlet form under the title, *The Equality of All Men before the Law Claimed and Defended*, 40-41. In the first edition 10,000 copies were sent out with an appeal for money to circulate 100,000.

[95] Stevens himself wished to go to the other extreme and confiscate Southern property and force the South to pay not only Northern pensions and reparation for all damage to Northern men or property, but three-fourths of the whole federal debt as well. Speech at Lancaster, Pa., Sept. 7, 1865, Stevens MSS., IV.

were sincere is indeterminable. Many of them were merely making political capital. George L. Stearns, for instance, one of the noisiest of them, said in a private letter to Johnson, "The return of those States is bound up with our financial condition, the prosperity of which rests entirely on faith in the wisdom of the government. Undue haste in admitting Southern members to seats in Congress, would impair this faith, and many timid persons, although perhaps a small proportion of the holders of the Government Debt, would be alarmed at the prospect of indirect repudiation, by refusal to levy taxes, or in some other mode, and these, added to the number who are obliged to sell on account of the tightness of the money market, would, it is feared by many of our leading capitalists, and other sagacious men, produce a panic in stocks." [96] It was not repudiation, then, that he feared but "a panic in stocks." Yet in spite of this admission that only "timid persons" and "a small proportion" of the bond-holders took the threat of repudiation seriously, Stearns sought by letters, speeches, and the dissemination of propaganda to spread this fear among thousands of others, because it would secure Radical votes.

Secretary McCulloch all but accused Sumner of creating a chimera for campaign purposes. "You and other good and able friends of the Government," McCulloch wrote, "are in danger of doing great harm by advancing the opinion that the preservation of the national faith may be contingent upon the policy of the Government with regard to the revolted States. Nothing can be more damaging to our credit than the openly expressed opinion by leading men, that there may arise contingencies in which the national debt may be repudiated. This debt has been created in the preservation of

[96] Nov. 13, 1865, Johnson MSS., LXXXI.

the Government, and is a sacred one. It is yet to be funded, and perhaps considerably increased; and I have been greatly alarmed at the disposition that seems to exist among our radical friends to induce the holders of our securities to take ground against the President's policy by the argument that under it there is danger of a coalition between the recent Rebels of the South and the Democracy of the North for the repudiation of the obligations which have been created in the prosecution of the War. . . . I entreat you, as a leader and a creator of public sentiment, not to encourage this idea." [97] But "to force the holders of securities to take ground against the President's policy" was a chief aim of Sumner's tactics, and few things did so more successfully than to persuade people that that policy led to repudiation. Regardless, therefore, of the government credit and the Treasury's entreaty, Sumner and his cohorts not only "encouraged" but helped to create "this idea."

Today this fear appears preposterous; even in 1866 reason or evidence would have dispelled it. But where fear rules, proof and reason are impotent. Thousands voted for Radical reconstruction to prevent repudiation of government bonds.[98] After the election *Fraser's Magazine* testified: "The panic among men of business . . . has been the chief reinforcement of the majority in Congress during its struggle with the President." [99]

*   *   *   *

Tariff fears were important in the Northeast, where a prominent element of the "disaster" in Radical defeat was danger of a repeal of protection. Not only would manufac-

[97] Aug. 16, 1866, Sumner MSS., LXXIV; McCulloch MSS., II.
[98] For further evidence see H. K. Beale, "Decision of Reconstruction," 479.
[99] *Fraser's Magazine*, LXXV (February, 1867), 249.

turers have suffered temporary hardship in the period of
readjustment to a revenue tariff, but their hopes of future
profits and of prosperity accompanying industrialization,
would have been blighted. In Northeastern manufacturing
centers, the thought of Southern tampering with the tariff
just when unheard-of protection was within reach, sent
voters scampering to the Radical fold.[1]

* * * *

Business men who depended upon stability and safety in
the South for their own prosperity, and investors who hoped
to make profits from rehabilitation of the South, were easily
alarmed into support of the Radicals. In pre-war days the
South had raised cotton, and Northern business and agriculture had supplied many of the necessities of life. Now
that the war demand was over, Northern farmers, merchants,
and manufacturers were eager to have the South reopened to
their products. Speedily to reopen the South was Johnson's
aim. But the Radicals succeeded in persuading interested
Northerners that he could not open it safely according to
his plan.

The South promised a fertile field for Northern enterprise. With a little encouragement from the government,
Northerners would soon be running stores, banks, railroads,
and even plantations in the South. Glowing reports of opportunity traveled northward. For example, Reid predicted,
"By-and-by . . . necessity will begin to pinch [the plant-
ers] more and more. Then . . . many of them will throw
their lands into the market, rather than honestly attempt to
work them with free labor. When that time comes, Northern
capital will have such an opening as rarely coffers [*sic*]

1 *Supra*, 271-299.

twice in one capitalist's lifetime." [2] "The whites," he reported, "too often were listlessly awaiting events, and talking of selling their houses or lands to get bread. The fresh tide of Northern enterprise will soon sweep rudely enough against these broken remnants of the *ancien régime*, and wash them under . . . 'New men' will soon be the order of the day, in Mobile and in many another center of Southern aristocracy." [3]

Northern capital did move South. General Morehead organized a cotton-planting company.[4] When the reorganized state of Alabama chartered a New Orleans, Mobile, and Chattanooga Railroad in 1866, Williams of New York, Radical Representative Ames of Massachusetts, and Chase's Radical son-in-law, Senator Sprague of Rhode Island, were among the incorporators.[5] Boston capitalists were ready to back a projected railroad from Hilton Head to the main South Carolina line eighty miles away, and, in the absence of a state government to authorize its construction, appealed to General Gillmore for military authority.[6] In 1866 de Fontaine raised money in Boston to start himself in business in Columbia, South Carolina, and Boston merchants arranged to send him goods to sell at a five to fifteen per cent commission; the same group supplied both advertising and financial backing for a Radical daily paper in Columbia.[7] Eighty discharged New England soldiers formed one company to buy an army reserve on which to erect a city, since the "rebels" of Pensacola were bitter against them, and another to build a railroad through the Perdido Valley to bring lumber out.

[2] W. Reid, *After the War* (at Savannah), 151.
[3] *Ibid.* (at Mobile), 226.
[4] T. E. Franklin to T. Stevens, Dec. 10, 1865, Stevens MSS., V.
[5] *New York Herald,* Dec. 8, 1866.
[6] W. Reid, *op. cit.,* 124-125.
[7] F. G. de Fontaine to "Professor," March 6, 1866, Wilson MSS.

They hoped eventually to connect their city of Northern men by a Northern-owned road with the Montgomery and Mobile line.[8] Reid found Lynchburg, Virginia, "swarming with representatives of Northern capitalists, looking for investments." Most of them went further South, but some stayed to exploit the mineral resources of the Virginia mountains.[9]

Opportunities in the South invited not only capital but men. Individuals and organizations were busy promoting emigration to the South.[10] Reid foresaw a great flow of Northerners from "all the over-crowded localities of the Middle States" into Tennessee when that state got "her long-sought railroad connection with Cincinnati and the North."[11] "Keep the States out," urged Haskins Taylor, "and protect and encourage the labor in them and encourage men of enterprise and industry to go there and build up the industry, and the whole Country will prosper."[12] An Ohio lawyer wrote Johnson for advice about his removal to Nashville.[13] A Lancaster friend sought counsel from Stevens on the best place to use twelve or fifteen thousand dollars in setting his son up as a cotton planter.[14] One Radical friend of Sumner's was assisting young men in going to Florida to take up plantations.[15] Colonies of poor families in Iowa were planning to move into Southern lands.[16] In Boston Winslow sought to form a new "Emigrant Aid Society," to colonize

8 G. J. Alden to C. Sumner, Oct. 7, 1865, Sumner MSS., LXXV.
9 W. Reid, *op. cit.*, 332.
10 For further evidence see H. K. Beale, "The Decision of Reconstruction," 483.
11 W. Reid, *op. cit.* (at Knoxville), 354.
12 H. Taylor to C. Sumner, Sept. 16, 1865, Sumner MSS., LXXIV.
13 J. J. Williams to A. Johnson, Jan. 20, 1865, Johnson MSS., LV.
14 T. E. Franklin to T. Stevens, Dec. 10, 1865, Stevens MSS., V.
15 S. S. Forbes to C. Sumner, Feb. 1, 1866, Sumner MSS., LXXVII.
16 A. F. Gillett to A. Johnson, Jan. 18, 1866, Johnson MSS., LV.

the South with "Emigrants and Northern whites." [17] Dignowity urged Johnson's acceptance of his plan to disfranchise the rebels and grant negro suffrage in Texas, and to
bring in German colonists to develop the state under scien-
tific methods.[18] As early as January, 1865, a German-
American Colonization Society in which Senators Sherman
and Sumner were interested, was hoping to send many of its
immigrants into Tennessee.[19] Governor Andrew of Massachusetts was involved in a Southern land company that kept
an agent to bring immigrants from abroad to buy farms.[20]
Southern economic despair made it possible for these newcomers to buy businesses or valuable cotton or sugar plantations for a pitifully small part of their value.

In spite of propitious circumstances, Northern enterprises in the South were frequently unsuccessful. Northern
confidence in Northern efficiency was boundless. But while
land was cheap, the legal title to it was often uncertain.
Besides, Northerners often knew nothing of running a plantation, making the negroes work for them, or carrying on
successful business in a Southern community. Their very
confidence made it difficult for them to learn. John Hay, for
instance, bought the orange grove of an ex-rebel soldier at
St. Augustine, but though he got it for arrears in taxes,
he could not make it pay.[21] "The elements are not altogether
to blame for a short cotton crop this year," wrote the *Herald*.
"Much of the disaster is owing to the bad management of
inexperienced planters . . . Considerable Northern capital
and many Northern men have gone South since the war, and
engaged in cotton culture. It is like the Southern planter

17 E. Winslow to A. Johnson, June 30, 1865, *ibid.*, LXIX.
18 A Texas Refugee to A. Johnson, May 3, 1865, *ibid.*, LXI.
19 G. O. Glavis to A. Johnson, Jan. 28, 1865, *ibid.*, LVI.
20 W. Nichols to H. Wilson, Dec. 8, 1865, Wilson MSS.
21 W. Reid, *op. cit.*, 172.

coming to Wall Street and undertaking to speculate amid our experienced bulls and bears. Northern cotton planters, when unallied with Southerners, have in nearly every instance failed." [22]

Southern unfriendliness toward this economic invasion was often to blame. Northerners who had had a good business in the South before the War, now found the welcome they received chilly at best. Newcomers were avoided or actually boycotted. Southerners resented outsiders' utilizing their temporary distress to gain control of the business, lands, and resources of the South. "Returning merchants," wrote Reid, "find sutlers behind their counters, reckoning up such gains as the old business men of Newbern never dreamed of; all branches of trade are in the hands of Northern speculators, who followed the army." [23] Boycott resulted partly from a bitterness that was the natural concomitant of war; many still hated the North. Very often, however, the Northerners provoked unfriendliness. Many had been failures in the North; others were adventurers, forerunners of the carpetbaggers; many were unscrupulous, like the tribe of dishonest treasury agents. Almost all of them labored under a handicap of self-conceit. They looked upon Southerners as an inferior, inefficient race. They tried to apply Northern methods to Southern conditions. They failed utterly, whether business men or planters.

Had some of the denouncers of Southern haughtiness been able to see their own boastful assurance and contemptuous rudeness through Southern eyes, they would have realized why they were not beloved. When they failed, however, they blamed not their own mistakes but Southern hostility, and

[22] *New York Herald,* Sept. 21, 1866.
[23] W. Reid, *op. cit.,* 30.

demanded protection, often meaning by that the power to coerce Southerners. Many Northerners did succeed, but they were accused of licking rebel boots. The *Herald* admitted that ill feeling in the South had almost closed that section to Northern capital and enterprise, but blamed the Radicals in Congress rather than Southerners, and pointed out that at the close of the War the South had been "inclined 'to let by-gones be by-gones,' to accept the altered condition of things in good faith, . . . to welcome Northern capital and enterprise." [24] But "conciliation" was a word not in the vocabulary of the Radical. The typical attitude was expressed by Stearns of Springfield, Massachusetts, who took up lands in Carolina and insisted that the rebels must be disfranchised for ten years; then "there will be sufficient Northern men to control the whole country, & we shall be forever safe." [25] The fears of Northerners economically interested in an unfriendly South were skilfully played upon by Radical campaigners.

* * * *

Two unfortunate riots in the South gave the Radicals at an opportune moment just the campaign material they needed. They had been talking vaguely of a new civil war if Northern control of the South were loosened. These riots gave apparent proof of organized Southern violence and bloodthirstiness that if properly used might terrify the North into support of the Radical cause. To claim that the riots had been instigated for campaign purposes by the Radicals was preposterous. They were spontaneous outbursts of post-war passion, in which both factions of Southerners lost their heads. But the riots did serve Radical campaign purposes well.

[24] *New York Herald,* Sept. 3, 1866.
[25] Sept. 15, 1865, Sumner MSS., LXXIV.

The first one, at Memphis, grew out of an impromptu quarrel between a negro and a white teamster in a city where negro troops had embittered the relations between blacks and poor Irish, who at best hated and distrusted each other. In an effort to restore order an Irish policeman was killed. Then police and the poorer whites, many of them Irish, raided the negro quarter, burning and killing promiscuously. The editor of the *Memphis Bulletin* wrote Johnson: The riot "was a literal verification of your prophecy to Fred Douglass" that negro suffrage "would beget an irrepressible conflict between the non slave-holding whites of the South and the blacks. This is the real cause of our difficulties here. Our police are all Irish. The negro soldiers are particularly down on the poor whites and Irish. Several skirmishes have occurred between them, and when the negro soldier no longer had an officer *to obey*, he was betrayed into unusual violence. The better class of citizens had nothing to do with the 'muss.' " [26] But the negroes were the chief sufferers in the riot, and this fact gave Radical campaigners in the North circumstantial evidence of their claim that it was maliciously premeditated work of "unrepentant rebels."

The New Orleans riot was the more damaging to Conservative chances in the election. New Orleans had long been a storm center in the quarrels between Southern Radicals and Conservatives.[27] Six weeks before the riot General

[26] J. B. Bingham to A. Johnson, May 17, 1866, Johnson MSS., XCIV.
[27] All through the year factional quarrels had annoyed Johnson. Governor J. Madison Wells, though he pretended impartiality, leaned toward the Radicals. When the legislature, duly elected under Johnson's plan of restoration, passed "an act appointing the twelfth day of March . . . for an election of mayor and other offices," Wells wired Johnson, "I shall veto it unless you direct to the contrary" (Jan. 29, 1866). Johnson did order him to do otherwise, and he reluctantly wired back, "Although I do not approve I will order the election for the 12th" (March 6, 1866). Wells averred that nine-tenths of the members of the Legislature were "unrepentant if pardoned rebels," and he promised to veto any bill passed for "reactionary

Granger sent a report on conditions in New Orleans that sheds new light on that unfortunate affair. He wrote:

"I deem it important to inform you that efforts are being made here to re-convene the State Convention of 1864. This movement is headed by Governor Wells, Gov. Hahn and other malcontents, and has for its object—first to reinstate themselves in office and power. Second—To disfranchise all persons Civil & Military who took part in the Rebellion against the U. S. all registered enemies & persons who left the State during the Butler & Banks regime—third, To declare & render null and void all Elections since the adjournment of the Convention in 1864. Wherein the radical element has not been successful—thereby violently vacating & refilling nine tenths of the- offices throughout the state. 4th To enfranchise all negroes who have served in the Army & Navy and Civil departments of the Government without further qualification than proof to that effect. It is further proposed to give the right of Suffrage to the Negro, based upon property or educational qualifications or both, as may suit the temper of the Convention—The motive of Govr. Wells and other officials is to forestall the next Legislature which they fear will call a Convention & either impeach or legislate them out of office—with the balance (office seekers) their

objects" (March 15, 1866). In the election Monroe was chosen mayor, and the Radical faction of the city, led by Mayor Kennedy, Governor Wells, and General Canby, began a fight to keep him out of office. "The Union sentiment is unanimous against him," wired Kennedy (March 17, 1866). General Canby told of severe charges against him (March 23, 1866), and recommended that his pardon be withheld (April 19, 1866). But Monroe claimed to be "fully determined in [his] sincere loyalty" (March 17, 1866); he was unquestionably more in sympathy with Johnson's policy than were his Radical opponents. To Kennedy's protests Johnson wired the answer, "We have no information showing that the election was not regular, or that the individual who has been elected cannot qualify. In the absence of such information, the presumption is that the election has been according to law, and that the person elected can take the oath of allegiance and loyalty required" (March 16, 1866). Johnson MSS., "Telegrams."

object is a lust of power and thirsting for the spoils. The great mass of the people & I may state, the industrious, peace-loving and law-abiding—those who are anxious and laboring diligently to reunite and restore the Country—are sternly opposed to upsetting and disturbing the present peaceful state of affairs which is daily improving & hourly becoming more generally satisfactory. It is unnecessary for me to point out to the President what this scheme, if they attempt to put it in execution, must inevitably lead to. In my opinion it will inaugurate revolution and terminate in anarchy. So fearful are the leaders of not being sustained or not being able to accomplish their ends, that they have already endeavored to ascertain if the military power would protect them in their deliberations, & enforce their mandates. I can further inform the President that the opposition Press of the North, with the same class of radical agents which did so much to fasten that atrocious 'Franchise Law' upon Tennessee, are here, coats off, hard at work trying to hurry forward the Convention." [28]

The dispute over the Convention was simply a factional one. Louisiana was being peaceably governed by officers elected by pardoned Confederates; the small Radical minority who claimed to be the only "loyal men" in the State and who opposed Johnson's policy, wished to regain the power they had held under the Banks régime in 1864. For this purpose they sought to reconvene the Convention of that year which represented only the "loyalists," now Radicals. Pardoned Confederates, who were the vast majority of voters under Johnson's plan, would have been disfranchised.[29] They

28 G. Granger to E. Cooper, June 11, 1866, *ibid.,* XCVI.
29 The testimony of General Granger as to the purpose of the Convention is borne out by James Harrison, a St. Louis friend of Browning who was in New Orleans at the time and talked with members of the Convention. J. Harrison to O. H. Browning, July 31, 1866, *ibid.,* XCVIII.

objected, and Johnson maintained that no convention was legal which did not represent the qualified voters of the state. Excitement was general; an attempt of this Radical Convention to meet to disfranchise a majority of the men who then had the vote, was certain to cause trouble.

On July 25 Mayor Monroe notified Baird, the general commanding in Sheridan's absence, that the old Convention proposed to reconvene, that a city ordinance declared unlawful "all assemblies calculated to disturb public peace," and that he intended "to disperse the unlawful assembly . . . by arresting the members thereof and holding them accountable to existing municipal law; provided they meet without the sanction of the military authorities." "I will esteem it a favor, General," he wrote, "if . . . you will inform me whether this projected meeting has your approbation, so that I may act accordingly." [30] Baird responded, "The assembly . . . has not, so far as I am aware, the sanction or approbation of any military authority. . . . The Military Commanders since I have been in the State have held themselves strictly aloof from all interference with the political movements of the Citizens of Louisiana. . . . I regret to differ with you entirely, I cannot understand how the Mayor of a City can undertake to decide so important and delicate a question as the legal authority upon which a convention claiming to represent the people of an entire State, bases its action. This, doubtless, will be decided upon in due time by the legal branch of the United States Government. . . . What we most want at the present time, is the maintenance of perfect order and the suppression of violence. If, when you speak of the proposed meeting as one calculated to disturb the public peace and tranquillity, I am

[30] July 25, 1866, *ibid.,* XCVIII.

to understand that you regard the number of persons who differ in opinion from those that will constitute it, so large, and the lawlessness of their character so well established, that you doubt the ability of your small force of police to control them, you have in that case only to call upon me, and I will bring to your assistance, not only the troops now present in the city, but, if necessary the entire force which it may be in my power to assemble, either upon land or water." [31]

Meantime Governor Wells [32] signed the writ of election to fill vacancies in the 1864 Convention.[33] Johnson wired in protest, "Please inform me under and by what authority . . . this convention can assume to represent the whole people of the State of Louisiana." [34] Wells quibbled, and claimed that he had not convened the Convention but had merely issued writs in response to what he deemed a legal summons by the president of the old convention.[35] Finally, the Convention members, all Radicals, gathered in the city.

On Friday night a "Radical mass meeting composed mainly of [a] large number of negroes" ended in a riot.[36] And on Saturday Johnson received this telegram from Lieu-tenant-Governor Voorhees and Attorney-General Herron: "Violent and incendiary speeches made, negroes called to arm themselves. You bitterly denounced. Speakers Field, Dostie, Hawkins, Henderson, Heinstand, & others. Gov. Wells arrived last night but sides with the Convention move.

[31] A. Baird to Mayor J. T. Monroe, July 26, 1866, *ibid.*, XCVIII.

[32] Governor Wells was a Radical; Mayor Monroe, Lieut.-Gov. Voorhees, and Att'y-Gen. Herron, were Conservatives.

[33] A. Voorhees and A. J. Herron to A. Johnson, July 27, 1866, *ibid.*, XCVIII.

[34] A. Johnson to Governor Wells, July 28, 1866, *ibid.*, "Telegrams."

[35] J. M. Wells to A. Johnson, July 28, 1866, *ibid.*, XCVIII.

[36] Dostie's inflammatory speech to the negroes is in the *Annual Cyclopedia* (1866), 454. Fleming prints it wrongly dated, *Documentary History of Reconstruction*, I, 231.

The whole matter before grand jury, but impossible to execute civil process without certainty of riot. Contemplated to have the members of the Convention arrested under process from the Criminal Court of this District. Is the Military to interfere to prevent process of Court?" [37] Johnson wired back: "The military will be expected to sustain and not to obstruct or interfere with the proceedings of the Courts." [38] Johnson wished to prevent incendiarism, and he opposed, as always, the convening of an assembly that was not representative.

On the same day Baird, perplexed and fearing violence, wired for instructions from Johnson. "A convention," he said, "has been called with the sanction of Gov. Wells to meet here on Monday. The Lieutenant Governor and city authorities think it unlawful, and propose to break it up by arresting the delegates. I have given no orders on the subject, but have warned the parties that I could not countenance or permit such action without instructions to that effect from the President. Please instruct me at once by telegraph." [39] No response came. Consequently, when the Convention assembled on Monday, and the riot ensued, the military, undetermined how to act, was useless in "maintaining order." It could only restore order after the damage was done. When Baird reported the riot he complained, "I regret that no reply to my dispatch to you of Saturday has yet reached me." [40] Stanton, as he afterward admitted, had deliberately withheld the telegram from Johnson. Had Johnson received this telegram he would have sent Baird orders to "sustain the civil authority in suppressing all illegal or unlawful assem-

[37] A. Voorhees and A. J. Herron to A. Johnson, July 28, 1866, Johnson MSS., XCVIII.
[38] A. Johnson to A. Voorhees, July 28, 1866, *ibid.*, XCVIII.
[39] A. Baird to E. M. Stanton, July 28, 1866, *ibid.*, XCVIII.
[40] A. Baird to E. M. Stanton, July 30, 1866, *ibid.*, XCVIII.

blies, who usurp or assume to exercise any power or authority without first having obtained the consent of the people of the State." [41] "If there is to be a Convention," was Johnson's decision, "let it be composed of delegates chosen fresh from the people of the whole state. The people must be first consulted in reference to changing the organic law of the state, usurpation will not be tolerated, the law and the Constitution must be sustained and thereby peace and order." [42] Had the military been actively on hand to "sustain the civil authority," it is probable that the riot would not have occurred.[43] Baird was "in full consultation with the City authorities, and had kept [his] troops well in hand for such an emergency. The riot commenced unexpectedly, and before the troops could reach the scene of action a number of persons were killed and wounded." [44] Voorhees testified that when he did call upon Baird, assistance was "cheerfully tendered." [45] But quiet had then been restored.

Reports of the riot conflicted. Radical papers ignored everything that was favorable to the city authorities; Democratic papers, everything that was unfavorable. Perhaps the most reliable account is a report of General Sheridan, Baird's superior and a Radical, submitted a week after the riot as the result of careful investigation:

"A very large number of colored people marched in procession on Friday night July 27th and were addressed from the steps of the City Hall by Dr. Dostie, Ex-Gov Hahn and others—The speech of Dostie was intemperate in language and sentiment. . . . The Convention assembled at 12. M.

[41] Instructions sent to A. J. Herron, July 30, 1866, *ibid.*, XCVIII.
[42] Instructions cited above.
[43] Johnson was certain he could have prevented it. W. G. Moore, "Notes," *Am. Hist. Rev.*, XIX (1913), 102.
[44] A. Baird to E. M. Stanton, July 30, 1866, Johnson MSS., XCVIII.
[45] A. Voorhees to A. Johnson, July 30, 1866, *ibid.*, XCVIII.

on the 30th, the timid members absenting themselves because
the tone of the general public was ominous of trouble. I
think there were but about twenty-six (26) members present—In front of the Mechanics Institute where the meeting
was held there was assembled some colored men, women &
children, perhaps eighteen or twenty, and in the Institute a
number of colored men, probably one hundred and fifty.
Among these outside and inside, there might have been a
pistol in the possession of every tenth man. About one P M,
a procession of, say, from sixty to one hundred and thirty
colored men marched up Burgundy Street, and across Canal
Street towards the Convention carrying an American flag.
These men had about one pistol to every ten men, and canes
and clubs in addition. While crossing Canal Street, a row
occurred. There were many spectators on the street, and
their manner and tone towards the procession unfriendly.
A shot was fired, by whom, I am not able to state, but believe
it to have been by a policeman, or some colored man in the
procession. This led to other shots, and a rush after the procession. On arrival at the front of the Institute, there was
some throwing of brick-bats by both sides. The police who
had been held well in hand, were vigorously marched to the
scene of disorder. The procession entered the Institute with
the flag, about six or eight remaining outside. A row occurred
between a policeman and one of these colored men, and a
shot was again fired by one of the parties, which led to an
indiscriminate firing on the building, through the windows,
by the policemen. This had been going on for a short time,
when a white flag was displayed from the windows of the Institute, whereupon the firing ceased and the police rushed
into the building. From the testimony of wounded men and
others who were inside the building, the policemen opened an

indiscriminate fire upon the audience until they had emptied their revolvers, when they retired, and those inside barricaded the doors. The door was broken in, and the firing again commenced when many of the colored and white people, either escaped out the door, or were passed out by the policemen inside, but as they came out, the policemen who formed the circle nearest the building fired upon them, and they were again fired upon by the citizens that formed the outer circle." [46]

In placing the blame,[47] Sheridan said, "The immediate cause of this terrible affair was the assemblage of this Convention. The remote cause was the bitter and antagonistic

[46] P. H. Sheridan to A. Johnson, Aug. 6, 1866, *ibid.*, XCIX. Spontaneously he had wired Grant on August 1: "A political body styling itself the convention of 1864 met on the 30th for, as it is alleged, the purpose of remodelling the present constitution of the State. The leaders were political agitators and revolutionary men and the action of the convention was liable to produce breaches of the public peace. I had made up my mind to arrest the head men if the proceedings of the convention were calculated to disturb the tranquillity of the Dept. but I had no cause for action until they committed the overt act." *Ibid.*, XCVIII. The next day he had sent a message to Grant that the Radical papers published with glee. "The more information I obtain, . . ." he wired, "the more revolting it becomes. It was no riot, it was an absolute massacre by the police which was not excelled in murderous cruelty by that of Fort Pillow. It was a murder which the mayor and police of this city perpetrated without the shadow of a necessity. Furthermore I believe it was premeditated and every indication points to this." Aug. 2, 1866, *ibid.*, XCIX. But the official report gives his final verdict after careful investigation.

[47] Mayor Monroe in his message to the Council blamed Baird as not willing to suppress riot and letting loose from jails the ringleaders "to make political capital for the radical enemies of the reconstruction policy of his commander, President Johnson." *New York Herald*, Oct. 3, 1866; *New York Semi-Weekly Tribune*, Oct. 5, 1866. The *Herald* (Aug. 11, 1866) blamed Baird. This seems unfair. He did sympathize with the Radicals, but in the absence of new orders, he was merely attempting to follow previous orders of non-interference. Of course a Sheridan, by taking the initiative himself, might have prevented trouble even without instructions. Johnson and the Democrats unjustly accused Northern Radicals of instigating the riot. Even the non-partisan *Herald* (Aug. 6, 1866) declared: "They hope that the riots which they have instigated at the South will create a false issue and blind the people to the issue already made. To our clamors against their taxes, tariffs, high prices, corruption and extravagances, they seek to reply by lauding negro rioters as 'martyrs,' and by loud outcries against the 'rebel barbarity' of those who will not allow the blacks to shoot down policemen."

feeling which has been growing in this community since the advent of the present Mayor." [48] He condemned Monroe for not having the confidence of "people of clear views," and for selecting "desperate men" for the police force. On the other hand he styled the Radicals "political agitators" and "revolutionary men." The brutalities were those that inevitably result when "roughs" resort to violence; the Southern negro, the Northern agitator in the South, and the police of New Orleans, were all ignorant, coarse-natured men. To fasten their deeds upon Southerners in general or upon Northern Conservatives was patently unfair.

Whoever was to blame for the riots, the Radicals gained great advantage from them. Some of their leaders undoubtedly believed them acts of premeditated murder. For others, exaggerated stories of these outbreaks were just good campaign propaganda. In any case, the dead and wounded were mostly Radicals and negroes.[49] That was a fact that Johnson men could not explain in the tense excitement of the campaign.

Radicals claimed that the President's attitude in the New Orleans riot made it unsafe for "Union men" to remain in the South.[50] "The hands of the Rebels are again red with loyal blood; Rebel armies have once more begun the work of massacre," wrote the *Tribune*. It mourned "brothers and friends . . . butchered by a Rebel mob," and held Andrew

[48] Aug. 6, 1866, Johnson MSS., XCIX.

[49] Sheridan, however, testified that one negro in ten had firearms and that many had clubs (*Supra*, 351); and Monroe, Voorhees, and Herron swore to what was scrupulously kept out of the evidence if true, that "the colored mob in unison with a few white rioters who were leading them in this affair were, no doubt, well organized," and that, "forty-two policemen and several citizens were either killed or wounded by them." *New York Herald*, Aug. 8, 1866.

[50] D. Richards to E. B. Washburne, Sept. 11, 1866, Washburne MSS., XIX.

Johnson responsible.[51] "The policy of Andrew Johnson [had] engendered the demon fury which [had] shed blood in the streets of the Crescent City"; "his statesmanship [had] again raised rebel flags in New Orleans."[52] "The radical press," Senator Dixon warned Johnson, "is exciting popular opinion most deeply, and I fear we are losing ground in consequence of it. What I would suggest is that some action be taken to show that the Administration is unjustly accused in regard to it. Some such step as the displacement of Mayor Monroe, by orders through Gen. Sheridan, would entirely counteract the radical effort to make Capital. Depend upon it, Sir, we are in danger of losing thousands of votes in the coming elections by the falsehoods circulated on this subject. It is all important that their effect should be counteracted."[53] Stanton was brazen enough excitedly to denounce "pardoned rebels" who had instigated "the murder," and to testify for the Radicals that Johnson was "author" of the riot.[54] Thousands of men listened with implicit faith to speeches like Stevens's at Bedford, where he said, "Behold the awful slaughter of white men and black—of a Convention of highly respectable men, peaceably assembled in New Orleans, which General Sheridan pronounces more horrible than the massacre of Fort Pillow. Even the clergyman who opened the proceedings with prayer was cruelly murdered. All this was done under the sanction of Johnson and his office-holders. It is the legitimate consequence of his 'policy.'"[55]

*   *   *   *

---

[51] *New York Semi-Weekly Tribune,* Aug. 31, 1866.

[52] *New York Herald,* Aug. 2, 1866.

[53] J. Dixon to A. Johnson, Aug. 27, 1866, *ibid.,* C.

[54] Welles MS. Diary, Aug. 3, 1866—(II, 570); C. Sumner to J. Bright, Sept. 3, 1866, Edward L. Pierce, *Memoir and Letters of C. Sumner,* IV, 298.

[55] Sept. 4, 1866, Stevens MSS., VIII.

TIMELY WARNING.

TO UNION MEN.

THE NEW ORLEANS

CONVENTION OR MASSACRE.

WHICH IS THE MORE ILLEGAL.

Harper's Weekly, Sept. 8, 1866

UNION MEN BUTCHERED BY REBEL MOB UNDER "MY POLICY"

The most effective stratagem of the campaign was attaching the appellation of "Copperhead" or "traitor" to every one who opposed the Radical Party. "Traitor" is always an opprobrious term, often unreasoningly applied, that has the peculiar quality of damning unheard the victim of its condemnation. It is questionable whether under the pretended American belief in self-determination of peoples, the effort of a third of the nation to set up an independent government was treason. The victorious theory of 1866 ruled that it was. But in 1866 the War was over, and most ex-rebels had been pardoned. By constitutional definition of the term, the only traitors in that year were the scattered individuals, if any could be found, who were still in arms against the government, and the small group of ex-rebels who had not been pardoned either by proclamation or by special grant. Johnson accepted as good citizens all who were ready to obey the laws in the future. The Radicals persistently spoke of all Southerners, except the few adventurers who espoused Radical principles, as still traitors. Senator Chandler, for instance, declared, "The same [rebels] are alive today, who have only changed their leader and their tactics. Then it was under Jeff Davis, now it is under Andrew Johnson. They mean to overthrow the government. These unwashed rebels . . . propose to control your government." [56] His auditors, in the excitement of the assembly-hall, did not perceive the contradiction between "overthrowing" and "controlling" a government. Chandler in his bigotry would have said that for any but Radicals to "control" government was to "overthrow" it.

Furthermore Radicals decried as "Copperheads" all Northerners who opposed them. To comprehend the oppro-

[56] *Detroit Free Press*, March 15, 1866.

brium of this designation, one must sense it in contemporaneous newspapers of the Northwest where Copperheads were best known and best hated, or in an Indiana scene where the women of the community with clubs and pistols were driving some prominent Copperhead out of town after a "soap-box" oration against the War in which their husbands were fighting and giving their lives. Some Copperheads were sincere believers in peace, forerunners of the twentieth century "conscientious objector," but many were adventurers, renegades, bad characters, who bullied the women of Northern towns while their husbands fought.[57] These latter furnished the popular and truer picture of a Copperhead. They not only had tried to defeat the government as the rebels had done in open battle; they had attempted it by the cowardly method of stabbing in the back. Successfully to brand a man a Copperhead ruined him socially and politically.

The full force of this attack was turned upon Johnson, though he had been one of the most loyal Union men of the War in a region where loyalty required high courage. "After whipping the rebels & Copperheads," wrote McCaully of Delaware, "to have to whip them again headed by Johnson is dreadful but we must do it—otherwise we will be financially ruined." [58] Senator Chandler declared, "The so-called policy of Andrew Johnson . . . is not his policy; it is the policy of the rebels to get back into this government to overthrow the government, and Andrew Johnson is merely a tool in the hands of the rebels to accomplish their new rebel-

[57] This same type of man provided also the Southern Radicals of 1866.
[58] Feb. 24, 1866, Stevens MSS., VII. Hannibal Hamlin assured a Philadelphia Radical mass meeting that "today there was more hostility to the North in the bosoms of rebels than there was when they were arrayed against the government, and that was because they had been encouraged by the President." *New York Herald,* Oct. 6, 1866.

lion." [59] "By the assassination of Abraham Lincoln," Sumner told his audience, "the rebellion . . . vaulted into the Presidential chair. Jefferson Davis was then in the casements at Fortress Monroe, but Andrew Johnson was doing his work. . . . Witness Memphis; witness New Orleans. Who can doubt that the President is the author of these tragedies? Charles IX of France was not more completely the author of the massacre of St. Bartholomew than Andrew Johnson is the author of those recent massacres which now cry for judgment. . . . The blood of Memphis and New Orleans must cry out until it is heard, and a guilty President may suffer the same retribution which followed a guilty King. . . . Next to Jefferson Davis stands Andrew Johnson as [the Republic's] worst enemy." [60] Schurz won applause by exclaiming, "If there is any man that ought to hang for supporting these principles it is Andrew Johnson." [61]

A similar campaign was waged against Johnson's supporters.[62] Welles was "an imbecile" and Fox "a scoundrel &

[59] Speech at Philadelphia, *New York Herald*, Sept. 5, 1866. *The Chicago Tribune* (June 1, 1866) warned that Johnson's policy would allow "rebels, Copperheads and renegades" to repeal the test oath, possess themselves of the government, repeal all the recent legislation, repudiate the debt, and elect to Congress "the worst rebels in the South . . . That is exactly what 'my policy' is intended to accomplish." One of the editors of that paper wrote as early as March 31: Johnson "has become a traitor to those who made him what he is. Every copperhead and rebel in the land are his fast friends. God knows what calamities are yet in store for us. He gave us the victory over the rebellion and he can ward off the machinations of Johnson & his co-traitors." W. Gross to H. McCulloch, McCulloch MSS., II.

[60] *New York Herald*, Oct. 3, 1866. Sumner's friend, Ben Perley Poore, felt it his "duty to inform the Northern people that they were being betrayed," because "rebels and copper-heads leave . . . the White House content." B. P. Poore to C. Sumner, Nov. 8, 1865, Sumner MSS., LXXV. Forney told an audience at Lebanon that Johnson was "the idol of the Copperheads and distrusted by others." *Chicago Tribune*, June 29, 1866.

[61] *New York Herald*, Oct. 24, 1866.

[62] Governor Brownlow, for instance, habitually styled Democrats "the Copperhead Democracy," and Johnson Republicans "other Northern traitors." E.g., letter printed in the *Press*, Nov. 21, 1865, Stevens MSS., IV.

a copperhead." [63] The Philadelphia Convention men were "traitors." [64] The *Chicago Tribune* announced that Young, one of the organizers of the Cleveland Convention of Soldiers and Sailors, was "the fellow from Worcester . . . who was discharged . . . from the Christian Commission for calling with five other flunkies to pay their respects to . . . Lee, immediately after his surrender." [65] After his letter of approbation of this convention, Beecher was made the butt of abuse. Greeley proclaimed that "in the conception of every blackleg, duelist, negro-killer and rowdy, from the St. John to the Rio Grande, [Beecher] has all at once ceased to be a fanatic, a bigot, a disunionist, and become an enlightened patriot and statesman." [66] So bitter did the attacks become that Beecher, while retaining his old views, ceased publicly to advocate them. "No man not a copperhead or rebel, supports Johnson's policy, unless he is paid for so doing by an office or a pardon," the *Chicago Tribune* assured its readers. [67] One of Chicago's Radical aldermen announced, "Few persons, comparatively, in this vicinity, are in a mood to lionize Mr. Johnson, excepting those who would have let loose the rebel prisoners from Camp Douglas to sack our city and murder defenceless inhabitants. . . . Wherever it is a crime to be faithful to our country, and reconstructed rebels are permitted to kill Union men by way of pastime, there the name of Andrew Johnson is praised." [68]

[63] Former Senator J. P. Hale to C. Sumner, April 28, 1865, Sumner MSS., LXXIII.
[64] Stevens's speech at Bedford, Pa., Sept. 4, 1866, Stevens MSS., VIII.
[65] *Chicago Tribune*, April 20, 1866.
[66] *The Amendment to the Constitution. Beecher's Letters and Greeley's Reply* (*Tribune Tracts, No. 3*), 6.
[67] *Tri-Weekly Chicago Tribune*, June 27, 1866. Senator Yates, the former war governor of Illinois, insisted that Johnson's party was composed only of "traitors in the South and peace democrats in the North, and a few republicans who were hungry for spoils." *New York Herald*, Sept. 5, 1866.
[68] *Ibid.*, Sept. 5, 1866.

Most acrid and perhaps most influential of all, were Stevens's diatribes, in Congress and out. "Not a single genuine Republican," he said, "has been seduced from his allegiance to principle. . . . I know there are a few soldiers of fortune who . . . have consented to take office under Cowan and Company. But they were men who were never trusted by the party, or who for years past have become so bankrupt in principle and fortune as to be ready to join any conspiracy that furnished rations. They are the army of Catiline. . . . I warn you to keep an eye on any professed Republican who consents to fill an enforced vacancy. However he may have stood before, there is villainy wrapt up in his composition. He is a moral leper whom you should not touch. He should be socially ostracised as unfit for decent society. Let him flit about in the twilight, and hide his averted countenance from the light of day." [69] Spoken with all the vigor of Stevens's dynamic personality, such words bound many a doubtful Republican to the party. In Congress a crack of his whip brought back wavering votes. With his eyes flashing, the lank, decrepit, but fierce, old man cried, "Let all who approve [Radical] principles rally with us. Let all others go with Copperheads and rebels. Those will be the opposing parties. Young men, this duty devolves on you. Would to God, if only for that, that I were still in the prime of life, that I might aid you to fight through this last and greatest battle of Freedom." [70]

There exists a type of man so devoted to a cause or so narrow of vision that he sincerely regards the man who differs with him politically as a traitor, religiously as a heretic, morally as a debauchee, and economically as an anarchist.

[69] Speech at Bedford, Pa., Sept. 4, 1866, Stevens MSS., VIII.
[70] Speech at Lancaster, Pa., Sept. 7, 1865, *ibid.*, IV.

Sumner's position may probably be explained on this ground of bigotry. The rank and file under able tutelage probably believed that everybody who opposed Radicalism was a menace to the nation.[71] But not many of the leading campaigners could honestly have believed that the Radical Party was the nation and that opposition to it constituted treason. With them the terms "traitor" and "Copperhead" were mere party catchwords. A keen observer of Ohio politics warned Johnson early that the Radicals were making a "great effort . . . to conceal the true issue under the cry of 'Johnson has gone over to the Copperheads, wishes to admit unwashed rebels to Congress and won't hang Davis.' "[72] Sumner's friends urged him to accept the issue and make the chasm complete between loyal men and Johnson.[73] "It ought to be made appear constantly," wrote an Illinois politician to Trumbull, that "the fixed purpose" of the "Randall Convention" is "to transfer the entire government from the control of loyal men to Copperheads and rebels."[74] Pillsbury, the Democratic nominee for the governorship of Maine, explained the success of Radicalism not only in that state but throughout the country when he averred: "The bitter vituperation and the employment of abuse instead of argument, now apparent, has always been characteristic of the radical party. When the temperance movement was started in this State every man who did not support the ramrod policy of Mowatt was branded as a drunkard; during the Know Nothing excitement all who did not fall in with their extreme views were held up to infamy as Roman

[71] A small number of Democrats and ex-rebels who would really have made mischief if given the chance, caused suspicion to be cast on the great mass who were good citizens.

[72] Maj. R. P. L. Baber to A. Johnson, March 29, 1866, Johnson MSS., XCI.

[73] E.g., J. M. Stone to C. Sumner, Feb. 26, 1866, Sumner MSS., LXXVII.

[74] D. L. Phillips to L. Trumbull, July 14, 1866, Trumbull MSS., LXVIII.

Catholics, and now every man who supports the wise and beneficent policy of the administration is called a traitor." [75]

In a democracy this method is eminently successful. The scheme was a shrewd one. Few could stand up against the scathing attacks of Stevens or the *Chicago Tribune*. Many conservatives voted the Radical ticket to avoid the suspicion of Copperheadism.

* * * *

Wild rumor and purposeful misrepresentation helped to defeat the Conservative cause. A few examples will suffice. Stanton and his Radical friends sought to silence Senator Reverdy Johnson by circulating the tale that he had been in Canada during the War plotting with the rebels.[76] In Ohio the report was widely published that McCulloch had instructed his agents "not to pay any bounty passed by the last Congress" because "the President does not intend a dollar of additional bounty shall be paid a Union soldier or his family if he can help it." [77] Wisconsin and Ohio Radicals charged that "Johnson was guilty of the assassination of President Lincoln," and that "he dared not dismiss Stanton and Gen. Baker for fear they would expose him." [78] Doolittle testified that in Wisconsin the story was believed and produced "such a state of phrenzy & insane madness, that no man can read the future." [79] The charge of drunkenness and immorality was repeated by those who knew it to be untrue.[80] The most daring and widely believed falsehood was the story that

[75] *New York Herald*, Sept. 5, 1866.

[76] J. A. Dix to E. M. Stanton, June 24, 1865, Stanton MSS., XXVII.

[77] J. C. Wetmore, J. H. Geiger, and J. G. Thompson to A. Johnson, Sept. 21, 1866, Johnson MSS., CII.

[78] In Ohio the charge was made publicly by Gibson while campaigning the state with Butler. H. C. Dean to C. Mason, Oct. 4, 1866, *ibid.*, CIV. In Wisconsin the *Milwaukee Sentinel* circulated the report. F. P. Blair to A. Johnson, Sept. 20, 1866, *ibid.*, CI.

[79] F. P. B. to A. J. cited above.

[80] *Supra*, 13-16.

Johnson was planning to recognize the Southern and Copperhead members when Congress met in December and to use the army against the Republican members.[81] Grant's refusal to go to Mexico was used as proof of his knowledge of the plan and determination to prevent its consummation. The *Philadelphia Ledger*, as we have seen, printed "authentic proof" in the form of a set of questions concerning the constitutionality of the project, submitted by Johnson to his Attorney-General. The questions were proved to be a fabrication of conjecture and falsehood.[82] But the denial did little good. Many honest men believed the conspiracy story to the end.[83]   *   *   *   *

Johnson's campaign trip to Chicago gave rise to a flood of misrepresentation and ridicule. Though it is certain he remained sober,[84] the Radical press persuaded the nation to hang its head in shame over his "drunken speeches." His harangues compared not unfavorably with other stump speeches of the day. What he said was worth saying. He pleaded for peace, conciliation, and the Constitution; he reiterated at every stop his unflagging reliance on the "intelligence, patriotism and integrity of the great mass of the American people." [85] He urged voters to rise above party.[86] He defended himself against the charge of treason, explained his vetoes and his policy, and maintained that not he but Congress had changed its aims. He pleaded for conciliation

81 E.g., Grand Rapids *Daily Eagle*, July 1, 1866; *Hendricks County Union* (Indiana), Sept. 20, 1866; the *Nation*, III (July 19, 1866), 50.
82 See *supra*, 320 ff.
83 As late as 1885 Depew repeated the conspiracy story and gave Grant, then dead and unable to deny it, as authority. C. Depew to F. D. Grant, *Boston Evening Transcript*, Oct. 21, 1885.
84 *Supra*, 13 ff.
85 E.g., speech at Philadelphia, *New York Herald*, Aug. 29, 1866.
86 E.g., speech at Utica, *ibid.*, Sept. 1, 1866; at Niagara, *ibid.*, Sept. 2, 1866.

and a restoration of the Union. His message was dignified
and statesmanlike. But his method of delivering it was unfortunate.

In the East the President was well received. The *Herald*,
whose correspondent traveled with the Presidential party,
reported a great ovation to the President as he trav-

*Determined to take a Summer trip, our noble Chief
Magistrate packs up a few indispensable articles.*

eled across New York State.[87] "The President," it wrote,
"speaks spontaneously—speaks from the heart. . . . Fas-
tidious writers may raise some objections to the construction
of his language; but that is a trifling matter compared with

[87] The *Herald* furnishes almost the only trustworthy reports of the trip;
it was non-partisan; its representative, Cadwalader, as Grant's press-
agent, would not have been biased in favor of Johnson; Cadwalader's reports had the merit of intimate accuracy, of freedom from either Democratic or Radical coloring, and to us the added value that we know the
Herald articles were first-hand testimony, instead of rumor or political
boilerplate. For these reasons the *Herald* has been used for an account of
the "Swing 'round the Circle." See also R. W. Winston, *Andrew Johnson*,
363-371 and L. P. Stryker, *Andrew Johnson*, 341-372, both published since
the present work was written.

the ideas expressed, the broad and exalted statesmanship of his views, the earnestness and sincerity of his purpose and the terse eloquence of his words." [88] From Niagara Falls Rawlins wrote his wife, "The enthusiasm everywhere along the route has been unbounded. . . . I feel from what I see

The President received by New York.   He leaves the Constitution HERE.

that the chances are favorable to the conservatives and Democrats in this State this fall. . . . Seward is delighted and is certainly a man unequaled in tact and shrewdness to manage an assemblage of men opposed to him in politics. . . . The President makes innumerable speeches every day, and the people cheer him lustily." [89]

[88] Of his visit to New York City it wrote, "There never has been any event in the city . . . calculated to make so profound an impression on the political affairs of the country as this reception of the President." *New York Herald,* Aug. 31, 1866.

[89] Sept. 1, 1866, in J. H. Wilson, *John A. Rawlins,* 335. Phillips of the *Herald,* wrote Johnson while he was in Cleveland, "We are all rejoicing at the extraordinary good effect of your journey to Chicago." Sept. 3, 1866,

But the Radicals persistently sought to make trouble. At Philadelphia the city officials refused to receive the President. At Cleveland the audience was packed with Radicals, who hooted and hissed, and insulted Johnson until they provoked him into the fatal expedient of parrying words with the crowd. The next day's Radical papers were shocked at his "drunken, maudlin speech"; their reports of the episode opened a campaign of bitter ridicule. At Battle Creek John-

Enthusiastic Reception of the President at Cleveland.

son was jeered and taunted. His friends began to fear that the hall in Chicago where he was to speak would be packed by the Radicals before his supporters arrived; the *Herald* feared a riot.[90] But the Chicago visit passed smoothly in spite of Radical machinations that secured a last minute refusal of the building where a large mass meeting was to have been held.

Johnson MSS., C. Even Chase wrote the day before the St. Louis speech, "Johnson, Seward, Grant, & Farragut make a strong four horse team, if they all pull one way." S. P. Chase to J. W. Schuckers, Sept. 8, 1866, Chase MSS., 2nd series, III.

[90] *New York Herald,* Sept. 4 and 6, 1866. At Fremont, Ohio, the Radicals circulated handbills stating that the President had changed his plans, and would not stop there. But their trick was discovered and a large crowd appeared to greet him after all. *Ibid.,* Sept. 5, 1866.

In St. Louis, however, heckling again exasperated the President to indiscretion. In his anger he accused the Radicals of instigating the New Orleans riot; he replied to Stevens's calling him a second Judas by suggesting that if he were Judas, Congress must consider itself the Christ; he declared that the Freedmen's Bureau maintained slavery, and merely transferred the profits from the old masters to Radical officers; he denounced Radical pandering to the Fenians, the "salary grab," and Congressional niggardliness to ex-soldiers; he defended his own "magnanimity," and urged the country to emulate Christ's spirit of forgiveness; he pictured himself as the defender of the working classes, and assured the crowd that the Radical program was merely an effort to retain power; he concluded by appealing as usual for union and peace, urging the people in the coming elections to preserve the Constitution which he confidingly left in their hands.[91]

At Indianapolis Morton and the other state officials fled his coming, and the Radical politicians staged a riot. Roughs knocked down the transparencies prepared to welcome him, shots were fired, one man was killed and several were seriously wounded by the Radicals, and after repeated efforts to speak, Johnson was forced to retreat from the bedlam without uttering a word.[92] At Pittsburgh he encountered similar insults.

The rioting and heckling were the work of Radicals, probably directed by their campaign managers. Goodman assured Johnson that the hecklers in Cleveland, "some thirty or forty in number *were hired* by notorious abolitionists in this vicinity for the purpose of disturbing you on the occasion, and

91 *Ibid.,* Sept. 10, 1866.
92 *Ibid.,* Sept. 11 and 12, 1866.

were paid for their services out of the Union League fund." [93]
The *Herald* was certain that the trouble-makers throughout
the tour were "purposely set upon his path to provoke him
to some indiscreet display of temper." [94] In fact Thomas
Ewing had warned him of this danger in advance, and had
urged him not to make the trip, as he would be exposed to
insult from Radicals and his conversation and actions would
be belied. [95]

Great enthusiasm along the Route. The President leaves the Constitution with the people out of the car window.

Johnson should never have made the Western tour. His
speech-making was disastrous. [96] But shrewd old Thomas
Ewing explained his February and April outbursts in words
which truly apply to the Chicago trip. "I concurred with
you," he wrote, "in censure of the President in making
speeches at all, and especially for hurling such denunciation
against those that denounced him, but on reflection I am

[93] Sept. 4, 1866, Johnson MSS., CI.
[94] *New York Herald*, Sept. 26, 1866. Welles agreed. MS. Diary, Sept. 17,
1866—(II, 593-594).
[95] Ewing even feared Johnson would be assassinated, so bitterly did the
Radicals hate him. T. Ewing to H. Stanbery, Aug. 27, 1866, Ewing MSS.,
"Letter-book."
[96] A Radical politician in Illinois expressed delight. "'Moses,'" he said,
"is doing a great work for us by . . . playing the blackguard all over the
country." D. Richards to E. B. Washburne, Sept. 11, 1866, Washburne
MSS., XIX.

inclined to think we required too much of him. He was very coarsely, even brutishly assailed in the two Houses & especially by the clerk of the Senate by whom they denounced & slandered him every day Sunday not excepted. . . . The President had no official organ & no official means of reply or defence—He had to sit and take it or make a speech—if he had been stoic enough to do so he had better kept quiet. A horse in a Yellow Jackets' nest kicks & plunges to little purpose, and so with him—there was a swarm upon him, whom strike as he would he could not hit. For a President or a Sovereign to reply to anything from anybody is bad taste, but Johnson had not acquired the habit of reigning and if we compare the abuse that was heaped upon him, with his retort we will not find the balance of propriety and good taste in favor of the two Houses." [97]

His speeches did compare well enough with those of his opponents. But where Radical leaders spoke every day to a different audience, Johnson spoke many times every day to the whole country, and after all, it was almost the same speech many times repeated. The country, eagerly expectant at first, wearied of it, then laughed at it, and finally became disgusted. Radical papers painted every speech as undignified. It was not Johnson, but the Radical roughs in the crowd, the riots, the hisses, and Johnson's helplessness before them, the unceasing ridicule in which Johnson was held for days beneath the Radical spotlights, the false charge of drunkenness, the Radical misrepresentation, and slanders— it was these and not the words or acts of Johnson that injured him. Stevens described the President's tour as the peregrinations of "a very remarkable circus" with Johnson and Sew-

[97] T. Ewing to W. P. Sheffield, Aug. 24, 1866, *ibid.,* "Letter-book."

ard as the chief "clowns," and Doolittle as the "monkey." [98]
With his overpowering personality to set it off, this masterpiece of ridicule must have won any crowd. In this vein Radical newspapers reported the trip. Few men could have stood
the attack. Johnson's error lay in having ever left the White
House, and thereby having exposed himself to it. Yet the
Western tour was but an incident in the Radical campaign
of ridicule. * * * *

Unadulterated abuse of the President helped the Radicals
to undermine his position with the people. The vituperative
spirit of the campaign cannot be described; it must be experienced through the words of those who helped to create it.
In welcoming the Southern Loyalists' Convention, the Philadelphia Loyal League passed a resolution "that in the
extraordinary sympathy recently manifested by Andrew
Johnson . . . with the prominent traitors of the country
and their political adherents; in his treachery to the loyal
people, who trusted and raised him to power, . . . in his
denial of the right of the people of the loyal states to exercise legislative power in Congress in the present condition of
the country, in his indecent and ribald attacks upon their
representatives for endeavoring to establish justice and protect a weak and helpless race from persecution, oppression,
and slaughter, in his fraternity with the rebels of New Orleans, resulting in the horrible and causeless massacre of
loyal, peaceful and virtuous citizens, wicked in conception
and fiendish in execution, we recognize with profound disappointment and sorrow a degree of moral and political depravity which has no parallel in our history." [99]

But this written attack was dignified in comparison with

Radical speeches. General Schenck, for instance, declared, "Mr. Johnson in his trip to Chicago, took occasion to debauch the public mind, and occupied the same relation that the rebels did when they presented their pistols and bowie-knives at the breasts of our Union soldiers." [1] In a campaign speech in Brooklyn Schurz said: Johnson's "sense of right and wrong is obscured by selfish influences. . . . When such a man is combative and vehement he is a dangerous man, and when he has a feeble intellect, he is both dangerous and foolish. The President's policy is the result of this happy combination." Johnson was the "victim of flattery. You might even tell him he was a gentleman and he would believe you." Johnson was worse than Vallandigham, shouted Schurz, yes, "worse than . . . Judas Iscariot or Benedict Arnold. . . . As he had been made President by assassination, he wanted to protect assassination." [2] Some of the epithets hurled at Johnson by the Radicals were "a demagogue . . . consumed with egotism," "trickster," "drunken tailor," "purjured and usurping traitor," a man with "the face of a demagogue and the heart of a traitor," "a culprit" with a "blood-stained and cowardly hand," a "calamitous and traitorous Executive," an "insolent, drunken brute, in comparison with whom Caligula's horse was respectable." [3]

At the Radical Philadelphia Convention a resolution was offered requesting Johnson to resign. "The delegates rose to their feet and cheered lustily, several voices exclaiming, 'good, good!' A voice amidst the confusion, 'No need for him to resign; Chicago will save him the trouble!' 'They'll throw him in the lake.' 'They'll poison the waters of Lake Huron

[1] *Ibid.*, Sept. 6, 1866.
[2] *Ibid.*, Oct. 24, 1866.
[3] See *supra*, 92.

with his carcass.' " [4] In the West, Logan said in imitation of Stevens's style, "When all things were created, in the Creation it was necessary to have animals for all kinds of work, and when the Almighty looked around for a demagogue he found Andrew Johnson and made him." [5]

But Stevens was the grand master of invective. To a Bedford, Pennsylvania, audience he declared, "The jesuitism, the imbecility, the impudence and vacillation shown by the Cabinet ministers perplexed, and for a while, paralyzed Congress—reluctant to make war upon the Executive of their choice, they sought every expedient to avoid it. But when it became inevitable, they accepted it. . . . A Congress elected by the people to resist armed traitors were not disposed to cower before the usurped sceptre of a single apostate." [6] In accepting his own renomination, Stevens told his constituents, "I cannot begin to attempt to unfold the policy of that man, in whom the people confided as a true patriot, and whom we have now found to be worse than the man who is incarcerated in Fortress Monroe. . . . You all remember that in Egypt the Lord sent frogs, locusts, murrain and lice, and finally demanded the blood of the first born of all the oppressors. Almost all of these have been sent upon us. More than the first born has been taken from us. We have been oppressed with taxes, and debts, and He has sent us more than lice, and has afflicted us with Andrew Johnson." [7]

* * * *

To passion, too, these men appealed—to the war-engendered, long rankling hatred which Conservatives sought

---

[4] *Ibid.*, Sept. 6, 1866.
[5] *Ibid.*, Aug. 10, 1866.
[6] Sept. 4, 1866, Stevens MSS., VIII.
[7] *New York Herald*, Aug. 20, 1866.

to sooth. Medill of the *Chicago Tribune* wrote Johnson, "The late civil war emancipated the *minds* of the Northern people from the dominion of the Oligarchy as well as the bodies of the Slaves. No scheme of reconstruction will ever again include the vassalage of the North to the Southern aristocracy. The day is passed forever of the rule of the chivalry. In the future they will stand before the country as whipped rebels, and not haughty dictators and swaggering task masters." [8] In a campaign speech at Gettysburg that contrasted strangely with Lincoln's words there, Edward Everett announced, "The people of loyal America will never take to their confidence or admit again to a share in their government the hard-hearted men whose cruel lust of power has brought this desolating war upon the land." [9] "Can it be possible," Ballard asked Sumner, that Johnson "really believes in the sincerity and repentance of the rebel devils?" [10] "The issue," asserted Senator Lane of Indiana, is this—Shall loyal people rule or red-handed traitors? . . . Andrew Johnson was created to cast respectability upon the treason of John Tyler." [11]

But deeper passion yet was appealed to. If the state of things revealed by the New Orleans riots cannot be altered, shouted Butler, "we will march once more, and wo to him who opposes us." [12] "What!" Stevens exclaimed in recounting the "strange, wild and wicked doctrine" laid down by the "traitors" of the Philadelphia Convention. "What! six millions of Rebels who had renounced the Constitution, who had

[8] Sept. 15, 1865, Johnson MSS., LXXVI.
[9] *New York Herald,* Oct. 30, 1866. Governor Curtin maintained that "he would rather trust the destinies of his country today to the uninformed loyal negro than to the rebels of the South or their sympathizers in the North." *Ibid.,* Nov. 3, 1866.
[10] Sept. 14, 1865, Sumner MSS., LXXIV.
[11] *New York Herald,* Sept. 6, 1866.
[12] *Ibid.,* Aug. 27, 1866.

murdered five hundred thousand of our citizens, who had loaded the nation with debt and drenched it with blood, when conquered had forfeited no right, had lost no jurisdiction or civil authority." [13] "This war," said Stevens, "had its origin in treason without one spark of justice. . . . In its progress our prisoners, by the authority of their government were slaughtered in cold blood. Ask Fort Pillow and Fort Wagner. Sixty thousand of our prisoners have been deliberately starved to death because they would not enlist in the rebel armies. The graves at Andersonville have each an accusing tongue. The purpose and avowed object of the enemy 'to found an empire whose cornerstone should be slavery,' render its perpetuity or revival dangerous to human liberty." Therefore the North has the undoubted right "to take the lives, liberty, and property of the belligerents of the South." [14]

Western oratory even more successfully stirred passions. Johnson's plan would "inaugurate another revolution and more bloodshed," vociferated Logan. He was opposed to temporizing with the South. "There [is] but one way to treat with rebels," he told a Springfield rally. "Take the torch in one hand and the sword in the other, and march to the music of the Union, with the flag unfurled, and sweep over their territory." He had no sympathy, he said, for the leading traitors, no commiseration for them. He could forget no man who had lost his life or who had been maimed in this war for the Union, and he could forgive no man who had fought against it. [15]

In a letter to Wade Hampton, John Quincy Adams bore witness to the success of this stirring of old hatreds. "It is

---

[13] Speech at Bedford, Pa., Sept. 4, 1866, Stevens MSS., VIII.
[14] Speech at Lancaster, Pa., Sept. 7, 1865, *ibid.*, IV.
[15] *New York Herald*, Aug. 10, 1866

declared," he wrote, "and I fear it is widely believed, that the spirit of secession still fires the Southern heart, and works through the Democratic party. A mass of honest men are taught and believe that the success of that party means the political re-establishment of the genius of revolt, and the elevation to power of the Southern leaders in the late war." [16] This cry was good strategy,[17] and the election to Congress in some of the Southern states of prominent rebel leaders under the Johnson plan of restoration but against Johnson's earnest advice, gave proof of Southern stubbornness and lent color to Radical prophecies. In the West, where the Radicals needed to counteract economic issues and prevent a natural gravitation toward friendly social and economic intercourse with the South, this rekindling of cooling passions was particularly effective.

*   *   *   *

To these attacks Johnson was more vulnerable than Lincoln would have been. But could any opponent have survived the Radical onslaughts? The Radicals bent all their efforts to exciting the people to an unreasoning state of mind; they appealed to every emotion and passion that could be aroused against their adversaries. They played upon every fear and every hatred that might serve a Radical purpose. To the invective the Conservatives could reply in kind. But Johnson's position would have been stronger had they remained silent, for Conservative success depended upon the abandonment of war animosities and prejudice, upon the soothing of passions, upon calm in which evidence could be dispassionately weighed. Every Conservative counter-attack merely

[16] *Massachusetts and South Carolina Correspondence. Correspondence between J. Q. Adams and Wade Hampton* . . . , Sept. 28, 1868.
[17] For abundant evidence of its use, see H. K. Beale, "The Decision of Reconstruction," 467.

added to the confusion that helped the Radicals cover dangerous issues with a smoke screen of vituperation and excitement. Radical stump speakers swayed the crowd at political gatherings to feelings that no man would have experienced in the quiet of his home. Huzzahing, emotionalism, keen excitement, were stimulated by all the tricks of the sensationalist. Under the tension thus aroused, men chose their parties and voted.

Chapter XII

THE ELECTION AND ITS EFFECT

EXCITEMENT became intense as the election approached. Wild reports of plotted violence flew about and were believed by many ordinarily calm men. Many Conservatives believed that the secret conclave of Radical governors in Philadelphia purposed arming the Radicals to carry the election by force.[1] Johnson dispatched Comstock to Tennessee to run down rumors of Brownlow's armed control of the state.[2] Comstock and O'Bierne were both sent into the Northwest to investigate insistent tales of large shipments of arms to be used against Conservatives by the Union League Clubs and the newly formed Grand Army of the Republic. O'Bierne reported mysterious cases of arms marked with a red diamond; he talked with a man in Toledo who confessed shipping thousands of muskets into Indiana and Illinois;[3] he thought all the railroads, telegraph and express companies, and post offices were privy to the "arms movement";[4] he claimed General Steedman had told him that "Morton, the Radicals, and the G.A.R. are determined to obtain possession of the President by deposing him through

---

[1] *New York Herald*, Sept. 8, 1866.
[2] Comstock MS. Diary, Sept. 22, 1866.
[3] Bulletin of J. R. O'Bierne, August, 1866, Johnson MSS., C.
[4] Oct. 9, 1866, *ibid.*, CIII.

impeachment and taking his life if necessary, and that the
G.A.R. when armed and equipped will march on Washington." He also reported that a St. Louis conference of Governors Morton, Yates, Oglesby, Fletcher, and Fairchild, and
General Logan, coolly discussed the question of appointing a
dictator.[5] Inflammatory bulletin after bulletin this excitable
agent sent to Johnson. Comstock, however, found no evidence
of "arms" or "plots" either in Indiana or Tennessee.[6] Johnson himself was distressed by fear of renewed civil war, in
North as well as South.[7] And many Radicals honestly believed that Johnson was plotting revolution and civil conflict.[8] That there was little or no foundation for these tales is
beside the point. They were current, and seriously believed.

Important, too, in the election excitement were the "Boys
in Blue" and the newly organized Grand Army of the Republic.[9] The chief purpose of the G.A.R. was probably to
perpetuate friendships, glorify the War, and keep alive the
love of Union for which men had fought. But it was a secret
organization, and Radicals predominated in it. To many of
the members, preserving the government from Democrats
was as great a duty as had been defeating the South. If this

[5] Oct. 12, 1866, *ibid.*, CIII. Johnson's life was threatened from time to
time. E.g., anonymous letter, Nov. 1, 1866, *ibid.*, CV.
[6] He reported that Brownlow did want to arm "loyal men" in Tennessee. Governor Morton assured him there would be no trouble in Indiana
unless Johnson aroused it by sending in troops. Comstock MS. Diary, Oct.
12, 1866.
[7] *Ibid.*, Sept. 22, 1866.
[8] E.g., W. W. Thayer who told Sumner that when Congress adjourned in
1866, Johnson, that "bold, bad, mad, ambitious traitor," would lead a
Southern revolution. About March, 1866, Sumner MSS., LXXVII.
[9] "You are right," an Illinois aide wrote Trumbull, "in attributing our
success in part to the Soldiers Love Feast. The evening prior to the election some 500 of the boys left here on a special train for Louisiana with
two bands, *hard tack* & *sow belly* in abundance and we enacted the scene
you witnessed in our Wigwam . . . The effect was magnificent, democrats
admit it gave us thirty votes. Had we inaugurated the Love Feast system
a month before the election we should have carried the county by 350."
A. C. Babcock to L. Trumbull, Nov. 12, 1866, Trumbull MSS., LXX.

had to be done by force, the military organization of the
G.A.R. might prove important.[10] In any case it aided the
Radical cause at election time. "The Grand Army of the
Republic," said the *Hendricks County Union*, "treated our
citizens to a splendid torch light procession on Saturday
night last. The organization was not out in full force, but the
display of flags, mottoes, lights, etc., was fine. The band
accompanied the procession, discoursing excellent music as
the procession moved through the various streets. The procession moved, with the steady step of old vets in double file,
each a line of light, and between them was borne the stars
and stripes by men who had carried them when shot and shell
fell thick and fast, and several transparencies bearing the
mottoes: 'Grand Army of the Republic,' 'Protection to soldiers' widows and orphans,' and 'Death to the traitors.'" [11]
However peaceful its· purposes, a secret military organization holding rallies and parading the streets urging "Death
to traitors" was not conducive to sane thinking and independent voting.[12]

But election excitement was not confined to rumors
and threats of violence, and parades of soldiers. Riots and
forcible disruption of meetings were common. In pugnacity
and quarrelsomeness the parties were well matched; neither

[10] "Nominally we are at peace," wrote Cook in justification of the found-
ing of a G.A.R. chapter at Springfield, Ill., "but does it never occur to you
that we may again be driven to arms? The persistent and unyielding course
of the Administration in a policy of reconstruction so foreign to the absolute demands of the country . . . will in the absence of the proper checks
imposed by a loyal and fearless Congress lead to a rupture that will sink
into insignificance the impoverishing war that has just ended. Can you then
think in our retaining our military organization with love to our country
and hate to treason any bad results will ensue?" J. Cook to L. Trumbull,
July 19, 1866, *ibid.*, LXVIII.
[11] *Hendricks County Union* (Danville, Ind.), Sept. 20, 1866.
[12] It did intimidate some into voting the Radical ticket. A. C. Babcock
to L. Trumbull, Nov. 12, 1866, Trumbull MSS., LXIX.

had a monopoly of violent methods. At Indianapolis the Radicals started a riot and prevented Johnson from speaking.[13] At Cairo, Illinois, the Democrats broke up a meeting to which two traveling delegates from the Southern Loyalists' Convention were trying to speak.[14] Only strenuous measures prevented a riot of ex-rebels in New Orleans.[15] At Connersville, Indiana, "a radical, who had been in the army and deserted, took some exceptions to speechmaking at a democratic meeting, and fired four shots in the crowd," severely wounding an old citizen.[16] In Philadelphia the campaign ended in a whirl of excitement with stump diatribes, fireworks, parades, and huge mass meetings. Radicals carried transparencies asking, "Shall liberty be lost, and the sway of a dictator begin?" Democratic transparencies declared, "We want a white man's government." The climax was two days of street fighting in which men on both sides were injured, shots were fired, bricks were thrown, transparencies were torn down, and a Conservative headquarters was demolished.[17] Responsibility could not be fixed; rioting started when parading Republican clubs and a disbanding Democratic meeting collided.[18] In Baltimore a riot threatened for days;[19] Johnson held an armed force ready to pre-

13 *New York Herald,* Sept. 11, 1866.
14 *Ibid.,* Oct. 7, 1866.
15 *Ibid.,* Oct. 22, 1866.
16 *Ibid.,* Sept. 1, 1866.
17 *Ibid.,* Oct. 6 and 7, 1866.
18 *Philadelphia Ledger* (Independent), Oct. 6, 1866. The Democratic *Philadelphia Age,* Oct. 6, 1866, called it a "disgraceful and dastardly attack" of Radical policemen upon the Conservatives. The Radical *Press,* Oct. 6, 1866, described an "unprovoked and cowardly attack" of a Democratic "gang of roughs" upon peaceful citizens.
19 The vote of the city depended upon the complexion of the Commissioners who interpreted the franchise law. Swann, under his unquestioned gubernatorial authority, sought to replace Radical commissioners with Conservatives, but the Radicals refused to relinquish their offices. Grant found Swann in such a predicament that if he attempted to oust

serve order if necessary,[20] and sent Grant to investigate;[21] ultimately tactful firmness on the part of Governor Swann and General Grant prevented trouble.[22] In Missouri excitement was so tense and brawls so frequent that Sherman and Johnson considered calling out troops to preserve order.

To understand the importance of this atmosphere, one must remember the mode of voting. Secret ballots were not used until a quarter of a century later. The candidate or party committee provided the ballots. Those of one party were easily distinguishable from those of the other by the size and color. Normally the voter was met at the polls by party agents urging him to take a ballot. Even when ballots were given out in advance, every one at the polls knew as the voter put one into a box how he was voting; some states even provided for signing of ballots. Employers lined up their men to vote a certain employer's ticket on pain of discharge; bribers watched their bought voters until the ballots were safely in the box. About the polls were political leaders and curious crowds to cheer or jeer as each man voted. Roughs often tore the opposition's clothes or staged mock riots to frighten timid men. During this very campaign the evils of the open ballot reached their height.[23] Courageous,

the commissioners by law, the delay would cost him the election; if by force, he might inaugurate a terrible riot. Grant urged the old commissioners (Comstock thought "not . . . quite so strongly as he ought") to offer no resistance to force and the new to appeal to law alone. Comstock MS. Diary, Nov. 1, 1866.

[20] A. Johnson to E. M. Stanton, Oct. 25, Nov. 2, 1866, Johnson MSS., "Letter-book."

[21] U. S. Grant to A. Johnson, Oct. 24, 1866, *ibid.*, CIV.

[22] Grant wired Stanton, Nov. 5, "This morning collision looked almost inevitable. Wiser counsels now seem to prevail and I think there is strong hope that no riot will occur. Propositions looking to the harmonizing of parties are now pending." *Ibid.*, "Telegrams." The new commissioners were at last peaceably installed, the riot averted, and the Radicals defeated.

[23] In 1867 Connecticut, Indiana, and Virginia, and in 1868 Ohio and West Virginia, passed laws prescribing a uniform ballot. Eldon C. Evans, *A History of the Australian Ballot System in the United States,* chap. I.

indeed, was the Republican who would brave the wrath, scorn, social ostracism, and business boycott of his friends, and march up in full view of his hooting neighbors to drop a "Copperhead" ballot in the box.

* * * *

The most significant factor in the election was the necessity men faced at the polls, of choosing between a Copperhead and a Radical.[24] The Philadelphia Convention was enthusiastically supported by moderate men, who were able to support it because it was untainted by the Democratic name or Copperhead participation.[25] When, however, the Convention leaders went back into their respective states to carry out their program, they found the party machinery and press in the hands of Radicals and professional Democrats. The greatest mistake of the Moderates was failure to organize a new party at Philadelphia. They could not get possession of the Republican Party because the Radicals controlled the machinery.[26] It was dangerous to act through the Democratic Party. Moderate leaders saw this peril.[27] But

[24] This determining circumstance is ignored by historians who interpret the election as a popular endorsement of the Fourteenth Amendment in preference to Johnson's policy.

[25] *Supra*, chap. IV.

[26] "Any cooperation with the radicals," Babcock of Connecticut testified, "is utterly impossible. They are despotic, unscrupulous, vindictive and abusive. At our first meeting in Hartford, I was for fighting the battle within our own lines; but I have seen the folly of that philosophy long since. The contest for Senator has cured me; and, further, I now think the Philadelphia Convention should take the Bull by the horns and *nominate Andrew Johnson for the Presidency* before they adjourn. That will draw the lines at once. It will commit the Democrats beyond retreat. It will sift the chaff from the wheat in our own late party." J. F. Babcock to G. Welles, July 12, 1866, Welles MSS., LXI.

[27] John Sherman assured his brother that Johnson realized that "the Democratic party is deemed . . . a disloyal organization and [that] no promise or platform they can make will redeem them from the odium they justly gained during the war." Nov. 10, 1865, W. T. Sherman MSS., XVII. "Those who sustained the Govt during the rebellion," Pratt of Connecticut wrote Welles, "have a horror of Copperheads; and I must confess, I cant fellowship with them until they repudiate their war record, declare the

by leaving the conduct of the Conservative campaign to local leaders, they fell victims to it. In some states where the Philadelphia Committee did attempt to organize a campaign and set up wisely selected moderate candidates, the Democrats opposed their plans, and by manipulation transformed the movement into a Democratic one. In other states where the Conservatives did not organize at all, the Democrats merely appropriated the Philadelphia program and sought through its popularity to return their party to power. Democratic politicians could not resist grasping the chance for personal rehabilitation.[28] They did not succeed in restoring the Democratic fortunes but they did carry the Conservative Party down to disaster with them.

Thousands of Northerners who had supported Lincoln, favored the Lincoln-Johnson Southern policy and abhorred both Radicals and Copperheads. But when faced with the dilemma of voting for one or the other, they instinctively chose the Radicals as the less obnoxious. Men of all political complexions agreed that the necessity of this choice made Radical victory inevitable. "The mere apprehension," averred one Johnson supporter, "that the Democratic Party might be brought into power, . . . and the unfounded allegation that Mr. Johnson and others had joined that party, so excited the nerves of the patriotic masses as to

Chicago platform, at least, a mistake, and agree to behave in future." (By Copperhead he meant Democrat.) July 19, 1866, Welles MSS., LXI. The *Springfield Republican,* July 21, 1866, estimated that even in Radical Massachusetts at least a third of the Republicans would gladly follow Johnson against Congress. But, it warned, "to reject Thaddeus Stevens and Charles Sumner and support Mr. Johnson is one thing, and to go to bed with Copperheads and rebels is another; and many eager for the first will hesitate long before doing the last." See also J. F. Babcock to G. Welles, March 24, 1866, Welles MSS., LX; G. Bancroft to A. Johnson, Sept. 30, 1866, Johnson MSS., CII; A. Smith to A. Johnson, Feb. 7, July 17, 1866, *ibid.,* LXXXVIII, XCVII; and J. F. Miller of Calif. to H. McCulloch, March 6, 1866, *ibid.,* XC.

28 Johnson's correspondence was cluttered with letters from Democrats praising his policy and then asking a favor.

make them blind to every other consideration." [29] After candidates were nominated, *Harper's Weekly* felt the issue was "virtually decided, because it [was] seen to be merely a question between the old Copperheads of 1864 and the Union party." [30] Earlier this had been merely Radical campaign talk. But the failure of Conservatives to organize a party made it an actuality. The Buffalo *Commercial Advertiser*, after supporting the Democratic ticket, thought the election showed that "the Democratic party, as it existed during the war, [had] become so odious that it [was] hopeless to seek to perpetuate and keep it alive." [31]

*   *   *   *

First among the 1866 elections was Connecticut's bitter gubernatorial contest in April, which showed how fatal the hesitancy of Johnson Republicans was to be. The state was divided into three groups, Radicals, Democrats, and Conservative Republicans who supported Johnson but refused to break with the Radicals.[32] The Democrats nominated English; after a struggle between Conservatives and Radicals, the Republicans nominated a Radical, Hawley, on a platform that commended Johnson personally but condemned his policy. Defeated within their own party, the Conservative Republicans were perplexed. Cleveland started to organize a Johnson meeting, but his courage failed, and he abandoned the plan. All depended upon Welles and the President. Welles, who knew and trusted Hawley, issued a guarded statement in his favor. Hawley assured Welles that they agreed in "general principles." Dennison wrote New

29 E. C. Benedict, *Constitutional Amendment*, 1.
30 *Harper's Weekly*, Oct. 13, 1866.
31 Quoted in *New York Herald*, Nov. 13, 1866.
32 Welles kept in close touch with leaders of all three factions. This story of the election has been taken from his correspondence with them. Welles MSS., LX, and the Welles MS. Diary, February to June, 1866.

Hampshire friends urging them to support the party that won the War, and his letter was used in Connecticut to win votes for Hawley. The Conservative leader, Babcock, and English and Hawley, representing the three groups, each went to Washington to consult the President. Johnson leaned to English, Welles to Hawley; [33] McCulloch felt "it would not do for us to disconnect ourselves from the War Party." Johnson finally issued an enigmatic statement, declaring, "I am for that candidate who is for the general policy and the specific measures promulgated . . . in my [messages]. . . . I presume it is known or can be ascertained, what candidates favor or oppose my policy." [34]

Hawley won by a meager 541 votes upon a platform that opposed the President's policy, yet claimed his support.[35] The Conservative, Babcock, was elated over the results.[36] He wrote Welles, "It is not intended to disrupt the Union party unless that party is bound to follow Stevens, Wade & Co. at the expense of all patriotism and decency. The friends of the President and his policy are a *power* in this state although they had no way of showing it at the recent election." [37]

Babcock was gradually disillusioned. In the Senatorial election in May, Conservative Senator Foster was defeated for reëlection and Ferry, a Radical, chosen in his place by

[33] Welles was really doubtful about Hawley, but felt that now, when nominations had been made and the only alternative was a Democrat, was no time to make an issue against the Radicals that should have been made several months earlier. MS. Diary, March 17, 1866—(II, 456).

[34] A. Johnson to W. S. Huntington, March 27, 1866, Johnson MSS., "Telegrams." But he did refuse to accept the resignation from the postmastership which Cleveland tendered because he had supported English.

[35] The vote was 43,974 for Hawley against 43,433 for English. *Tribune Almanac* (1867), 49.

[36] J. F. Babcock to G. Welles, April 8, 1866, Welles MSS., LX.

[37] April 6, 1866, *ibid.*, LX. "It is better," he thought, "that the radicals should drive us out of their ranks for no greater offence than the effort to make ourselves heard, than that the Conservatives should bolt without an effort to make their counsels prevail among their associates." April 19, 1866, *ibid.*, LX.

effective use of the party whip and the votes of several
Republican legislators who favored Johnson's views but did
not dare break with the party. Babcock now saw the folly of
a hesitant policy, and wrote Welles, Weed, Randall, and
Raymond that it was "time to carry the war into Africa."
"We made a great mistake," he continued, "in not electing
English. . . . I have been greatly cramped here by *some*
that ought to have cooperated with me, but who seem anxious
to ride the two horses; but I shall pay no regard to them
hereafter, but cooperate with such democrats as will go into
the work heartily, and there are enough of them. The passive
defensive policy of the past will be our ruin and the ruin of
the country." [38] Had Conservatives heeded this lesson, they
might yet have defeated the Radicals by the formation of
a new party.

In Connecticut, however, in spite of the Conservative
failure to organize a party, in spite of the fact that Hawley
claimed the administration's support, in spite of Republican
unwillingness to vote a Democratic ticket, the Republican
majority of 1865 was cut down from 11,035 to 541; the
Democrats polled 49.7 per cent of the votes; and the next
spring Connecticut Democrats carried the Congressional
elections by 1,394 votes, won three out of the four Congressmen, and chose English for governor over Hawley by 987
votes. [39] Wiser Conservative tactics might have carried the
state overwhelmingly for Johnson in 1866, and turned the
tide that rose to Radical victory in the fall.

In Maine's September election the Radicals won all the
Congressmen and a majority of 26,843. [40] The decisiveness
of the vote resulted partly from the lethargy of the Demo-

[38] July 12, 1866, *ibid.*, LXI.
[39] *Tribune Almanac* (1866), 53; (1867), 49; (1868), 43.
[40] This was a large increase over the 18,841 of 1864. *Ibid.* (1867), 49;
(1865), 46.

crats, and partly from Radical vigor that brought speakers
from all over New England and held as many as fifty-one
mass meetings in one day.[41] The repudiation bogy,[42] anti-
Southern prejudice,[43] defamation of Johnson,[44] and violence [45] were effectively used by a Radical organization that
controlled the press.[46] Minor factors may have influenced the
result: in Portland, for example, a fire which opportunely
wiped out a large Democratic vote, the necessity of many
Irish who remained dependent upon Radical authorities for
housing and food, the Fenian excitement, and the power of
the city marshal over little liquor-store keepers whose votes
he watched at the polls.[47] But these were mere details, for
the Maine voter had to choose between a Radical and a Copperhead. The Democrats had imported as campaigners not
only Montgomery Blair, but actually Fernando Wood of
New York Copperhead infamy, and Parsons of Alabama.

[41] *New York Herald,* Sept. 7, 1866.

[42] "If the President's policy were successful," warned the Radical campaigners, "the first thing Congress would do would be to repudiate the
national debt in favor of the four thousand millions of Confederate scrip
. . . The next . . . would be to order compensation for all Southern slaves
emancipated by . . . Mr. Lincoln." Jewett's speech in the *New York
Herald,* Sept. 7, 1866.

[43] Clay eaters were described as proof that "the whole Southern people
were a dirty, contemptible race, unfit for any share in government, and
inferior to their own negroes." *Ibid.,* Sept. 7, 1866.

[44] Voters were told that when Johnson was in the Senate "his habits were
such that no respectable man would associate with him." *Ibid.,* Sept. 7, 1866.

[45] When an ex-colonel attempted to address a Johnson meeting at Kittery,
the Radicals extinguished the lights and shut the doors in his face amidst
great excitement. *Ibid.,* Sept. 6, 1866.

[46] "No newspapers but the most rabid radical sheets are allowed to
penetrate into the State," testified the *Herald* correspondent. The people of
Maine, he added, "have conceived one set of ideas and have never listened,
nor do they care to listen to any other . . . Many a barroom loafer of New
York has a broader idea of the nature of the present constitutional crisis
than have these Yankee farmers, shrewd, intelligent and thrifty though
they be. Early education and training have fixed their minds in one set
groove, and nothing but a strong volcanic convulsion can ever drive them
out of it. They read no newspapers but those which advocate the views
they have already imbibed, and listen to no argument that tends not in
the same direction." *Ibid.,* Sept. 5 and 7, 1866.

[47] *Ibid.,* Sept. 11, 1866.

And their candidate for governor, Pillsbury, was a prominent Copperhead who had been identified with draft riots
and had made himself offensive by verbal violence against
the War. No Republican or War Democrat, however strong
his approval of Johnson's policy, could support these men.
The psychological effect of this Maine election upon doubtful men in other states was important.[48]

In the remaining New England states, Radicals won huge
majorities; [49] it was New England's interests that their program best served. But even in these states Johnson would
have had strong support had there been a way of expressing it. His followers faced the usual dilemma of choosing
between a Radical and a Democrat. In Massachusetts the
Democrats seized even the Philadelphia movement. "The
natural leaders of a conservative party in Massachusetts
were conspicuously absent" from the state gathering of
Philadelphia men, wrote the *Springfield Republican*.[50] "Instead there were the old hack leaders of the Democratic
party . . . ; of Republicans who voted for Abraham Lincoln in either 1860 or 1864 hardly a dozen all told, and none
of these conservative in temperament or education." Francis
J. Parker wrote Johnson, "I believe that even Massachusetts
would cordially place the decision in your hands but one
party is so fully controlled by extreme men and the other by
opposition to the war is in so bad odor that most men like
myself find it impossible to make themselves felt through the
ordinary political channels." [51]

---

[48] It convinced the *Herald* of the hopelessness of Johnson's cause.

[49] New Hampshire and Rhode Island did not elect until 1867.

[50] "Mr. Winthrop was not there, nor Mr. Ticknor, nor Judge Curtis,
nor Judge Abbott, nor Mr. Ashmun, nor Caleb Cushing, nor any Lawrences,
nor any Adamses, nor any Lincolns, nor a Parker, nor any F. F's. of Boston or the Connecticut valley." Aug. 9, 1866, quoted in Edith E. Ware,
Political Opinion in Massachusetts during Civil War and Reconstruction,
163.

[51] Oct. 13, 1865, Johnson MSS., LXXIX.

The old Northwest, too, was carried by the Radicals, but not easily. In Ohio the Republicans were troubled by conflicting views and policies. In their convention, the Western Reserve delegates persistently demanded a negro suffrage plank and repudiation of Johnson. Conservatives wanted neither. Even Conservatives did not agree, however, for the Campbell-Geiger faction wanted to force the issue by standing firmly on Johnson's policy, while Governor Cox sought a compromise with the Radicals that would reunite the party. Cox was successful. Reservist delegates agreed to omit the negro suffrage plank; Conservatives gave up their demand for repudiation of the Fourteenth Amendment. Campbell and Geiger were disgusted.[52] But Cox was sanguine; he thought the platform "a real and substantial victory, which assures . . . final triumph." [53] A sorry victory it was, for it forced the Conservative Republicans to an organized effort to defeat at all hazards the nominees of their own party by coöperating with Democrats. Baber, chairman of their Committee of Five, hoped "by judicious management" to defeat "at least 8 or 10 of the Radical Congressmen." "It partly depends," he said, "on the co-operation the Democracy may give by allowing independent Johnson candidates to run. . . . The great want is to have a fair and square canvass on the merits of your Restoration Policy unembarrassed by old issues—it would tell on the country." [54]

[52] L. D. Campbell to A. Johnson, June 22, 1866, *ibid.*, XCVI.

[53] "It is better for what it omits than for what it contains. You will notice that it does not affirm that the acceptance of the Constitutional Amendment shall be a condition precedent to representation. It does not endorse any expected measure which Congress may add to its programme. It does not advocate or advise negro suffrage. It does not endorse any specific act of Congress whatever, but simply and solely 'the amendment as it stands and makes it a party measure in Ohio to vote for it." J. D. Cox to A. Johnson, June 21, 1866, *ibid.*, XCVI.

[54] R. P. L. Baber to A. Johnson, June 21 and 28, 1866, *ibid.*, XCVI.

The Democrats based their fight on the question of "whether less than one-third of the people should despotically govern more than two-thirds." "Civil war," they warned, "the disfranchisement of white men and the confiscation of their property as well as other dire calamities" would follow Radical victory.[55] They tried to arouse economic issues, but were unsuccessful.[56] The Radicals resorted to the usual abuse and firing of passions.[57] The appeal, however, which carried the state, Hayes made at Cincinnati when he assured his constituents that there were only two plans of reconstruction before the country—that of Lincoln and that of the rebels. "There was another . . . ," he said, "which may properly be called the Administration plan, [but it] never had many supporters outside of the influence of the executive patronage, and has now been . . . for all practical purposes, abandoned." [58] Here it was again Radical or Democrat. The Conservative Republicans coalesced with the Democrats in some districts, but always upon a Democratic candidate. Judge Thompson, chairman of the Democratic Central Committee, was a Vallandigham man who would support none but "regular Democratic nominees." [59] The outstanding candidate of the state was George Pendle-

[55] "Address of Democratic Executive Committee, Oct. 3, 1866," in Geo. H. Porter, *Ohio Politics during the Civil War Period*, 233.

[56] Hayes claimed these were "either unimportant . . . or matters which are in no sense party questions." R. B. Hayes, *Speech at Sidney, Ohio, Sept. 4, 1867.*

[57] Hayes was dignified and mild among Radicals; yet he urged opposition to Conservatives because "men who abused and hated negroes did not usually hate rebels." *Speech at Lebanon, Ohio, Aug. 5, 1866.* He told his constituents that Johnson's policy would mean ruin because a "rebellious people" would "demand compensation for their emancipated slaves" and "the repudiation of every national obligation to creditors and the nation's defenders, and their families." *Speech at Townhall in 17th Ward of Cincinnati, Sept. 7, 1866.*

[58] *Ibid.*

[59] R. P. L. Baber to A. Johnson, June 28, 1866, Johnson MSS., XCVI.

ton, who had been a "peace Democrat" and McClellan's running mate in 1864.

Nevertheless, the Radicals' victory was not overwhelming. They won sixteen out of nineteen representatives and an aggregate majority of 39,642; but some of the districts were always Radical by inheritance, and of the 39,642 majority, 22,133 were rolled up in the three Northeastern districts where the new manufacturing interests particularly in the Cleveland district, great wool-growing counties, and a concentration of the New England abolitionism, combined to make Radicalism so inevitable that the Moderate Republicans did not even enter the contest. Outside of these three districts the Democrats polled 47.8 per cent of the votes, and in the state as a whole actually 45.8 per cent. When Democrats and Moderate Republicans combined the next year on an "independent Republican" candidate for the vacancy created by Hayes's resignation, they reversed Hayes's majority of 2,558, and defeated the Radical by 959 votes. In that next year, too, the legislature elected to choose Wade's successor in the Senate was Democratic in both houses, and a Radical negro suffrage amendment was defeated by 50,629 votes.[60] An analysis, then, shows Ohio really for Johnson against the Radicals but with no means of expressing that preference.

The contest in Indiana was close and exciting, characterized by huge mass meetings, vituperation, and riots.[61] The Republican platform straddled the reconstruction quarrel by endorsing both Congress and the President. The Democrats condemned secession and praised Johnson.[62] The Radicals imported aid from far and near. Wilson of Massachusetts

[60] *Tribune Almanac* (1867), 59; (1868), 46.
[61] E.g., *New York Herald*, Oct. 5 and 18, 1866.
[62] Logan Esarey, *History of Indiana*, II, 820.

stumped the state abusing the President, but avoiding the negro suffrage issue.[63] Logan lent his soldierly popularity and malignant tongue to the cause. Julian toured the state making violent but effective speeches which stirred up hatred of Southerners by blood-curdling stories of their depravity.[64] Speaker Colfax returned from Washington in time to regale credulous crowds with the story that Mrs. Lee on a visit to Arlington had said that "when she got possession of the place not a Yankee bone should stay in the ground." [65]

Victory in Indiana was largely won, however, by one man —Governor Morton. He had stood with Johnson against the Radicals until June. Then rather than fraternize with Democrats he threw his vigor, his magnetic personality, and his prestige as war governor into the Radical balance. Although Indiana Republicans had generally supported Johnson against the small Julian faction of extremists, Morton's influence now converted them to Radicalism.[66] Even Julian, who distrusted him,[67] testified that his "vigor in action and great personal magnetism so rallied the people to his support, that with the rarest exceptions the prominent leaders of his party quietly succumbed to his ambition, and recoiled from the thought of confronting him, even when they believed him in the wrong." [68] Morton's key-note speech, on

63 E.g., his speech at Indianapolis, *New York Herald*, Sept. 24, 1866.

64 He preached negro suffrage and confiscation of Southern property, and threatened repudiation and civil war as the result of a Copperhead-rebel victory. G. W. Julian, *Speeches*.

65 *New York Herald*, Aug. 26, 1866. Mrs. Lee, who was an invalid in a wheel-chair, had not been to Arlington or Washington since 1861. Capt. Robert E. Lee, *Recollections and Letters of General Robert E. Lee*, 195-197, 235-251. But excited partisans did not think of that.

66 The *Herald*, Oct. 18, 1866, thought "no other man in the State could, in the short space of three months, have effected so complete a revolution in the public sentiment of the republican party."

67 He privately wrote Sumner, "Morton is a very aspiring and very much overrated politician." Oct. 11, 1865, Sumner MSS., LXXIV.

68 G. W. Julian, *Political Recollections*, 270.

the pronouncements of which the campaign was fought and won, is not a discussion of issues, but a bitter condemnation of rebels and Copperheads and a recitation of their past offenses.[69] Conservatives had no chance to express an opinion except to answer the challenge, "Will you put the Copperheads into power?"

Yet in spite of their stupendous effort and the odds in their favor, the Radicals won by only 12,445 out of 323,959 votes. They secured eight of the eleven Congressmen; but three of the eight won by less than one thousand votes, one by only 205 out of 29,661. The Democrats polled 48.8 per cent of the ballots.[70]

The Radicals won decisive majorities in the newer Western states where New England influence had always been strong. In Illinois and Missouri the vote was closer. A large factor in the success of Illinois Radicals [71] was the personal popularity and tireless campaigning of General Logan; by sheer dint of personality he swung the two "Egypt" districts, usually strongly Democratic, to the Radical side. In Missouri a registry law which Sherman termed "extremely Radical" disfranchised many of the Democrats, and riots, Radical militia manœuvers, suspicion, and fear, controlled the state. There, as in Kentucky and Tennessee, the election gave no clue to the feeling of the people. In Delaware the Democratic candidate was elected by 1,380 votes out of 18,486. Maryland Democrats won four out of five seats in Congress and a majority of 15,388 out of 69,224 votes.[72] No Confederate state but Tennessee was allowed representation in Congress.

* * * *

[69] O. P. Morton, *Speech Delivered at Masonic Hall . . . June 20, 1866.*
[70] *Tribune Almanac* (1867), 60.
[71] They secured ten out of thirteen Congressmen, and a popular majority of 54,254.
[72] *Tribune Almanac* (1867), 57 and 64.

The two largest and most important states were Pennsylvania and New York. Pennsylvania elected in October. Her Radicals nominated a popular general, J. W. Geary, for governor. To run against him the Democrats chose Heister Clymer, a widely known opponent of the War. There was the issue ready-made, and it did not take the Radicals long under the guidance of Kelly and Stevens to grasp their opportunity. The campaign was desperately fought.[73] The Radicals won by the small margin of 11,439 votes out of 596,141. They elected eighteen out of twenty-four members of Congress, but four of them by less than 1,000, and three of these by less than 500, majority. The Democrats told 292,-351, or over 49 per cent of the votes.[74]

"Look at the kind of man selected to run for governor," wrote Johnson's friend, Cochrane. "A *democrat* and an *opposer of the War* or simply a *secessionist:* and how could conservative men work with any heart for such a man.—The whole matter has been most bunglingly handled." [75] Truly did Wilson of Erie write Johnson, "The result of this election is a substantial victory for *you*—and had the *only* issue been with us, Congress or the President, *you* would have swept the state. Thousands who were your friends could not

[73] A sidelight on the methods is provided by a letter of Senator Cowan to the President. "I am contesting Penna. as well as I can," he wrote, "but we must have *some money* as it is impossible to contend with the Radicals who have thrown $13,000 into my Congressional District to elect Covoda over me, and my influence. I am poor myself and have no money to put into the issue of any acct. but I have found Maj. Hall who wants to be a paymaster and Wharton White who wants to be a Lieut. (2nd) in the Army and they each agree to give for the purposes of election $2000,—each, this will enable me to pay the expenses of speakers who have been speaking day and night and to pay canvassers and wagons to bring out the votes of 2 or 3 close districts in this State." Oct. 1, 1866, Johnson MSS., CII.

[74] *Tribune Almanac* (1867), 62.

[75] October, 1866, Johnson MSS., CV. "Thousands of the supporters of President Johnson," said the *Herald* (Sept. 19, 1866), "can not conscientiously vote for Heister Clymer, and the President himself cannot desire the defeat of such a candidate as Geary."

be induced to vote for Clymer and other anti-war Democrats." [76]

In New York, the Philadelphia Convention men went
actively to work to organize a separate Conservative group
that would be neither Radical nor Democratic. Preparatory
to nominating conventions, a Philadelphia committee and a
Democratic committee met in Albany to work out details.
After a long discussion they decided to hold two simultaneous
conventions and agree upon candidates, but to keep the
Philadelphia movement independent of the Democrats so
that all Conservative Republicans might support it. Weed
left for New York, and then the Democrats pressed the
Philadelphia men into rescinding the earlier plan of two
simultaneous meetings, in favor of one joint convention.
Weed, dismayed, called a caucus at the Astor House which
decided to summon separate simultaneous conventions anyway. The next day Dean Richmond conferred with Weed and
others and persuaded them to hold a joint convention after
all. [77] Richmond recognized the wisdom of coöperation with
Johnson Republicans, but before the Convention met, his
death removed the one man in the New York Democracy
who could have controlled the Democrats in the joint convention that met September 11.

Without Richmond to guide it, that body fell victim to
the intrigues of political cliques. Among various factional
candidates for the governorship, two were important, Hoffman and Dix. Hoffman, the Tammany nominee, represented
the Democratic machine and had a dubious war record.
Dix, the choice of the Philadelphia Convention Republicans,
was a highly respected War Democrat who had been a

[76] Oct. 11, 1866, Johnson MSS., CIII.
[77] *New York Herald*, Aug. 22, 26, and 31, 1866.

popular general. Weeks before, Johnson had picked him out as an ideal candidate and had suggested him to Bennett of the *Herald*, who approved and began a persistent campaign for his nomination.[78]

When the Convention met, the Tammany forces tried to force an adjournment until the next day, because they feared Dix's nomination if a vote were taken at once, but hoped that before the morrow his country support would get discouraged over expenses, and go home. Adjournment was defeated in the morning by a large vote. But before any business was transacted at the afternoon session, the motion was repeated. It was clearly voted down, but Church, the Tammany temporary chairman, declared the meeting adjourned, put on his hat, and left the hall. Bedlam broke loose. Out of it came cheers for Hoffman and hisses and groans for Dix, probably all from the roughs Tammany had imported. The hisses and scurrilous attacks made on him later in the day discouraged Dix's supporters. But Tammany played its trump card the next day, when, in seconding Hoffman's nomination, Judge Pierrepont announced that he was authorized to withdraw the name of "that gallant, excellent, noble, perfect gentleman and statesman, . . . General Dix, . . . my personal friend, whom I respect, whom I personally like." It was inconceivable that Dix's friends should entrust the withdrawal of his name to an opponent. Pierrepont had from the first supported Hoffman. Weed was chagrined; he claimed that both he and Richmond had understood that "the Democratic party consented, for the accomplishment of a great national reform, to temporarily merge itself in the National Union Movement."[79] Dix maintained dignified

[78] W. B. Phillips to A. Johnson, Aug. 7, Sept. 3, 1866, Johnson MSS., XCIX, C.

[79] *New York Times,* Oct. 9, 1866.

silence, but his letter to Johnson indicates that he did not withdraw, and his son testifies that Pierrepont acted without his father's "knowledge or consent." But the trick worked. The effect was immediate—Hoffman was nominated and the election was lost.[80]

In New York, then, in spite of the efforts of the Philadelphians, Conservatives had no means of expressing their preference. Hoffman was a "Copperhead"; he was a Tammany man at a time when bitterness between Tammany and upstaters made a Tammany connection disastrous. Certainty of his defeat sent the *Herald* scurrying to the support of the Radicals.[81] Even ex-Governor Seymour refused to support him.[82] Again the choice was between a Copperhead and a Radical. Intelligent observers were certain that the Conservative Party would have carried the state had Dix been nominated. Dix himself wrote Johnson, "I foresaw the inevitable result in this State from the moment that the democratic party was put prominently forward in the Albany Convention as the leading interest to be promoted. The understanding at Philadelphia was that in the movement we were inaugurating we were to follow the lead of the Conservative republicans. Our failure in this State is due to the utter selfishness and folly of the democratic managers."[83] Yet the defeat was not decisive. The Conservatives elected

[80] This account is taken from the *New York Herald*, the *New York Tribune*, and the *New York Times*, for Sept. 12 and 13, 1866. See also H. A. Stebbins, *Political History of New York*, 99-105, 112; DeAlva S. Alexander, *Political History of the State of New York, III*, 156-159; and Morgan Dix, *Memoirs of John A. Dix*, II, 173.

[81] W. B. Phillips to A. Johnson, Sept. 16, 1866, Johnson MSS., CI. The *Herald* (Sept. 29, 1866) commented, "The people wanted a man of broad, comprehensive views, able to cast aside partisan considerations and think and act for the good of the country." They got "a narrow, hidebound partisan, belonging to a little clique, in a little ring, in a little corner of this city. How . . . can they vote for him?"

[82] *Ibid.*, Oct. 23, 1866.

[83] Nov. 8, 1866, Johnson MSS., CV.

twelve, and the Radicals nineteen, of thirty-one Congressmen. The Radical majority was only 22,092 out of 713,018 votes.[84] In the only two districts [85] where the Conservative Republicans did have candidates of their own they were elected.

In no Northern state did Johnson men have means of expressing their preference. The election did not decide that men favored the Radical rather than the Conservative plan of reconstruction, but that they disliked Copperheads more than Radicals. One may well exclaim with Dix in his condolent letter to Johnson, "How aggrieved you have a right to feel by the selfish policy of making the success of your measure to tranquilize the country and place the government on its constitutional footing, secondary to personal and local interests." [86]

* * * *

In the face of the decisive Radical victory, why did Johnson not accept the situation and urge the Southern States to make the best of it by ratifying the Fourteenth Amendment?

This study of the election provides a partial answer. Johnson realized that there were many vital issues before the country beside the much discussed Amendment: the larger question whether to restore or remake the South, the remodeling of our government into a centralized parliamentary form, negro suffrage, the tariff, the currency, national banks, the incidence of taxation, governmental extravagance, funding of the debt, control of monopolies, government aid to corporations, regulation of railroads and of nascent big

[84] *Tribune Almanac* (1867), 52.
[85] One of these was the strongly Republican up-state twenty-eighth district.
[86] Nov. 8, 1866, Johnson MSS., CV.

business. To read into the election a clear verdict on *any* of these was presumptuous.

Johnson saw how successful the Radicals had been in conjuring up bogies to play upon Northern fears, and in using the excitement which they had aroused to conceal the issues behind a screen of misrepresentation and vituperation. He was only too painfully aware that the Radical purpose had been abetted by his own tactical mistakes: bungling of the patronage power,[87] failure to organize a moderate third party early in the struggle, his own campaign speeches, and his failure to counteract the anti-Southern sectional hatred that the Radicals invoked, by exploiting Western distrust of the Northeast on economic questions.[88] Too late Johnson realized that he should have kept steadily before the public an explicit statement of his objections to the Amendment, his willingness to accept certain of its principles once the excluded states were back, his recognition that Congress had

[87] Too late to benefit him, but just in time to create a bad psychological effect on the eve of election, Johnson did begin making removals (e.g., in Iowa, *New York Herald*, Aug. 22, 1866); and worse yet, he put Democrats in some of the places vacated. Welles and Weed urged against these last-minute removals, and Sherman accredited much of the discontent in Congress in December to them. G. Welles to ——, Sept. 25, 1866, Welles MSS., LXII; T. Weed to A. Johnson, Oct. 2, 1866, Johnson MSS., CII; J. Sherman to W. T. Sherman, March 14, 1867, W. T. Sherman MSS., XX.

[88] Men like Sumner, Wilson, and Stevens were perpetually doing and saying things that, save for the overshadowing reconstruction problem, would have turned the West against them. The West felt a latent hostility toward the East that, if utilized, might have rent the Radical Party in two. This sectional jealousy infected at once so moderate a man as General Sherman, who wrote his brother, "It won't do to impose pure New England notions on the West and South" (March 24, 1866, W. T. Sherman MSS., XVIII); and so inveterate a Radical as Julian, who urged confiscation of the lands of Southern planters to prevent "rich Yankees" from getting possession of them. "I don't want to abuse the Yankees," he said, "for they have made this country what it is; but there are Yankees who believe that the almighty dollar is the only living and true God, and it is said some of them would wade into the mouth of hell after a bale of cotton . . . There are men who would go down and buy up these estates, and establish a system of wages-slavery, of serfdom over the poor, that would be as intolerable as the old system of servitude." G. W. Julian, *Speeches*, 269. The depths of sectional feeling that separated New England and the West were never even sounded.

full power to pass upon the qualifications of its members, his approval of the exclusion of prominent and unpardoned rebels, and agitators, and his willingness to acquiesce in a Congressional test for members, provided Congress applied it to individuals and admitted from *all* states any members who conformed. Johnson knew that the election had voiced opinion on none of the issues, not even on the Fourteenth Amendment. He felt certain that on many of the issues which Radical tactics had evaded, and above all on the question of a Southern policy, public opinion would have backed him against the Radical leaders if only the smoke could have been cleared away and the issue fairly faced.

Nevertheless the people had elected a Congress that would be almost omnipotent. The part of wisdom seemed to be for the South to accept the inevitable, and ratify the Amendment. The terms were hard, but in the face of election returns the South could not hope for better, and might by opposition invoke even worse. So reasoned many of the South's best friends and Johnson's advisers. However obnoxious the Amendment was, if Johnson, their only hope, had urged Southerners to submit to it in order to get back into the Union, it would have been accepted.[89] Because Johnson did not follow this course, he has been almost universally condemned,[90] even by historians who agree with his earlier position. He has been denounced for staking his policy upon the people's verdict and then failing to abide thereby. By pride of opinion and pigheadedness, say his accusers, he brought upon the South the disaster of ten years of reconstruction. These critics overlook one determining fact: Johnson did de-

[89] E.g., General Sickles testified, "North and South Carolina would have adopted it, if [the President] had favored the acceptance of that vital guarantee of peace and Union." G. D. E. Sickles to E. M. Stanton, July 19, 1866, Stanton MSS., XXX.
[90] See e.g., J. F. Rhodes, *op. cit.,* VI, 5.

cide at election time not to oppose the Amendment; then shortly before Congress convened, he became convinced that acquiescence was futile.

In defeat Johnson atoned in dignity and calmness of judgment for the excesses of his Chicago trip. In the face of conflicting counsel [91] from equally trustworthy sources, Johnson listened patiently, held his tongue, and prepared his message. Through October and November thousands were advising him and predicting what his course would be, but nobody knew what decision he had really made.

The message Johnson prepared was able, conciliatory, and wise. Not once did he criticize Congress for its past acts. He reviewed what he had done toward reconstruction; he recited the evidences of renewed Southern loyalty. "The people of the States which have thus been reorganized," he told Congress, "have, without exception, chosen Senators and Representatives to represent their several States and districts in the two Houses of Congress. Of those so chosen, the Senators and Representatives of the State of Tennessee have been admitted to seats, while those appointed by other States are awaiting the action of the Houses of Congress upon their credentials." Then in the friendliest manner he continued, "It belongs exclusively to Congress to decide upon the eligibility of the person so chosen and it is believed that the persons so chosen as well as their constituencies are ready and willing to acquiesce in and conform themselves to the decisions respecting which the Senate and House of Representatives shall pronounce." He next told of the submission of the Fourteenth Amendment to the states, and listed the states

[91] Phillips of the *Herald* personally (Oct. 7, Nov. 8, 1866, Johnson MSS., CIII, CV), the *New York Herald* editorially (Sept. 13 and 15, 1866), and ex-Governor Cox of Ohio (June 21, 1866, Johnson MSS., XCVI), urged Johnson to accept the Amendment. Welles (MS. Diary, Dec. 4, 1866) advised continued opposition.

that had ratified, and those that had rejected it. Instead of commenting upon it himself, he took an entirely new departure. "A careful survey of our social condition," he suggested, "sustains the belief that the United States have now no exceptional or unusual domestic disturbances to apprehend, and that our attention may therefore be directed to financial and other measures having for their objects amelioration of the burdens, and a removal of the restraints which the late civil war unavoidably rendered necessary, and the sure and steady development of the resources of the continent. In all judicious and constitutional measures directed to that end, I can promise Congress my cheerful concurrence and cooperation." He pictured the need of industry and enterprise in the South, and the prosperity that might accrue to the whole nation from a development of Southern resources. Without a suggestion that Congress had sought to interfere, he conceded that "exceptional interference" in the local affairs of states, and proscriptions and disabilities, were effective weapons, the use of which during civil war to embarrass and defeat insurgents was legitimate. But he warned Congress that the continued employment of these war-time expedients after the War had ceased and those who had been misled into revolution had again become loyal to the Union, "would in every way be injurious to the public safety and welfare and inconsistent with the Constitution." "The interest, passions and sentiments," he concluded, "which for so long a time, and so deeply alienated the population of different portions of the nation, have proved to be transient and epherial, while the necessity for constant and perfect union is absolute and eternal." [92]

[92] MS. draft of Message not sent to Congress, Johnson MSS., "Messages," IV.

Sometime between November 17 when he dated a proclamation that was to have accompanied the original message,[93] and November 30 when he read the final draft in cabinet, Johnson rewrote his message. The conciliatory tone of the earlier document was gone, as were the suggestion that reconstruction troubles were about to end and his promise of "cheerful concurrence and cooperation" if Congress would lead in a new consideration of "financial and other matters." The new message ignored the Amendment and the election, reviewed the old quarrel with Congress, and calmly but sternly criticized Congress for its failure to admit Southern members. The message actually delivered met Congress with futile and bitter defiance.

At the same time Johnson abandoned his position of neutrality on the Amendment, and actually advised the South not to ratify. When in December Governor Perry of Alabama recommended ratification, and a favorable vote seemed likely, ex-Governor Parsons consulted Johnson in Washington, and then sent a telegram urging the Legislature not to ratify,[94] whereupon the Legislature adjourned without a vote. When the question did come up after the holidays, Johnson wired Parsons, "What possible good can be attained by reconsidering the Constitutional Amendment. I know of none in the present posture of affairs. I do not believe that the people of the whole country will sustain any set of individuals in attempts to change the whole character of our Government, by enabling acts or otherwise. I believe, on the

[93] The message mentions as issued a proclamation which was further to decrease the excepted classes, leaving exceptions much like those of the second bill that originally accompanied the Amendment in Congress. The proclamation was never issued, but was written, and remains to help date Johnson's rejection of this message. *Ibid.*, "Proclamations."

[94] W. Swayne to S. P. Chase, Dec. 10, 1866, "Chase Correspondence," Am. Hist. Assoc., *Annual Report* (1902), 516; *New York Herald*, Dec. 8, 1866.

contrary, that they will eventually uphold all who have patriotism and courage to stand by the Constitution, and who place their confidence in the people. There should be no faltering on the part of those who are honest in Co-ordinate Departments of the Government, in accordance with its original design." [95]

The Radical attitude explains Johnson's change of program. From the beginning it had been doubtful whether Congress would admit Southerners even if they did ratify the Amendment. The Radicals had won the election upon the understanding that the Amendment presented their final terms of readmission of Southerners.[96] The admission of Tennessee had made this plausible. But the bill guaranteeing admission upon ratification was tabled. Extreme Radicals had refused to bind themselves by promises [97] and regarded the Amendment as merely a first step in their full program for subjugating the South.

Victory merely emboldened these men for new extremes. They redoubled their attacks on Johnson. "Let us pray to God," urged Wendell Phillips, "that the President may continue to make mistakes, that he may continue to speak, and that his text may be furnished by the people of the South." "Congress, before they look at the Amendment or utter the word reconstruction, [should] impeach the Rebel in the White House." [98] Shortly after the election, Butler actually

---

[95] Jan. 17, 1867, Stanton MSS., XXXI.

[96] E.g., Hayes (*Speech at Lebanon, Aug. 5, 1867*), Sherman (*The Sherman Letters*, 271, 284), the *New York Herald* (Sept. 21, 1866), and the *Cincinnati Commercial* (Sept. 26, 1866).

[97] E.g., Stevens, who said, "Remember that I do not say, and never mean to, that when these amendments, which I now propose, are adopted the rebel States shall be allowed to come in until they present constitutions containing the essence of liberty." Speech at Lancaster, *New York Herald*, Sept. 29, 1866.

[98] *Ibid.*, Nov. 7, 1866; speech at Cooper Institute, *New York Tribune*, Oct. 26, 1866.

listed charges of impeachment.[99] Wendell Phillips described
the Radical program when he said, "Reconstruction . . .
means that North making over that South in its likeness, till
South Carolina gravitates by natural tendency to New England. . . . The South must be won to the capital and to the
energy, to the brains and to the habits of the North. . . .
Reconstruction begins when the South yields up her idea of
civilization, and allows the North to permeate her channels
and to make her over, throughout the route which victory
has given to the better and the dominant idea. . . . Until
that process commences, reconstruction has not commenced."
Anything else is "only rebellion in a new form." [1]

But Radical leaders did not confine themselves to words.
Stevens wrote to trusted co-workers, urging subjugation of
the South and proposing a conference of assured extremists
preliminary to the party caucus.[2] Several days before Con-

[99] *New York Herald*, Nov. 25, 1866.

[1] Speech at Cooper Institute, *New York Tribune*, Oct. 26, 1866.

[2] Broomall's answer is instructive. "I have received and read yours of
October 16th.," he writes Stevens, "with a good deal of interest and
thought much of the plan you propose. If a consultation could be brought
about among fifteen or twenty of the radical members and Senators without
its appearing that the remainder were excluded I can see that great good
might result from it. A caucus of the entire party would result in nothing,
as we both well know. Bingham and myself would agree upon nothing.
You would help me to disagree. I take it that the inevitable question—
whether all the adult males of the South are to be consulted in the reconstruction, will find you the leader on one side and Bingham on the
other . . . Now if we could get together those who would be upon *our*
side of that question alone I would like it very much but after the first
dozen who can tell who they are. Would it not be better if you agree with
me in thinking this to be the great question coming for us to communicate
by letter with Boutwell, Kelly, Williams, Wilson of Iowa and such others
as we feel sure of, and getting an interchange of views without a caucus
which if general will amount to nothing and if selected will look like forestalling opinion in the party. I regret that the public press persisted in
putting forth the Constitutional Amendment as the terms of reconstruction.
I never assented to that proposition. It will go hard with me to consent
to any reconstruction against the will of the loyal men of the South of
either race. The Amendment is the means of protection of the Government
and the North. It will do no good to the loyal majority of the South, three-
fourths of whom are disfranchised. Please think of these things and write
me. If you still think a conference desirable I will yield to your better
judgment and aid in bringing it about." Oct. 27, 1866, Stevens MSS., VIII.

gress met, Stevens and his friends were in Washington organizing their forces to secure military rule, negro suffrage, impeachment, and the other drastic measures that the next year and a half witnessed. Completely ignoring Radical campaign pledges in regard to the Amendment, they now claimed that it had never been intended for more than a first step, and that the election had given them a mandate from the people to proceed to whatever extremes they could concoct.

Somehow the shrewd Washington correspondent of the *Herald* learned of the significant first message whose existence was unknown to future historians. On December 4 that paper printed inconspicuously a news item which seems to explain Johnson's position. "The more intimate friends of the President," it ran, "assert today that his message as sent to Congress, in all that relates to our domestic troubles, is an entirely different document from that first prepared. The Johnson party now say that on the appearance of Thad Stevens here last week in his great efforts to forestall the action of Congress by committing individual members to extreme measures of hostility to the administration, the President saw but little likelihood of any favorable reception of such conciliatory propositions as he had designed making, and inasmuch as but kicks and cuffs were to be his portion, he could receive such treatment with better advantage on his own grounds. Hence he revised the message and reasserted his former line of policy."

Welles undoubtedly voiced administration opinion when he wrote, "The extreme Radicals are very vindictive and revolutionary. Their language in regard to the President is such as shows the unfitness for their places, and [is] most disgraceful to the country. This will be likely to work its own cure; certainly will if the President does not temporize under bad advisers." [3]

Probably it made little difference which message Johnson used. The election had given the Radical Congress complete power over President and South alike, and Congress seemed already determined to proceed to extremes. The significant fact is that the election which gave it this power was not a popular referendum upon Johnsonian and Radical plans of reconstruction. A study of that campaign shows that the Radicals forced their program upon the South by an evasion of issues and the clever use of propaganda in an election where a majority of the voters would have supported Johnson's policy had they been given a chance to express their preference on an issue squarely faced.

[3] Welles MS. Diary, Dec. 4, 1866—(II, 632).

BIBLIOGRAPHY

NO ATTEMPT has been made to list all of the works dealing with the early reconstruction period, or even all of those that a study of the temper of the times made it necessary to peruse. Only those which have been specifically useful are given. Many speeches, pamphlets, and contemporary histories have been included which are prejudiced, repetitious, and historically untrustworthy, but none the less important in understanding what influences determined the popular choice between Johnson and the Radicals.

MANUSCRIPTS

Most useful of the manuscript collections are the Johnson papers in the Library of Congress. They contain some fifty-one volumes of bound letters received during the years 1865 and 1866, a volume of "Executive Mansion Letters" containing copies of outgoing correspondence, two volumes of "Telegrams" preserving the messages exchanged between Johnson and the civil and military authorities in the South, two volumes of "Messages" including the original conciliatory message that was not delivered in December, 1866, a volume of draft proclamations, and a "Scrap-book." Unfortunately the letter-books of outgoing correspondence were lost by a New York woman to whom Johnson's family had loaned them. During his presidency Johnson suffered from writer's cramp and therefore wrote little; that little was always in pencil. Few, then, of the President's own letters remain. But his other papers were preserved with meticulous care; in fact, it was he who first systematized the filing arrangements of the executive offices. His correspondence was voluminous. Many of his letters, to be sure, were from office-seekers and unknown, unsought advisers. But even these present a full and varied record of all shades of opinion.

Equally valuable are the Sumner manuscripts at Harvard. They include nine chronologically arranged volumes of miscellaneous letters received during 1865 and 1866, and separate volumes of letters from Governor Andrew, S. P. Chase, R. H. Dana, Wendell Phillips, and others. The Sumner collection is extremely important because of the extensive correspondence that that Senator carried on with leading Radicals throughout the country. Again the absence of press copies of his own letters is regrettable. Copies of the illuminating Schurz-Sumner letters are also at Harvard, only some of which were printed in Schurz's *Correspondence.*

The Welles papers in the Library of Congress are indispensable in a study like this. They contain bound volumes of letters received, two volumes of letter-book copies of letters sent, a volume of newspaper clippings, seven volumes of articles prepared for publication, and the manuscript of the famous diary. Welles, as Secretary of the Navy under both Lincoln and Johnson, was an important figure. Furthermore, he maintained intimate friendships with men of all shades of opinion in Connecticut and Washington, even with political enemies like Sumner. His correspondence is large, and his diary, kept with scrupulous care, provides an unequaled record of public affairs. It is necessary, however, to use the manuscript diary, as the printed edition includes, as of the original text, many emendations, corrections, and additions, and makes a few important omissions.[1] For this reason quotations and citations from the diary are always from the manuscript. For the sake of convenience, the parallel reference to the printed *Diary* is given in parentheses, if, as is usually the case, there is a printed form that approximately follows the original.

Other manuscript collections in the Library of Congress proved useful. The Salmon P. Chase papers contain both letters received, and letter-press copies of letters written in Chase's own almost illegible hand. The original papers of Senator J. R. Doolittle of Wisconsin are few, but the Library has transcriptions from the letters in Duane Mowry's possession. The Thos. Ewing collection is made up of bound volumes of letters received and letter-press copies of those sent. This veteran Democrat, who had turned Republican during the War, was at home in Ohio in 1865 and 1866 actively corresponding with leaders of the Conservative movement in Washington. The W. P. Fessenden and the Horace Greeley collections contain a few letters of importance. The Joseph Holt manuscripts give an admirable indication of the hysteria which seized the country after Lincoln's death. Francis Lieber's and George B. McClellan's papers afford little that is useful. The Hugh McCulloch collection is small but important. Edward McPherson's papers consist chiefly of essays and speeches by that gentleman. The papers of Senator John Sherman of Ohio are not as complete as one would wish. But his position as a leading Mod-

[1] See the author's article, "Is the Printed Diary of Gideon Welles Reliable?", *Amer. Hist. Rev.*, XXX (April, 1925), 547.

erate who felt himself forced into Radicalism, makes his letters important. Especially valuable are several from his brother, W. T. Sherman. His brother's papers comprise a large collection. Unfortunately it is less complete for this period than for the War, but it does contain important letters from his senator-brother. Not many of the papers of Edwin M. Stanton are preserved. That gentleman probably discreetly destroyed the most illuminating ones. But the importance of his position as Secretary of War, his treachery to Johnson, and his close connection with leading Radicals make what papers do remain, significant. The Thaddeus Stevens papers are not numerous but contain valuable material. Those of Senator Lyman Trumbull give Illinois opinion on public questions. More valuable, however, is the collection of Elihu B. Washburne. Unfortunately his papers are badly arranged. They were bound before they came to the Library of Congress, without regard to chronology or any other easily determinable scheme. But they do give many examples of Illinois political sentiment. A few scattered letters to Henry Wilson of Massachusetts complete the tale.

Beside the Welles diary, the Library of Congress possesses several other interesting journals. The diaries of Edmund Ruffin, a rabid Southerner who finally closed his record by ending his life because of the South's defeat, and of William Owner, who wrote in Washington, both present the extreme Southern point of view. The journal of a Northerner named McCarter who had lived in South Carolina for several years presents one of the few trustworthy accounts of the South after the War. McCarter was sympathetic toward the South and liked Southerners, and yet he saw their weaknesses. He was critical, yet friendly. He seems to have written entirely free from prejudice or bias. Several years' life in the South and first-hand information in the days after the War enabled him to write with knowledge. The private diary of Gen. Cyrus B. Comstock, Grant's aide, who traveled widely in the South during 1865 and 1866, gives further reliable testimony.

PERIODICALS

Newspapers were important not only in gathering information, but in studying the factors that influenced men of 1866 in choosing between Johnson and the Radicals. Newspapers were themselves a powerful element among those factors. The great New York dailies exercised an important influence throughout the North. Of these the *World* was in disgrace and could affect no one not already a determined Democrat. But Greeley's *Tribune*, almost a Bible unto the Radicals, was powerful, and has been extensively used in this work, both in its daily form and in the semi-weekly edition that reached the rural districts. The *Times* expressed orthodox yet moderate Republican opinion, but was less influential. Most useful for this work, however, was the *Herald*, daily and weekly. Its sensationalism led it to gather much material that the others did not discover. Its desire for popularity induced it to try to read and follow the majority opinion. James Gordon Bennett, its editor, had an uncanny faculty for sensing public sentiment. Its freedom from party affiliations made the *Herald* more independent and hence more trustworthy than the party sheets. Its avidity in news-gathering made it the most nearly modern paper of the day. The *Chicago Tribune*, ably edited and more liberal than in recent years, was already the most powerful organ of the Middle West, and has been extensively used in both daily and tri-weekly editions. It combined extreme Radicalism on reconstruction with dislike of high protection. The *Hendricks County Union* of Danville, Indiana, has been consulted throughout the period as an example of a Western country paper. Besides, scattered issues of other newspapers have been used: the *Boston Daily Advertiser*, the *Boston Evening Commercial*, the *Boston Evening Transcript*, the *Boston Pilot* (Catholic), the *Chicago Times*, the *Commercial and Financial Chronicle* of New York, the *Cincinnati Commercial*, the *Detroit Free Press*, the *Illinois State Journal* of Springfield, the *Memphis Commercial and Argus*, the *Norristown Herald* of Pennsylvania, the *National Intelligencer* of Washington, the *Evening Post* of New York, the *Ledger* and the *Press* of Philadelphia, the *Springfield Republican*, the *Universe* (Catholic) of Philadelphia, and the *Utica Herald*. These random issues were found in the American Antiquarian Society Library, the Widener Library at Harvard, the New York Public Library, the Chicago Public Library, the John Crerar Library of Chicago, and in scrap-books at Harvard and in the Library of Congress. Particularly valuable are Johnson's and Welles's scrap-books, a collection of clippings of Sumner, and scrap-books compiled by Charles E. Norton.

Edward McPherson's annual *Political Manual* contains valuable reprints of public documents, messages, telegrams, proclamations, state laws, and letters. The *Tribune Almanac* and Appleton's *American Annual Cyclopaedia* are useful and reliable. *Harper's Weekly* with G. W. Curtis as its editor and Thomas Nast as its inimitable cartoonist was the great popular periodical of the day. The *Atlantic Monthly*, the *Christian Examiner*, the *Galaxy*, first appearing in 1866, the *Independent* edited in New York by Theodore Tilton, the

Nation established in 1865 by a group of Liberals and Radicals under the editorship of E. L. Godkin, and the rather heavy *North American Review* under James Russell Lowell, each had its public. All were interested in the problems of reconstruction and the quarrel between Johnson and the Radicals. None was friendly to Johnson.

GOVERNMENT DOCUMENTS

Of public documents of the United States, James D. Richardson, *A Compilation of the Messages and Papers of the Presidents* (*House Misc. Docs.*, 53 Cong., 2 Sess., ser. no. 3265, doc. no. 210), and the *Congressional Globe* for the years 1860 to 1868 are the most valuable. There is also a *Congressional Directory* for each year. Among the *Senate Executive Documents* are a number of important papers including some of Johnson's veto messages, Grant's, Schurz's and Ben. C. Truman's reports to Johnson on conditions in the South (39 Cong., 1 Sess., ser. no. 1237, doc. no. 2, and ser. no. 1238, doc. no. 43), and an important "Report of the Special Commissioner of the Revenue" made by David A. Wells in December, 1866 (39 Cong., 2 Sess., ser. no. 1276, doc. no. 2). The *House Executive Documents* include other veto messages, the "Annual Reports of the Secretary of the Treasury" of which the one for 1896 (54 Cong., 2 Sess., ser. no. 3498, doc. no. 8) contains statistics important for this study, the "Report of the Commissioner of Agriculture for the year 1866" (39 Cong., 2 Sess., ser. no. 1297, doc. no. 107), D. A. Wells, "Report of the Special Commissioner of Revenue" for 1867 (40 Cong., 2 Sess., ser. no. 1332, doc. no. 81), and an important "Report of the U. S. Revenue Commission" (39 Cong., 1 Sess., ser. no.

1255, doc. no. 34). The *Reports of the Committees of the House of Representatives* contain the "Report of the Joint Committee on Reconstruction" (39 Cong., 1 Sess., ser. no. 1273, doc. no. 30), a most important document, also printed and distributed as a separate publication, and the *Impeachment Investigation—Testimony Taken before the Judiciary Committee of the House . . . in the Investigation of the Charges against Andrew Johnson* (40 Cong., 1 Sess., ser. no. 1314, doc. no. 7). The *Census* for 1860 and 1870, the *Statistical Abstracts*, especially the first one, published in 1878, and the *U. S. Statutes at Large* are useful.

Of the many state documents of the period, those giving state laws in regard to negroes, and those furnishing agricultural and industrial statistics are the most important. The *Illinois Session Laws* for the years 1845 to 1867, the *Revised Statutes of the State of Illinois* for 1865, the *Indiana House Journal, Indiana Senate Journal*, the *Brevier Report* of the Indiana Legislature for 1865, and the *Indiana Session Laws* from 1845 to 1867 give the first kind of information. A compilation of the State Department of Michigan entitled *Statistics of the State of Michigan* for the years 1860 and 1870, the *Annual Reports* of the Ohio Commissioner of Statistics, the *Annual Reports* of the Ohio Secretary of State and the *Annual Reports* of the Ohio State Board of Agriculture provide the second.

PRINTED WRITINGS OF CONTEMPORARIES

Most important among collections of writings of contemporaries is James D. Richardson, *Messages and Papers of the Presidents* (see documents), printed for sale in 11 volumes (Bureau of Nat. Lit. and Art, 1908). Walter L. Fleming, *Documentary History of Reconstruction, Political, Military, Religious, Educational, and Industrial, 1865 to the Present Time* (2 vols., A. H. Clark, Cleveland, 1906-07) is useful, as is Edward McPherson, *Political Manual* (D. C. Philp & Solomons, Wash., annually, 1866-69). Other important collections are: James G. Blaine, *Political Discussions, Legislative, Diplomatic, and Popular, 1856-1886* (Henry Bill, Norwich, 1887); *Speeches of Andrew Johnson*, with a biographical introduction by Frank Moore (Little, Brown, Boston, 1866); Geo. W. Julian, *Speeches on Political Questions*, 1850-68 (Hurd & Houghton, N. Y., 1872); *Complete Works of Abraham Lincoln*, eds., John G. Nicolay and John Hay (12 vols., F. D. Tandy, N. Y., 1905); Carl Schurz, *Speeches, Correspondence, Political Papers*, ed., Frederic Bancroft (6 vols., Putnam's, 1913); *Home Letters of General Sherman*, ed., M. A. De W. Howe (Scribner's, 1909); *The Sherman Letters; Correspondence between General and Senator Sherman from 1837 to 1891*, ed., Rachel S. Thorndike (Scribner's, 1894); *Works of Charles Sumner* (15 vols., Lee and Shephard, Boston, 1875-94); "Diary and Correspondence of Salmon P. Chase," Amer. Hist. Assoc., *Annual Report*, 1902, II; "The Correspondence of Robert Toombs, Alexander H. Stephens, and Howell Cobb," Amer. Hist. Assoc., *Annual Report*, 1911, II, and letters of Dix and Doolittle in "Some Political Letters of the Reconstruction Days Succeeding the Civil War," *Amer. Historical Mag. (Americana)*, IV, 331-336.

The most important printed diary of the period is the *Diary of Gideon Welles, Secretary of the Navy under Lincoln and Johnson* (3 vols., Houghton Mifflin, 1911). "Extracts from the Journal of Henry J. Raymond" published in *Scribner's*, XX (1880), 275, also proved useful.

A number of reports of observers of conditions in the South were printed and given wide circulation during the campaign of 1866. Most important among these are: Sidney Andrews, *The South since the War as Shown by Fourteen Weeks of Travel and Observation in Georgia and the Carolinas* (Ticknor & Fields, Boston, 1866) ; U. S. Grant, *Letter Concerning Affairs in the South* (Gov. Printing Office, 1865) ; Whitelaw Reid, *After the War: a Southern Tour* (Moore, Wilstach & Baldwin, Cincinnati, 1866) ; Carl Schurz, *Report on the States of South Carolina, Georgia, Alabama, Mississippi and Louisiana* (Gov. Printing Office, 1865) ; John T. Trowbridge, *The South: a Tour of its Battle-fields and Ruined Cities, a Journey through the Desolated States and Talks with the People* (L. Stebbins, Hartford, 1866) ; and Ben C. Truman, *Report on the Condition of the South* (Gov. Printing Office, 1866).

Reports of two political conventions of 1866 were printed as campaign material: *Proceedings of the National Union Convention, Held at Philadelphia, August 14, 1866* (Nat. Union Ex. Com. Phila., 1866), and *The Southern Loyalists' Convention, Philadelphia, 1866* (McGill & Witherow, 1866). Business men and farmers alike were organizing into associations. The reports of some of these and of their meetings were published: American Iron and Steel Association, *Bulletins* (Phila., weekly, 1866-1912) ; John L. Hayes, *Address before the National Association of Wool Manufacturers at the First Annual Meeting in Phila., Sept. 6, 1865* (J. Wilson, Cambridge, 1865) ; J. L. Hayes, *Protection a Boon to Consumers: an Address Delivered before the National Association of Knit Goods Manufacturers, May 1, 1867* (J. Wilson, Boston, 1867) ; *Joint Report of the Executive Committee of the National Association of Wool Manufac-*

turers, and the Executive Committee of the National Wool-growers' Association, Addressed to the United States Reve-nue Commission, Feb. 9, 1866 (J. Wilson, 1866) ; National Association of Wool Manufacturers, *Annual Reports* (J. Wilson, 1865-67; *Report of the Joint Committee of the Chicago Board of Trade and Chicago Mercantile Associa-tion (Feb. 1866)* (Chicago, 1866) ; Wool Growers and Wool Manufacturers, *Report of Proceedings of Convention at Syracuse, New York, Dec. 13, 1865* (J. Wilson, 1866) ; and Henry S. Randall, "Address Delivered before the Ohio Wool Growers' Association, in Columbus, Jan. 6, 1864," Ohio State Board of Agriculture, *Annual Report* (1863), 340 (Columbus, 1864).

A vast literature in campaign pamphlets testifies to the interest and excitement of the struggle between Johnson and the Radicals, and throws light upon the determining factors in the outcome of the election. An extensive list of these pamphlets is given in my manuscript dissertation, "The Decision of Reconstruction" at Harvard. Here only a few examples can be cited. Some of these pamphlets were speeches printed and widely distributed for campaign purposes. Many of them were speeches in Congress published at gov-ernment expense in the Congressional Globe office, such as, J. M. Ashley, *Impartial Suffrage, the Only Safe Basis of Reconstruction . . . May 29, 1866;* J. G. Blaine, *Reim-bursement of the Loyal States for Expenses Incurred in the War for the Union . . . March 21, 1866;* Z. Chandler, *Legal and Political Disabilities . . . Jan. 31, 1872;* W. D. Kelley, *Speech . . . in Favor of Negro Suffrage, Jan. 16, 1865;* L. Myers, *Speech . . . March 24, 1866. The Respon-sibilities of Congress. Acceptance of the Results of the War the True Basis of Reconstruction;* J. W. Nesmith, *Recon-*

struction . . . Jan. 18, 1866; T. A. Plants, *Reconstruction . . . Feb. 24, 1866;* H. J. Raymond, *Peace and Restoration . . . Dec. 21, 1865, and Restoration and the President's Policy . . . Jan. 29, 1866;* C. Sumner, *No Compromise of Human Rights. No Admission in the Constitution of Inequality of Rights, or Disfranchisement on Account of Color . . . March 7, 1866,* and *The Equal Rights of All; the Great Guarantee and Present Necessity, for the Sake of Security . . . Feb. 6, 1866;* T. Stevens, *Reconstruction, Dec. 18, 1865;* and B. F. Wade, *Against the Immediate Restoration of the Seceded States . . . Jan. 18, 1866.* Other speeches in Congress were privately reprinted and distributed, such as H. S. Lane, *Reconstruction and Amendments of the Constitution . . . Feb. 8, 1866* (H. Polkinhorn, Wash., 1866) and H. J. Raymond, *Restoration and the Union Party* (Baker & Godwin, N. Y., 1866). Speeches delivered in the campaign were printed and broadcasted, such as, Gov. J. A. Andrew, *Address to the two Branches of the Legislature of Mass., Jan. 6, 1865* and *Valedictory Address . . . Jan. 4, 1866* (Wright & Potter, Boston, 1865-66); G. S. Boutwell, *Reconstruction: its True Basis . . . Speech Delivered at Weymouth, Mass., July 4, 1865* (Wright & Potter, 1865); R. Conkling, *Congress and the President. The Political Problem of 1866 . . . Speech at Mechanics' Hall, Utica, Sept. 13, 1866* (Roberts, Utica, 1866); R. H. Dana, *Speech at a Meeting of Citizens Held in Faneuil Hall, June 21, 1865, to Consider the Subject of Reorganization of the Rebel States* (Wash., 1865); *The Absolute Equality of All Men before the Law, the Only True Basis of Reconstruction. An Address by William M. Dickson at Oberlin, Ohio, Oct. 3, 1865, with John Stuart Mill's Letter on Reconstruction* (R. Clarke, Cincinnati,

1865); *Influence of the War on our National Prosperity
. . . Baltimore . . . March 13, 1865* (W. C. Martin, N. Y.,
1865); Anthony P. Dostie, *A Loyal Voice from Lou-
isiana. Speech before the Union Association of New Orleans,
Jan. 27, 1866* (Reconstruction Print, New Orleans, 1866);
W. D. Kelley, *The Dangers and Duties of the Hour, An
Address at Concert Hall, Phila., March 15, 1866* (Chronicle
Bk. & Job Print., Wash., 1866); G. B. Loring, *Speech . . .
upon the Resolutions on the State of the Union, Delivered in
the Massachusetts House of Representatives, March 12,
1866* (C. D. Howard, So. Danvers, 1866); O. P. Morton,
*Reconstruction and Negro Suffrage . . . Richmond, Ind.,
Sept. 29, 1865,* and *Speech Delivered at Masonic Hall . . .
June 20, 1866* (Holloway, Douglass, Indianapolis, 1865-
66); and C. Sumner, *The National Security and the National Faith; Guarantees for the National Freedman and the
National Creditor . . . Republican State Convention, in Wor-
cester, Sept. 14, 1865,* and *The One Man Power Vs. Con-
gress! Address . . . at the Music Hall, Boston, Oct. 2, 1866*
(Wright & Potter, 1865-66). The Union Republican Con-
gressional Committee published a number of speeches, for
example, C. C. Andrews, *Early Steps in Reconstruction.
Speeches . . . in Texas and Arkansas* (1865) and W. D.
Kelley, *The South—its Resources and Wants . . . His
Address to the Citizens of New Orleans . . . Address at
Montgomery, Ala., . . . and his Address to his Constitu-
ents* (1866).

Three pamphlets are useful beyond all others: *Mass Meeting of the Citizens of New York, Held at the Cooper Institute, Feb. 22d, 1866, to Approve the Principles Announced
in the Messages of Andrew Johnson* (N. Y., 1866) containing speeches of Cutting, Field, Seward, Dennison, Raymond,

letters of Dickinson and Walker, and resolutions of the meeting; a National Union Club Document under the title, *Speeches of Hon. Edgar Cowan, of Pennsylvania; Hon. Jas. R. Doolittle, of Wisconsin; Hon. Hugh McCulloch, Secretary of Treasury; Letter of Hon. O. H. Browning, of Illinois; and an Address by a Member of the Club; also, The Condition of the South; a Report of Special Commissioner, B. F. Truman* (Wash., 1866) ; and J. Parton, *Manual for the Instruction of "Rings," Railroad and Political; with a History of the Grand Chicago & North Western "Ring," and the Secret of its Success in Placing an Over-Issue of Twenty Millions; with a Margin of Three Millions in Three Years* (New York, 1866. Suppressed and republished by the Illinois Republican State Central Committee, Chicago, 1876. In John Crerar Library, Chicago). The following examples indicate the type of material with which pamphleteers deluged the country, much of which has been preserved in the Widener and Congressional libraries: *All Governments Derive their Just Powers from the Consent of the Governed! . . . Free Suffrage Tried for the First Time, Succeeds; Aristocracy and Caste, on the Same Theater, Tried for the Thousandth Time, Fails as Usual* (Cleveland, 1865) ; Amicus, *The Rebel States, The President and Congress. Reconstruction, and the Executive Power of Pardon* (E. S. Dodge, N. Y., 1866) ; *The Reconstruction of States. Letter of Maj.-Gen. Banks to Senator Lane* (Harper, N. Y., 1865) ; *Letter of Hon. M. F. Conway to Senator Doolittle, of Wisconsin, in Support of President Johnson's Policy of Reconstruction* (Republic Bk. & Job Office, Richmond, 1865) ; A. M. Dignowity, *Reconstruction!! An Appeal to the Patriotic National Republican Members of Congress; in Behalf of All Loyal Residents of the South* (Wash., 1869) ; *The Equality*

of Men Before the Law Claimed and Defended . . . by
Kelley, Phillips, Douglass, Wright, and Heighton, ed., G. L.
Stearns (G. C. Rand & Avery, Boston, 1865) ; *Nationality
vs. Sectionalism* (McGill & Witherow, Wash., 1866) ; *The
Great Struggle between Democracy and Absolutism Impend-
ing; Being the Alarm Bell Published in 1863, with Addi-
tional Matter. America Threatened. By a Constitutionalist*
(N. Y., 1865) ; C. P. Kirkland, *A Letter to Peter Cooper on
"The Treatment to be Extended to the Rebels Individually,"
and "The Mode of Restoring the Rebel States to the Union"*
(Randolph, N. Y., 1865) ; *Letter from MM. de Gasparin,
Martin, Cochin, and Laboulaye to the Loyal Publication
Society of New York* (Westcott, N. Y., 1866) ; C. G. Loring, *Reconstruction. Claims of the Inhabitants of the States
Engaged in the Rebellion to Restoration of Political Rights
and Privileges under the Constitution* (Little, Brown, Boston, 1866) ; *Massachusetts and South Carolina. Correspondence between John Quincy Adams and Wade Hampton and
Others of South Carolina* (1868) ; *The Real Question before
the Country. What the President Proclaims!! What Congress Has Actually Done* (N. Y., 1866) ; J. H. Serment,
*La Question des Nègres et la Reconstruction du Sud aux
Etats Unis* (J. G. Frick, Genève, 1866) ; J. Y. Smith, *Review of Senator Doolittle's Speech at Madison, Sept. 30,
1865, on the Reconstruction of Rebel States* (Madison,
1865) ; D. A. Wells, *Wool and the Tariff. An Argument
against Interference* (N. Y., 1873) ; and E. P. Whipple,
The Johnson Party (E. C. Markley, Phila., 1866).

Important in the campaign were the jibes of humorous
pamphlets, such as *Moses, or, the Man Who Supposes Himself to be Moses, no Moses at All* (Am. News Co., N. Y.,
1866) ; Zedekiah Comitatus, *Reconstruction on "My Pol-*

icy"; or, its Author at the Confessional (Timberlake, N. Y., 1866) ; *Andy's Trip to the West together with a Life of its Hero. By Petroleum V. Nasby* (Haney, N. Y., 1866) ; and *"Swingin round the Cirkle"—By Petroleum V. Nasby . . . Illustrated by Thomas Nast* (Lee & Shepard, Boston, 1867).

A number of contemporaries have left memoirs : James G. Blaine, *Twenty Years of Congress* (2 vols., Henry Bill, Norwich, Conn., 1886) ; Geo. S. Boutwell, *Reminiscences of Sixty Years in Public Affairs* (2 vols., McClure, Phillips, N. Y., 1902) ; *Autobiography and Personal Reminiscences of Major-General Benj. F. Butler. Butler's Book* (A. M. Thayer, Boston, 1892) ; Samuel S. Cox, *Union, Disunion, Reunion. Three Decades of Federal Legislation 1855-1885* (J. A. & P. A. Reid, Providence, 1885) ; *Through Five Administrations; Reminiscences of Colonel William H. Crook, Body-Guard to President Lincoln* (Harper, 1910) ; Shelby M. Cullom, *Fifty Years of Public Service, Personal Recollections* (A. C. McClurg, Chicago, 1911) ; Chas. A. Dana, *Recollections of the Civil War* (Appleton, 1898) ; Grenville M. Dodge, *Personal Recollections of President Abraham Lincoln, General Ulysses S. Grant, and General William T. Sherman* (Monarch Print. Co., Council Bluffs, Ia., 1914) ; *The Life and Times of Frederick Douglass from 1817-1882 Written by Himself* (DeWolfe, Fiske, Boston, 1893) ; *Personal Memoirs of U. S. Grant* (2 vols., Century, 1885) ; Geo. F. Hoar, *Autobiography of Seventy Years* (2 vols., Scribner, 1903) ; Oliver O. Howard, *Autobiography* (2 vols., Baker & Taylor, 1907) ; Geo. W. Julian, *Political Recollections, 1840-72* (Jansen, McClurg, Chicago, 1884) ; Capt. Robt. E. Lee, *Recollections and Letters of General Robert E. Lee* (Doubleday, Page, 1904) ; Mary S. Logan, *Reminiscences of a Soldier's Wife; an Autobiography* (Scribner's,

1913); Alex K. McClure, *Abraham Lincoln and Men of War Times* (Times Pub. Co., Phila., 1892); *Colonel Alexander K. McClure's Recollections of Half a Century* (Salem [Mass.] Press, 1902); Hugh McCulloch, *Men and Measures of Half a Century* (Scribner's, 1888); Col. W. G. Moore, "Notes," *Am. Hist. Rev.*, XIX (1913), 102; Benjamin F. Perry, *Reminiscences of Public Men with Speeches and Addresses* (Shannon, Greenville, S. C., 1889); B. Perley Poore, *Perley's Reminiscences of Sixty Years in the National Metropolis* (2 vols., W. A. Houghton, 1886); John M. Schofield, *Forty-six Years in the Army* (Century, 1897); Carl Schurz, *Reminiscences* (3 vols., McClure, 1907-08); John Sherman, *Recollections of Forty Years in the House, Senate, and Cabinet* (2 vols., Werner, Chicago, 1896); *Memoirs of General William T. Sherman by Himself* (2 vols., Appleton, 1875); Alex. H. Stephens, *Recollections* (Doubleday, Page, 1910); and Sen. Wm. M. Stewart, *Reminiscences* (Neale, N. Y., 1908).

Among the many contemporary articles some of the most interesting are: Sidney Andrews, "Three Months among the Reconstructionists," *Atlantic Monthly*, XVII (Feb., 1866), 242; "Differences of Administration," *Christian Examiner*, LXXXI (Nov., 1866), 400; M. Elsner, "The Production of Wool on Earth," Ohio State Board of Agriculture, *Annual Report*, 1864; (Jas. R. Lowell) "The President on the Stump" and "The Seward-Johnson Reaction," editorials in *North Am. Rev.*, CII (April, 1866), 530, and CIII (Oct., 1866), 520; Robt. D. Owen, "Political Results from the Varioloid," *Atlantic Monthly*, XXXV (1875), 660; "President Johnson's Tour and his Policy," *New Englander*, XXV (Oct., 1866), 711; "The Purpose and the President of the United States," *Fraser's Mag.*, LXXV (Feb., 1867), 243;

"Three Presidents of the United States," *Blackwood's Edin-burgh Mag.*, C (Nov., 1866), 623; and Gideon Welles, "Lincoln and Johnson," *Galaxy*, XIII (1872), 521, 663.

A few contemporary books have been useful: Gen. Lafayette C. Baker, *History of the United States Secret Service* (L.C.B., Phila., 1867); Wm. H. Barnes, *History of the Thirty-ninth Congress of the United States* (Macauley, Indianapolis, 1867); Orestes A. Brownson, *The American Republic* (P. O'Shea, N. Y., 1866); Edward A. Pollard, *The Lost Cause Regained* (Carleton, N. Y., 1868); Henry Wilson, *History of the Reconstruction Measures of the Thirty-ninth and Fortieth Congresses, 1865-68* (J. A. Stoddard, Chicago, 1868); and David A. Wells, *The Recent Financial, Industrial, and Commercial Experiences of the U. S. A Curious Chapter in Politico-Economic History* (J. H. & C. M. Goodsell, N. Y., 1872).

SECONDARY MATERIALS

Most general histories of the United States deal with reconstruction. A few deal adequately. James F. Rhodes, *History of the United States from the Compromise of 1850* (8 vols., Macmillan, 1899-1919), V-VI, covers the period thoroughly and accurately, but sees only the political side of reconstruction, and even in that is faulty in interpretation. E. P. Oberholtzer, *History of the United States since the Civil War* (3 vols., Macmillan, 1917- —) is interesting, accurate, and detailed, but fails to cast interpretive light on the period at all. Much less known, but sounder in understanding and analysis of this decade than any of the larger works is James Schouler, *History of the United States under the Constitution* (7 vols., Dodd, Mead, N. Y., 1894-1913),

VII. Of briefer treatments, Charles A. and Mary Beard, *The Rise of American Civilization* (2 vols., Macmillan, 1927) and Samuel E. Morison, *Oxford History of the United States* (2 vols., Oxford University Press, 1927) are by far the best in their treatment of Johnson and reconstruction. Morison gives an excellent analysis of Johnson and his problems; the Beards suggest the economic factors at work though they do not pause long enough to develop them. At last we have an excellent social history of the period in Allan Nevins, *The Emergence of Modern America*, in Arthur M. Schlesinger and Dixon R. Fox, *A History of American Life* (12 vols., Macmillan, 1927- —), VIII. Of the numerous economic histories Harold U. Faulkner, *American Economic History* (Harper, 1924) is on the whole the best. For the purposes of this work Victor S. Clark, *History of Manufactures in the United States, 1607-1929* (3 vols., McGraw-Hill, N. Y., 1929), Ida Tarbell, *The Tariff in Our Times, 1860-1911* (Macmillan, 1911), and Frank W. Taussig, *The Tariff History of the United States* (Putnam's, 7th ed., 1923) are extremely valuable. Katherine Coman, *Industrial History of the United States* (Macmillan, 1905) and Davis R. Dewey, *Financial History of the United States* (Longmans, Green, 8th ed., 1922) are also useful. A few state histories are useful, DeAlva S. Alexander, *A Political History of the State of New York* (4 vols., H. Holt, 1906-23), Arthur C. Cole, *The Era of the Civil War, 1848-1870* (*The Centennial History of Illinois* [Ill. Centennial Com., 1919], III), and Logan Esarey, *A History of Indiana from 1850 to the Present* (2 vols., B. F. Bowen, Indianapolis, 1918).

A number of valuable works have appeared dealing particularly with reconstruction. Some of the more important are here given: Mrs. Myrta Avary, *Dixie After the War*

(Doubleday, Page, 1906) ; H. K. Beale, "The Decision of Reconstruction" (my own unpublished doctoral dissertation at Harvard, now in the Widener Library) ; John W. Burgess, *Reconstruction and the Constitution, 1866-1876* (Scribner's, 1902) ; Chas. E. Chadsey, *The Struggle Between President Johnson and Congress over Reconstruction* (Columbia University Studies in Hist., Econ., & Public Law, VIII, 1896) ; Powell Clayton, *The Aftermath of the Civil War in Arkansas* (Neale, N. Y., 1915) ; E. Merton Coulter, *Civil War and Reconstruction in Kentucky* (U. of N. Carolina, 1926) ; Wm. W. Davis, *The Civil War and Reconstruction in Florida* (Columbia U. Studies, LIII, 1913) ; Wm. A. Dunning, *Essays on the Civil War and Reconstruction* (Macmillan, 1898) ; W. A. Dunning, *Reconstruction, Political and Economic, 1865-1877* (Harper, 1907) ; Hamilton F. Eckenrode, *Political History of Virginia during Reconstruction* (Johns Hopkins U. Studies in Historical and Political Science, XXII, 1904) ; Jas. W. Fertig, *The Secession and Reconstruction of Tennessee* (U. of Chicago Press, 1898) ; John R. Ficklen; *History of Reconstruction in Louisiana* (Johns Hopkins U. Studies, XXVIII, 1910) ; Horace E. Flack, *Adoption of the Fourteenth Amendment* (Johns Hopkins U. Studies, Extra Vol. XXVI, 1908) ; Walter L. Fleming, *Civil War and Reconstruction in Alabama* (Macmillan, 1905) ; W. L. Fleming, *The Sequel of Appomattox; a Chronicle of the Reunion of the States* (Yale U. Press, 1919) ; Jas. W. Garner, *Reconstruction in Mississippi* (Macmillan, 1901) ; Joseph G. deR. Hamilton, *Reconstruction in North Carolina* (Columbia U. Studies, LVIII, 1914) ; Alex. Harris, *A Review of the political Conflict in America, From the Commencement of the Anti-Slavery Agitation to the Close of Southern Reconstruction* (Pollock,

N. Y., 1876) ; Paul L. Haworth, *Reconstruction and Union, 1865-1912* (H. Holt, 1912) ; Hilary A. Herbert, *The Abolition Crusade and its Consequences—Four Periods of American History* (Scribner's, 1912) ; H. A. Herbert, *Why the Solid South? or, Reconstruction and its Results* (R. H. Woodward, Balt., 1890) ; John P. Hollis, *The Early Period of Reconstruction in South Carolina* (Johns Hopkins U. Studies, XXIII, 1905) ; Benj. B. Kendrick, *The Journal of the Joint Committee of Fifteen on Reconstruction* (Columbia U. Studies, LXII, 1914) ; Stephen D. Lee, *The South Since the War* (C. A. Evans, ed., Atlanta, Ga., 1899) ; Chas. H. McCarthy, *Lincoln's Plan of Reconstruction* (McClure, Phillips, N. Y., 1901) ; Edward McPherson, *Political History of the United States of America during the Period of Reconstruction* (Philp & Solomons, Wash., 1871) ; Joseph B. Morrison, *The Chapter on Reconstruction from the "Life of Thaddeus Stevens," now in preparation* (Maysville, Mo., 1903) ; Chas. C. Pearson, *Readjustor Movement in Virginia* (Yale U. Press, 1917) ; Paul S. Pierce, *The Freedman's Bureau* (State U. of Ia. Studies in Soc., Econ., Pol., & Hist., III, 1904) ; Chas. W. Ramsdell, *Reconstruction in Texas* (Columbia U. Studies, XXXVI, 1910) ; John S. Reynolds, *Reconstruction in South Carolina, 1865-1877* (State Co., Columbia, S. C., 1905) ; Eben G. Scott, *Reconstruction during the Civil War* (Houghton Mifflin, 1895) ; *Studies in Southern History and Politics, Inscribed to William A. Dunning* (Columbia U. Press, 1914) ; Richard Taylor, *Destruction and Reconstruction* (Appleton, 1879) ; Clara M. Thompson, *Reconstruction in Georgia, Economic, Social, Political, 1865-1872* (Columbia U. Press, 1915) ; and Edwin C. Woolley, *The Reconstruction of Georgia* (Columbia U. Studies, XIII, 1901). Since the completion of the present work Claude G. Bowers's *Tragic Era* has appeared. After his admirable *Jefferson and Hamilton* it is a great disappointment. Written in his usual readable style, this book displays Bowers's power of vivid characterization, his keen sense of the dramatic, and his familiarity with newspaper material. But Bowers has used surprisingly little new material; even Julian's diary yielded nothing startling. His sources are meager, and his use of them sometimes superficial. The book is amazingly partisan, better as a Democratic campaign document than as sober history. In fact, Bowers employs against the Radicals as much bias and prejudice as he rightly condemns them for using for political ends against Johnson. His unmitigated praise of the South is as far from the truth as the Radical condemnation of it. The economic factors in reconstruction he hints at but does not develop. Bowers has not given us the definitive work that many of us hoped for. Yet withal Johnson's point of view needed stating; Bowers has presented it vigorously; and his book will appeal to a wide public.

Biographies of Johnson and his contemporaries exist in quantity, but few are really satisfactory. Geo. W. Bacon, *Life and Speeches of President Andrew Johnson . . .* (Bacon, London, 1865), Lillian Foster, *Andrew Johnson . . . His Life and Speeches* (Richardson, N. Y., 1866), *Life, Speeches, and Services of Andrew Johnson* (T. B. Peterson, Phila., 1865), Frank Moore, *Speeches of Andrew Johnson* with a Biographical Introduction (Little, Brown, Boston, 1865), Kenneth Rayner, *Life and Times of Andrew Johnson* (Appleton, N. Y., 1866), and John Savage, *Life and Public Services of Andrew Johnson* (Derby & Miller, N. Y., 1866) were poor campaign biographies, valuable only for the speeches they collected. Rev. James S. Jones, *Life of*

Andrew Johnson (E. Tenn. Pub. Co., Greenville, 1901) was
little better. For one phase of his career Clifton R. Hall,
Military Governor of Tennessee (Princeton U. Press, 1916)
is good. Only since the appearance of Robert W. Winston,
Andrew Johnson, Plebeian and Patriot (H. Holt, 1928) and
Lloyd P. Stryker, *Andrew Johnson, a Study in Courage*
(Macmillan, 1929) have we had a creditable biography of
our seventeenth President. Stryker has the zeal and the
shortcomings of an ardent partisan. His general defense of
Johnson is sound, but in details his judgment is faulty. His
venom in dealing with Johnson's enemies is understandable,
and in some cases, particularly Stanton's, justifiable; but
often it leads him to regrettable misunderstanding of other
public men. The work is readable, but not scholarly. More
thorough and less biased is Winston's book. It is sound, fair-
minded, sympathetic but not uncritical; yet it suffers from
an uninspired style and surprising inaccuracy of citation.
A. Badeau, *Grant in Peace* (Scranton, Hartford, 1887),
Wm. G. Church, *U. S. Grant* (Putnam's, 1897), and *Life
and Services of U. S. Grant, Conqueror of the Rebellion*
. . . (Republican and Cong. Com., Wash., 1868) are instructive as anti-Johnsonian perversions of history. Better
as biographies but still prejudiced in regard to Johnson
are H. Garland, *U. S. Grant* (Macmillan, 1920) and L. A.
Coolidge, *U. S. Grant* (Houghton Mifflin, 1922). The fairest
view of Grant's part in early reconstruction is presented by
F. S. Edmonds, *U. S. Grant* (G. W. Jacobs, Phila., 1915).
Other biographies useful for this study are: Henry G. Pearson, *Life of John A. Andrew, Gov. of Mass. 1861-1865* (2
vols., Houghton Mifflin, 1904); Lyman Abbott, *Henry
Ward Beecher* (Houghton Mifflin, 1903); Paxton Hibben,
Henry Ward Beecher (Doran, 1927); Edward Stanwood,

James Gillespie Blaine (Houghton Mifflin, 1905); Geo.
S. Merriam, *Life and Times of Samuel Bowles* (2 vols., Century, 1885); Emory Speer, *Joseph E. Brown of Georgia* (Foote & Davies, Atlanta, 1905); Detroit Post & Tribune, *Zachariah Chandler* (C. Drew, N. Y., 1880); Wilmer C. Harris, *Public Life of Zachariah Chandler* (Mich. Hist. Com., 1917); A. B. Hart, *Salmon Portland Chase* (Houghton Mifflin, 1899); Jacob W. Schuckers, *Life and Public Services of Salmon Portland Chase* (Appleton, 1874); Orando J. Hollister, *Life of Schuyler Colfax* (Funk & Wagnalls, N. Y., 1886); Alfred R. Conkling, *Life and Letters of Roscoe Conkling* (C. L. Webster, 1889); Ellis P. Oberholtzer, *Jay Cooke, Financier of the Civil War* (2 vols., G. W. Jacobs, Phila., 1907); Edward Cary, *George William Curtis* (Houghton Mifflin, 1894); Morgan Dix, *Memoirs of John A. Dix* (2 vols., Harper, 1883); John D. Hicks, "The Political Career of Ignatius Donnelly," *Miss. Valley Hist. Rev.*, VIII (1921), 80; Duane Mowry, "An Appreciation of James Rood Doolittle," State Hist. Soc. of Wis., *Proceedings*, 1909; Francis Fessenden, *Life and Public Services of Wm. Pitt Fessenden* (2 vols., Houghton Mifflin, 1907); Lindsay Swift, *William Lloyd Garrison* (G. W. Jacobs, 1911); *Life and Letters of Edwin L. Godkin*, ed., Rollo Ogden (2 vols., Macmillan, 1907); Wm. A. Linn, *Horace Greeley, Founder and Editor of the N. Y. Tribune* (Appleton, 1903); Wm. Salter, *Life of James W. Grimes* (Appleton, N. Y., 1876); Chas. E. Hamlin, *Life and Times of Hannibal Hamlin: By his grandson* (Riverside Press, 1899); Johnson Brigham, *James Harlan* (State Hist. Soc. of Ia., 1913); Russell H. Conwell, *Life and Public Services of Gov. Rutherford B. Hayes* (B. B. Russell, Boston, 1876); Jas. Q. Howard, *Life, Public Services, and Select Speeches of*

Rutherford B. Hayes (R. Clarke, Cincinnati, 1876) ; Wm.
D. Howells, *Sketch of the Life and Character of Rutherford
B. Hayes* (Hurd & Houghton, 1876) ; Chas. R. Williams,
Life of Rutherford B. Hayes (2 vols., Houghton Mifflin,
1914) ; Bernard C. Steiner, *Life of Reverdy Johnson* (Nor-
man, Remington, Baltimore, 1914) ; Mrs. Grace Clarke,
George W. Julian (Ind. Hist. Com., 1923) ; *Life and Letters
of Francis Lieber,* ed., Thos. S. Perry (J. R. Osgood, Boston, 1882) ; John G. Nicolay and John Hay, *Abraham Lincoln* (10 vols., Century, 1890) ; Geo. F. Dawson, *Life and
Services of Gen. John A. Logan* (Bolford, Clarke, Chicago,
1887) ; Wm. D. Foulke, *Life of Oliver P. Morton* (2 vols.,
Bowan-Merrill, Indianapolis, 1899) ; Albert .B. Paine,
Thomas Nast, his Period and his Pictures (Macmillan,
1909) ; Jas. H. Wilson, *Life of John A. Rawlins* (Neale,
N. Y., 1916) ; Augustus Maverick, *Henry J. Raymond and
the New York Press, for Thirty Years* (A. S. Hale, Hart-
ford, 1870) ; Frederic Bancroft, *Life of William H. Seward*
(2 vols., Harper, 1900) ; Frederick W. Seward, *Story of the
Life of William H. Seward* (3 vols., Derby & Miller, N. Y.,
1891) ; Theodore E. Burton, *John Sherman* (Houghton
Mifflin, 1917) ; Frank A. Flower, *Edwin M. Stanton, the
Autocrat of Rebellion, Emancipation, and Reconstruction*
(Saalfield, Akron, O., 1905) ; Geo. C. Gorham, *Life and
Public Services of Edwin M. Stanton* (2 vols., Houghton
Mifflin, 1899) ; Richard M. Johnston and Wm. H. Browne,
Alexander H. Stephens (J. B. Lippincott, Phila., 1878) ;
Edward B. Callender, *Thaddeus Stevens: Commoner* (A.
Williams, Boston, 1882) ; Samuel W. McCall, *Thaddeus
Stevens* (Houghton Mifflin, 1899) ; Jas. A. Woodburn, *Life
of Thaddeus Stevens* (Bobbs-Merrill, Indianapolis, 1913) ;
Edward L. Pierce, *Memoir and Letters of Charles Sumner*

(4 vols., Roberts, Boston, 1893) ; Moorefield Storey, *Charles Sumner* (Houghton Mifflin, 1900) ; Pleasant A. Stovall, *Robert Toombs* (Cassell, N. Y., 1892) ; Horace White, *Life of Lyman Trumbull* (Houghton Mifflin, 1913) ; Albert G. Riddle, *Life of Benjamin F. Wade* (W. W. Williams, Cleveland, 1886) ; Thurlow W. Barnes, *Life of Thurlow Weed* (2 vols., Houghton Mifflin, 1884) ; and Ralph D. Williams, *The Honorable Peter White* (Penton, Cleveland, 1907).

Pertinent monographs are: Jas. W. Angell, *The Theory of International Prices; History, Criticism, and Restatement* (Harvard U. Press, 1926) ; Arthur C. Cole, *Whig Party in the South* (Am. Hist. Assoc., Wash., 1911) ; David M. Dewitt, *Impeachment and Trial of Andrew Johnson* and *Assassination of Abraham Lincoln and Its Expiation* (Macmillan, 1903, 1909) ; Harriette M. Dilla, *Politics of Michigan 1865-1878* (Columbia U. Studies, XLVII, 1912) ; Eldon C. Evans, *A History of the Australian Ballot System in the United States* (U. of Chicago Press, 1917) ; Alex. L. Holley, *The Bessemer Process and Works in the United States* (Van Nostrand, N. Y., 1868) ; Claudio Jannet, *Les Etats-Unis Contemporains; ou, les Moeurs, les Institutions et les Idées depuis la Guerre de la Sécession* (M. Le Play, Paris, 1876) ; Oliver H. Kelley, *Origin and Progress of the Order of the Patrons of Husbandry in the United States: a History from 1866 to 1873* (Wagenseller, Phila., 1875) ; Willford I. King, *The Wealth and Income of the People of the United States* (Macmillan, 1915) ; Isaac Lippincott, *A History of Manufactures in the Ohio Valley to the Year 1860* (Knickerbocker Press, 1914) ; John M. Mathews, *Legislative and Judicial History of the Fifteenth Amendment* (Johns Hopkins U. Studies, XXVII, 1909) ; Clarence L. Miller, "The Attitude of the Northwest Toward the Tariff, 1864-1883" (an interesting unpublished M. A. thesis at the University of Chicago, 1919); Wesley C. Mitchell, *Gold, Prices, and Wages under the Greenback Standard* (U. of California Press, 1908); Henry R. Mussey, *Combination in the Mixing Industry: a Study of Concentration in Lake Superior Iron Ore Production* (Columbia U. Studies, XXIII, 1905); Geo. H. Porter, *Ohio Politics during the Civil War Period* (Columbia U. Studies, XL, 1911); Chalfant Robinson, *A History of Two Reciprocity Treaties* (Tuttle, Morehouse & Taylor, New Haven, 1904); Harry E. Smith, *The United States Federal Internal Tax History from 1861 to 1871* (Houghton Mifflin, 1914); Oliver P. Temple, *Notable Men of Tennessee from 1833 to 1875* (Cosmopolitan Press, N. Y., 1912); Harrison C. Thomas, *Return of the Democratic Party to Power in 1884* (Columbia U. Studies, LXXXIX, 1919); Edith E. Ware, *Political Opinion in Massachusetts during Civil War and Reconstruction* (Columbia U. Studies, LXXIV, 1916); and Chester W. Wright, *Wool-Growing and the Tariff* (Houghton Mifflin, 1910).

Of the many articles dealing with the period the following are particularly helpful: H. K. Beale, "The Tariff and Reconstruction," *Am. Hist. Rev.*, XXX (Jan., 1930), 276; A. C. Cole, "President Lincoln and the Illinois Radical Republicans," *Miss. Valley Hist. Rev.*, IV (1918), 417; L. G. Connor, "A Brief History of the Sheep Industry in the United States," Am. Hist. Assoc., *Annual Report* (1918), I, 89; H. B. Converse, "Sheep and Wool Industry, its Growth and Development from 1800 to the Present," Ohio State Board of Agriculture, *Report* (1894), 352; R. E. Cushman, "Voting Organic Laws: the Action of the Ohio Electorate in the Revision of the State Constitution in 1912," *Political Science Quarterly*, XXVIII (1913), 207;

W. E. B. DuBois, "The Freedmen's Bureau," *Atlantic Monthly*, LXXXVII (1901), 354; W. A. Dunning, "The Second Birth of the Republican Party," *Am. Hist Rev.*, XVI (1910), 56; C. R. Fish, "Lincoln and the Patronage," *Am. Hist. Rev.*, VIII (1902), 53; W. L. Fleming, "The Freedmen's Savings Bank," *Yale Rev.*, XV (1906), 40-67, 134-146; C. B. Galbreath, "The Vote on the Ohio Constitution," the *Independent*, LXXIII (1912), 1407; L. H. Gipson, "The Statesmanship of President Johnson: A Study of the Presidential Reconstruction Policy," *Miss. Valley Hist. Rev.*, II (1915), 363; F. D. Graham, "International Trade under Depreciated Paper; The United States, 1862-1879," *Quarterly Journal of Economics*, XXXVI (1922), 220; E. B. Greene, "Some Aspects of Politics in the Middle West, 1860-72," State Hist. Soc. of Wis., *Proceedings* (1911), 60; Harvard U. Com. on Econ. Research, "Business and Financial Conditions Following the Civil War in the United States," *Rev. of Econ. Statistics*, II (1920), Supplement 2; J. B. Henderson, "Emancipation and Impeachment," *Century*, LXXXV (1912), 196; H. A. Hilary, "The Conditions of the Reconstruction Problem," *Atlantic Monthly*, LXXXVII (1901), 145; G. Hunt, "The President's Defense," *Century*, LXXXV (1913), 422; S. W. McCall, "Washington during Reconstruction," *Atlantic Monthly*, LXXXVII (1901), 817; F. W. Moore, "Representation in the National Congress from the Seceding States, 1861-1865," *Am. Hist. Rev.*, II (1897), 279 and 461; H. G. Otis, "The Causes of Impeachment," *Century*, LXXXV (1912), 187; T. N. Page, "The Southern People during Reconstruction," *Atlantic Monthly*, LXXXVIII (1901), 289; A. Phelps, "New Orleans and Reconstruction," *Atlantic Monthly*, LXXXVIII (1901), 121; S. F. Rederus, "The

Dutch Settlements of Sheboygan County," *Wis. Mag. of Hist.*, I (1917), 256; L. B. Shippee, "Steamboating on the Upper Mississippi after the Civil War: A Mississippi Magnate," *Miss. Valley Hist. Rev.*, VI (1920), 470; St. G. L. Sioussat, "Andrew Johnson and the Early Phases of the Homestead Bill," *Miss. Valley Hist. Rev.*, V (1918), 253; G. M. Stephenson, "Nativism in the Forties and Fifties," *Miss. Valley Hist. Rev.*, IX (1922), 185; N. W. Stephenson, "Lincoln and the Progress of Nationality in the North," Am. Hist. Assoc., *Annual Report* (1919), I, 351; F. W. Taussig, "International Trade under Depreciated Currency" and "The Tariff Act of 1922," *Quarterly Journal of Economics*, XXXI (1917), 380 and XXXVII (1922), 1; W. Wilson, "The Reconstruction of the Southern States," *Atlantic Monthly*, LXXXVII (1901), 1; and J. A. Woodburn, "Party Politics in Indiana during the Civil War," Am. Hist. Assoc., *Annual Report* (1902), 223.

INDEX

Abolition of slavery, agitation for, 51-52; Emancipation Proclamation, 52, 53; Lincoln and, 212; South's recognition of, 38, 44, 45, 134. *See also* Thirteenth Amendment.

Abolitionists, oppose Lincoln, 52, 54-55; effective Radical propagandists, 66, 142-143, 153, 215, 332, 366

Abuse in campaign, 16, 17, 19, 76, 77, 78-79, 87, 88, 91-92, 131, 152-153, 205-206, 212-213, 303, 309, 314, 325, 330-332, 353-362, 365-372, 386, 389-391

Adams, Charles Francis, praises Johnson's message, 49; offends Fenians, 302

Agriculturalists, antagonism toward business men, 114, 144, 145, 231, 247-249, 255-260, 281, 288-290; associations and conventions, 256-260, 279, 281-284, 289; hard times, 230-231, 240-241, 255-256, 279-282; support Conservatives, 145, 289; tariff, 231, 278-284; taxes, 229-232; other economic issues, 238, 240-241, 247-249, 255-260, 264, 287-290, 296-297

Alabama, reorganized, 31; unpardoned rebel denied office, 39; militia, 42

Amendments, proposed, 46, 77, 93, 196-197. *See also* Thirteenth, Fourteenth.

Amnesty, oath, 31, 39, 40; universal, 90, 197

Andrew, Gov. John A., supports Johnson, 48; considered for cabinet, 121-122; on negro suffrage, 122, 146; conciliation toward Southerners, 122, 169-170; won to Radicalism, 132; objects to methods of Radicals, 146; on tariff, 274, 291; investment in South, 341; speeches, 122, 274, 291

Arkansas, provisional government, 31-32, 55

Atlantic Monthly, offers Stanton space against Johnson, 102

Babcock, James F., supports Johnson, 47, 384-385; Conservative Party, 130, 381, 384-385

Baird, Gen. Absalom, conditions in South, 162, 163; New Orleans riot, 105, 347-350, 352

Baker, Gen. Lafayette C., defames Johnson, 16-17, 79; Johnson said to fear, 361

Bancroft, George, praises Johnson's policy, 49

Banks, importance in reconstruction controversy, 8, 145, 247-248, 297-298; opposition to, 229, 231, 246, 247-253, 263; power to issue currency, 248-252

Beard, Charles A. and Mary, economic issues, 4

Beckwith, General, conditions in South, 163, 191

Beecher, Edward, attacks South, 331

Beecher, Henry Ward, supports Johnson, 48, 170; centralization and military rule, 221; Civil Rights Bill, 91; Johnson's immorality, 16, 78-79; patronage, 119; Radical desire to retain power, 313; silenced by Radical attacks, 358

Bennett, James G., Conservative Party, 116, 395; economic issues, 248, 291, 297-298; patronage, 119

Bingham, Rep. John A., moderate views, 82; Civil Rights Bill, 109, 220; Committee of Fifteen, 82, 220;

reconstruction, 149; relations with Schurz, 70-73; tariff, 296; speeches, 19, 67, 68, 77, 102, 115, 357

Surratt, Mrs., trial, 34, 104

Swing 'round the Circle, effect of, 24, 228, 299, 305-306, 363-364, 367-369; events of, 362-369; Grant and, 305-306, 307-308; Radical use of, 13, 328, 362, 365-369

Syracuse Convention. *See* wool-growers.

Tariff, importance in reconstruction, 8, 144, 146-147, 223, 271-273, 284, 287, 293-295, 297, 299; adjustment to taxes, 234, 235, 271-273; Bill of 1866, 233, 284, 289, 291-296; factors counteracting opposition, 278-287, 297; legislation, 271-272, 291-294; Johnson opposes, 236, 297; Northeasterners oppose, 229, 276, 296-297; Northeasterners support, 144, 271-277, 291-295; Westerners oppose, 276-277, 279, 281, 287-291; Westerners support, 109, 223, 278-284, 287

Taxation, importance in reconstruction, 8, 228, 229, 230-236; amendment to Constitution concerning, 46, 200-201; apportionment, 46, 200, 230-236, 246; Moderates, 200-201; protest over taxes, 226, 228, 229, 230, 235, 289-290

Tennessee, provisional government, 31-32, 55; recognition of, in Congress, 74-75, 80-84, 97-98, 209; Fourteenth Amendment, 97-98, 105, 209

Texas, reorganized, 31, 81; convention, 81; Freedmen's Bureau, 157

Third Party. *See* Conservatives.

Thirteenth Amendment, problem created by, 46; ratification urged by Johnson, 38-39, 44

Thomas, Gen. Geo. H., supports Johnson, 48; arming negro, 43, 156; Tennessee Legislature, 105

Tilden, Samuel, railroad stocks, 262-263; Fenians, 304

"Traitor," Radical meaning of term, 3, 30, 153-155, 159, 202, 275, 355; term used to injure opponents, 9, 76-77, 78, 112, 306, 314-315, 344, 353-357, 372-374

Travelers in the South. *See* South, travelers.

Treason, definition of, 30, 32-33, 153, 154-155, 277, 355

Trials. *See* Mrs. Cobb, Jefferson Davis, Mrs. Surratt.

Truman, Benj. C., conditions in South, 167; Johnson's sobriety, 16

Trumbull, Sen. Lyman, works with cabinet against Johnson, 102; Civil Rights Bill, 111; won to Radicalism, 111, 132; Freedmen's Bureau Bill, 80, 111; Johnson and, 48, 80, 111; Stockton, 88; tariff, 288; speech, 111

Union League clubs, in election, 366-367, 376

Union Party, conventions, 67; during war, 52, 54, 113. *See also* Republican Party.

U. S. Revenue Commission, 233-235

Vallandigham, C. L., Philadelphia Convention, 133; unpopularity, 154

Vetoes, Admission of Colo., 92-93; Admission of Neb., 92-93; Civil Rights Bill, 89-92, 324-327; Davis Bill, 53; Establishment of New York and Mont. Iron Co., 92-93; Freedmen's Bureau Bill, 80-84, 88, 92-93; Organization of Mont., 92-93

Vindictiveness at North, criticized by Lincoln, 57; examples, 51, 57, 151-153, 173, 331, 371-373. *See also* Radicals.

Violence, threats of, 376-378, 379-380, 392. *See also* riots.

Virginia, advised by Johnson, 40; provisional government, 31-32, 35, 55

Vituperation, 9, 111, 300, 369, 375, 390

Voorhees, Lieut.-Gov. A., New Orleans riot, 348-350, 353

Voters, difficulty in knowing how to vote, 141, 208-210, 381-383; choice between Copperhead and Radical, 381-383, 386-387, 389-390, 392, 393-394, 396-397

Voting, methods of, 380-381

Wade, Sen. Benjamin, denounces Johnson, 49, 314, 325; hopes for Johnson's support, 36, 62; opposes Johnson, 73; opposes Lincoln, 53, 54, 58; desire to retain power, 314;

VERMONT COLLEGE
MONTPELIER, VERMONT